THE
BUILDINGS OF ROMAN BRITAIN

Guy de la Bédoyère

B.T. Batsford Ltd, London.

© Guy de la Bédoyère 1991.

First published 1991

All rights reserved. No part of this publication
may be reproduced, in any form or by any means,
without permission from the Publisher

Typeset by Tek-Art Ltd, West Wickham, Kent
and printed in Great Britain by
Courier International, East Kilbride
Published by B. T. Batsford Ltd
4 Fitzhardinge Street, London W1H 0AH

A CIP catalogue record for this book is
available from the British Library

ISBN 0 7134 6311 2

CONTENTS

FIGURES

COLOUR PLATES

FOREWORD

This book has been in a sort of preparation for a very long time. As a boy I dragged my parents to every Roman site I could find and once even persuaded an RAF pilot to fly me over Silchester. In more recent years my long-suffering wife and children have tolerated interminable detours across field walls, bogs and rivers to view the derelict remains of a bygone world. To them I should express particular gratitude. This sort of book is necessarily dependent on the published work of others; I make no apology for this as there seems to be a pressing need to attempt to synthesise the vast amount of material which has appeared over the years, but any mistakes or errors of interpretation are entirely my own. I would like to thank Graham Webster and Catherine Johns who were both very supportive of the project and particularly helpful with various aspects of the text, and also the various excavators, too numerous to mention here, who were kind enough to express their views about the reconstructions of their sites. I should also thank Philip Crummy and Graham Webster for their help with some of the colour illustrations and Philip Clarkstone for preparing some of the black-and-white prints. I am particularly grateful to Peter Kemmis Betty for his enthusiastic reception of the original idea. Finally I owe a special debt to Tony Poole whose enthusiastic teaching of Romano-British history at sixth form gave me a love of this subject which has endured.

Note about the illustrations: the drawings were all prepared by the author though a small number were based directly on the work of others – where appropriate they have been credited; with the exception of four of the colour plates all the photographs were taken by the author between 1986 and 1990. For those with a technical interest they were taken with a Pentax ME Super camera using 50mm and 28mm lenses.

Map of Roman Britain showing the location of sites illustrated throughout the book. The column capital is from the site of the basilica at Silchester. Grid references for other sites mentioned in the text can be found in the bibliography.

INTRODUCTION

This book is an innovative experiment in drawing together as many different types of Romano-British buildings as possible and to reconstruct many of them on paper. Unfortunately with very few exceptions the buildings of Roman Britain are not amongst the most impressive historical monuments this island boasts. For the most part the surviving examples form disappointing chunks of shapeless masonry. Even the remains of country houses with their colourful mosaics present a challenge to the most inspired imagination. The sad fact is that not a single Romano-British building has survived even nearly intact, though complete examples are not uncommon elsewhere in the former Empire.

In the fifth century Britain gradually drifted out of the sphere of classical influence. During this period a great deal of change took place, and although many details are obscure it is clear that by the eleventh century England had emerged as one of the most stable and influential Christian states in Europe. The growth of towns and the small distances involved meant that it was virtually impossible for ancient settlements to rot in peace – Roman settlements were either built over, for example London and York, or if not, the stone was carried away, as at Verulamium and Silchester (see Chapter 7). Only the walls of towns which survived into the Middle Ages and the military buildings of the remote west and north stood a reasonable chance of surviving as recognizable ruins.

But to judge the architecture of Roman Britain from crumbling stumps of flint and tile is rather unfair. The Romans were responsible for the first major buildings to be built in Britain. A number of public buildings would have borne comparison with the medieval cathedrals. The colossal basilica in London is a case in point. The contrast with pre-Roman Britain is particularly important – houses are known but there is no evidence for any sort of ordered architecture or building programmes. The material culture of the Mediterranean world was well known to the wealthy members of Celtic tribes in south-east England. They enjoyed imported luxury goods and stored their wealth in silver and gold, but the cultural borrowing went no further. In many ways the buildings of Roman Britain represent the most radical feature of a new age because they symbolize not just the concept of cities, civic identity and urban-based local government but also the more generalized spread of wealth amongst the population expressed in more robust housing. In particular, religious cult centres were consolidated with the building of temples, which appear to have been rare before the invasion in AD 43.

In a paradoxical way the ruin of Roman Britain has made it easier to understand. For example, the dereliction of the third-century fort at Richborough has allowed the extensive excavations which have revealed much of its past. It would be inconceivable to damage a house in Herculaneum for the sake of what might lie underneath. Equally no one would consider demolishing Westminster Abbey for the sake of the Saxon abbey beneath. But ruined Roman buildings can sometimes be judiciously removed in part to reveal not only the construction sequence but perhaps also a late Iron Age round-house beneath. When modern development makes destruction a certainty then there is no reason not to trace a site's history at all its stages. So it has been possible to learn far more about the buildings of Roman Britain than would ever have been possible had they been much better preserved.

Excavation since the nineteenth century has revealed that Roman Britain was a place rich in buildings of all kinds. On the one hand the island was very far from being a centre of classical architecture – there were no Parthenons or Pantheons for instance – but on the other its towns were bigger than some of its medieval counterparts and some of the large country houses were remarkable for their complexity. There were also some astonishing structures, like the monumental building at Castor, or the triconch hall at Littlecote. However, few buildings have been completely excavated and naturally attention has always been drawn to the more dramatic examples. These excite the attention of the public (and of not a few archaeologists). On the whole they include the fourth-century country houses with their colourful mosaics and wall-paintings, for example Bignor and Lullingstone. The colossal building developments in modern towns have led to occasionally dramatic discoveries like the temple of Mithras in London and also a wealth of evidence for Roman civic public buildings. The forum and basilica at Lincoln have recently been identified, and more parts of the huge London basilica have been revealed in the last few years. In 1988 the amphitheatre of Roman London was finally located. In most cases these urban buildings have to be analysed from fragmentary traces of walls. While this may be frustrating, it does provide a stimulating basis for piecing together the known components into a coherent whole.

The excavation of buildings discovered in land which is now open, and not under threat from modern construction, is a more leisurely process. But even after several years of careful digging the building and its associated features rarely form more than a ground-plan. Of course people do not live and work in ground-plans, and trying to interpret the structure as a building with form and the history of its development is far from easy. Visualizing its original appearance can be even more difficult; it depends on understanding which parts of a building existed at the same time and trying to reconcile what has been found with intelligently imagined walls and roofs.

This book is an attempt to try and give *form* to ground-plans and ruins. Of course we will never know for certain what Romano-British buildings looked like, but this is no justification for sometimes ignoring the fact that all the ground plans which have been recovered are the skeletons of buildings which once had walls and roofs. Reconstructions on paper are often attempted now but the fact that very few reports of excavations known to the author include contour maps and elevations of surviving remains against the Roman ground level along with the plan shows how little serious attention is paid to recording the evidence of the structure itself in a comprehensive format. It is even quite rare to include photographs which illustrate the site within the landscape. This is really quite remarkable when one considers how many pages are usually given over to recording dozens of pot rims and other finds, or providing a meticulous record of mosaic panels and fragments of painted wall-plaster.

These omissions can occasionally make it extremely difficult to make sense of the excavator's description, of particular regret when the site no longer exists. And, occasionally, assertions are made about a building's original appearance without experimenting with different alternatives. Orthographic projections based on the ground plan can show some ideas to be very unlikely, while at the same time suggesting alternatives. Charting falls of roof tiles would give invaluable information about the likely lay-out of roofs, but even this apparently obvious record is hardly ever made, or at least published. Alan Sorrell, famous for his artistic reconstructions of Romano-British settlements, bemoaned these shortcomings some years ago and it is sad that so little note has been taken. The authors of recent reports of excavations at the temple in Bath and the forum site in London are to be congratulated for paying so much attention to recording the structural details. The excavation is, after all, generally designed to record the remains and history of a building, and without these details the plan is almost meaningless in terms of how the building was integrated into the landscape and of visualizing its form.

So how should one attempt to show a three-dimensional building in two dimensions? For the most part the drawings in this book use the techniques of orthographic projection which are discussed in more detail in Appendix 1. This does have the disadvantage of creating an unreal world of parallel lines and right angles. The truth of course is that buildings work because they have parallel lines and right angles (amongst others) – it just so happens that they do not look to the eye as if they do. So when reconstructing a building we have to begin with the unreal world because that shows us if the structure we are imagining can be reconciled with the plan we have found. This does not mean that the reconstruction is right but that it is possible; a problem when beginning with an artistic interpretation is that one can unwittingly ignore a detail of the plan which makes the restoration a technical impossibility. Orthographic projections force one to take note of the consequence of every feature of the plan – armed with the result, an artistic version can be produced and it is hoped that some of the drawings here will provide a stimulus. One problem is distinguishing between what is fact and what is imagined. It is not practical to do so without making the drawings look even more contrived. As far as Roman Britain is concerned almost anything above ground level has to be imagined, and so long as the reader recognizes this he/she will not be misled.

The range of buildings in Roman Britain must have been quite considerable, running from the most basic kind of rectangular strip house to the basilicas. This book sets out to reconstruct as many different types as possible, though obviously this has involved great selectivity and inevitably there will have been omissions. A bias has been adopted towards buildings which are structurally interesting and distinct, and/or published in accessible form and/or which can be visited today. The book is designed to be as self-contained as possible, and has a number of appendices which supply additional information about access to some sites considered worth visiting, and inscriptions referring to some of the buildings mentioned. The bibliography follows the pattern of the chapters and lists the individual sites alphabetically, thus avoiding the need to disrupt the text with references or foot-notes.

This book follows the topical divisions used in the author's *Finds of Roman Britain* and is based on a concise general text; the illustrated buildings are accompanied by extended captions in order to make them as self-contained as possible, thereby saving the reader from having to trace a single building's history through numerous references in the index. As with *Finds* places are referred to with the names in common usage – thus Verulamium and Vindolanda appear throughout for St Albans and Chesterholm. Naturally there are examples of buildings which could be assigned to more than one category. In recent years it has been suggested that some of the great 'villas' such as Chedworth were actually cult centres, designed to house pilgrims visiting nearby temples, though of course it may have functioned in both capacities. A conservative approach has been adopted here simply because it will be easier for the reader to find something where he expects to find it, though it is hoped that as much note of modern thinking and different points of view has been taken as possible.

Even so it is very important to be realistic about our interpretations of ancient buildings and the limitations imposed on us – we have very little positive evidence and debates about the use of some curious buildings, like Littlecote's hall, are based on really very limited material. The tendency to place too much emphasis on the iconography of a mosaic, or the design of a ground-plan, is quite understandable, but all too often these arguments become accepted as facts when in truth we often simply do not know. Sometimes it is suggested that, say, abandonment of a particular site may be linked to known historical events such as the repercussions following the defeat of Clodius Albinus by Septimius Severus. While it may be possible, with reservations, to suggest a link between a general phenomenon found at a number of sites and such an historical event, it is quite misleading to associate any one site with the event unless there is much more specific evidence which refers to the site in question. This is very rare, for example Tacitus' description of the burning of London, Colchester and Verulamium during the Boudican Revolt. This is not a defeatist approach, merely realistic – we actually have very little historical material to work from, and we know nothing about most of what happened during the Romano-British period. This makes it very difficult to link the ruins of a building with what we know did happen.

Although a number of the sites mentioned can be visited today it is always worth bearing in mind that much of the inspiration behind this book is to be found in France, in Italy, on the fringes of the desert in North Africa and in western Turkey. Nothing in Britain now can compare with a cool *atrium* of a house in Herculaneum in Italy, the majestic capitol at Sbeitla in Tunisia or the Great Theatre of Ephesus in Turkey – but the points of this book are to show that this was not always so, to provoke discussion about a subject which has often been ignored and to give a little life to stumps of walls which have given the author an immense amount of pleasure ever since, at the age of five, he confidently asserted to American tourists visiting the newly discovered palace at Fishbourne that the hypocaust tile stacks were where the Romans sat and passed the time of day. Considering the debate which is currently taking place about the future of architecture in modern Britain it seems particularly appropriate now to recall a period of intensive new building which was both functional and often inspired. We may never be able to stand in the sunlight and look across the temple precinct at Bath or fly low over Verulamium in high summer but we can at least imagine what may once have been.

I

CONSTRUCTION TECHNIQUES

Introduction

Hardly a single Romano-British building survives in a form that would be recognizable to the men who built it. This makes it difficult to try and understand how a building was erected and the techniques used to create a durable structure. The archaeologist is usually confronted with the pitiful remains of a building which is likely to consist of no more than wall footings and remnants of the superstructure, though fragments of roof tile usually abound. If he/she is lucky, the superstructure will lie where it fell and the walls will bear traces of plaster. In unusual circumstances the walls will stand to a significant height, for example at Beauport Park in East Sussex. At this remarkable site, buried by a collapsing slag-heap, the whole roof was found in pieces in and around the bath-house (fig. 44). Waterlogged or burnt conditions may even preserve traces of organic components, such as rafters or the frames from wattle-and-daub walls.

But in most cases the building will have been reduced to a mere ground plan, usually by centuries of stone-robbing and ploughing. If the building was made entirely of timber this will have long since rotted away and only aerial observation followed by careful excavation of the bedding trenches and post-holes is likely to reveal anything of its form. Re-using stones from Romano-British building, was regarded as a convenient alternative to quarrying from the later part of the Roman period up until modern times (see Chapter 7).

Despite the disappointing lack of impressive surviving evidence we have a reasonably good idea of what many Romano-British buildings must have once looked like. The extraordinary towns of Pompeii and Herculaneum in Italy are probably the best examples, but there are many other sites with very well-preserved ruins not only in Italy, but also in France, Spain, North Africa and Turkey. Although there may have been regional styles of architecture and building design, one of the remarkable features of the Roman world was its relative uniformity. So we can often be reasonably confident about what a building looked like, especially when its plan identifies it as an example of a well-known stereotype, like a theatre or a basilica.

Selection of sites and the planning of buildings

Surveyors

There were various reasons why particular sites were selected as suitable plots for buildings. Agricola, governor of Britain from 78-84, was said by Tacitus to have had a remarkable eye for suitable ground on which to build a fort (*Agricola*, 22). This was a comment on his tactical judgement, rather than his ability as a surveyor. He would have been advised by a military surveyor, *mensor*, such as Attonius Quintianus attested on a lost inscription from the fort at Piercebridge, County Durham (Appendix 2). Many towns, such as Verulamium or Wroxeter, grew up around early forts which had themselves been sited close to a native settlement. In other cases the fort alone provided the stimulus by acting as a market on one of the new roads – for example Cirencester, or London, which almost certainly grew up around an early fort guarding the crossing over the Thames. Subsequently some of these towns received official status and were properly laid out when the fort was given

11

1 Depiction of buildings and surveying equipment:
a drawing of a *pharos*(?) on a tile from London. The tile seems to show a cross-section of a stepped tower. The internal diagonal lines are a little hard to make sense of. It may be a drawing of something else entirely, perhaps a cross-section of a basilica, a finial (it resembles one found at the villa at Dewlish, Dorset), or even a component from a heating system like a boiler.
b drawing of a house (?) on wall-plaster from the villa at Hucclecote. It seems to show a gabled roof, a row of windows and two arches beneath. The vertical line at centre bottom suggests there may be another floor below but the picture is clearly incomplete.
c wall-painting from Trier (Germany) showing a country house with towers and colonnaded portico.

Some of the winged-corridor houses in Roman Britain may have looked more like this than conventional reconstructions (compare figs. 98 and 108 for example).
d bronze *norma* (mitre/set square) from the construction level of a second century building in Canterbury. It bears the name G(aio) Cu(. . .) Valeno, 'for Gaius Cu.. Valenus' and was probably used by a joiner (after Hulse; see Chapman, 1979). Architects and surveyors would have used similar, but larger, examples.
e *groma*, used for laying out the axes of a right angle. This is based on an example from Pfünz in Germany, other examples have the supporting staff offset to avoid obstructing the view.

up. In the countryside rural houses of early Roman date are often found to have been built over pre-Roman round-houses and similarly rural temples are often found on sites which had clearly previously functioned as the focus of a native cult, even if no earlier 'temple' had been involved. Obviously in such cases surveyors played no part in the choice of location, though they may have been used to lay out the new building.

Surveyors were men educated in arithmetic and geometry and were often slaves or freedmen. They worked with various pieces of equipment such as the *groma*, which was a device for sighting straight lines by suspending two pairs of weighted lines (fig. 1e). In this way the right angle of an insula or the direction of a road could be set by looking across one of the pairs of weights towards an assistant in the distance. As such it resembled a modern theodolite. In addition the surveyors would have used measuring instruments based on units of feet, *pedes*, and a mitre/set-square, *norma* (fig. 1d).

Surveyors were mainly responsible for laying out land on which buildings were to be erected. Normally this happened on new sites where forts or towns were planned. Vegetius described how the surveyors measured out the ground for the tent-parties and allocated the soldiers to their individual quarters (*epitoma rei militaris*, iii.8). In such cases it was important that the correct amount of land was allocated for individual buildings and that the plots were laid out in the correct relationship. In practice this was flexible, though all towns and forts conform to fairly similar patterns. In forts for example, surveyors started from a central point in front of the head-quarters which was also called the *groma*. At Inchtuthil the headquarters building was dispro-portionately small but the surveyors had correctly allowed a much larger area (fig. 17). Presumably the building would have been recon-structed on a larger scale if the fortress had remained in occupation. Similarly the surveyors had allowed space for the commanding officer's house, but this was never built. Military surveyors were not always reliable: building in a new province was likely to be unpredictable, particularly when it concerned forts being erected in the front line under military and political pressure. The Neronian legionary fortress at Usk in south Wales seems to have been abandoned by *c.* 75 in favour of the site further

south at Caerleon, possibly because it turned out that Usk was prone to flash floods, something evidently initially unforeseen. At Easter Happrew in Scotland the curious diagonal Flavian fort plan has been attributed to poor surveying.

Most of the major Romano-British towns show evidence for regimented planning of blocks and public buildings. In general it seems that sites were chosen for military, religious, social or geographic reasons rather than the specific conditions of a particular plot. This is hardly surprising and certainly reflects the writings of the first-century BC architect Vitruvius. He described the priorities for siting a public building as 'general convenience and utility' (i.7.1). Silchester and Verulamium are the best examples because the sites have never been significantly built on in later periods. However, local factors often created eccentricities. At Verulamium the street grid was complicated by the approach of Watling Street from London at an angle. One of the results was the unconventional 'Triangular Temple' (fig. 129). Minor towns were not usually laid out in this rigid way but grew up haphazardly along the line of a main road, like Kenchester in Herefordshire. The substantial town of Water Newton seems to have been a product of the very successful Nene Valley pottery industry; it, too, developed irregularly around a road, in this case Ermine Street, the main route to the north.

The Flavian Fishbourne 'palace' was laid out on a site previously occupied by military buildings and the so-called 'proto-palace', but the new building was so large that extensive levelling was necessary. Soil was moved from the western half of the site and used to build up the eastern side. The eastern part remained lower, but instead of there being a slope two terraces had been created, with the west wing slightly higher than the rest of the structure. This can be seen in Figure 119. The building's early date and complexity make it certain that surveyors had been used to plan out and organize the site.

Academic debates exist about the basis of measurement used on different sites because the inaccuracies, in both the original laying out and modern plans, found at different places makes it difficult to be certain what the original scheme was. It has been argued recently that Silchester and Caerwent were laid out on a basis of units called *pedes Monetales* (Walthew, 1987), used to lay out the insulae and the buildings within them.

These units were 2.21m (7ft 3in) in length, though a half unit 1.1m (3ft 9in) was also used. This is made even more complicated by the fact that some places, for example Silchester, were apparently re-surveyed on slightly different alignments. Traces of the original plan survive in the orientation of earlier buildings. At the fort of Gellygaer in south Wales it appears that the various fort buildings were measured out on multiples of five or ten Roman feet, a Roman foot (*pes*) being 0.296m (about 11½ modern inches).

Architects

Surveyors worked closely with architects, and may even have been employed by them. We know the names of a few architects who lived in Britain, such as Amandus, *architectus*, who erected an altar to Brigantia at Birrens (Appendix 2 and *Finds*, fig. 87a), though we know nothing of his work. Another, called Quintus, dedicated an altar to Minerva at the fort of Carrawburgh on Hadrian's Wall and was probably a soldier (*RIB* 1542). Like the surveyors they were educated men and would have used some of the same equipment. Even so the architects of major public buildings seem sometimes to have either lacked access to civic records (if they existed) or been remarkably careless in their preparatory work. The basilica at Cirencester was built of high-quality masonry in the last quarter of the first century, but curiously the site chosen lay partly over the ditches of the earlier fort. The fort had been abandoned as late as the 70s so it seems odd that the architect was ignorant of either the ditches' existence, or the possible consequences of building on top of them. In any case the basilica had begun to subside by the middle of the second century. Even the major basilica in London was built over filled-in brick earth quarries with similar results (figs. 63-5). More peculiarly the second century basilica and forum at Wroxeter were built on the site of unfinished public baths which were simply demolished to make way for the new project. A new set of baths was built in the adjacent insula. The reasons are unknown but may have been connected with problems over water supply. At Colchester the theatre was apparently built over the levelled eastern defences of the Claudian legionary fortress though too little is known about the theatre to know if this had any disastrous results.

All these examples suggest a strange lack of co-ordinated long-term planning, perhaps because there was a lot of administrative pressure to erect public buildings swiftly – we don't know, but even at Bath the late vaulted cover building for the sacred spring created apparently unforeseen problems with the huge weight of the vault (fig. 137) despite the provisions that had been made for the cover building for the Great Bath (figs. 10, 11). This haphazard approach to some major building projects seems also to have occasionally prevailed in private projects – the ambitious *frigidarium* at Lufton (fig. 106) needed propping up with substantial buttresses when it began to subside. The temple at Nettleton had to be strengthened internally to support a similar structure and eventually collapsed possibly because the precautions found necessary at Lufton were not adopted (figs. 147-50). The villa at Great Witcombe was built on an unsuitably steep hillside right over a spring, though this may have been for religious reasons (figs. 124, 125); thereafter the owners seem to have been pre-occupied with keeping the house in serviceable form. At Littlecote the fourth-century Orphic hall was built partly over an earlier road. Eventually subsidence occurred and one of the apses seems to have been damaged (fig. 159).

An interesting and related topic is the extent to which buildings were maintained. There are many military inscriptions, and some from other sites (see Appendix 2) which commemorate the restoration of buildings that had been allowed to deteriorate completely (if we can take them at face value). As it happens most of these date from the third century and as far as the military ones are concerned probably result from the general lack of military activity in the period. But it seems strange that a temple of Isis in London could have been allowed to decay in this way, especially as it was important enough to be rebuilt by the governor or his deputy. Similarly a temple to Diana was restored by the legionary legate at Caerleon. At Bath a cryptic and incomplete inscription appears to record the repair and repainting of an unspecified structure in the temple precinct (*RIB* 141). There is also the restoration of a *principia* at the imperial estate(?)/villa at Combe Down. Whether these are more generally representative of a lack of investment in maintenance, particularly of official buildings, we cannot be sure. On the other hand they may be yet more examples of structures which were not well designed in the first place.

These various examples suggest that many Romano-British architects belonged to the 'suck it and see' school of thought, contrasting with the popular image of Roman building as the product of competent planning and techniques. In other words, if the building started falling down it was either patched up or abandoned. If it didn't fall down there wasn't a problem. If correct this suggests that successful projects were as much a result of luck as of design. The great majority of simple ordinary buildings would have been designed by the owners themselves more or less as they went along, erected perhaps with help from neighbours or locally hired labour. In most cases the building would have belonged to a stereotype adapted to local circumstances and requirements with various alterations taking place as the project progressed. Although this must have been true of ordinary houses it may also have been true of substantial public buildings. Most major Romano-British public buildings, especially the basilica and forum, are all very similar and often derive from military prototypes (compare the plans on figs. 29 and 63). This raises an interesting point if we assume that many early major Romano-British public buildings were designed by military architects, or people trained by them. Such men would have been accustomed to working on virgin sites, or consolidating in stone an earlier timber fort. They may not always have fully appreciated the kind of structural problems which could arise when erecting massive masonry buildings on previously disturbed land. However this does not explain the lack of foresight found in private or religious projects such as Lufton, Littlecote or Nettleton.

Needless to say we have no actual plans of Romano-British buildings. Vitruvius said that it was essential for an architect to be able to draw so that he could communicate his ideas effectively. He also describes the preparation of ground-plans, elevations and perspective as well as the conception of new ideas through a flexible approach to specific problems (i.2.2). Some copies of plans, carved in stone, have survived from other parts of the Empire, for example a mausoleum and attendant buildings at Perugia in Italy, but are very far from being accurate blue-prints of the intended projects because the proportions of the various elements do not match the stated measurements. However they must have served as guides, aided by the sketching of buildings 'on site' perhaps by the architect in order to help him explain his intentions to the workmen. A tile found in London may be one of these. It seems to bear a sketched cross-section of an unspecified building. This has been identified as a *pharos* which is certainly a possibility (fig. 1a). It may also represent the cross-section of a basilica, or something else entirely – perhaps a stone finial, or even part of a pump or similar hydraulic system. A scratched representation of a building on plaster from the house at Hucclecote in Gloucestershire seems to represent a two-storied house with a gabled roof. The upper storey seems to have square windows and the lower storey seems to have two arched entrances. However, the illustration is clearly incomplete (fig. 1b).

We have practically no example of a single Romano-British architect whom we can associate with a specific structure. Building inscriptions generally record the emperor, governor, community or private individual who commissioned the project. But at Beauport Park in East Sussex a remodelling of the bath-house in the early third century seems to have been carried out by a man called Bassus or Bassianus under the orders of the *vilicus* (director) of the ironworks. Bassus is described as a *curam agens* which means he was in charge of the work in hand. So he was probably responsible for designing the extension to the bath-house (fig. 44 and Appendix 2). He was an architect or builder of poor quality despite his almost unique status of having escaped Romano-British architectural anonymity. His extension is of conspicuously poor work when compared to the neatly laid stones of the earlier part of the building.

From an archaeological point of view all these points raise a number of problems. It would be unwise to make assessments on the probability of there having been an upper storey, or other architectural complications, on the basis of the thickness of a stone footing or depth of a foundation as it is quite obvious that this sort of theoretical application was not applied, or if it was it was quite likely to be wrong. We rarely have any evidence for the extent to which timber had been used in a wall, and obviously a largely timber wall would have required less in the way of foundations. So one house might have had an excessively thick wall without an upper storey and another might have had an upper storey built on an inadequate wall and foundations. This did happen, and one needs to mention only how the new gable end of the house at Meonstoke fell down (fig. 104), probably because of inadequate foundations or bonding, to make the point. Had there been more time it would have probably been propped up with buttresses.

One important point worth considering is that the poor survival of Roman buildings in Britain makes it very difficult to be certain whether they were ever actually finished. Medieval cathedrals often took centuries to finish, and it may well be that some major Romano-British buildings were never completed, making discussions about whether the structures were viable irrelevant. The headquarters building at the legionary fortress of Caerleon had a huge basilican cross-hall (fig. 28). Some of the foundations and wall-footings have been located, but the whole area was covered over with a thin layer of packed soil and no remains of columns were found even though the positions of their bases were. Of course it could have been comprehensively demolished, but fragmentary traces of the super-structure might then have been expected. With public buildings the problem of local money may have had an even more significant effect on construction projects which could easily have lasted longer than the patience, fortunes or lives of their benefactor(s). From an archaeological point of view such situations are almost impossible to identify, and the details are lost in the untraceable machinations of Romano-British local politics and finance.

With so little specific evidence it is not easy to draw general conclusions about Romano-British architects and surveyors. Possible examples of poor planning or design are not isolated, and the impression is of a provincial profession occasionally out of its depth. There were obviously many reasons for this and it will never be possible to isolate those which complicated any one instance. But we only have to consider the kind of problems which befall modern buildings to know that poor-planning, hasty construction, shortage of money and the use of inadequate materials are usually behind most of those that prove structurally unsound. However it would be unfair not to point out that many of the simpler (and not necessarily smaller) Romano-British buildings exhibit no evidence at all for subsidence or collapse resulting from an inherently unstable design, or unsuitably prepared ground.

Timber

It is almost certain that the vast majority of buildings in Roman Britain were made of timber, either fully or in part. This is based on the fact that timber, at the time, must have been far more readily obtainable than building stone. It would have been felled locally and would have required a minimum amount of effort to convert into fort buildings, dwellings and even public buildings like the first basilica at Silchester (fig. 62). The availability of suitable timber may even have helped dictate the distribution of buildings, particularly country ones, but we have no idea of the extent of initial deforestation and subsequent forestry management that took place in Roman Britain. It has been calculated that the fortress at Caerleon would have required the equivalent of 150 hectares (380 acres) of woodland (Brewer, 1987, 16; about seven times the area of the 20.5 hectare/52 acre fortress; 495 x 420m/1618 x 1373ft), though obviously maintenance and rebuilding would have used up even more. A writing tablet from an early well on the site records that some men were concerned with the collection of timber for building (*materia*). Presumably as the province developed stocks of properly seasoned timber would have been built up, though during the early stages of military building such long-term considerations would have been ignored. Wood was prepared by either sawing or splitting the trunks to make planks and posts. Later on a new problem may have emerged. At the New Fresh Wharf in London examination of quayside timbers suggested that substantial exploitation of mature trees during the second century had created a shortage of supply. By the late third century the quay builders were having to turn to younger trees. If correct this gives us some idea of the massive scale of Roman use of timber.

Archaeological evidence for timber buildings is usually relatively poor – remains of such buildings are almost always confined to post-holes and sleeper beam trenches – but many buildings which appear to be made of stone may have only had stone footings to inhibit rot. Even so very few first century buildings in Britain seem to have had any stone at all. Only in the second

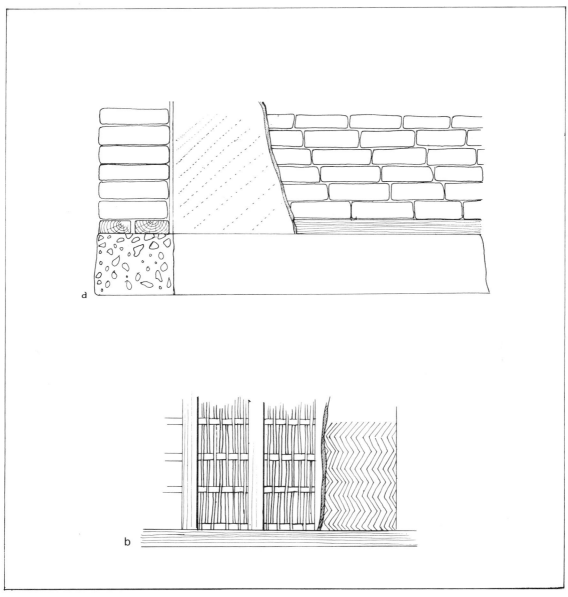

century and after did it become commonplace to consolidate a structure in stone. Verulamium is an excellent example: it took a major fire in c. 155 to provoke the townspeople into building stone houses, or at least with stone footings.

Buildings made entirely of timber were generally secured to the ground in one of two ways. They are found most frequently in early military sites, because these were often occupied for a short period of time before being abandoned. On longer period sites where later stone buildings were erected on the same plots it can be difficult to identify traces of earlier timber structures. In the simplest method, the upright

2 Early daub and timber wall types (after Crummy but adapted):

a daub-and-timber wall. A mortar plinth provided a footing, a layer of timber provided a level base for the wall of sun-dried bricks. The surface was then rendered and could be plastered to provide a perfectly adequate, if not particularly strong, wall which could be painted. Internal walls could dispense with the mortar plinth.

b wattle-and-daub internal wall made out of a timber frame laced with wattles and packed with daub and then rendered and plastered. More basic walls omitted the timber horizontals, the vertical members being hammered straight into the ground.

Based on mid-first-century walls excavated in the legionary fortress at Colchester (c. 43-47).

17

posts which formed the frame were inserted straight into post-holes which were then packed to make the posts secure. The building's super-structure was then nailed or pegged on and around the timber uprights. The iron nails used could be quite substantial, for example 30cm (1 Roman foot) in length. The use of prefabricated components would have hastened the whole process. The early military granary at Fishbourne is a very good example of this, and the archae-ological product is a pattern of post-holes. Some-times the waterlogged remains of the base of an upright may remain in the hole or even as no more than a 'ghost' of discoloured soil. Unfortunately they tell us nothing of the super-structure. The mid-first-century granaries at the fortresses of Usk and Inchtuthil were built with the more complicated method. In this case a series of trenches were dug into which sleeper beams were laid (figs. 17, 36). These horizontal beams were designed to form the base for the uprights which would have been inserted into holes designed specially to receive them. Like-wise there is no information about the super-structure because the only product of archae-ological excavation is the sequence of sleeper trenches. A remarkable recent discovery in London is the almost complete floor and parts of the walls of an early-second-century timber ware-house (fig. 172). We can be sure that carpenters were skilled men who used precision equipment, much of which has not changed up to modern times (see *Finds*, 61). The mitre square from Canterbury (fig. 1d) has been interpreted as the possession of a skilled joiner who was probably preparing timber on the site of a second-century domestic structure. His name was Gaius Cu . . . Valenus.

Whether or not the footings were of timber or stone, timber walls must have been made up of a series of uprights between which horizontal beams were inserted or laid across. This created a timber frame which could be filled with wattle and daub, timber, brick or stone. Timber-framed walls filled with brick can still be seen at Herculaneum in southern Italy. Here the unique conditions of being buried under a mass of boiling mud and lava carbonized the wood. The careful excavations of modern times have shown that upper storeys were often built in this way. The structure is lighter and stronger as a result, though obviously normal weathering must have meant that such buildings would have needed considerable periodic repairs. While this technique must have been used in Britain it is more likely that the timber-framed buildings of Roman Britain would have had wattle-and-daub fillings in the walls. Fortunately the circum-stances of the Boudican Revolt in 60 have left well-defined burnt layers at London, Colchester and Verulamium from the sack of each settle-ment. This has preserved the footings of wattle-and-daub walls (fig. 2). Waterlogged deposits can preserve wattle and daub as well. Vitruvius was very critical of wattle and daub because of its instability and inflammability. He considered it only as an expedient solution to a lack of time or money (ii.8.20) and emphasized how vital it was to build the wattle and daub on a raised base in order to prevent damp which would rot the timber frame and cause the wall to sag and crack its plaster skin. The overall impression of such structures must have resembled the half-timbered houses which are still a common feature of Britain and northern Europe.

Apart from wattle and daub the other most likely walling would have been planks of timber. The reconstructed granary at the first-century fort of the Lunt, near Coventry, was re-erected in this way. The effect is similar to the 'clapper-board' technique still visible on some older houses from the eighteenth and nineteenth centuries in England, particularly East Anglia and Kent.

Stone

Building partly or entirely in stone did not become commonplace in Roman Britain until the second century. It was not only durable and practical but also the only viable means, along with concrete, of building walls strong enough to support vaults. It was also the most desirable medium for constructing elaborate buildings of any type, for example classical-style temples and basilicas. The practice of enjoying baths heated by furnaces made stone an essential material for bath-houses. There are a number of rural sites where a bath-house has been located but no house, suggesting that the latter was built of perishable materials – a risk which could not be taken for baths (for example Baston Manor, at Hayes, Kent).

Stone was quarried locally wherever possible, and sometimes inscriptions are found that confirm the quarry was worked in Roman times (fig. 3). Foundations are not always examined closely in excavation but they probably varied extensively depending on either the height of the building or the experience of the man who was building it. Normally a trench was dug and filled with rubble courses set in some sort of cement. These foundations might be narrower than the walls they supported as in the house at Plaxtol (figs. 96, 97), or they might be wider. Where the land was damp, or the walls were to be built to a considerable height, stone foundations might be laid on top of a timber raft which was itself set on piles driven several metres into the subsoil. This may sound rather unreliable but it was a very well

established technique and is usually found under major fortifications, for example the late riverside wall in London (fig. 170), or the Saxon Shore fort at Pevensey (fig. 52). Where a building was set into a hillside the slope might be cut back and the stone set directly onto the surface, for example at the Huggin Hill baths in London which were terraced into the slope leading down to the river (fig. 4).

Evidence of attempts to restrict the effects of rising damp and rain passing through porous masonry are extremely rare. Hypocaust systems may have helped dry walls, and indeed the purpose of the system may have been as much to combat condensation as to heat rooms. However, hypocausts were not as common as is sometimes popularly imagined and were in any case usually confined to bath suites. A building at 25-6 Lime Street in London put up after *c.* 125 had a cellar built at least 1.6m (5ft) below the surrounding ground level. Three rows of roof-tiles (*tegulae* – see fig. 8) had been mortared vertically to one of the exterior walls in what has been interpreted as an attempt to create a barrier against damp (see London in bibliography for Chapter 4). Even if it was effective no other examples are known from London, so the technique cannot have been very widespread.

---

3 Carved stone removed from a quarry at Fallowfield Fell, near Hadrian's Wall about 6.5km (4 miles) east of Chesters fort. It bears the inscription [P]ETRA FLAVI CARANTINI, which means 'Flavius Carantinus' rock'. Carantinus would have been a legionary, of unknown rank, detailed to work in the quarry, supplying stone for the Wall. The stone has been removed to Chesters museum. Such inscriptions are well-known from other quarries near the Wall and elsewhere in Britain and the Empire. (Photo: author, 1988.)

There were two basic methods of building in stone in the Roman period. Masonry construction involved the use of accurately sawn and placed blocks of stone. Their weight made mortar unnecessary and it was extremely durable. However, it required a great deal of unskilled effort to transport stone to the site and a great deal of skilled effort to erect the building. The unfinished remains of a stores building at Corbridge (fig. 5) give an idea of what this could involve. Concrete construction, *structura caementicia*, was much better suited to Roman Britain where it was usually based on mortared rubble. This formed the core of a wall which was faced with small blocks of stone or brick. A few courses of the faces were built first and the rubble core poured in. When this had set the height of the faces was raised and more core poured in, and so on. The facing and the core can be clearly seen in Hadrian's Wall at Poltross Burn (fig. 6). As the wall's height increased it was supported with wooden scaffolding set into putlog holes. These can be seen in the 'Old Work' at Wroxeter and in the 'Mint Wall' at Lincoln (fig. 68) but few surviving Romano-British walls are high enough to show this. However Vitruvius pointed out that

rubble construction, however beautifully finished, was not durable (i.8.8). If the facing stones became displaced then the internal core is exposed and as the cement bonding decays so the rubble begins to break up. This is why Romano-British buildings cannot be exposed to public view unless modern consolidation of the core and facing has been undertaken.

It does seem to have been general practice, as elsewhere in the Empire, to use rectangular or square tiles as levelling and bonding courses, as quoins for corners and to create a frame for openings (fig. 7). The effect of this was to use the tiles almost as a kind of frame filled with stone. This, combined with cement or concrete used as pliable filler, made up for irregularities in the stone. In this way flint nodules could be used as facing

---

4 The baths at Huggin Hill, London during excavation. The huge complex of public baths was terraced into the slope down to the Thames. On the right of this view a substantial wall can be seen abutting directly onto the slope which has been cut back to create two levels. (Photo: author, 1989.)

5 Unfinished masonry at Corbridge, Northumberland. Part of a substantial building, possibly a store, which may have been built during the late second century but which was never completed. Although the blocks have been dressed on the sides lying against other stones their faces are still rough. Had construction continued the faces would probably have been chiselled and polished to create a smoother surface. (Photo: author, 1989.)

stones in substantial walls, and this is particularly evident in city walls in south-east England, for example at Silchester and Verulamium. Even in these cases the facing stones were worked to create a relatively smooth surface, but such a useful commodity was readily carted off in the Middle Ages and few traces of the old surface survive. It was not always necessary to use tile, Hadrian's Wall was built entirely of stone. Although the width varied according to the zone and period in question the Wall was made up of a core of concreted rubble with sides of dressed stone.

The external appearance of many stone walls may have been quite different from that popularly imagined. Recent work on Hadrian's Wall has suggested that the curtain was rendered and whitewashed. At the temple on Maiden Castle traces of external rendering and painting were found. This may have been far more common than we will ever appreciate and it may be that Romano-British towns and houses resembled modern Mediterranean settlements in having rendered and brightly painted walls. Unfortunately the British climate has destroyed most of the evidence.

6 Hadrian's Wall at milecastle 48 (Poltross Burn). The Wall's facing stones can be seen in contrast to the rubble core. This particular section also shows where the milecastle's wing walls (left of centre) had been built to 'Broad Wall' specifications (see Chapter 2). The foundation for the Wall had been prepared for the same gauge but when the Wall was actually constructed on this stretch plans had changed and it was being built to the new 'Narrow Wall' width. (Photo: author, 1989.)

7 Tile arch inserted in the masonry wall of the commandant's baths at Binchester, built by the *numerus Concangiensium* (a low status auxiliary infantry unit). The arch was one of a number which helped circulation of warm air beneath the floors of the fourth-century bath-house. Neatly constructed of splayed tiles cemented into the masonry it is a good example of a typical feature of Roman architecture. A similar technique was used for windows in walls though obviously these rarely survive (see fig. 104). (Photo: author, 1988.)

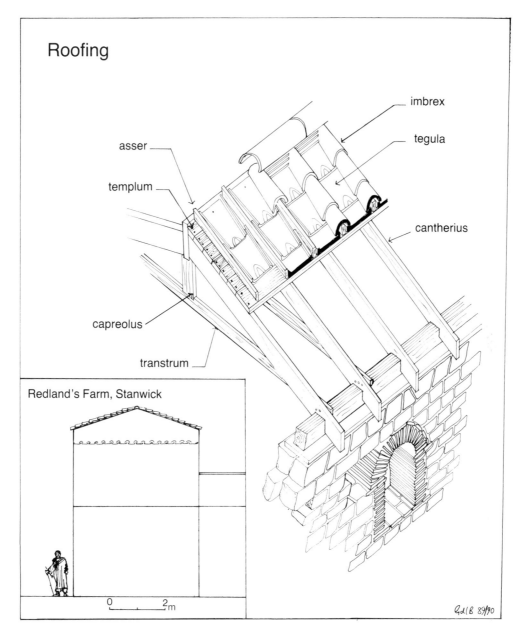

Roofing

asser

templum

capreolus

transtrum

imbrex

tegula

cantherius

Redland's Farm, Stanwick

0   2 m

GdB 89/90

8 Diagrammatic view of a Roman tile roof. This diagram is based on and adapted from a modern Italian roof illustrated in Barry (1980, fig. 183) which makes sense of the Vitruvian description. The problem concerns the upper strips of wood (*asseri*). Vitruvius describes these as simply over-lying the layer of *templi* and consequently they seem rather superfluous. This modern Italian roof shows how the *asseri* were laid at a distance from one another in order to create channels for the *tegulae*. The *tegulae* were wedged in and consequently it would not have been necessary to nail each one in – particularly as the *asseri* would have expanded when damp. The joins were covered in mortar and the *imbrices* laid over. A ridge of *imbrices* was laid along the apex of the roof, any gaps being filled with mortar and pieces of broken tile. The inset shows a reconstructed view of the collapsed gable end wall found at Stanwick, giving a roof pitch of about 20°.

23

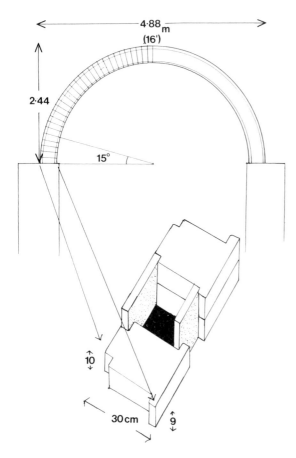

9 Vaulting at the bath-house, Chesters fort, Hadrian's Wall. A number of the tufa components of the vault were found during the excavation in the late nineteenth century. The vault had been made out of a series of ribs of solid, shaped blocks. Each rib was connected to its neighbours with flat blocks sitting on shoulders cut into the solid blocks thus creating voids to lighten the vault. By using the measurements of the blocks and the known diameter of the room (G; see figs. 45, 46) it is possible to reconcile the vault with the room. It can be seen that the vault blocks were less wide than the wall. Therefore it may be that the external wall (on the left; the right wall abuts another room) rose higher to support a pitched roof above the vault (similar to fig. 83).

Roofing

Although the shattered fragments of roof tile are one of the most obvious clues to locating a Romano-British building, little is known about how roofs were constructed. Roofs were obviously essential but they create certain problems. Firstly they had to be strong but as

10 Lower portion of a reinforced pier of the Great Bath at Bath (see fig. 11). (Photo: author.)

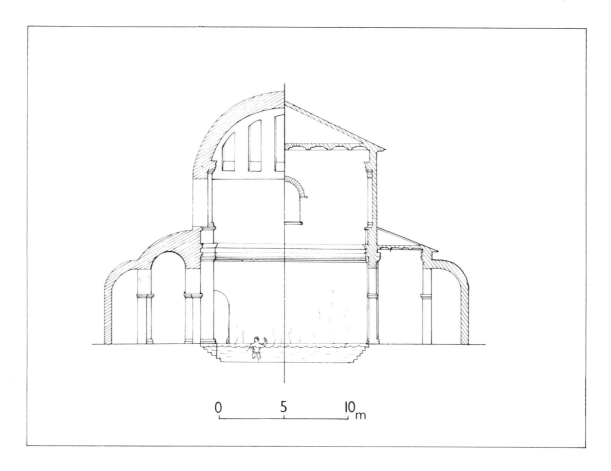

0 5 10 m

light as possible; secondly the weight had to be distributed so that it was directed down through the supporting walls. Most tiles were made of fired clay, but in some areas where the stone was suitable slates made of stone could be used instead. Slate or Cotswold limestone was ideal. Many buildings must have been thatched, especially the outbuildings on villa estates and the more basic houses. However the only evidence for this is a lack of tiles amongst the building's debris, and in any individual case this may be because the tiles had been removed for re-use.

The individual tile types are discussed in more detail in *Finds* (p. 110ff). There has been a great deal of debate about exactly how the tiles were secured to the roof. The same tiles are in common use in Mediterranean buildings today, and Figure 8 shows how a modern Italian roof is constructed. The discovery of a collapsed gable end wall at Stanwick, Northants, has shown that the roof here had a pitch of about 20 degrees and a height

11 Cross-section of the Great Bath at Bath, Avon (after Cunliffe, but adapted). The Great Bath was 22m (72ft) long by 8.8m (29ft) wide and was built in its original form in the late first century. At this period it has been assumed that the bath had a pitched roof supported by a colonnaded arcade with two storeys (*right*). However this created long-term structural problems because of the predominantly warm and wet atmosphere created by the thermal waters of the spa. The timbers of the roof would have decayed quite rapidly under such conditions and there must have been costly maintenance work underway all the time. Eventually, by the late second century at the earliest the building was completely re-roofed, this time with a barrel vault. The weight and thrust was far too great for the existing piers and consequently they were substantially thickened (*left*). The surviving stumps show this very clearly (fig. 10). The side-walls were equipped with additional piers to help absorb the thrust. The vault itself was made of hollow box-tiles (to save weight) with a concrete skin capped with tiles. It may very well have had a pitched roof to protect it against wind and rain.

of only 0.61m (2ft).

It was possible for a decorative effect to be created by using tiles of different colours, achieved through the use of different clays and firing conditions. At Lullingstone, Kent, the second-century house was roofed with red tiles occasionally interspersed with yellow tiles. At Piddington, Northants, the *imbrices* (curved roof tiles) were over-fired to create a deep blue colour. They were laid over yellow *tegulae* (flat roof tiles). This particular roof was supported by plastered columns painted red and purple-brown, reminding us that the ancient world's appreciation of garish colour schemes was much stronger than surviving remains usually imply.

Many tiled roofs may have covered and concealed vaulted roofs, though this would generally have been confined to bath-houses where the warm and damp air would have had a destructive effect on roof timbers (see Caerleon and Wroxeter, figs. 43, 83). Tile was also used in the vault at Beauport Park which covered one of the warm rooms. Large fragments of the vault lay on the floor where it had collapsed, and it was possible to see that the central row of keystones had been flanked on either side by a row of tiles (fig. 44). The bath-house at Chesters used tufa sections in the vault which created voids and thus saved weight (fig. 9). Vaulting did mean that the lateral walls had to be substantially stronger in order to withstand the forces. The Great Bath at Bath shows this to good effect (figs. 10, 11) and shows just how much reinforcement work had to be done even though extensive use had been made of weight-relieving voussoir tiles.

Windows and doors

Romano-British buildings must have had windows but hardly any survive either *in situ*, or in fragments. The Beauport Park and Chesters bath-houses and the town house at Colliton Park, Dorchester, retain window sills (fig. 12). The Dorchester house's window had collapsed into the house but it could be partially reconstructed and shows that the stone was moulded to take a wooden frame for the glass, splinters of which were found about. The collapse of the gable end of the house at Meonstoke has preserved brick-arched windows which had been blocked up at a later date (fig. 104) and the collapse of Duncan's

Gate at Colchester has preserved part of another (fig. 89). On the northern frontier round-headed windows were often created by carving a semi-circle into a single piece of stone and this is how the gate at South Shields has been reconstructed (fig. 27). The depictions of buildings from Hucclecote and Trier though seem to show square windows (fig. 1). Although we also have sections of iron window grilles from other sites (see *Finds*, fig. 62), the truth is that we have no idea of how common windows were. Too many may have been considered a disadvantage in houses which were designed to be warm and comfortable, too few would have made expensive artificial lighting essential. But we can assume that glass would have been essential for the heated chambers in a bath-house, while shutters and grilles were probably more usual for other windows.

The only evidence of doors which usually survives is a space in the wall as, with a single exception, all Romano-British doors had perished before discovery. When the vault in the headquarters building at Chesters was excavated in the nineteenth century the door was found in place. Made of oak it was strengthened with iron bands and studs but it rapidly disintegrated on exposure to air. Sometimes sections of the door frame are found but this is generally only when the frame was made of stone. Many houses at Caerwent had stone sills, and at Great Witcombe a complete frame, made of four single pieces of stone, was found. Stone sills have recesses in them for the door pivots and these show if the door was single– or double-leaved. Timber frame members very rarely survive but sometimes an impression of a timber sill can be found in wall cement, as in the recent excavation of a house at Plaxtol in Kent.

Internal decorations and features of Romano-British buildings

Amongst the most interesting aspects of Romano-British houses are their decorations. Many have yielded traces of wall plaster but this is rarely preserved well enough to allow reconstruction, and in any case a large number of the houses were excavated before the techniques had been developed. More important are the mosaics because enough are known to make it possible to have some idea of their frequency and origin.

This is such a huge subject that it would be quite impossible to do more than consider just a few general points here.

Mosaics and tessellated flooring

Villas and town houses seem hardly to have existed in the first century beyond the very simplest types of buildings (see Chapter 4). Correspondingly very few mosaics are known from the period though the large houses which were built, like Fishbourne (the 'proto-palace' which preceded the better-known Flavian house) and Eccles in Kent, were decorated with mosaics as early as the 60s. These were simple monochrome geometrical designs which reflected the wider tastes of the period: better preserved contemporary examples are known from Pompeii and Herculaneum. It seems reasonable to assume that such isolated examples were laid by professional craftsmen who had come from the Continent to do the job.

Throughout the period simple tessellated

12 Reconstructed window recess in the south wall of a room in the town house at Colliton Park, Dorchester, Dorset. Note the seating for the window frame. Glass from the window itself was found within the room. The wall is made of flint nodules cemented together but around the window larger pieces of roughly dressed stone consolidated the opening. (Photo: author, 1989.)

floors, made up of small pieces of stone or tile, were fairly common. Normally they were either uniformly red or simple geometric patterns and were ideal for corridors or houses owned by the less well-off. An alternative was *opus spicatum* where narrow rectangular tiles were laid in a herringbone pattern. This seems to have been particularly durable. The cheapest option of all was *opus signinum* where crushed tile and brick were mixed with concrete to create flooring with a red-brown hue. At Verulamium this first appears around 100, but much later on it was occasionally used to patch damaged mosaics which had once been of the highest quality, for example the Seasons mosaic from Cirencester (see below).

In the second century the better-appointed town houses seem to have been fitted with mosaics and tessellated floors more as a matter of course and this suggests a developing Romano-British tradition of the art. Verulamium and Colchester have produced the largest number of examples, and stylistically the mosaics were based on geometric backgrounds and panels containing representations of animals, fantastic or natural, human beings, divine or mortal, or inanimate objects like vases. Colour was now commonly used. The panels may have been pre-fabricated and chosen from stock by the customer. The Verulamium examples tend to be rather restrained whereas some of the panels found at Cirencester show that some Romano-British mosaicists of the late second century were inspired artists of the highest order. The head of Dionysus as Autumn in the Seasons mosaic from Dyer Street is one of the most vital mosaic portraits from anywhere at any time, despite having been crudely repaired with *opus signinum*. Although town houses had mosaics at this period there is comparatively little evidence for them in the countryside and only about 20 are currently known, for example at Boughspring near Chepstow and Great Witcombe, both in Gloucestershire, and Brislington in Avon.

Few Romano-British mosaics have been attributed to the third century, but by the fourth the elaboration of a number of villas seems to have stimulated a revival. Students of the subject have been particularly fond of trying to identify regional 'schools' based on designs and the topics depicted. Interesting though this is, such theories are necessarily based purely on the products and we really cannot distinguish the products of one workshop from the works of another though geography and distance make it likely that designs and topics might tend to be regional. This is as likely to reflect the customers' tastes as those of the craftsmen. 'Influence' is as likely to come through the medium of demand as it is through those who supply it – this applies equally to architecture in this context – and a mosaicist interested in staying in business would have made what his customers wanted; style and subject matter can be easily imitated. Probably the most interesting are the remarkable mythological series from Brading in the Isle of Wight, and the Orpheus mosaics from Barton Farm near Ciren-

cester and Woodchester. These are highly complicated geometric designs which use a number of stock components in a highly sophisticated way combined with naturalistic animals and humans. Whether they were of religious significance or not is quite another matter. A similar problem of interpretation affects the mosaics from Frampton and Hinton St Mary in Dorset (plate 13). The villa at Bignor has a particularly dramatic series of mosaics (plate 1) which includes the monogram signature TR possibly standing for 'Terentius', perhaps the man responsible for designing and supervising the laying of the floors. Unfortunately no other mosaics have been found which also bear the monogram, highlighting the problem of identifying schools without such evidence.

The kind of mosaics referred to above were the most expensive and would certainly not have been the kind of decoration most Romano-British would have taken for granted, any more than they would have expected to live in large courtyard houses. Even for those who did, mosaics rarely covered more than a very few floors, the remainder being consolidated with simple red *tesserae* or *opus signinum*. There would probably have been rugs or carpets as well but naturally these do not survive.

Very few mosaics are known from non-domestic contexts in Britain. One of the rare military examples is from Caerleon, found in the second-century headquarters building there. However, it was laid in a single small room in the north-east range, and the design is a very simple geometric one surrounded by an equally simple scroll. The fourth-century temple of Nodens at Lydney had a mosaic depicting a marine scene and cryptic inscription recording its funding from temple offerings and laying under the supervision of one Victorinus who may have been an interpreter of dreams (see Appendix 2). It is an equally unusual example though rather more elaborate in design. These rare instances mean that mosaics in Roman Britain can only really be studied in the villas and town houses.

Wall-plaster

The walls of any house with even limited pretensions would have been rendered with plaster. Those who could afford it would have paid for the walls to be painted with designs, probably in rooms with mosaic floors. Public buildings would certainly have been extensively painted. Whereas many mosaic floors are known from Britain, painted wall-plaster is much rarer and is usually so fragmentary that it is extremely difficult to restore the original design.

In recent years techniques have been developed which have made it possible to 'lift' shattered sections of wall or ceiling plaster from where they fell. So instead of the occasional recovery of larger fragments of plaster modern excavations can sometimes produce enough pieces to reconstitute quite elaborate schemes. These include second-century examples from town houses in Verulamium (plate 2) and Leicester, and the very remarkable series of fourth-century panels depicting Christian motifs and disciples from the celebrated villa at Lullingstone in Kent. Other buildings had painted wall-plaster too, for example the panels from the so-called *macellum* in Leicester and a mausoleum in the cemetery at Poundbury outside Dorchester, Dorset. In very rare instances the original walls stand high enough to preserve large portions of painted wall-plaster *in situ*, for example the exceptional 'Painted House' at Dover (fig. 116) or the villa at Iwerne Minster in Dorset.

As with mosaics it would be quite impossible to venture deeply into this subject. However, as more and more painted wall-plaster is recovered it is probably safe to say that it must have been far more common than mosaics and far more common than we will ever be able to appreciate fully. Most internal walls in public buildings, houses or temples would have had some sort of rendering and these would at the very least have been painted a single colour or embellished with simple designs. The temple at Maiden Castle had external walls which were plastered and painted red (figs. 141, 142). Weathering is obviously far more damaging to external walls and again we probably have no idea of how widespread external plastering and painting was.

Wall-plaster was normally built up in layers graduating from coarse layers which bonded the plaster to the wall to a fine skim which provided the painting surface. In Roman Britain two or three coarse layers around 1cm (0.4in.) in thickness normally provided the base. Plaster was derived from lime and sand as it still is. Rough stone surfaces were ideal, but wattle and daub, or tile surfaces, needed keying first. Plaster from the fourth-century house in Colliton Park,

Dorchester, had traces of reeds on the reverse and these may have formed part of the backing required for ceiling plaster, though this is not certain. The skim was achieved by using powdered calcium or powdered marble; the latter was unlikely to be used in Britain for obvious reasons. It seems that the main background colours were painted on before the plaster had dried, as the drying process created a smooth surface on which to paint the more detailed elements of the design. In order to make the whole process easier plaster was sometimes laid in sections. Unfortunately we know nothing of how Romano-British wall plaster artists operated, or even the name of a single one of them.

With limited resources available archaeology has obviously only concentrated on the more exciting compositions, and it is clear that the affluent Romano-British were able to afford competent artists. In the first century it was much less common, reflecting the early state of the province's development. However, the Flavian house at Fishbourne (fig. 119) and another house of similar date at Boxmoor in Hertfordshire are amongst a small number of examples. Not surprisingly they followed a well-established basic Roman lay-out which divided a wall into three horizontal zones: the lower dado (not more than about 80cm/2.5ft in height); the main section which was divided into vertical panels containing the most elaborate scenes or topics (around 2m/6ft in height); and a narrow upper which created a border with the ceiling. The main section is invariably the most interesting because it usually incorporated smaller panels depicting mythological figures engaged in some activity or a motif, alternatively they might form part of a larger scheme involving fantastic architecture. Amongst the most complete series we possess are the paintings from the 'Painted House' at Dover (fig. 116), the Norfolk Street villa in Leicester and the house known as *Insula* xxi.2 at Verulamium (plate 2). Ceiling designs were more two dimensional in concept but often no less complex and they must have been even more difficult to execute satisfactorily. Generally they involved repeated sequences of motifs contained within square, circular or polygonal panels. It is probably safe to assume that floors, walls and ceilings were often decorated with a theme based on a single concept but it is unusual to recover the remains of a single panel, let alone a scheme.

Other decorations

The only other kinds of decoration which might have been installed in Romano-British buildings are stucco (decorative plasterwork) and carved stonework (architraves, columns and the like). Not surprisingly both are rare, stucco particularly because it is so prone to fragmenting. As far as houses are concerned Fishbourne is one of the few sites which have produced traces of it but it may have been much more widespread than we can appreciate. Certainly towns like Pompeii and Herculaneum show that it was commonplace in first-century Italy, decorating ceilings and walls in all kinds of buildings. It was particularly suitable for decorating the internal surface of vaults.

Ornamental stonework is better known. We can be confident that extensive use of it was made in public buildings and major religious buildings, for example the temples at Colchester and Bath (figs. 129-36). London has produced a large number of fragmentary traces which suggests that ornamental stonework was widespread in the province's capital (fig. 163). Various pieces have been recovered from recent excavations along the riverfront including fragments of columns and capitals. Other major towns have produced more substantial pieces of stonework which almost certainly came from major public

---

13 South-west gate at Lincoln showing the re-use of masonry. The gate was built in the early fourth century but was substantially redesigned later in succeeding decades to include two projecting towers. Part of the north tower's plinth included a section of carved entablature, possibly from a temple. While the carved stonework was approximately the right shape it must have looked curiously displaced and suggests that the gate was built either with an eye to economy or haste. The carved stone now visible is a cast of the original. (Photo: author, 1989.)

buildings like the basilica or forum. Ornate carved stone capitals have been found at several sites, for example Silchester, Cirencester and Caerwent. At Bath the recovery of a very large quantity of the carved stonework from the temple and its precinct gives us a very good idea of its original appearance. Most of these provincial pieces would have been carved locally from stone which had been quarried in the vicinity. We even have the names of a few of the Romano-British craftsmen (see Appendix 2 and *Finds*, fig. 36 and p. 62). Such ornamentation even extended to the northern frontier where forts seem to have been decorated with appropriate figures like a figure of Mars from Housesteads on Hadrian's Wall, carved in a niche. It probably once stood in the headquarters.

As far as private houses are concerned we have really very little evidence except for stone columns, but again these tend to reflect local availability of stone. The houses at Bignor, Gadebridge Park, Keynsham and Chedworth are amongst those which have yielded remains of columns, balustrades or cornices but like mosaics

they were probably the preserve of the rich rather than a commonplace fitting. Columns were normally turned on lathes but where the stone was not of good enough quality to allow this they might be built up of stone or tile discs and covered with moulded cement and plaster before being painted, as at Piddington. Roof-finials, made of stone or fired clay, were designed to act as attractive terminals, probably at the apex of a gable, and have been found at several other sites, for example Dewlish, Llantwit Major and Rockbourne. Some of these were made of fired clay and normally had triangular cut-outs and trimmings made with finger-pressed frills, for example one from Norton (see *Finds*, fig. 65). The villa at Piddington has produced fragments

---

14 Hypocaust at Rockbourne villa, Hants. This is a unique example of a heated floor standing on *pilae* made of curved roof tiles, *imbrices*. The room was built as part of an extension to the villa house around the first half of the third century. (Photo: author, 1989.)

of at least 15, suggesting that they may have been much more common than hitherto suspected.

Very few Romano-Celtic temples have produced ornamental stonework. The temples at Bath, Nettleton and Corbridge are exceptional in this respect. The problem is that large pieces of stone have always been prone to robbing, even in the late Roman period when it became common to remove stone and use it for new defensive structures. The west gate of the lower town at Lincoln, built in the fourth century, was found to contain a particularly ornate piece of a cornice which had obviously been removed from another building (fig. 13), possibly a temple of classical form.

But stone is difficult to transport and unless available very locally it was more convenient to use it sparingly but effectively as veneers or inlays secured to a brick or concrete core. This applies particularly to exotic coloured stone which is not found in Britain. London has produced numerous examples of exotic stonework, for example porphyry from Egypt and Sparta (Greece), and marbles from various sites in the Mediterranean as well as Purbeck in Dorset. However, while examples are common, most of them are no more than chippings or fragments and give us very little idea of how the material was distributed, or whether it comes from private as well as public buildings. The Neronian 'proto-palace' and the later Flavian palace at Fishbourne has produced some of the very earliest evidence for the use of stone in this way, though it is an exceptional assemblage. Numerous sections of marble mouldings, pieces of *opus sectile* (flooring made up of various coloured stone shapes like squares and triangles) and traces of masons' debris were recovered.

Hypocausts, water-supply and baths

The hypocaust system of heating is a feature so commonly associated with Roman life that it is rather easy to assume that it was far more widespread than it actually was. The principle is very simple and is described so frequently that it needs only a brief summary here. Hot air from a furnace was channelled under the floors of rooms and up through the walls, escaping out of the roof. The cavity under the floor was created by either supporting the floor on tiles (figs. 14, 15) or by building channels into a solid floor (fig. 16). Hot air from the furnace, which was invariably a small

external structure, usually entered through arches which might also carry the heat to an adjacent room (fig. 7). The air was carried through special hollow tiles in the wall (see *Finds*, figs. 66, 67).

15 Tile stacks in the commandant's fourth-century baths at Binchester, Durham. The stacks, at a little over 1m (3ft 5in) in height, are unusually tall but exceptionally well-preserved. Some bear the stamp N CON for the *numerus Concangiensium* (the infantry unit responsible for the construction work). See fig. 7 as well. (Photo: author, 1988.)

16 Hypocaust in Room N1 at Fishbourne palace. The heating was being added to this room around the end of the third century when the whole building was destroyed by fire. The hypocaust, built of upturned roof-tiles in a room in the north wing, had never been fired and no floor had been laid above it though abandoned heaps of mortar suggest it was soon about to be. Note the four channels directing heat from the centre of the room to the four corners where vents would have been sited to allow it to escape up through the walls. Heat would have entered through the separate fifth channel in the north wall. (Photo: author, 1989.)

The most common use of hypocaust systems was in bath-houses in order to create the correct temperatures in the warm room, *tepidarium*, and the hot room, *caldarium*. Public bath-houses could involve huge floor areas supported on tiles, for example at Huggin Hill in London (fig. 84). The furnaces also heated water for the hot and warm baths. Depending on the circumstances water was collected locally from rain-water, springs or wells, or was supplied to the building via a civic water supply. Water-pipes are known from a number of towns (see *Finds*, fig. 68). The water was contained in a cold lead or stone tank from where lead or wood pipes with bronze taps carried a supply to a large bronze boiler which was supported above a furnace with huge iron beams. The furnace naturally made a bath-house an enormous fire risk, so it is not surprising that many baths were built away from villa houses or forts (though this was not always the case – integral baths are known at a number of villas, and some military baths were built within the fort). For the same reason they were built of stone. The plumbing arrangements are known from intact systems in houses in and around Pompeii and Herculaneum. However, very little evidence apart from lead pipes has survived in Britain because the materials were so readily re-usable. But at Chedworth a number of massive iron bars were found in the northern baths which must have been used to support boilers (though they had been displaced by the final period); most of the other examples known have also been found in bath buildings, for example at Catterick. The largest weighs 230kg (484lbs) and is 1.61m (5ft 4in) long. Once heated the water was carried to the baths in more pipes. The circulating hot air in the wall cavities helped to keep it warm.

But apart from these, hypocausts are comparatively unusual and if fitted, like most of the luxuries associated with 'Roman villas' such as mosaics, they were generally confined to a small number of rooms. Most rooms in practice would have been heated by braziers. In addition, unless the function of the room(s) is otherwise beyond doubt it is always a possibility that the underfloor heating channels were actually designed for the less luxurious purposes of drying clothes, fabric and/or grain rather than the wet and cold Romano-British. They may also have helped combat rising damp. It would have been hopelessly impractical to try and heat most public buildings, but the enigmatic 'tower' at Stonea (fig. 72) does seem to have been fitted with a hypocaust, and so too was one of the tribunals in the basilica at Caerwent.

2

MILITARY BUILDINGS

Introduction

Britain was a frontier province of the Roman Empire. It began that way and remained so. The Roman Empire was divided into two types of province: the senatorial provinces, mostly grouped around the Mediterranean; and the imperial 'province', which was all the rest. The imperial 'province' was made up of frontier provinces which were governed by the emperor's personal delegates, the *legati*, who were usually ex-senators or ex-praetors. Apart from this geographical distinction, these imperial territories contained the vast bulk of the Roman imperial army, dispersed as considered appropriate by the emperor for both his own defence and that of the frontiers.

Throughout the period there were about 30 legions, though this number varied. With about 5000 men each this makes about 150,000 in total, almost all of whom were infantry. There were probably at least the same number of auxiliary troops divided into rather smaller units of about 500 or 1000 strong. These were infantry, cavalry or mixed.

Of course these troops had to be accommodated, fed, provided for and equipped. In addition they had to be defended, whether in a permanent fort or in temporary, perhaps even overnight, quarters. Britain had never less than three legions, occasionally four, and numerous auxiliary units. As an insecure, hostile and recalcitrant province for much of its early life there was a considerable amount of troop movement. So, in Britain, we have many examples of military buildings and defences. These range from early Claudian forts to Hadrian's Wall and the Antonine Wall, and include substantial legionary fortresses, the late forts of the Saxon Shore, signal towers on the coast, marching camps and a whole host of other conventional forts. There were a number of different construction techniques, and it is as well to be aware that as far as the Roman army was concerned turf, earth, timber and stone were all perfectly suitable.

British weather, agriculture and stone-robbing have combined to level many Roman forts, but the large numbers known and the very considerable effort expended in excavation and analysis has produced an unparalleled body of evidence making this a particularly rich archaeological resource. Moreover the uniformity of army habits means that much of the knowledge gained about Roman military building from Britain is relevant to the Empire as a whole. In general apart from size there is no need to distinguish between legionary and auxiliary military building techniques. Almost all forts might serve for either, or even both, depending on the circumstances. The forts on Hadrian's Wall were built by legionaries but occupied by auxiliaries. Only the legionary fortresses were built by legionaries for their exclusive use.

Forts and their buildings (first to early third centuries)

Types of forts

The Roman fort was really a military settlement. It was a self-contained unit where troops could be fed and sheltered. Siting was important (see Chapter 1): a fort had to be secure but close to communications for supplies. Forts were not the same as camps. A camp was essentially an overnight bivouac – normally a simple rectangle of

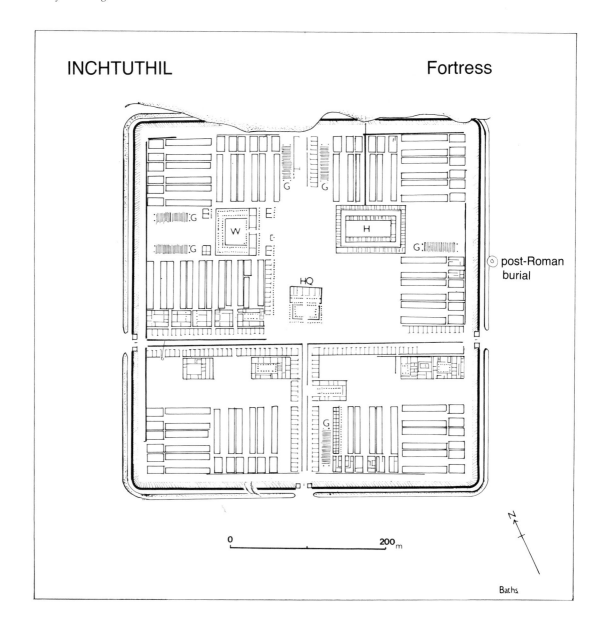

17 Plan of the Flavian legionary fortress at Inchtuthil, Perthshire (after Richmond), *c.* 83-86/7. This well-known plan exhibits a number of peculiarities which means that it cannot be regarded as wholly typical of a legionary fortress. But as it was occupied briefly it does offer a snapshot of Roman military organization and logistics. It had stone defences but contained only timber buildings because it was so short-lived. The fortress was undoubtedly the centre of Agricola's consolidation operations in the north and was almost certainly built and garrisoned by *legio* XX.

The headquarters building (HQ) is unusually small; there is no house for the legate, though a space has been set aside to the east of the headquarters building; the ten barracks and five houses to the west seem to represent the enlarged first cohort. By the end of Vespasian's reign (69-79) the first cohort was apparently enlarged so that it contained five double centuries of 160 men each (total: 800), rather than six centuries of 80 men (total: 480). Consequently there were only five centurions, hence the five houses (instead of the normal six). The first cohort was the most prestigious, which explains the unusually lavish accommodation for its centurions. Granaries are marked G; the workshop W; and the hospital H.

mound and ditch built as large as was necessary to accommodate a unit in tents, and levelled the following morning or within a few days or weeks. Many have been identified in Britain, usually from aerial photography, but they are not 'buildings' in the true sense of the word.

Roman forts were much more permanent establishments, though in practice 'permanent' might mean 5 or 250 years. The fort is distinguished from the camp by having much more elaborate defences and also internal buildings. From the first to early third centuries – the

18 Plan of the Flavian turf and timber fort at Elginhaugh, near Edinburgh (after Hanson). This fort, excavated during the 1980s, is one of the very few whose entire plan has been recovered in the whole Roman Empire even though it was discovered only recently by aerial photography. The fort is at least big enough (1.2 ha/3 acres) to have housed an auxiliary infantry, or infantry and cavalry, cohort of about 480 men (six centuries of 80 soldiers) plus officers. The purpose of all the timber buildings is not known and it is possible that the garrison was a larger one. The buildings were indicated by sleeper trenches and postholes. An annexe, *c.* 1 ha (2.4 acres) in extent lay to the west and would have served a number of purposes such

as protecting stores, and perhaps horses. The fort seems to have been occupied for around a decade and then deliberately dismantled, around the same time as Inchtuthil (see fig. 17) *c.* 86-7 and forms a similar snapshot of fort building, albeit on a much smaller scale.

a commandant's house
b headquarter's building
c granaries
d a stone building of unknown purpose, possibly a workshop where fires would have made timber hazardous

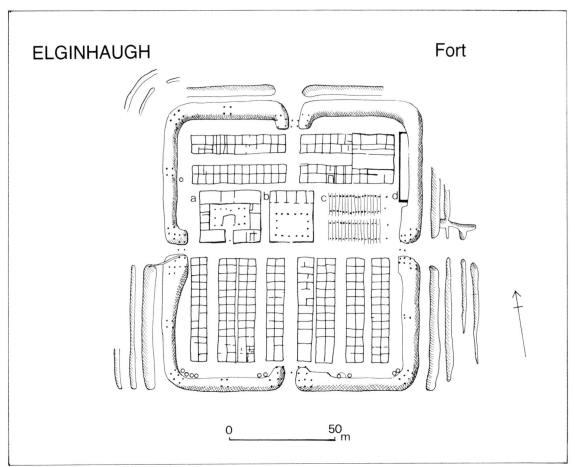

ELGINHAUGH   Fort

a   b   c   d

0   50 m

main period of military activity in Britain – they were designed as variations on a basic format which is found throughout the Empire. The only differences tend to be those of scale and sophistication, as a comparison between the plans of the legionary fortresses at Inchtuthil, Elginhaugh and Housesteads show (figs. 17-19). Apart from the defences the main features are the headquarters building, the commander's house, the granaries, and the barracks. Most forts had a hospital, stables, ovens, latrines and baths. While examples of all these buildings are known from many sites in Britain, relatively few are well preserved, well studied and visible today.

19 Plan of the auxiliary fort at Housesteads, built *c.* 122-6 in the central sector of Hadrian's Wall. The forts were added after the initial phases of construction. The former line of the Broad Wall foundation (see fig. 54), and the site of turret 36b, are marked by the dotted line, though the peculiar position of the north-east angle tower suggests that the Narrow Wall curtain was not actually built until the fort was in place. The first garrison was the *cohors I Tungrorum* though the fort was probably built by legionaries. The plan shows the fort as it probably appeared in the second century. A number of the individual buildings are reconstructed elsewhere in this book (see figs. 26, 29, 31, 41, 42).

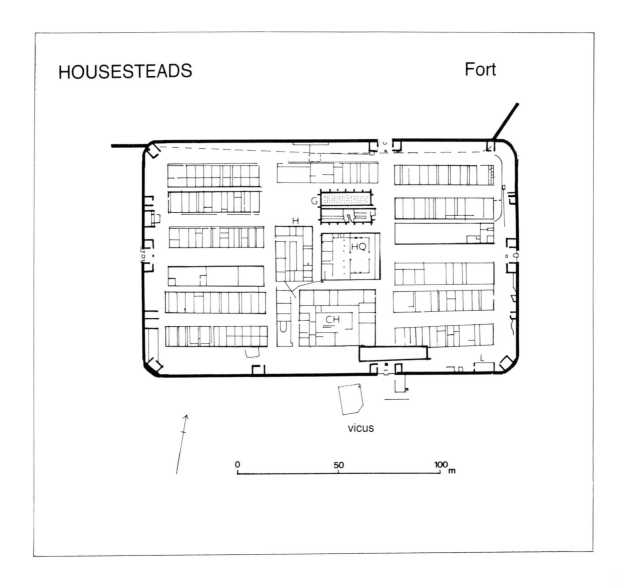

Defences

During the first century most forts were built in Britain with turf and timber ramparts, broken only by timber gateways. The archaeological evidence is usually slight but where burning has taken place or the site is waterlogged there may be more remains of timber. In general ramparts may survive as gentle mounds, if at all, and gates are usually only identifiable as arrangements of post-holes. Only a few sites are visible on the ground today, for example at Hod Hill in Dorset (see Chapter 1 and fig. 20).

---

20 View of the fort at Housesteads on Hadrian's Wall looking north. The fort is often illustrated with aerial photographs but this view shows how the commanding stronghold straddles a ridge. The Wall itself lies on the far side where the ground falls away steeply. On the slope below the fort to the south lay the civilian settlement (*vicus*). The Military Way joined the fort at the east gate on the right hand side after crossing the Knag Burn. (Photo: author, 1989.)

In the simplest form a turf rampart with sloping sides supported a walkway, probably fronted by a timber parapet. More elaborate versions, called 'box ramparts' (fig. 21), involved an array of planks and beams used to 'lace' and strengthen the turf. The most interesting site to visit is the mid-first-century fort at the Lunt, Baginton, near Coventry, where experimental reconstruction in the 1970s has highlighted long-term problems, such as rotting timbers and sagging of the ramparts. However, labour-intensive repair work, uneconomic in today's terms, would have been quite acceptable to the Roman army, which was being paid anyway and enjoyed unlimited access to local raw materials.

Timber gateways are rather harder to understand simply because a pattern of post-holes supplies no information about the superstructure. The simplest timber gates were supported on four or six posts between a break in the rampart, for example the south gate at the Claudian fort on Hod Hill, Dorset. They may have supported a tower as well, or perhaps simply a bridge for the

rampart walkway. The reconstructed gate at the Lunt fort, Baginton, was based on representations of timber gates shown on Trajan's Column, a source which also suggests that towers may have been roofed. More elaborate plans would have formed the basis for double-portalled gates equipped with towers, and in some cases were recessed, for example the south-east gate at Great Casterton (fig. 22). The gates themselves were probably made of timber posts and beams, plated with iron against attackers trying to fire them. Fragments of iron sheathing were found on the site of a gate at Fendoch. The gates swung on pivots and were closed against raised thresholds. The representations of gates on Trajan's Column, mentioned above, also suggest that pitched roofs might have been used. Interval and angle towers were used along the ramparts and at the corners of the fort to provide extra observation posts and artillery platforms. They are usually represented by much simpler patterns of post-holes, for example at Elginhaugh (see fig. 18), and are not associated with breaks in the rampart.

Stone defences in Roman Britain belong mostly to the second century and later though it would be quite wrong to give the impression that turf and timber had become obsolete. Some evidence from Trajan's Column suggests that stone gates may actually have had timber superstructures, though artistic licence or error may be responsible for this impression. A number of stone fort gates and portions of walls have survived in Britain to a reasonable height but none supplies conclusive information about roofing and parapets. The well-preserved Severan north gate at the fort of Bu Njem in Libya appears to have had crenellations. Crenellations also appear on various walls which appear on Trajan's Column. A collapsed section of the fort wall at Wörth in Upper Germany showed that the walkway was on average 4.5m (15ft) above ground level. It was marked by a projecting chamfered course of stone. The parapet appears to have been 1.6m (5ft) high and was equipped with crenellations. The legionary fortresses may have had elaborately carved stonework in the defences; recently, substantial and ornate cornice stones have been found in the fortress wall at Chester.

Stone defences were frequently added to forts that had already been built with turf and timber. The simplest way of incorporating the stone was to cut away the front of the turf rampart and replace it with stone facing. New forts had walls which were built of rubble cores and which were faced on either side. Once completed the wall was reinforced with an earth bank which was built up against the internal face. Earth banks were not used on Hadrian's Wall or later forts (see below). At Gellygaer the Trajanic defences were built of two stone walls separated by a narrow void filled with earth. Units which were equipped with artillery sometimes built special ramps up against the earth banks. At the Claudian fort of Hod Hill these took the form of chalk slopes next to both gates. Not many other examples are known but at High Rochester inscriptions record the building and repair of masonry platforms in the early third century (see Appendix 2). These are the only dated Romano-British examples and it may be that they represent a new defensive policy in the third century. However, it is not possible to be certain because artillery platforms were always built separately from walls and ramparts to prevent recoil pressure from damaging the defences.

---

21 Military defences (**a-g** after A. Johnson). All these types might be used at any time in Roman Britain up to the late second century though **a** & **b** were the most common in the late first century. In structural terms the problem was to prevent the earth or rubble rampart collapsing outwards under its own weight – each type represents a different solution to the same problem. Choice would have been dictated by habit and availability of raw materials, especially timber. In the third and fourth centuries, military defences were built as free-standing masonry walls, creating different problems for the builders.

a single turf revetment
b double turf revetment
c double turf revetment with rubble core, enabling a vertical face to be constructed
d double turf revetment with timber lacing for stability
e single timber revetment (**e** & **f** were not commonly used in Britain)
f double timber revetment
g clay rampart with stone foundation
h stone revetment with earth bank

Defences

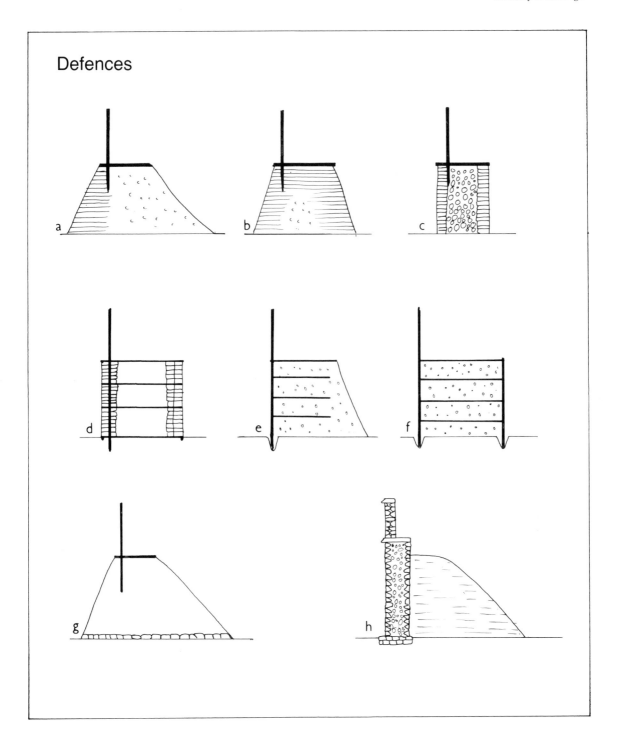

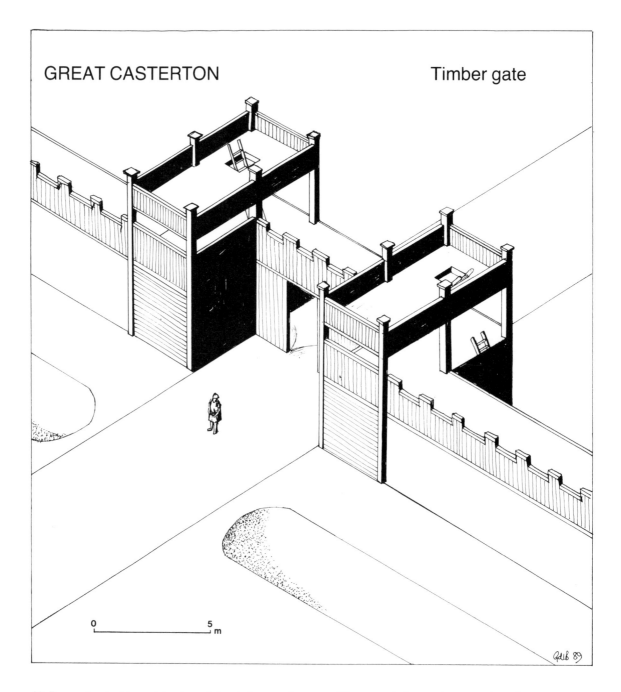

GREAT CASTERTON — Timber gate

22 Reconstructed isometric view of the timber southeast gate of the auxiliary fort at Great Casterton, Leicestershire. The gate was a double-portalled example, flanked by towers and was recessed behind the ramparts. It was built *c.* 60-70 as part of new southeast defences which reduced the fort's size. As the plan consists solely of post-holes there are many possible ways of reconstructing such a gate.

The most informative remains of gateways are to be found on the northern frontier, especially the west gate at High Rochester (fig. 23), and the east and south gates at Birdoswald (figs. 24, 25) but also at Housesteads (fig. 26) and South Shields (fig. 27, plate 3) – all these forts belong primarily to the second and early third centuries.

23 The west single-portal gate at High Rochester, Northumberland, an outpost fort first built in timber in the late first century but not consolidated in stone until the mid-second century. It remained occupied thereafter. The field wall and blocking to the gate is modern. The north jamb survives to the height of the springer for the arch. (Photo: author, 1989.)

A number of reconstructions of the west gate at Housesteads was prepared a number of years ago, showing this type of gateway with crenellations and rooms above the portals. They may be correct but the modern rebuilding of the west gate at South Shields is equally likely. The most obvious difference is the use of gabled and tiled roofs, for which there is a certain amount of evidence from Trajan's Column. It is also possible that the same gate had different superstructures at different times.

No doors survive but holes in flagstones show that they swung on pivots, probably made of iron (fig. 24). The doors were inserted by sliding the pivot through a channel cut in the floor stone. Once the pivot had dropped into the specially carved hole the channel was filled with lead and the door could then swing without sliding out of position. These pivot holes can be seen at a number of gates. The four main gates were normally twin portal, though in many cases, especially on Hadrian's Wall, one of the portals was subsequently blocked up. Single-portal gates were normally used for subsidiary gates, or those which were likely to have less traffic passing through, for example the west gate at High Rochester (fig. 23) which overlooks a steep slope while the main road, Dere Street, passes the fort to the east.

As with timber and turf forts the defences were augmented with angle and interval towers along the ramparts. They seem to have been simple stone towers attached to the internal face of the wall and were probably designed as observation posts and shelter. Sometimes the ground floor was used to house an oven.

In general, up until the reign of Antoninus Pius (138-61), stone gates and interval or angle towers were built flush with the defences. This can be seen particularly clearly at Birdoswald and Housesteads (fig. 26). However from then on it

24 View of the south twin-portalled gate at Birdoswald fort on Hadrian's Wall looking across the east portal. Note the pivot hole for one of the east portal's gates in the right foreground beside the base of the arch. (Photo: author, 1989.)

25 View of the east gate at Birdoswald fort on Hadrian's Wall, one of the best preserved military gates in Britain. In the foreground is the centre support for the twin arches and beyond is the north jamb which survives to the springer of the arch. (Photo: author, 1989.)

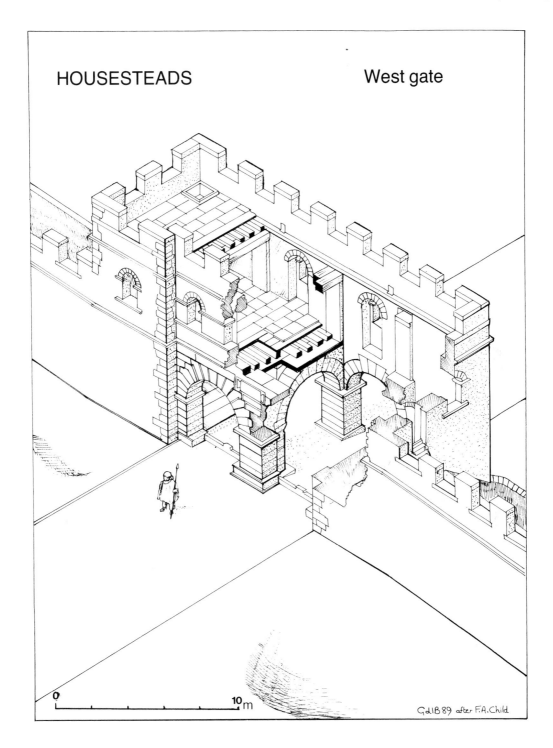

HOUSESTEADS   West gate

0   10 m

GdIB 89 after F.A.Child

26 West gate at Housesteads (isometric reconstruction after Child, but adapted). Built *c.* 122-6 this gate survives well enough to show that it was twin-portalled. Naturally the superstructure is purely hypothetical but this reconstruction shows a version where the whole gate is of a single height capped with crenellations and a flat roof. It should be contrasted with fig. 27.

became increasingly common to use projecting gate-towers. Whether this marks a change in tactics or a move towards a more defensive posture overall is not certain. Nevertheless the effect was to create individual gates which could be more easily defended, for example the west gate at Brecon y Gaer. By the beginning of the third century it was also becoming common to do away with square gate-towers and build semi-circular projecting towers. This became especially marked in the Saxon Shore forts (see below and fig. 52).

Gates were particularly suitable for embellishment and decoration. Normally they carried inscriptions which described who had built the gate and when. One of the most explicit comes from the south gateway at Risingham, an outpost fort on Dere Street, north of Hadrian's Wall (see Appendix 2). This is an elaborate example – earlier inscriptions were probably briefer and more succinct, though it is consequently less certain that they come from a gate unless there is a specific reference to it. Gates might also be decorated with sculptures. The east gate at Housesteads bore a relief depicting Victory. These carvings and inscriptions were probably painted and the whole gate itself might have been rendered or whitewashed.

Internal buildings

The internal buildings of Roman forts of the first, second and early third centuries follow very standard plans, though with considerable variation in detail. Nevertheless it is quite possible to discuss them as general types because most of the differences are usually in scale.

---

27 View of the reconstructed west gate at the fort of South Shields. Dates of the stone defences here are still uncertain but it has been suggested that the first stone fort on the site, including this gate, was built around the middle of the second century. The height of the reconstructed gate may be higher than the original – there may not have been a range of rooms above the entrance portals for example – but it undoubtedly must recreate something of the imposing presence of a Roman military gateway. (Photo: author, 1989; see also plate 3.)

Headquarters

As with the Roman town the most important building was the administration centre. It is no coincidence that the civil forum and basilica bear much resemblance to the military headquarters building (*principia*), especially in a province where troops may have contributed to civic development. The principia consisted of a square or rectangular courtyard with an ambulatory and offices on three sides. On the fourth side, opposite the entrance, was the covered cross-hall, behind which lay offices and shrines for the unit's standards, sometimes including a strong-room dug into the ground. In cavalry forts a fore-hall seems to have been built along the front of the building, parallel with the cross-hall on the other side, for example at Brecon y Gaer. These may or may not have been roofed but would have allowed the mounted troops to parade and perhaps perform drill.

28 The headquarters building at the legionary fortress of Caerleon (isometric reconstruction). The great hall was about 64m (210ft) long by 25m (82ft) wide but excavation revealed no traces of superstructure despite the existence of column bases and substantial foundations. It may therefore never have been completed. Its intended form is a little difficult to understand because of a very wide gap between the columns in the centre of the two arcades supporting the nave roof. This has been resolved here by restoring the building in cruciform shape. Such a form has the advantage of focusing attention on the main shrine of the legion's standards which were contained in the *sacellum*. At either end of the hall there would have been a raised tribunal where the legion's officers could preside over administrative and disciplinary matters.

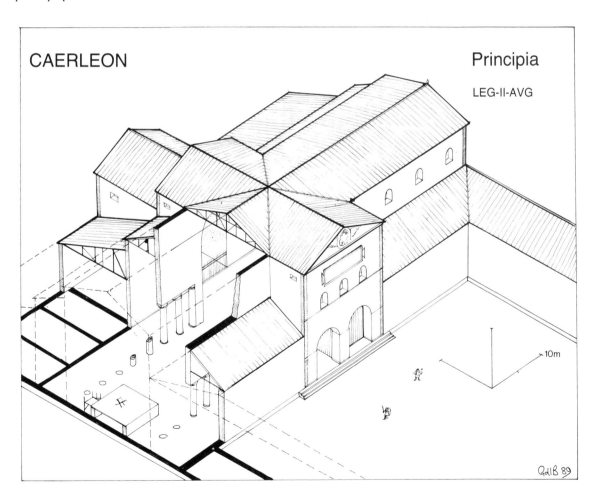

CAERLEON

Principia

LEG-II-AVG

10m

QdB 89

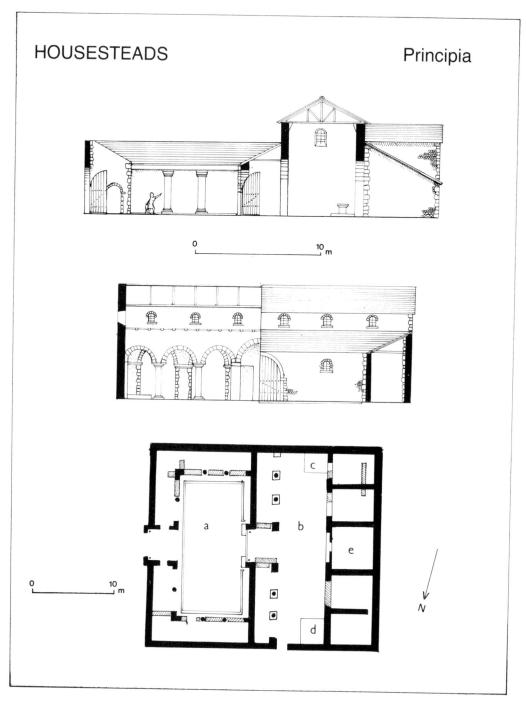

29 The headquarters building at Housesteads in elevations and plan. This is based on the plan of the building currently visible which dates from the third century, replacing the Hadrianic version. The plan is fairly typical in having a forecourt (a), cross-hall (b) and administrative/ceremonial chambers (e). The colonnade around the forecourt was later walled up, either to strengthen the building or perhaps to provide more storage space. The hall contained raised tribunals (c, d).

As such an important building the principia was probably the most architecturally ambitious structure in the average Roman fort. The surviving pieces of column from the principia at the legionary fortress of York show that it was monumental – the columns from the cross-hall

---

30 The headquarters building at Vindolanda (axonometric reconstruction). Like the Housesteads example (fig. 29) the visible remains belong mainly to the third century. The most interesting feature is the survival of stone screens to separate the administrative rooms from the cross-hall (fig. 34). Unlike Housesteads the forecourt was apparently surrounded by solid walls.

were just a little under 7m (22 ft) in height. Unfortunately none of the legionary fortresses have yielded much of their principia except for the Flavian fortress at Inchtuthil. However, the internal buildings here were built of timber and the principia seems to have been disproportionately small. No doubt it was built in haste as an essential facility with the intention of replacing it when time allowed (fig. 17). It was only 42 by 45m (138 by 148ft), compared to 74 by 100m (243 by 328ft) at Chester and 66 by 94m (217 by 308ft) at Caerleon (fig. 28); though this may never have been finished, but space permitted a building 66 by at least 69m (217 by 226ft).

Caerleon's principia is not visible today but other examples can be seen at Housesteads,

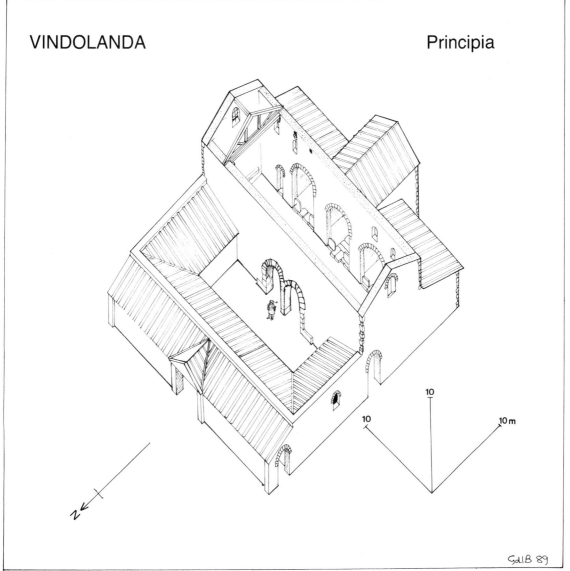

VINDOLANDA   Principia

10

10   10 m

2

GdlB 89

31 The cross-hall of the headquarters building at Housesteads looking south. Note the steps leading up to the hall on the left and the arch bases within the hall. (Photo: author, 1989.)

32 The vault for the strongroom in the headquarters building at Chesters. Steps in the foreground lead down to the vault in which the unit's standards and valuables would have been stored. (Photo: author, 1989.)

33 The vault for the strongroom in the headquarters building at Great Chesters on Hadrian's Wall. This fort has barely been touched by excavation but incongruously part of the vault still protrudes from beneath the turf. (Photo: author, 1988.)

Chesters and Vindolanda (figs. 29-34). The principia served a number of practical purposes. It provided open and covered assembly areas, rooms for storage and administration, and a strong-room where the unit's standards, valuables and money could be safely locked away. At Chesters the steps leading down to the sunken chamber and also the vaulted roof can still be seen (figs. 32, 33). When the Chesters vault was excavated its oak and iron door was found in place although it soon disintegrated. The central room of the rear range of rooms behind the crosshall was called the *sacellum*. Containing the strong-room it lay on the main axis of the building, facing not just the entrance to the principia but also the main entrance to the

fort. The standards formed the focus of the various rituals which took place in the military calendar (*fasti*); these included worship of the gods, the imperial cult, the *genius* of the unit and the very standards themselves. These rooms were secured with low stone screens into which iron grilles were inserted (fig. 34).

Headquarters buildings were naturally a subject for architectural embellishment. Typically the date of construction or dedication was recorded on a monumental inscription. Carved reliefs decorated the building, perhaps on either side of the entrance. Those from the principia at Housesteads, depicting a Victory poised on a sphere and Mars, are amongst the few surviving examples, though their exact original position is unknown. The *sacellum* at Corbridge contained a relief of Hercules killing the Hydra, assisted by Athena. Hercules was popular amongst soldiers for obvious reasons, and this piece of sculpture emphasized the religious associations of the principia in a military unit's life.

34 Carved stone screen in the headquarters building at Vindolanda. The rooms at the rear contained the standards when they were on display. Access to the rooms was restricted with stone screens and iron grilles (see fig. 30). (Photo: author, 1988.)

Accommodation

Most of the average fort's area was taken up with accommodation in the form of barrack blocks. In rare cases a fort which had a special function might differ – the Severan period fort at South Shields, for example, was adapted to house a very large number of granaries to support Septimius Severus' campaign in Scotland (209-12). Almost every fort had a house (*praetorium*) for the commanding officer and his family; legionary fortresses had individual houses for the six military tribunes (one *tribunus laticlavius* and five *tribuni angusticlavii*), the camp prefect (*praefectus castrorum*) and the five centurions of the first cohort.

Legates' houses are not known in great detail from Britain. At Inchtuthil an area had been left aside next to the principia, but no building had taken place by the time the fortress was

dismantled *c.* 86/7 (fig. 17). However, many examples are known from smaller forts. They differ from most Romano-British houses by being built in Mediterranean style: inward looking, they consisted of four continuous ranges of rooms built around a rectangular courtyard (see Chapter 4 and figs. 114, 115). The best surviving example can be seen at Housesteads where this plan was adapted, despite being terraced into the hillside on which the fort was built. Occasionally such houses enjoyed the addition of a private bath-suite, for example at Chesters, but in general the houses were modest by civil standards (especially in later centuries) though some have produced traces of window-glass and wall plaster. The officers' and centurions' houses at Inchtuthil show that these were modelled on similar but smaller and more modest plans.

The barracks, *centuriae*, as implied by their ancient name, were built to house individual centuries of soldiers. In practice for infantry this meant 80 men plus centurion and a handful of 'non-commissioned' officers. The 80 men were divided into ten groups of eight, the 'tent-parties' (*contuberniae*), and this is reflected in the minimum of ten parallel pairs of rooms which appear in most barrack blocks. The centurion and his assistants occupied the block at the end of

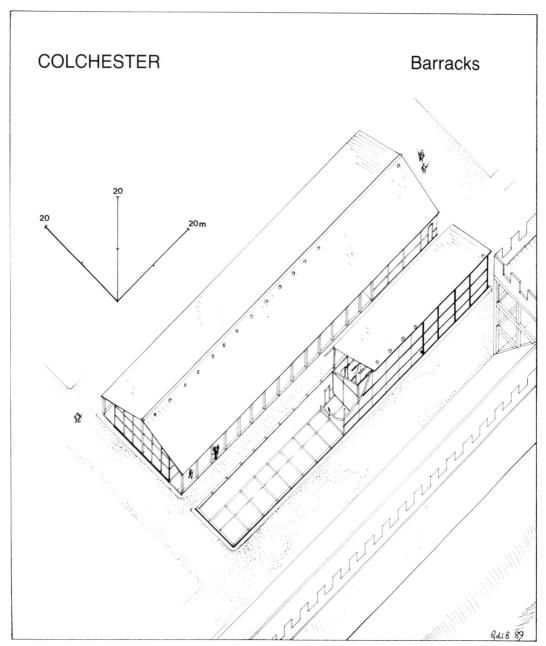

COLCHESTER

Barracks

20
20
20m

35 Early-first-century timber barracks at Colchester. For about four years following the conquest in 43 Colchester seems to have acted as a legionary fortress for *legio* XX. A number of recent excavations have identified traces of timber and wattle-and-daub barracks which were subsequently used when the fortress was given up. The axonometric reconstruction is based on plans of the southernmost barracks on the Culver Street site, adjacent to the ramparts and south gate, using details from other contemporary barracks in the fortress. The narrower building is a single block, the wider is two barrack blocks back to back. Each barrack block was about 69m (226ft) long and had a large room for the centurion at the east end, and 14 pairs of rooms for the ten groups of eight legionaries and other 'non-commissioned' officers. Some of the rooms had hearths and, while traces of drainage gullies have been found in front, the verandahs are hypothetical.

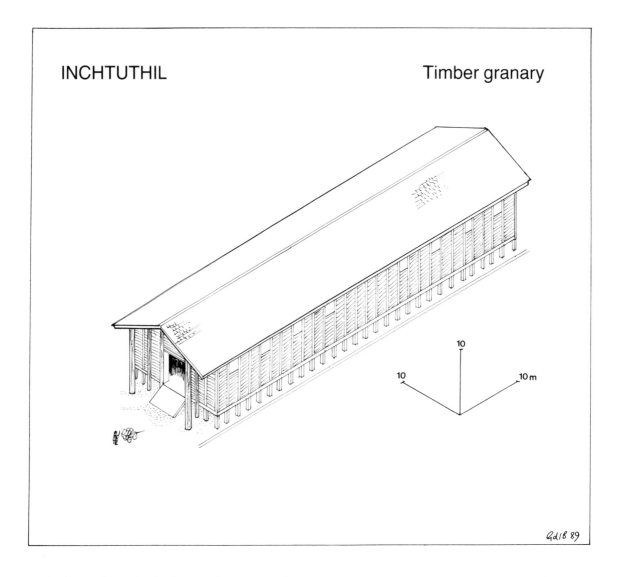

INCHTUTHIL   Timber granary

10

10   10 m

GdIB 89

each barrack – in legionary fortresses the assistants would have occupied a pair of rooms each, making 14 parallel pairs (fig. 35). The building grew directly out of the lay-out of tents in a marching camp and served the purpose of making sure that when on the march every soldier knew where he would pitch his party's tent in relation to the whole unit. Cavalry barracks were slightly smaller and were probably designed to accommodate two *turmae* (64 men) in eight pairs of rooms plus extra space for the officers. Although they must have been cramped, evidence from the early-first-century timber legionary barracks at Colchester shows that internal walls may have been plastered, some

36 Timber granary at Inchtuthil, Perthshire (isometric reconstruction). The presence of a covered loading area is implied in the two very large post-holes found at the end. The other posts were set into sleeper beams laid in transverse trenches (see fig. 17). Evidence for at least five others was found. About 83-86/7.

rooms had hearths, and drains were placed in the street outside the barracks.

Stables
Stables are difficult to identify from archae-ological evidence though the large number of

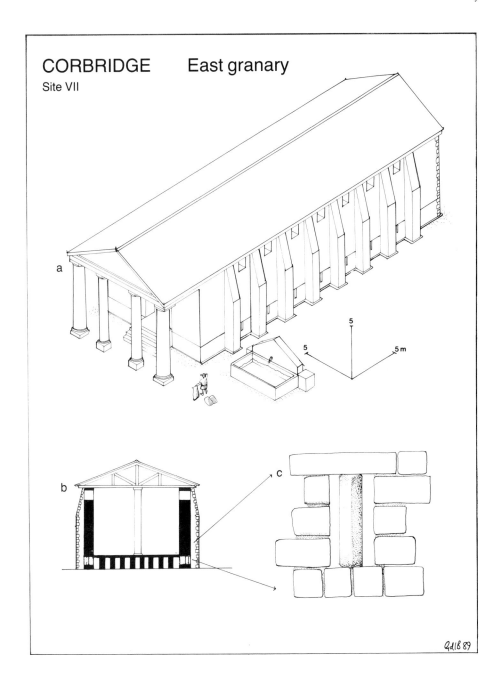

CORBRIDGE   East granary
Site VII

37a East stone granary at Corbridge (isometric reconstruction). Two stone granaries have been found at this site, dating to the third century. They are amongst the best preserved specimens in the whole country. Sections of the floor and the remains of the ventilation slots in the side walls survive. Column bases and steps on the street front show that each had covered porches. The large buttresses give an idea of the kind of lateral forces (from the settling grain within) which were anticipated.

37b cross-section view shows the under-floor channels, ventilated by air which entered through the ventilation slots, **c**, which contained a mullion to restrict the access of larger animals and rain.

auxiliary cavalry regiments stationed in Britain makes it certain that many forts contained them. Some of the structures which appear to be barracks but lack some internal divisions may have accommodated horses, though any simple building of unspecified purpose may have served. The most likely supporting evidence is the presence of internal drains. Drains would have helped to create a dry, more hygienic environment. Such drains have been identified at Brough on Noe, Ilkley and Halton Chesters but they were not essential and have not been found in some other forts which certainly had auxiliary cavalry garrisons. Other possible evidence might take the form of wear on flooring, for example at Hod Hill. A number of forts on the Antonine Wall have been found to have enclosures attached to one side. Their purpose is unknown and while they may simply have been used as storage areas they may also have been used to corral horses.

Granaries

A hungry army is a useless army, and the logistics of supplying Roman troops with enough to eat

were well organized. Granaries (*horrea*) appear in most forts. As we have already seen some forts might be almost entirely given over to them in order to act as supply-bases, as at South Shields. Granaries presented three major problems to their builders: controlling the effects of both damp and rodents, and withstanding the lateral forces created by the grain itself as it settled.

Military granaries were normally rectangular, though there was considerable variation in size depending on the needs of the garrison. Timber examples were built on posts inserted into either the ground or sleeper beams laid in trenches. The posts allowed air to circulate freely below and helped prevent rodent attacks (fig. 36). Stone granaries were rather more imposing. Usually the floors, of either timber or stone, were laid on

38 Granary and fountain at Corbridge. This view looking north-west shows the front of the granary reconstructed in fig. 37. Years of re-metalling in antiquity raised the level of the road above the column bases. Years of knife sharpening(?) wore down the walls of the fountain. Note the drainage gullies in the foreground. (Photo: author, 1989.)

dwarf walls or pillars which created a series of air channels; granaries with solid floors, for example at Caerhun, may have been adapted for other purposes. Air was allowed in through narrow ventilator slots with mullions. The best surviving example can be seen in the east granary at Corbridge (figs. 37, 38) which retains the dwarf walls, flagstones and ventilator slots.

Access to a granary was by a loading platform or steps, usually beneath a covered portico. Platforms, indicated by slots or post-holes, meant that grain could be transferred from a wagon straight onto the raised floor. The timber granary at the mid-first-century fort of the Lunt was reconstructed with a platform running beneath a portico, with steps at either end. It is not known exactly how the grain was stored but, as most stone granaries were equipped with substantial buttresses, it seems likely that grain was poured into bins which lay alongside the walls. It was quite usual to build granaries in parallel pairs, for example at Housesteads and Corbridge (figs. 19,

38), probably for convenience and to help support one another.

Hospitals

The hospital (*valetudinarium*) was sited in the central part of the fort. The principles of construction seem to have been access and seclusion.

---

39 Perspective reconstruction of the hospital at Inchtuthil looking north-east. The building consisted of four wings with concentric ranges of rooms built around a courtyard. The inner range of rooms did not continue around the west wing (see fig. 17). The outer range was made of up of a series of groups of rooms. Each group was accessible only from the central range which seems to have been one long corridor. The inner range was a further series of rooms. Each concentric range was separated by a gap and the reason for this was probably to create as much peace and quiet as possible. In view of this windows have been omitted from the outer walls. About 83-86/7.

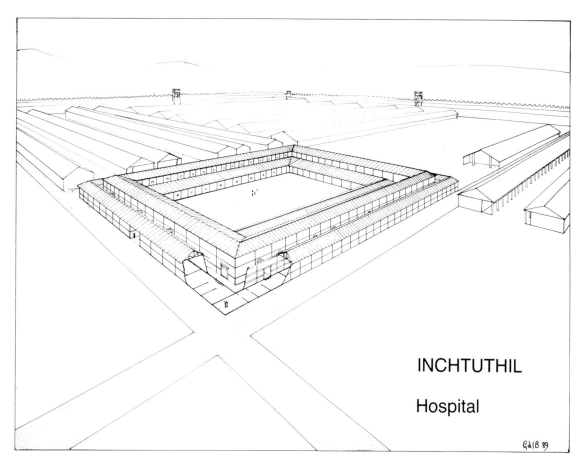

INCHTUTHIL

Hospital

The product in its most elaborate form was a series of concentric rectangles of wards and corridors built with double walls. The corridors allowed access to the rows of wards on either side. The ranges and corridors might even be separated by spaces in order to reduce noise levels. This can be seen particularly clearly from the plan at Inchtuthil (figs. 17, 39), though the only visible example now is the auxiliary hospital at Housesteads. This is a rectangular building with four ranges of rooms around a corridor and a central courtyard. The fort at Fendoch had an even simpler example where two parallel ranges of rooms were separated by a central corridor.

It should be borne in mind that unless specific evidence in the form of surgical equipment is found the identification of such buildings in forts is very uncertain. The buildings may have been workshops and/or storerooms and unless another building within the fort can be assigned to these purposes (for example at Inchtuthil) a firm identification cannot be made. Only in the legionary fortresses where the most sophisticated versions were built can the plan be regarded as conclusive evidence.

Workshops
The Roman army consisted of small, independent, self-contained units. It was absolutely essential that each unit could service and repair its equipment and facilities. Many forts have

40 The workshop at Inchtuthil, Perthshire, looking north-west. This seems to have been a courtyard building with a portico. The reconstruction has been made deliberately high on the assumption that the need to disperse noise and smoke would have made low roofs unacceptable. The building contained a pit into which more than a million nails and other pieces of redundant ironwork were sealed in order to prevent them being used by a potential enemy, following withdrawal of the Roman forces. (About 83-86/7.)

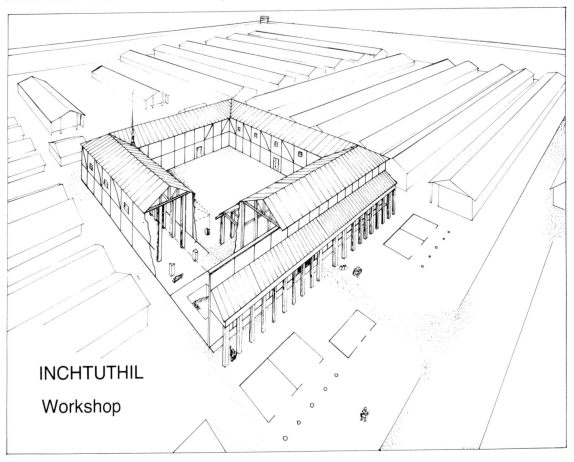

INCHTUTHIL

Workshop

yielded evidence for workshops (*fabricae*) and although identification is not always certain, as we have seen with hospitals, the workshops are more likely to contain evidence of the activities which went on. Typically these are hearths or traces of smelting. Sometimes, as at Inchtuthil and Elginhaugh where the forts were abandoned, the metal goods like nails were sealed in pits to prevent them being of use to the enemy. The design of the buildings seems to have been a range of rooms around a central courtyard (fig. 40). Considering the need for ventilation and the claustrophobic effects of low roofs in a hot and noisy atmosphere the workshops probably had quite high walls. Some of the rooms may have been open to the sky.

Latrines

The most outstanding example of Roman toilet facilities in Britain is at Housesteads (figs. 41, 42). The remarkable latrine was sited in the south-east corner and was built early in the fort's life. It underwent considerable alteration but the basic design remained unchanged. The latrine

was fed by two supplies of running water from several different tanks and cisterns, built at higher levels. Some of this water was provided for washing, and more water carried waste away out of the fort from beneath the seats in the latrine (fig. 42). A centurion's quarters at Chester was equipped with a lead-lined latrine of early-first-century date. Relatively few traces of similar buildings have been found at forts elsewhere in Britain, though provision for hygiene must have been made everywhere.

41 Details of the plumbing system for the latrine at Housesteads looking south. One of the tanks which supplied washing and flushing water can be seen to the left. Within the latrine a washing basin can be seen. See figs. 19 and 42 for plans. (Photo: author, 1989.)

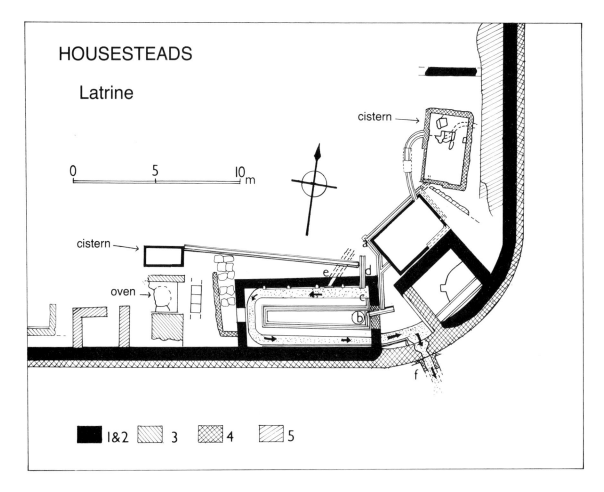

HOUSESTEADS

Latrine

0   5   10 m

cistern →

cistern →

oven →

1&2   3   4   5

Bath-houses

Bath-houses were usually built outside forts, but in the case of legionary fortresses substantial *thermae* were erected within the central area, for example at Exeter and Caerleon (fig. 43). It made good sense to site such a fire risk outside, especially if the fort was a small establishment. The two best-preserved military bath-houses are at Beauport Park in East Sussex (fig. 44) and at Chesters on Hadrian's Wall (figs. 45, 46), but only the latter is currently accessible. The fragmentary remains of the bath-house outside the fort at Ravenglass in Cumbria include some of the highest standing walls of any Roman building in Britain.

All these examples vary from the basic design of the Roman bath-house but they conform to the general theme. The structure had to be durable and was often quite sophisticated, for example at Caerleon (fig. 43). At Chesters the bath-house

42 Plan of the latrine at Housesteads (after F.G. Simpson). The numbers refer to the sequential periods of construction beginning in the Hadrianic period (see fig. 41).

possessed a latrine, a changing room and a complicated series of rooms. Set into the slope below the fort it was strengthened with buttresses. The bath-house at Beauport Park, while a modest building, possessed two vaults and had undergone substantial alterations. It may have been associated with a nearby fort, but if so, the fort has remained undiscovered.

Arenas

The Roman military arena (*ludus*) was very similar to the civic amphitheatre (see Chapter 3).

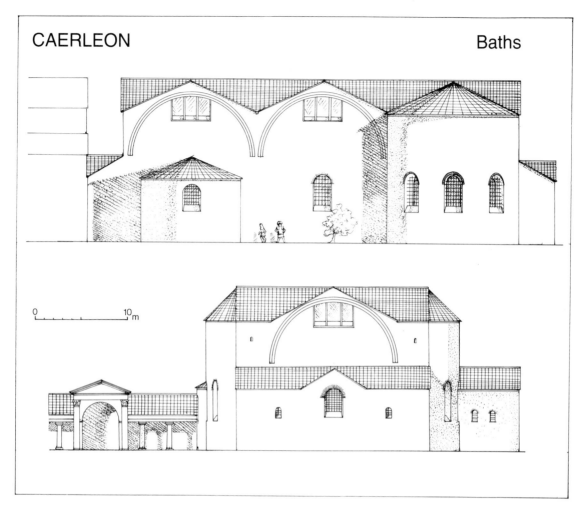

0 ———— 10 m

43 The Flavian fortress baths at the legionary fortress of Caerleon in elevation. The drawings show the main block of vaulted halls which served as the cold, warm and hot chambers. The western façade (above) overlooked a swimming pool installed in the 80s in the adjacent courtyard. A covered exercise hall was certainly planned and begun but like the great hall of the headquarters building (fig. 28) it may never have been finished.

Several are known from Britain and are usually described as amphitheatres despite having a slightly different purpose. The two best-known are at the legionary fortresses of Caerleon (figs. 47-9) and Chester, because they were partially built of stone and have therefore survived comparatively well, making them impressive monuments for public display (though half the Chester arena remains buried). Not all forts had permanent arenas, though one has been identified near the auxiliary fort at Tomen-y-Mur in north Wales.

Typically a military arena was sited just outside the fort walls and provided seating for most of the garrison. It would have been used for weapons training and public displays of fighting skills. The niche in the side of the arena at Caerleon may have been dedicated to Nemesis (Fate) who was associated with gladiators, so it is probably safe to assume that the garrison was also entertained by matched pairs (fig. 49). The recently discovered amphitheatre in London is well within the city walls but also lies adjacent to the Hadrianic fort in the north-east part of the settlement. It may therefore have originally been a military arena, perhaps adopting a civilian role in later years. The Neronian auxiliary fort at the Lunt, Baginton, has revealed traces of a unique circular building identified as a possible horse training arena, *gyrus*. This was a circular arena, 34m (112ft) in diameter, contained within the

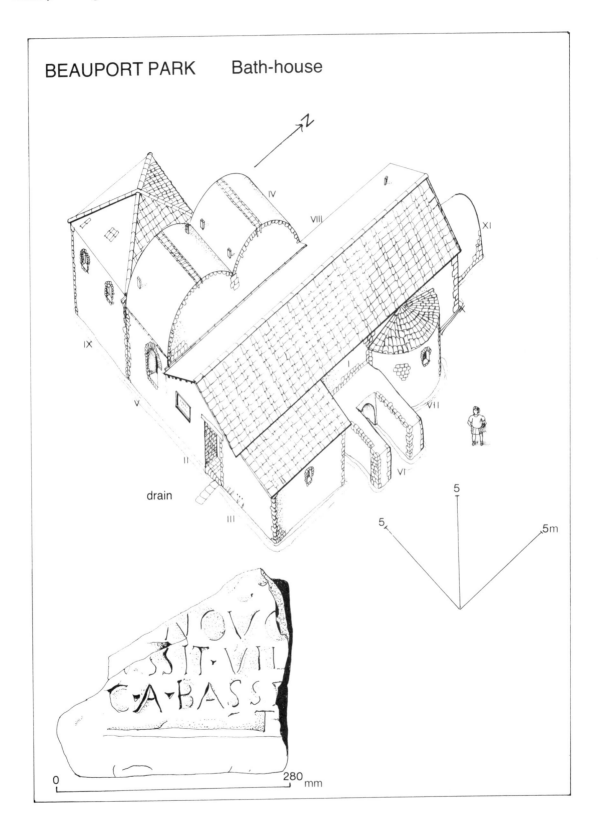

BEAUPORT PARK   Bath-house

44 The bath-house at Beauport Park, near Battle, East Sussex (axonometric reconstruction). The bath-house is one of the most remarkable buildings to have survived from ancient times. Despite being located in the congested south-east of modern Britain it was only discovered in 1969, having been buried during the Roman period by a landslip of industrial slag. It lies in woodland which was probably more or less undisturbed until early modern times.

The bath-house formed part of a large settlement concerned with the extraction of iron ore. The nature of the settlement is little known but the fact that the majority of the bath-house's roof tiles bear the stamp of the *Classis Britannica* suggests that detachments of the fleet were involved. This may seem curious but it is worth noting that Bodiam, which lies a few miles to the north was originally the site of a large inland harbour.

The bath-house itself survives largely intact having lost only its roof and upper walls. Even so much of the roof was found collapsed in and around the building. There were two distinct periods. Period 1 dates to the earlier part of the second century, but by the early third century the building had been enlarged (Period 2). The expansion was commemorated with a clumsily carved inscription, part of which survived just outside the

entrance (illustrated here but see Appendix 2 for details).

The new rooms were tacked on to the old walls with little attempt to bond them in. In fact the new walls are conspicuously tatty by comparison. The changing room (IX) was built into a fresh cutting in the hillside complete with niches for clothing, and a new furnace (XI) was installed at the northern end next to an extra hot room and annex (VIII). The two warm rooms (IV, V) were now vaulted – parts of the collapsed vaults were found. The southern one retains a window sill. The curious arrangements of the baths meant that the conventional route of: changing → warm rooms → hot rooms → cold room (III) involved a complicated series of comings and goings. Water supply came from a nearby stream, and there seems to have been a wooden water tank sited a few metres to the south-east. In later years the bath-house seems to have been used as somewhere to live by people who knocked an entrance through the apsed room, and one of their dogs was found amongst the *pilae* of floor-supporting tiles. Subsequently the building was finally wrecked by the accumulation of iron slag to the west – it slipped down the hillside, burying it completely until it was located in 1969.

---

fortifications; in fact the fort walls were built on a twisted path in order to go round the gyrus. The identification is by no means certain and an alternative possibility is that it was a stockade for prisoners.

Later forts

All the fort buildings discussed above refer to the buildings which belong to the period of conquest in the first century, consolidation during the second century and re-conquest in the early third century. Thereafter, following a period of peace, military strategy in the Western Empire became wholly defensive. This can be seen particularly clearly in the building of town defences on the Continent. In Britain the old forts continued to serve, often with significant amounts of repair work because the long peace in the middle years of the third century had allowed many forts to fall literally into ruin (see Appendix 2).

With the growth of a maritime threat to the

southern and eastern shores a new phase of fort building began. The sequence is complicated and poorly dated but the result was the system of forts of the Saxon Shore, the *Litus Saxonicum*. As monuments, a few of these forts are amongst the most impressive remnants of Roman Britain, particularly at Richborough, Pevensey and Portchester, but this applies entirely to their massive curtain walls and bastions (figs. 50-53). Of their internal buildings very little is known because with few exceptions these appear to have been built of timber. The remains of some of the forts were attractive to castle builders in the Middle Ages, and consequently post-Roman activity has tended to destroy details of these timber structures. Only a single wall-stump remains of the fort at Bradwell-on-Sea in Essex, Dover is known from fragments of walls and bastions identified in recent years, Walton Castle near Felixstowe in Suffolk disappeared over a cliff many years ago, and Brancaster's stone walls have been entirely robbed out.

CHESTERS

Baths

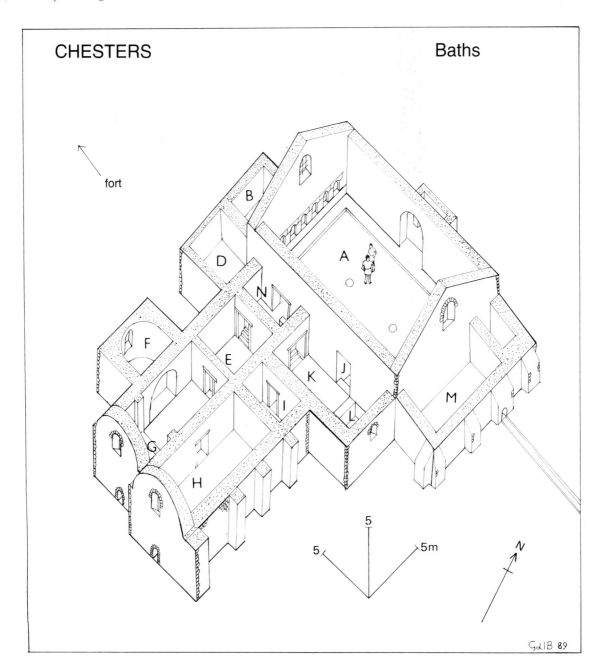

fort

5
5
5m

N

GdlB 89

45 The bath-house at Chesters (axonometric reconstruction). Shortly after their discovery in the 1880s John Collingwood Bruce described the baths as a 'large and lofty range of buildings'. Built into the slope below the fort the baths lay close to the west bank of the River Tyne. Movements of soil down the slope covered the building from view, and preserved it, until 1885, in a similar manner to Beauport Park (fig. 44). Its history is extremely complicated and the letters used to identify the rooms follows the scheme used by MacDonald (see bibliography). Some of the rooms were vaulted (see fig. 9 for details).

A = *apodyterium* (changing room) – note the niches, perhaps for storing clothes
N = a vestibule
K = *frigidarium* (cold room)
L = early cold bath
J = later cold bath
E = *laconicum* (dry-heat room)
I = *tepidarium* (moist warm room)
H = second *tepidarium*, with buttresses to support the building against the downward slope to the river.
F & G = *caldaria* (moist hot rooms). **G** contained a number of tufa and tile components which have been identified as parts of a vaulted roof. Ribs of tufa were connected with two rows of flat tiles to create cavities between each rib, thus saving weight.
M = latrine
Furnaces were sited by **B**'s north wall, and by **G**, and **H**'s south walls.

46 The bath-house at Chesters fort looking north across room G (see figs. 9 and 45). The solid quality of the masonry can be seen, an essential requirement for a bath-house which had vaulted roofs. The fort lies above the bath-house to the left up the slope. Erosion of the slope covered the bath-house and helped preserve its walls. (Photo: author, 1989.)

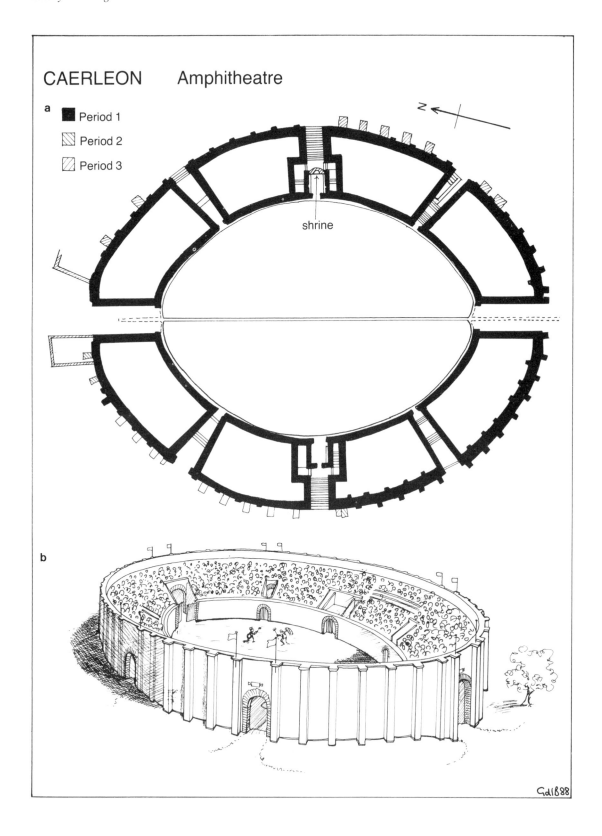

CAERLEON   Amphitheatre

a
- ■ Period 1
- ▨ Period 2
- ▨ Period 3

shrine

b

47 The arena (*ludus*, at Caerleon, *Isca*, fortress of *legio* II *Augusta* from the late first century until the beginning of the fourth.

a plan of the arena (after Wheeler). The building was built in the late first century (Period 1) in an area to the south-west of the fortress walls, cut in part from a low slope. It was based on earthen banks, created from soil dug from the arena. Wooden seats were laid across the banks and these were revetted by a stone wall. During the Hadrianic period, perhaps as a result of parts of the legion returning from construction duties on Hadrian's Wall, the structure was repaired and more buttresses added (Period 2) but thereafter it was allowed to deteriorate. At the beginning of the third century it was repaired and remained in use until the late fourth century. The amphitheatre was built by centuries from the legion, each assigned a sector. They recorded their efforts with centurial stones placed in the arena wall. One, for example, reads:

> **> C FVL MAC**

Which means: '[built by] the century of C. Fulvus Macer'. There were eight entrances, the main ones being at the ends of the long axis (see fig. 48). The entrances on the short axis incorporated small chambers, the easterly example adding a small shrine (see fig. 49). These two entrances supported ceremonial seating (omitted in the reconstructions to show the substructure). There were four small additional entrances. The arena was drained by a culvert running its full length.

The area of the arena, relative to the seating, is large and it should be borne in mind that this is primarily a military structure, not a civic amphitheatre and should be more accurately described as a *ludus*. It should be compared with the examples at Chester and at London, both also built in association with forts. Its main purpose was probably to act as a compound for weapons training, cavalry training and displays by units of the legion (these would have included religious dedications and ceremonies). Even so it must have also served as a source of entertainment.

Seating capacity can be estimated on the same principle as used for the Verulamium theatre (see figs. 79-81). The area of the auditorium at Caerleon is approximately 1670 sq. m, (18,000 sq. ft), which at 0.3 sq. m (about 3½ sq. ft) for each member of the audience, provides room for over 5500 individuals, not allowing for structural components and stairs. It can hardly be coincidence that the establishment of a legion was nominally around 5000 so it seems clear that the amphitheatre was designed to hold the whole legion when necessary.

b reconstruction of the amphitheatre (after J. A. Wright). This shows the walls as being completely of stone. However, they may actually only have served as footings supporting a timber revetment for the earthen banks.

48 The amphitheatre at Caerleon today looking north through the south entrance. Note how much lower the ground level of the arena was – this created flooding problems and eventually the main entrances had to be blocked up. (Photo: author, 1989.)

49 Recess in the east wall of the arena in the amphitheatre at Caerleon. It was probably a shrine to Nemesis (Fate) where those about to engage in combat could seek reassurance. The niche would probably have contained a statue, with an altar for sacrifices on the floor below. See also fig. 76. (Photo: author, 1989.)

Despite variations in detail the forts all share a location on or near the coast, though suitable high ground was exploited if available. The earliest forts seem to have been those at Reculver and Brancaster. Their plans resemble those of the more traditional 'playing card' forts of the northern frontier zone and Wales. Even so such archaeological evidence as exists suggests that, while Reculver may have been built by *c.* 225 Brancaster could be as much as 50 years later. In fact the main series of forts seems to belong overall to the period *c.* 260-300. The others differ radically from earlier Roman military tradition by lacking internal berms, i.e. the walls were free-standing, and in possessing colossal projecting bastions, some of which were solid masonry. These reflected developments in artillery machines which had become larger and more powerful (figs. 50, 52, 53). Not only did the defences have to be strong enough to support these but upheavals within the Empire had also made it more likely that a Roman fort would be assaulted with Roman military equipment (fig. 50). Some of the forts show that plans changed during building. Burgh Castle was built with rounded corners and an internal earth rampart (probably), with the external bastions added during the process of construction. This is clear from the fact that the bottom parts of the towers are not bonded to the walls though the upper courses are. Similarly, at Richborough, one of the towers was added after the walls had been built. Here there is clear evidence of the walls being built by separate gangs (fig. 51).

Unfortunately, apart from Reculver, no inscriptional evidence has survived to indicate who built the forts and whether they formed part

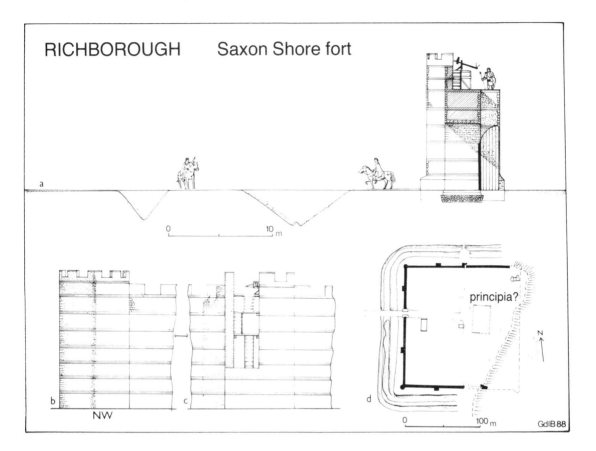

RICHBOROUGH   Saxon Shore fort

principia?

50 The Saxon Shore fort at Richborough, Kent. Now land-locked, Richborough was one of the most important sites in Romano-British history: the Claudian army seems to have landed here in 43 and subsequently a monumental arch was erected to commemorate the event (fig. 86).

The Saxon Shore forts present a number of archaeological and historical problems. This is largely because they appear as a unified system in the late Roman military document, the *Notitia Dignitatum*, but archaeology and structural analysis have shown that they were not built at the same time.

Richborough was one of four forts built in fairly close proximity to one another around the east coast of Kent. The others are at Reculver, Dover and Lympne. Construction of the fort, shortly after *c*. 273, involved destroying all the other structures on the site. The original garrison is unknown but by the late fourth century *legio* II *Augusta* seems to have been based here. The fort was built with integral circular corner bastions and square interval towers but a number of irregularities in detail, plus a misaligned ditch show that changes took place during building work.

The illustrations show catapults on the towers. There is no specific evidence for their use here, but on balance this seems a reasonable function for the towers.

a section through the west gate and two external ditches. The plan shows three at this point but the middle one seems to have been dug in error and was filled in. The height of the wall is estimated but the surviving sections show that it was at least this high. It had a flint and mortar core faced with dressed stone and bonding courses of tile. Different gangs built different sections and changes in pattern of stone laying show the joins (fig. 51).

b the north-west bastion (solid)

c interval tower (between north-west bastion and west gate). These towers had stone bases but timber superstructures, perhaps to store ammunition for catapults.

d plan of the site. Few internal buildings of this period were revealed by excavations in the first half of this century, probably because contemporary techniques did not usually help in identifying timber buildings. The east wall has fallen away since the Roman period but would have originally overlooked both the sea (which is now some kilometres away) and also the port buildings.

69

of a concerted policy to build a chain of coastal defences. The Reculver inscription appears to credit the building of a shrine in the *principia* to the governorship of Aradius (?) Rufinus. His name is otherwise unknown in Britain but, if he was governor, the building might have taken place in *c.* 225-30 (See Appendix 2). This does not help date the main sequence of forts, and arguments have tended to hinge on coin evidence, but this is not particularly conclusive. Stephen Johnson has presented a convincing argument in favour of the Emperor Probus (276-82) being responsible. In 276 Gaul was overrun by barbarian tribes, and subsequently many of the cities and towns received new defences. The Saxon Shore forts, which have counterparts on the Gaulish coast, may have been part of this grand strategy of concerted defence. The existing forts at Reculver and Brancaster (?), which presumably represent earlier less concerted efforts to resist a growing maritime threat, were incorporated into the new scheme. Burgh Castle,

already under construction, was adapted to the new style of military architecture which was paralleled in town walls and forts alike.

The system was not confined to the shores of the English Channel and the North Sea. Late forts are known at Cardiff and Lancaster, and military enclosures have been identified on the Isle of Anglesey. None are closely dated and it is possible that, like Pevensey, they represent supplements, added during the fourth century as the need arose. Pevensey differs from the other Saxon Shore forts in having an irregular plan. The evidence of a single coin beneath a bastion has been used to suggest that the fort was added in or after the mid 330s. Unfortunately the late-Roman military document, the *Notitia Dignitatum*, is both too late and too inaccurate to help us understand in detail how these forts were operated. The *Notitia* seems to be based on information of troop dispositions in *c.* 395, with various updatings for the next 40 or so years incorporated, but not necessarily excluding out-of-date information.

Most of the names on the list can be matched with known sites, but one, *Portus Adurni*, creates a problem. It represents Portchester, Walton Castle, or an unknown site. Whichever case is right leaves us with the problem that we have at least one more fort than the *Notitia* lists. The debate is an inconclusive one because the

---

51 The north wall of Richborough fort. To the left of centre the join between two sections of wall built by different gangs can clearly be seen because of the styles of stonework. To the right is the simple north postern gate. See fig. 50. (Photo: author, 1989.)

52 The west gate of the Saxon Shore fort at Pevensey, East Sussex. Originally the gate bastions would have been joined by arched portals. The projecting gate bastions illustrate the radical changes in military architecture towards a more overtly defensive posture (compare with figs. 26, 27). Pevensey seems to be later in date than most of the Saxon Shore forts and was probably built towards the middle of the fourth century filling a long gap between the forts at Lympne and Portchester (fig. 53). (Photo: author, 1987.)

evidence does not exist to resolve it. While the forts may eventually have been incorporated into a cohesive system, we cannot say when that was; it seems changes of plan had taken place all along – perhaps one of the forts had been abandoned by the time the *Notitia* was drawn up. There is also the role of Carausius to consider – it seems likely from archaeological evidence that Portchester was put up during his rule, and it has even been argued that the main sequence of fort construction was his responsibility in an effort to defend his new empire from a Roman invasion.

The archaeological evidence is poor, so we can only see the forts as broadly belonging to a late-third-century imperial initiative to defend the north-west provinces from a maritime threat. There is no specific evidence to attribute them to any one emperor, or any particular threat – the history of the period shows that threats had existed intermittently for some decades and as a result there were already some fortifications available. Subsequently changes were made where necessary, but none of these ideas detracts from the fact that these late forts belong to a new style of military thinking. These were not Agricolan forward camps, or forts designed to hold hostile passes in mountainous territory. Instead they were designed to secure the coastline by acting as strongholds for units which could defend themselves with an array of artillery. We have no evidence for any of the forts being involved in a campaign, but the general growth and development of rural lowland Roman Britain in the third and fourth centuries suggests their existence may have contributed to a sense of security.

These were not the only military provisions made during the later period. As we will see, the

53 The west wall with bastions at Portchester, Hants. Standing almost to original height because of medieval repair work, this is the best preserved section of Roman military defences in Britain. The crenellations which can be seen near the second tower are probably post-Roman work. (Photo: author, 1989.)

northern frontier of Hadrian's Wall required extensive rebuilding in the fourth century, and a number of signal towers were built on the north-east coast. The legionary fortress at York had its western defences extensively remodelled during the fourth century. Originally built for *legio* IX *Hispana* in *c.* 71 it later emerged as the military and civilian capital of northern Britain. It was also the place in which Constantine I, the Great, was declared emperor. Around this time the section of wall which overlooked the River Ouse was augmented with a series of polygonal towers. These may have been designed to make the fortress as impressive as possible in accordance with its new status as headquarters of the *Dux Britanniarum* (Duke of the Britons). The *duces* were regional commanders of frontier troops

54 Hadrian's Wall.

a the different methods used to construct the Wall. Initially the Wall was designed to be built in *c.* 121 as the Broad Wall in the eastern sector and turf in the western. After *c.* 124 unfinished stone sections and the turf sector were completed as the Narrow Wall (though the turf alignment was not always followed, for example in the vicinity of Birdoswald fort). The stone wall was built with two different foundations as shown here – however, these were used for both the Broad and Narrow Walls depending on different units responsible for construction.

b cross-section of the Wall with forward ditch and vallum to rear. The vallum's distance behind could vary quite considerably depending on local terrain.

c-d milecastle plans (37 and 48). Milecastles have been given modern numbers starting from the eastern end of the Wall.

e-f other types of milecastle gates.

g-h different turret plans (7b & 18a), built about every 0.5 km (1/3 mile) between milecastles. The numbers of turrets follow those of the milecastles, thus turrets 7a and 7b are the next two turrets west of milecastle 7.

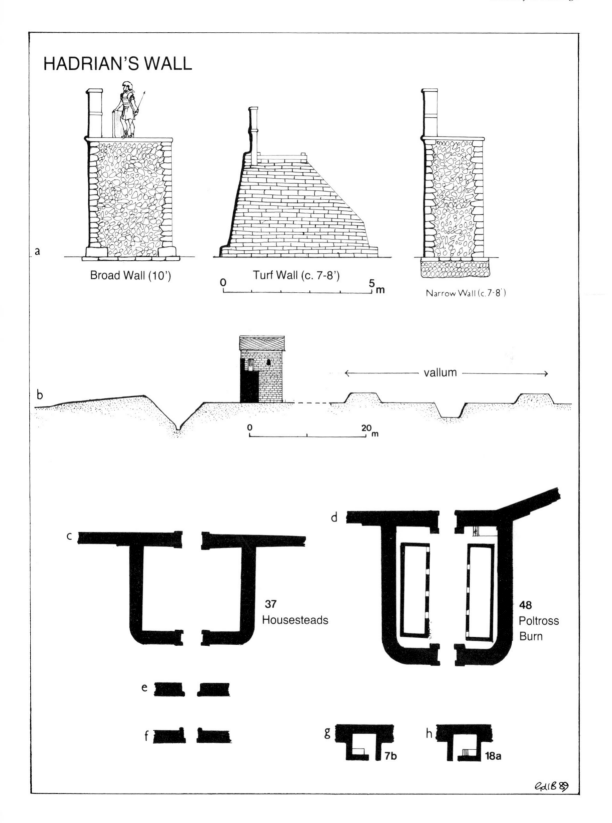

HADRIAN'S WALL

a

Broad Wall (10')   Turf Wall (c. 7-8')

Narrow Wall (c. 7-8')

0   5 m

b

vallum

0   20 m

c

37
Housesteads

d

48
Poltross
Burn

e

f

g   7b

h   18a

appointed initially by either Diocletian (284-305, who instituted the system) or Constantine I (307-37). The west corner tower has survived to an impressive height of 5.8m (19ft) with a medieval superstructure. Known as the 'Multangular Tower' it has ten projecting faces based on a plan of 14 faces. The other four faces are omitted to allow access to the tower from within the fortress. Supported on a concrete raft and piles it would have had internal floors of wood but its original height is unknown.

Frontier works

At no time during the Roman occupation of Britain did military control extend over the whole island. During the reign of Domitian (81-96) and Septimius Severus (193-211) considerable advances were made into Scotland but these were never consolidated. As a result the frontier always lay within the island. Like elsewhere in the Empire the second century was a period in which these frontiers were made permanent. In Britain this policy resulted in the walls of Hadrian (117-38) and Antoninus Pius (138-61) the former of which is amongst the most famous of all Roman construction works at any time. They belong to a more general range of Roman frontier works, particularly those in Germany, though Hadrian's Wall in particular forms a uniquely coherent group of buildings and military works.

Although Hadrian's stone Wall had a much longer life than the earthen Antonine Wall, both projects were similar in concept and form. Unfortunately we have little evidence for the reasoning behind the walls – we are told that Hadrian was the 'first' to build a wall in order 'to separate the Romans and barbarians' (*Scriptores Historiae Augustae, Hadrian*, xi.2). This seems to have followed from a general inability of the Roman army to control northern Britain effectively during the reign of Trajan (98-117). Following the abandonment of Agricola's northern conquests by Domitian in *c.* 86/7 Roman policy in Britain becomes very difficult to understand because we have no literary or epigraphic references available until Hadrian's reign. This incidentally highlights the inadequacy of archaeology under such circumstances and, realistically, we have to accept that the beginning part of the second century is something of a 'dark age'. A number of military installations between

Corbridge and Carlisle appear to belong to this phase. They may have formed a frontier zone based on the east-west road known now as the Stanegate, though whether they were conceived as such is quite another matter. If so Hadrian's Wall may have been designed as a re-working of the idea, based on an actual wall. By the reign of Antoninus Pius it had apparently failed because another war was fought following which Pius 'built another wall, this time of turf' (*SHA, Antoninus Pius*, v.4). But we should always be wary of attributing these projects to specific events – they may represent political and military responses to more general situations.

Hadrian's Wall

Unfortunately Hadrian's Wall has acted as a convenient source of building stone for centuries, and much information has had to come from the more remote central sector which is the only part in a reasonable state of preservation. Most of the eastern section lies under modern Newcastle upon Tyne and the Military Road built between 1752 and 1757. However, a century of study and excavation has produced a coherent picture of the Wall's development revealing the most important aspect of the system: radical alteration of the original plan and reconstruction through-out its history (fig. 54).

Hadrian's Wall was begun about the year 122, following the emperor's visit to Britain. Whether Hadrian played a significant part in its design or not is unknown. Considering his interest in architecture it is not improbable that the scheme was based at least in part on his ideas. It seems to have been conceived as a stone wall 10 Roman feet (about 3m) broad with a forward ditch separated by a berm about 20 Roman feet (6m) wide (fig. 54b). The stone curtain ran from a bridge on the River Tyne at Newcastle, *Pons Aelius*, running westwards to the River Irthing at Willowford. From this point the Wall was continued westwards in turf to Bowness-on-Solway. The stone wall, as planned, is now usually described as the 'Broad Wall'. The total length was around 76 Roman miles (111km).

Inscriptions indicate that the units responsible were detachments of the II, VI and XX legions which built it in approximately five-mile units. Differences in the way the Wall was built correspond with these and it seems that there were two basic methods now known as 'Standard

A' and 'Standard B'. Standard A consisted of a single course of large stones above the foundations followed by an offset, and is associated with the II and VI. In Standard B three or four smaller courses preceded the offset and is associated with XX (fig. 54a). The Wall had milecastles every Roman mile and turrets (or perhaps more accurately described as signal towers) every third of a mile in between (figs. 54c-h, 55-57). These measurements were adhered to sometimes with a perplexing disregard for tactically disadvantageous locations, but careful surveying has shown that quite significant variations in distances were allowed. For example milecastles 37 and 38 are separated by a distance of 0.99 of a Roman mile (*c.* 1.4km), 38 and 39 by 0.94 of a mile (*c.* 1.3km), and 39 and 40 by 1.11 miles (*c.* 1.6km). The main forces of auxiliary units were located behind the Wall at forts already in existence on the east-west Stanegate road (for example at Vindolanda). The system of milecastles and turrets, but no Wall, continued some way down the Cumbrian coast. Recent excavations have suggested that where necessary additional structures were incorporated. At Peel Gap, between Turrets 39A and 39B, a tower was added to fill a gap. Other recent work at Denton Burn suggests that the Wall curtain may have been whitewashed. If so its original appearance may have been rather different to that popularly imagined.

By 124 a number of radical alterations had been introduced. The sequence is very complicated, and minor details need not concern us here. Unfinished sections of the stone wall were now built on a narrower gauge. The new design is known now as the 'Narrow Wall', and though usually said to be 8 Roman feet (*c.* 2.4m) wide it actually varies considerably sometimes being less than 7 feet (*c.* 2.1m) wide. Standard A and Standard B continued in use. The change of policy is manifest in the fact that the foundations and some milecastles and turrets had already been prepared for the 10 foot (*c.* 3m) Broad Wall, and the change in thickness is quite clear at a number of sites (fig. 6). Rather more significant was the decision to build 12 forts on the Wall itself, in some cases involving the demolition of existing turrets, for example at Chesters and Housesteads. The new forts were sited around 7 Roman miles (*c.* 10km) apart. Each was to be garrisoned by an auxiliary unit and were built either up against the Wall's south side, or

projecting in part to the north – this depended on local conditions (fig. 20). The reason must have been that the older forts to the south were simply too far away to allow a speedy response to an incursion, and possibly because it was easier to supply the frontier garrison when it was concentrated into a single zone.

At around this time the Vallum was added. This was a ditch flanked by northern and southern mounds which ran south of the Wall. Although the ditch to the north of the Wall was sometimes dispensed with when it was made superfluous by precipices the Vallum was constructed almost regardless of the local landscape. Just how regardless can still be seen at Limestone Corner where colossal pieces of the local stone were hacked out to form a ditch. They still lie where they were hauled and form a vivid reminder in an age of explosives and power drills of the power of disciplined muscle (fig. 59). At Down Hill, near the site of milecastle 21, the Vallum runs like a switchback over the hill despite the fact that the ground drops steeply away immediately to the south. In general the Vallum lay around 120 Roman feet (*c.* 33m) behind the Wall but this varies very considerably depending on the terrain (fig. 54b). It thus created a 'military zone' with the Wall. Crossings were built at each fort and this suggests that the Vallum was also devised as a means of funnelling trans-Wall traffic into easily policed channels. The Vallum sometimes diverts to go round forts, demonstrating that it was either contemporary or later. However at Carrawburgh the Vallum lies beneath the fort and was filled in, showing that this fort was added later in order to fill the long gap between Chesters and Housesteads.

In the east the Wall was extended to the fort of Wallsend where it ran down into the River Tyne. In the west the stone forts had been built into the turf wall but this was itself subsequently built in stone, probably under Hadrian. At Birdoswald, which had projected north, the new stone wall was re-aligned to meet the fort's north wall, thus placing the whole fort south of the Wall. In essence this was the completed form of Hadrian's Wall. In time the purpose of the components altered – gates were blocked up, others were opened (for example at Knag Burn by Housesteads) and the Vallum was given crossings throughout its length. Much of the dereliction which has been identified on the Wall resulted from the time when the Antonine Wall was in use. It needed so much repair in the early third century and later that some post-Roman chroniclers believed Septimius Severus had built the Wall from its foundations. The long period of peace during the third century also contributed to decay.

Much space has been given to discussing the strategic intentions behind Hadrian's Wall and the tactical plan behind the various components. The fact that the Wall was altered during construction implies that its purpose changed according to circumstances – it is thus hopelessly simplistic to try and attribute the Wall's construction to a single idea. There were probably many reasons. The Wall must have provided a psychological boost not just to local inhabitants who wished to become peaceably romanized, but also to the population further south. Likewise it must have appeared as a potent statement of Roman power to those beyond the Wall to the north. It cannot have really been intended as an absolute barrier because outpost forts to the north, for example at Bewcastle, indicate that Rome regarded land immediately to the north as under its control. In any case a determined 'raider' would have had little difficulty in scaling the Wall if he so desired. It is rather more likely that the Wall and its various crossing points made it possible to supervise local movements. From a military point of view the forts and milecastles may well have enabled a swift response to incursions, and it seems an unavoidable conclusion that the various turrets and milecastles were designed to make observations and communications easier.

55 Milecastle 48 at Poltross Burn looking north, showing the remains of the flight of steps which led up to the wall-curtain (see fig. 57). It is possible though that they only led up to a low flat platform on which a ladder stood. This would have had tactical advantages had the curtain been scaled by an attacker because a ladder could be swiftly removed. (Photo: author, 1989.)

56 The north gate of milecastle 37 during repair work looking north. The survival of the springers makes it possible confidently to restore the arch and therefore a minimum height for the wall. See also plate 4. (Photo: author, 1989.)

However it is worth remembering that the Wall garrison of about 5000 men was dispersed along the whole length. Consequently the number of men available in any given area was limited to a few hundred. If this was effective then it seems that the scheme was designed more to deal with small-scale skirmishes than with major invasions.

All these are possibilities, and the Wall was probably designed to deal with them all; it is not strictly necessary to see the Wall purely as a response to a pressing military crisis. Where the plan seemed inadequate it was altered and in time the Wall probably became so integrated a part of military routine and local civilian life that its original intention was largely forgotten. There is no doubt that Hadrian's Wall was an astonishing project. It is the kind of ancient structure that invokes modern incredulity, particularly with regard to cost. This is quite irrelevant. Hadrian's Wall cost nothing at all. The materials were free and the soldiers were being paid regardless. It made no difference to the Imperial treasury whether they fought wars, sharpened their swords or built walls if that seemed a good idea at the time. This makes it easier to understand why

Hadrian's Wall was more or less abandoned 20 years after it was built.

The Antonine Wall

The Antonine Wall runs between the Firth of Forth and the Firth of Clyde in Scotland, about 160km (100 miles) north of Hadrian's Wall. It was built by the early 140s and was permanently abandoned in the 160s. There may have been several reasons: a new emperor or governor needing a new reputation; idle soldiers; the tying up of too many troops in the numerous garrison posts of Hadrian's Wall; or the difficulty of supplying the remote central sector forts.

The new frontier was closely modelled on its predecessor but was built entirely of turf. This does not appear to have been the original plan because the fort of Balmuildy, one of the earliest on the frontier, was built of stone and was prepared with wing walls of stone. This suggests that a stone curtain had been intended, but that this plan was altered after the project had been begun.

The most obvious advantage the new frontier had was its length. It is only 37 Roman miles (59km) long, or around half the length of Hadrian's Wall. The use of turf should not be interpreted as an economy measure employed under duress because Roman frontiers were usually built of turf. Like Hadrian's Wall the new wall had a forward ditch but this was separated from the wall by a broader berm 20 to 30 Roman feet (7 to 9m) wide.

Unlike Hadrian's Wall forts were associated with the new frontier right from the very beginning. They were interspersed with fortlets, but there is no positive evidence for a regular series of turrets. These strongholds are distinctive for their slightly irregular plans and considerable variation in size. This may be explained in part by the idea that some of the forts were built before the Wall and some after, perhaps after having discovered that the original provision was inadequate. At any rate the forts and their capacity mean that the total garrison cannot have been very much less than that on Hadrian's Wall. In military terms this means there were twice as many men per mile of frontier than before. An important tactical difference was that the Antonine Wall appears to have had no equivalent to the Vallum on Hadrian's Wall. This is curious because the Vallum was built with such diligence that this suggests it was regarded as an indispensable component of the frontier.

The Walls as buildings

The Antonine Wall was abandoned permanently by the 160s and thereafter Hadrian's Wall served as the northern frontier. More details of their fascinating history can be best pursued by reading the excellent summaries of the archaeology by Stephen Johnson, and Breeze and Dobson, and the most recent edition of John Collingwood Bruce's handbook, edited and revised by C. Daniels.

We are concerned here more with the building of the Walls and their associated structures. No part of Hadrian's Wall stands to full height today nor in recorded times. One of the highest sections, at Hare Hill, still stands to 3m (10ft). However the surviving lower part of a flight of steps at the milecastle of Poltross Burn (MC 48) suggests, if extended at the same angle, that the walkway on the rampart within the milecastle was 4.8m (15ft) from the ground (fig. 55). The remains of the north gate at milecastle 37 (fig. 56) support this. This does not necessarily mean that the Wall itself was this high, or even that it was the same height throughout its length. However, assuming that a parapet existed to protect patrols the Wall must have presented a face of around at least 5-6m (17-20ft) high to the north. It is likely, but not certain, that the Wall had crenellations. The Rudge Cup, a small bronze vessel, is decorated with what appears to be a stylized representation of the wall with crenellations and may be a souvenir of a visit (see *Finds*, plate 3). No collapsed upper sections of the Wall have been found but occasionally bevelled stones do turn up in the general tumble of fallen masonry. These may have capped crenellations.

The material used was mostly local sandstone and a number of quarries have been identified in the vicinity of the Wall (fig. 3). The facing stones were crudely dressed and laid in horizontal courses on a stone foundation. About two courses were laid and then the core, a mixture of rubble, clay or mortar, was poured in. Another two courses were then laid, more core poured in and so on (fig. 6). In order to relieve pressure from water forming ponds in natural dips or depressions drains were built into the structure. Similar arrangements also allowed streams to run under the Wall. Recent archaeological work on the Wall has produced evidence to suggest that whitewash and/or a hard white lime mortar may have been used to cover the whole curtain, perhaps in order to make the frontier conspicuous from a distance.

Milecastles were miniature forts attached to the south face of the Wall and were equipped with sheltered accommodation (fig. 57). Most had gates in their north and south walls, making it possible to cross the Wall, but there are exceptions. Turrets were even simpler and were not equipped with gates through the Wall (fig. 58). The turrets probably had at least two floors, the upper of which was reached by either ladder or wooden stairs. Normally the turrets were recessed into the Wall, though additions, like that at Peel Gap (see above), were just tacked on to the existing curtain. When a turret was demolished the wall recess was filled in. These structures all served the important purpose of allowing access to the walkway on the Wall itself. However, the milecastles and turrets were also built along the southern shores of the Solway Firth to extend the system, albeit without the actual wall curtain.

As with forts discussed earlier there is no evidence at all for the roofing of the milecastles and turrets. Traditional reconstructions show these with crenellations in the manner of a medieval castle. It has been argued that the lack of roof tiles from Hadrianic destruction levels is evidence for crenellations. But there is no specific evidence for crenellations either, and in any case it would have been perfectly feasible to roof the buildings with perishable materials like wooden shingles. As with the forts it is not entirely easy to accept the idea of flat roofs in Britain. These posts were presumably intended as observation bases. If so it is logical to assume that a dry, comfortable soldier is more likely to do his observing than a wet, cold one. Quite apart from personal comfort is the problem of structural maintenance of flat-roofed buildings, particularly in such exposed places. Gabled or pitched roofs on turrets and milecastle gates are more likely to have been suitable. The general evidence from Trajan's Column is that timber superstructures of gates might be flat roofed but that the majority of stone structures and free-standing towers portrayed seem to have had pitched roofs. It is quite possible that the turrets may have resembled the signal towers described below in having external wooden platforms, in which case

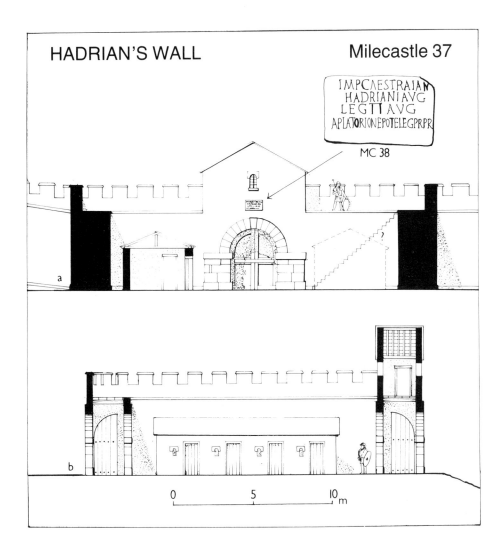

HADRIAN'S WALL   **Milecastle 37**

IMPCAESTRAIAN
HADRIANIAVG
LEGTTAVG
APLATORIONEPOTELEGPRPR

MC 38

0   5   10 m

57 Cross-sections of a milecastle, based on the dimensions of number 37 (Housesteads), using information from other milecastles. Changes of ground level have been ignored for simplicity. Milecastle 37 is a 'short-axis' milecastle and a fragmentary inscription shows that it was built by *legio* II *Augusta*. The inscription was probably identical to a complete example found at milecastle 38 (illustrated – *RIB* 1638) indicating that building took place under Hadrian during the governorship of Aulus Platorius Nepos. Milecastle 37 contained few traces of internal buildings, and no trace of a stairway but more substantial evidence from milecastle 48 (Poltross Burn) suggests these were normal features (see fig. 55).

Milecastle 37's claim to fame is that it retains its north gate up to the first springers on the two arches (fig. 56). This gives the height of the arch, and therefore, probably the wall too. The gatehouse, if one existed, has been reconstructed at the minimum convenient height, and with a pitched roof. Reconstructions of milecastles frequently show the gatehouse as projecting from the wall of the milecastle. In this particular case it is evident from the surviving remains that only the massive blocks of the door jambs project – the rest of the gatehouse was flush with the flanking walls. Subsequently the north gate was narrowed and some of the partial blocking is still visible on the site. In fact the ground falls away so steeply to the north that this gate must have been useless except for foot-traffic, though narrowing of milecastle gates seems to have been a general phenomenon. See also plate 4.

a cross-section east-west 17.5m (58ft)
b cross-section north-south 15m (50ft)

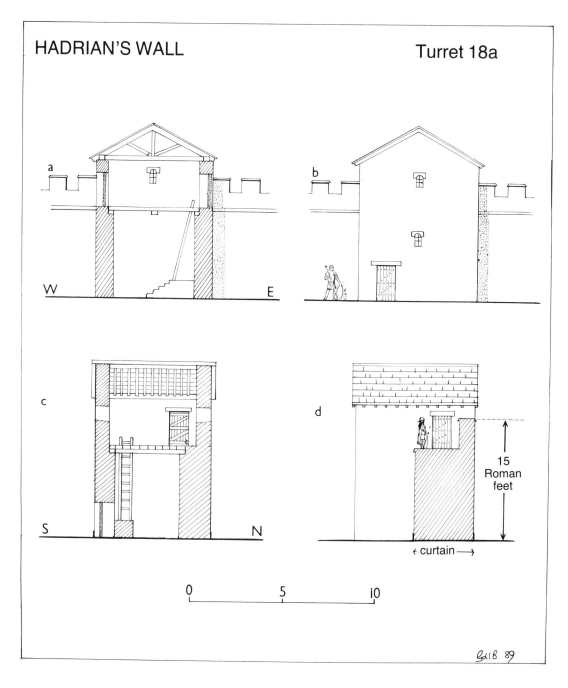

HADRIAN'S WALL

Turret 18a

a

W   E

b

c

S   N

d

15 Roman feet

← curtain →

0   5   10

GdlB 89

58 Hadrian's Wall, turret 18a (Wallhouses East, east of the fort at Haltonchesters, see fig. 54h). This turret, when excavated, was in an exceptional state of preservation and retained a ladder platform though height and roofing remain conjectural. They may have resembled the reconstruction shown in fig. 60 of a timber signal tower with an external gallery but the Wall probably served this purpose (assuming it had a walkway along the parapet, but even this is not certain).

a cross-section west to east showing the ladder platform and access to the upper floor
b the same, externally, showing ground-floor access
c cross-section south to north
d the same, showing the curtain itself in cross-section

they would have been a little higher than reconstructed here (figs. 57, 58, plate 4).

The turf Walls were built differently. Although the western sector of Hadrian's Wall was eventually replaced in stone the new curtain did not always follow the same course. This has allowed examination of the turf version. It was made of cut turves sometimes laid on a cobbled base 20 Roman feet (6m) wide. Its height is unknown but in order to have been effective it would have had to have been around at least 3m (10ft), and probably supported a timber palisade. The Antonine Wall was built on a cobble base 14 Roman feet (45m) wide. The continuous stone base increased stability, facilitated drainage and probably meant that with parapets the wall was at least as high as Hadrian's. Either this followed a lesson learned, or there was better planning. There was nothing particularly unsatisfactory about using turf; the technique is fast and durable – parts of the Antonine Wall are still visible

today, and it was the normal method of building Roman frontiers.

Signal towers

An organized army is dependent upon communications. Hadrian's Wall and the Antonine Wall provided a fairly rigid system of linear communications with the various turrets and milecastle towers incorporated into the structure. Signal towers were also built in isolation, though in a series, and they formed a vital component of military communications. For example a sequence of ten, averaging less than a mile apart, are known from eight miles of road between Perth and Strageath.

Signal towers were generally built of timber because this was the quickest and most efficient way. Consequently the archaeological evidence is limited usually to post-holes and ramparts. However a number of square timber signal towers appear on Trajan's Column. These provide the basis for the reconstruction of the Beattock tower (fig. 60). The design was simple and presumably effective. The tower supported an external gallery and a brazier and was defended by a palisade and ditch. The remains of a tower's circular surrounding rampart and ditch

59 The Vallum at Limestone Corner close to the fort at Carrawburgh. Huge boulders extracted with wedges and water still lie littered about (see fig. 54). One of the subsequent crossings of the Vallum can be seen in the centre. (Photo: author, 1989.)

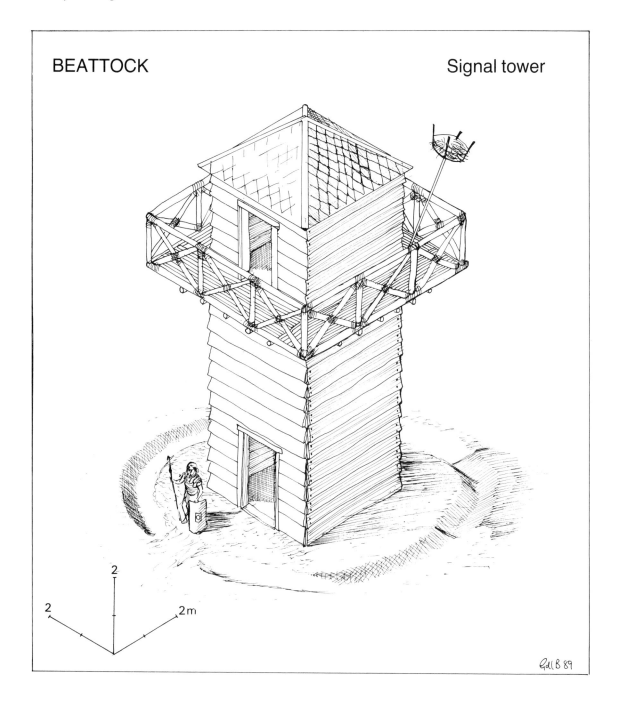

BEATTOCK　　　　　　　　　　　　　　　Signal tower

GdlB 89

60 Timber signal tower at Beattock Summit, Lanarkshire (isometric reconstruction). One of a series of towers this site is represented by only four post-holes and a shallow encircling ditch so there is little obvious evidence for its original appearance. However, signal towers are portrayed on Trajan's Column and they appear to have had an external gallery which would have served, as not only a look-out platform but also a support for a brazier. The brazier would have been lit when the need arose. Access is not so certain – here an entrance on ground level is shown but an alternative method would have been by ladder; this could then be pulled up for security.

can still be seen at Bowes Moor, 6.5km (4 miles) west of Bowes in North Yorkshire. Trajan's Column shows that a palisade of stakes capped the rampart.

Not all towers were timber. A square stone tower at Pike Hill on Hadrian's Wall pre-dated the system. The Wall was diverted to incorporate it and turret 52A lies less than 200m (650ft) to the west showing how it lies 'out of sequence'. It lies at an angle of 45 degrees to the Wall because it was aligned with a series of signal towers and forts.

Much later in Roman Britain's history it proved necessary to defend the eastern and southern coasts with the forts of the Saxon Shore (see above). Subsequently it also proved necessary to augment coastal defences with much more elaborate signal towers. These are better described as signal stations and really amount to small forts. In fact during the first century coastal fortlets were built for signalling, as for example at Martinhoe in Devon which contained accommodation for a century of troops (about 80 men) and an outer fortification for the beacons.

The late-fourth-century stations were much more elaborate and involved an outer ditch, and a stone wall for the compound which contained a stone tower possibly up to 30m (100ft) in height. A series is known from the east Yorkshire coast and they seem to have been built in or after 369. An inscription from Ravenscar (see Appendix 2) specifically describes the station as consisting of a tower and fort. The site at Scarborough is probably the best known and can still be seen in part today, though the height of the tower as reconstructed (fig. 61) is purely hypothetical; the large piers suggest a substantial building, perhaps resembling a Norman castle keep but without the corner towers. Occupation seems to have lasted into the fifth century.

---

61 Signal tower at Scarborough, East Yorkshire, restored in elevation. A series of these towers were built along the Yorkshire coast in the late fourth century. They were probably designed to warn against sea-borne raiders from northern Europe. All the examples known seem to have consisted of a tower surrounded by a walled courtyard and an outer ditch. They may have resembled later Norman keeps. The height is purely speculative, but the towers must have been high enough to allow the garrison to see into the ditch.

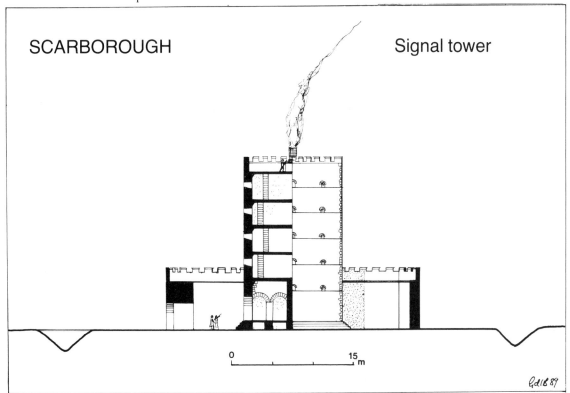

SCARBOROUGH   Signal tower

0   15
m

3

PUBLIC
BUILDINGS

Introduction

All organized communities need administrative centres. In the relatively sophisticated government of the Roman world this was true not just at imperial level but also at provincial and local level. The Roman state had to delegate its power through local communities because ancient transport and technology was so primitive that it would have been impossible for it to have functioned otherwise. So in Roman Britain we find that many of the settlements which we call 'towns' contained a public hall (*basilica*) and associated market place (*forum*).

Public life was more than just provincial and civic administration. The Roman world contained many monuments to past events, local pride and ostentation such as triumphal arches, theatres and circuses. Discovering exactly who paid for public buildings in the Roman world is a subject in itself. Inscriptions from Britain, and to a far greater extent from elsewhere, show that buildings were put up by the emperor and civic governments alike. City funds were derived from local taxes on trade and rents on civic property as well as from cash paid by local magistrates in return for their offices. Sometimes buildings were erected at the expense of a single man or family. Although town governments had employees who must have contributed to the labour required for public buildings it would be wrong to think in modern terms of costing because of the availability of forced labour. We might even include the army in this category because soldiers were being paid regardless of what they actually did with their time and may well have been obliged to participate in civic building works as part of the policy of romanization. On the other hand it may be that some towns actually could not afford such projects, causing financial problems for their communities – our lack of detailed knowledge leaves this as pure speculation.

It is certainly quite wrong to imagine that all Romano-British towns had fully functioning public buildings in the second century – evidence from North Africa (where far more inscriptions have survived) shows that work could go on for decades. The Agricolan inscription from the forum at Verulamium (see Appendix 2) might belong to an early stage of a project that could have stretched on till late in the second century, absorbing large quantities of the town's money (though it is fairly certain that the state made a contribution) and perhaps explaining why the theatre was not erected until after *c*.155 on a site apparently reserved for it long before.

A few other inscriptions supply us with factual information but they are usually tantalizingly vague or incomplete (see Appendix 2). We also have Tacitus' reference to Colchester's possession of a senate-house and theatre by the year 60. Beyond that we have only the stumps of walls, reconstituted ground plans and guess-work to base our reconstructions on. It is impossible to know what the different parts of public buildings were used for even if one can be certain about what was a forum or a basilica: a description of rooms in a basilica as municipal offices is no more than an educated guess. Although this is not going to change, the large amount of building activity which has gone on in Britain over the last few decades has affected all of Britain's towns to a greater or lesser degree. So many towns have Roman origins that much new information about the structure of ancient public buildings in Roman Britain has emerged, even if most of the new evidence is fragmentary.

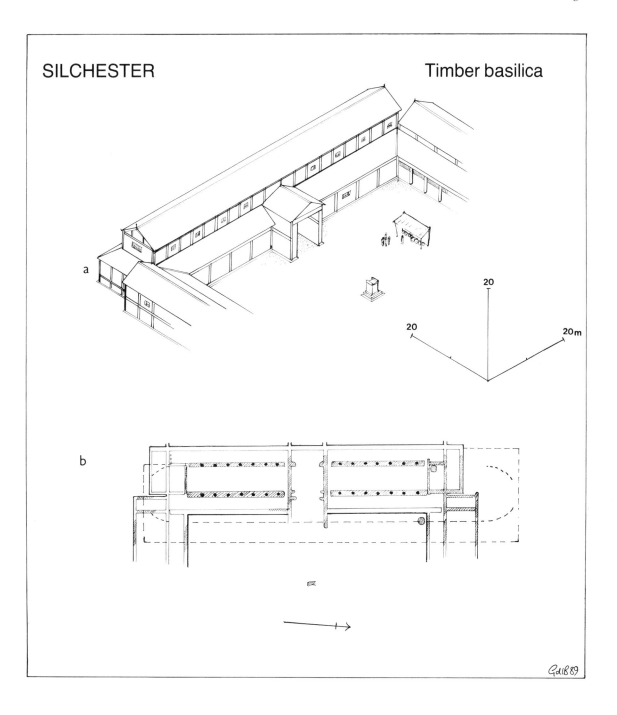

SILCHESTER   **Timber basilica**

a

b

62 The Flavian timber basilica at Silchester (isometric reconstruction). Missed by Victorian excavators this early basilica lay beneath the later stone version (see fig. 66). It seems to have been built in the 80s replacing an even earlier rectangular timber building with a portico, perhaps a market, up by the 50s or 60s. Apart from the entrance, which split the main hall in two, the timber basilica seems to have been conventional in form with a nave and two aisles.

Basilica and forum

In practice the towns which had a forum and basilica were the provincial capital, the *coloniae* (settlements of Roman citizens) and the administrative capitals of the tribal cantons, for example Silchester. There seems little doubt that these buildings were derived indirectly, in architectural terms, from the headquarters buildings of the military forts. This is an important distinction, and it would be wrong to imagine a Romano-British forum on the lines of the much earlier surviving example at Pompeii in southern Italy. Here the forum is an elongated piazza with temples and arches at either end; the basilica forms an appendage to the south-west corner of the forum. Nevertheless the collective function was the same: to act as the centre for local government, administration, trade and commercial activity.

The basilica and forum was also an important expression of civic pride and display and these buildings individually must represent the largest and best the local community could afford (or thought they could afford), though there may have been a certain amount of state assistance and patronage. Consequently there is a fair amount of variation in scale – contrast the basilica in London with that at Caerwent, for instance – but we can only guess at the variation in decoration and adornment. The plans of these buildings look a little spartan but originally they would have been surrounded by statues of emperors, local worthies, military heroes and gods and goddesses, quite apart from carved stonework, wall paintings and marbled veneers. The forums were thriving markets – the late-second-century fire at Wroxeter was followed by demolition which covered the collapsed remains of the abandoned stalls, thus preserving their stock. This included pottery (Romano-British mortaria and Gaulish samian) and whetstones, though obviously perishable commodities left no trace.

As we saw in Chapter 2 the principia was the administrative centre of the Roman fort. It consisted of a hall, in front of which was an open area surrounded on the other three sides by an ambulatory and a range of rooms. The Romano-British civic equivalent of this building was usually rather larger, though size varies, but it is quite possible that the architects were either ex-soldiers or on loan from the army, or that architects in Britain derived their ideas from what they saw around them in military forts. Verulamium's is usually considered an exception because of the three temples and side entrances in the forum (plate 5) though in fact it only differs in detail and the general plan is fairly conformist. Unfortunately we have relatively little information about when such buildings were put up. We know that the Verulamium forum had been dedicated by the year 79, and that the forum at Wroxeter had been built by 130-1 (Appendix 2). Archaeological investigations have indicated that the second-century basilica at Silchester overlies a timber predecessor dated to the 80s, as at London (fig. 62).

London was the capital of Roman Britain. We do not know this for a fact but it is a more than reasonable supposition because the town was the biggest in the province and its Hadrianic basilica was also the largest. We also know that the post-Boudican *procurator provinciae Britanniae*, Julius Classicianus, died at London. The site of London's basilica has been the subject of a number of intermittent excavations since the nineteenth century. Only a small portion of its plan has been recovered, but by extending known walls a very reasonable complete plan has been drawn up.

---

63 Elevation (western half) and plan of the Hadrianic basilica and forum at Gracechurch Street, London, built *c.*100-50 but the evidence is so sparse that no greater precision is possible. It was aligned on the approach to the bridge over the Thames, and roads in the vicinity were given a new layout. The basilica was certainly a very substantial building. Late-Roman churches which still stand show that the height should be roughly equivalent to the width of the nave and one aisle which for this building was about 25m (82ft). The gaps between the piers are known and these suggest an arcade of the dimensions shown which corresponds very well with the suggested height. The hall was about 150m (492ft) in length. Excavations in the north-east corner (fig. 65) have shown that there were two distinct construction phases, followed by third century refurbishment and early fourth century demolition.

No traces of the decoration of the building have been recovered apart from fragments of painted wall-plaster. It is certain that there must also have been various architectural embellishments such as detached columns and capitals, decorated cornices, inscriptions and statuary. The well-known bronze bust of Hadrian (see *Finds*, fig. 77b) is likely to have come from here.

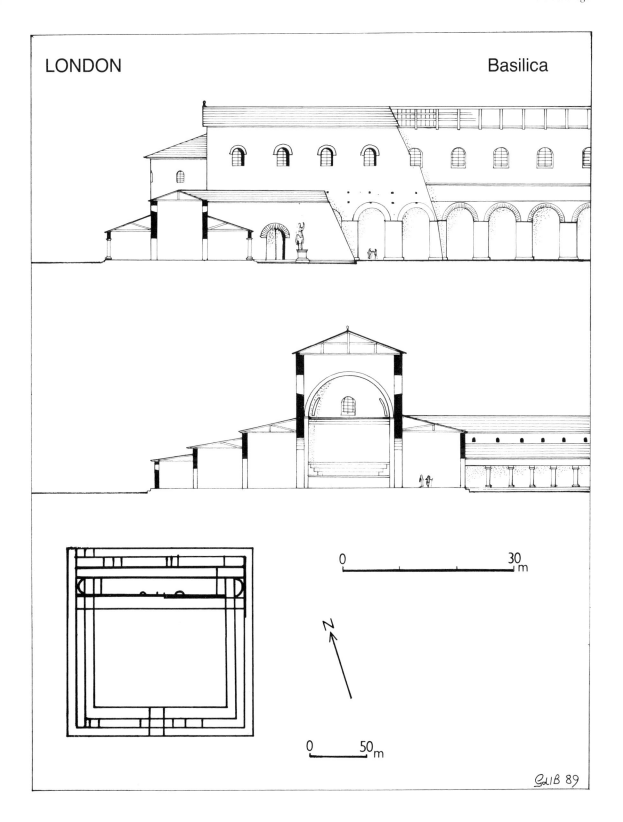

LONDON

Basilica

0 _____ 30
                m

N

0 _____ 50
            m

GdIB 89

London had two consecutive basilicas and forums built on the same site, but the first pair was much smaller and simpler. It seems to belong to the mid-Flavian period and probably represents part of official policy to reconstruct Britain after the Boudican Revolt of 60. Its scale is surprisingly small, smaller in fact than contemporary structures in cantonal capitals in Britain, for example at Silchester. Perhaps it was an expedient project, designed to get a working building into commission as fast as possible, as may have been the case with the principia at Inchtuthil (fig. 17). At around 5500 square metres (59,000sq.ft) it was very unassuming in comparison to the replacement which was built around, and finally over, its predecessor covering

nearly 30,000 square metres (323,000sq.ft) in the process. The later building must have been a particularly magnificent construction which may have taken decades to build (figs. 63, 64). We know nothing about its date except that a coin of Hadrian in excellent condition found sealed in the mortar implies that building work was underway by the end of his reign and after. Of course it could have begun much earlier, and ended far later but it is tempting to associate its inception with Hadrian's known visit early in his reign, particularly as Hadrian is known to have promoted civic development elsewhere (see Wroxeter above). The truth is that we do not know if he was involved, but its function was evidently to act as the centre of provincial administration and justice.

The great basilica of Roman London consisted of a hall about 35m (115ft) wide, and about 150m (492ft) in length, oriented roughly east-west on the long axis. Its north-south axis seems to have been aligned on the road which ran downhill to the bridge across the Thames. The hall was divided into two side aisles, separated from the central nave by two rows of brick piers. These

---

64 London basilica and St Paul's.
a the Hadrianic basilica of Roman London super-imposed against St Paul's Cathedral to show its scale.
b superimposed outline plans of the same buildings – in actuality the site of the basilica and forum lay some way to the east of where the cathedral now stands.

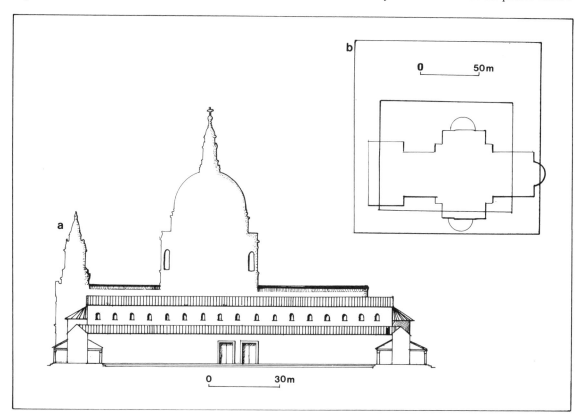

65 The north-east part of the Hadrianic basilica of London by Leadenhall and Gracechurch Streets under excavation. The wall in the foreground is the north wall of the complex and the walls in the background running at right angles represent internal divisions. The site has since been destroyed to make way for a modern building. (Photo: author, 1986.)

probably supported arches, possibly embellished with either pilasters or detached columns. We cannot know the height of the nave but, by taking the parallels of similarly designed early churches which are still standing, we can assume that it was approximately equivalent to the sum of the diameter of the nave and one aisle; in this case about 27m (89ft). The roof was tiled but whether this was supported by vaulting or timber rafters

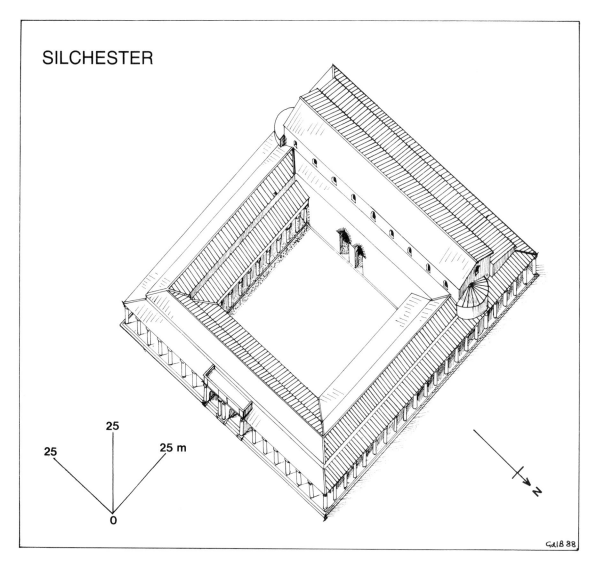

SILCHESTER

25

25

25 m

25

0

N

GdlB 88

66 The second-century basilica and forum at Silchester (axonometric reconstruction). Recent excavations have revealed the presence of a timber basilica, of similar size, beneath a mid-second-century replacement in stone 82m (269ft) in length (see fig. 62). These excavations have also proved that the stone basilica had an unusual plan. Instead of the two arcades to support the superstructure there was only one. Traces of the columns suggest they were a little under 9m (29ft) in height and had ornate Corinthian-style capitals. At either end there was a raised apse for the magistrates concerned with dispensing justice. The forum was a roughly square piazza with internal and external ambulatories. There seems to have been a monumental entrance to the forum and this may have been modelled on a triumphal arch.

During the third century it seems that the building was taken over by various metal-workers who left traces of their smelting and casting activities. The building certainly contained monumental bronze sculptures, some of which may have been broken up at this time (see *Finds*, figs. 31d and 77c).

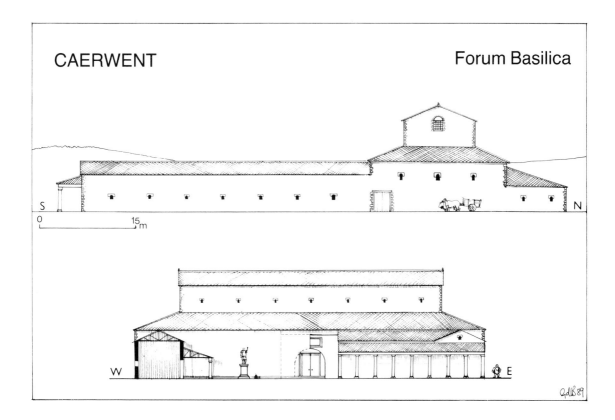

CAERWENT   Forum Basilica

67 The basilica and forum at Caerwent in elevation. One of the smallest of all the civic administrative centres in Roman Britain this building was built on a similar model to most of the other, much larger, examples. It only had an external portico on the south side and instead of having apsidal tribunals at either end of the basilica there were simple rectangular rooms, though one of these was heated. Despite its modest scale it had columns with carved stone capitals. At a late point in its history the west range of offices or shops in the forum had a temple-like building inserted into it. The building has been recently re-excavated (see *Britannia*, 20, 1989, pl.XVIII).

we do not know. At the east end of the building was an apse with a raised floor level. This would have been used by the presiding dignitaries, depending on the occasion. There may have been a similar apse at the west end. On the northern side of the building there was a row of rooms running off the north aisle, and beyond that a further row. These would probably have been used as offices, and perhaps for the storage of the government and judicial records.

Unfortunately the limited excavations on the basilica site have yielded no evidence for elaborate architectural decorations in the form of carved columns and capitals, cornices and architraves (fig. 65). However, in this case it is certainly safe to assume that they must have been there, and were carried off or broken up in later centuries. It would be unthinkable for this colossal and prestigious building to have been built merely of plastered brick – some fragments of painted wall plaster have been found. The end of the London basilica is, like everything else in Roman Britain, an enigma. The remains of some of the walls are fairly substantial but they formed no part of later, medieval, buildings. The fact of course is that the building had a specific function that became redundant once provincial and civic government came to an end. Structural problems may have played a part because the building, like a number of major Romano-British buildings, was put up on ill-prepared ground (Chapter 1).

Almost all the basilicas of Roman Britain seem to have been similar to the London example. The only difference is that they were without exception smaller. Some have been excavated in their entirety, for example the Silchester basilica, now entirely under grass. This building is particularly interesting because recent excavations, designed to make up for the shortcomings of Victorian archaeologists, have shown that the second-century masonry building was preceded by a similarly planned wooden basilica, put up in the 80s. The stone building was modest by London's standards and was only 82m (269ft) long, by 17.5m (57ft) in width (fig. 66). It had two apses but only one aisle, separated from the hall by a single row of columns about 8.6m (28ft) in height. The even smaller basilica at Caerwent resembles London more closely but was only 50m (164ft) long and 20m (66ft) wide (fig. 67). Even this modest and comparatively remote example of classical architecture had columns embellished with ornately carved Corinthian capitals and painted wall-plaster. None of the Romano-British basilicas is now visible apart from the north wall of the basilica at Lincoln. Known for years as the 'Mint Wall', only recent excavations in the city centre have shown that it formed part of the civic centre (fig. 68).

The basilica was always built in association with a forum. This was a much simpler building and consequently there is little variation in the basic plan (fig. 69). The forum was an open square or rectangle which was surrounded on three sides by covered and colonnaded ambulatories. The ambulatory normally ran along a central row of rooms, which were probably shops, on the other side of which a further ambulatory formed the external part of the building (see figs. 62-7). The ambulatories were only broken by entrances or, rarely, temples. The fourth side was crossed by the basilica which itself had civic offices to the rear.

---

68 The 'Mint Wall' in Lincoln, now identified as the north wall of the basilica surviving to a remarkable 21m (70ft) in length and 5.5m (18ft) in height. Putlog holes in the wall were probably for scaffolding during construction. The lack of windows seems strange but if this was the basilica's north wall then there may have been practical reasons for this. (Photo: author, 1989.)

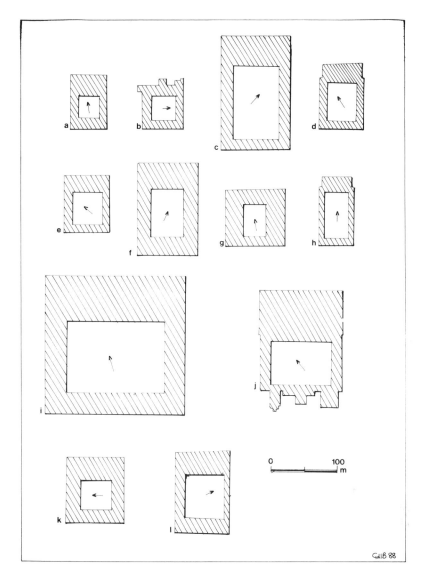

69 Comparative sizes of basilicas and forums. In each case the basilica forms the upper part and the internal space indicates the forum piazza. The majority of the examples are known from traces but enough evidence exists to indicate the extent of the structure. The size of London's period 2 building is apparent, followed by Verulamium and Cirencester. It is also worth noting how the *coloniae* at Gloucester and Lincoln, despite being of superior urban status, had smaller buildings than the tribal capitals of their cantons (Cirencester and Leicester respectively). This emphasizes the need for tribal capitals to have the facilities to govern more than just the towns themselves. The arrow indicates north for each case, and it is apparent that the basilica was normally on the northern side. A number of other towns in Britain have produced probable traces of forums and basilicas but their plans cannot yet be estimated accurately and are therefore omitted.

a Caerwent *Venta Silurum*
b Caistor-by-Norwich *Venta Icenorum*
c Cirencester *Corinium Dobunnorum*
d Exeter *Isca Dumniorum*
e Gloucester *Glevum*
f Leicester *Ratae Coritanorum*
g Lincoln *Lindum*
h London, period 1 *Londinium*
i London, period 2 *Londinium*
j Verulamium
k Silchester *Calleva Atrebatum*
l Wroxeter *Viroconium (Cornoviorum?)*

Vitruvius said the forum's size should reflect the number of local inhabitants, being neither too small to be useful nor so large that it looked like an empty desert (v.1.3).

The evidence available seems to suggest that there were two periods in which towns built their administrative centres. The first was during the Flavian reconstruction of Roman Britain. However, the buildings were on a modest scale and it was only after the second decade of the second century that the towns began to embark on more extravagant projects. The later history of these monumental building complexes is not very clear. That London and Cirencester suffered subsidence has already been mentioned. There are a number of cases where later churches seem to be associated with the sites, for example in London, Lincoln and Verulamium. Even the great hall of the principia at York now lies beneath the great medieval minster. It is quite possible that the basilicas served a Christian function in their later years and that the religious associations of the sites continued, even once the basilicas had crumbled. In several cases churches were founded on the sites. At Lincoln the church of St Paul-in-the-Bail was founded in the old forum. Its early history is obscure, but some of the associated burials seem to date back to the fifth and sixth centuries. However, the Romano-British basilicas probably decayed because in the fifth century and later the technology, skill and will needed to maintain them simply did not exist any longer. As the biggest and most complicated buildings the basilicas and forums were the least likely to be maintained, especially as their administrative purpose had disappeared.

Other market buildings

While the forum functioned as the main centre of urban commercial activity it could sometimes be supplemented by a separate market building known as the *macellum*. These were not apparently very common in Britain but this may reflect a difficulty of interpretation; examples have been found at Cirencester, Leicester, Verulamium (fig. 70) and Wroxeter and it seems inevitable that any reasonably sized town would have outgrown the facilities afforded by its forum. Of course there would have been shops like those in Insula xiv at Verulamium (see Chapter 4; fig. 111) arranged along a street front, but markets were essential for non-residential

traders, such as farmers or merchants. At Pompeii the macellum not only contained shops and booths for changing money but also a shrine and meeting place for the priests of the imperial cult. Unfortunately we cannot be certain whether the Romano-British examples were public or private, but their central locations makes it very likely that they were civic projects provided as a supplementary facility.

Official residences and other monumental buildings

As a province Roman Britain was administered by official staff under the control of a governor. The governor was officially known as the *legatus augusti*, which means literally 'the emperor's delegate'. He was usually a man of high social rank, a senator who had almost certainly commanded a legion earlier in his career. He was assisted by a procurator, usually of equestrian status. The governor lived in and worked from what we would describe as a palace. Assuming that London was the official capital of Britain for most of the period we are concerned with it was also the most likely site for the governor's palace.

A building which lies partially beneath Cannon Street Station is thought a likely candidate but no evidence has been found which makes this certain. A number of stamped tiles indicate it was an official building. The plan (fig. 71) is very incomplete, but there seems to have been a very substantial building set in terraces by the Thames including an ornamental garden with a large pool overlooked by a large hall. Around the garden were ranges of rooms. The better preserved remains of the so-called governor's palace at Aquincum show a series of 'state rooms' opening off a corridor with the rooms and baths of the private residence to the rear. Unfortunately the remains of the London building are so fragmentary that it is impossible to be sure of its original appearance. A number of massive walls have been recorded in the vicinity during various building operations since the nineteenth century. However, the jaunty lay-out of the rooms that are known in better detail makes it impossible to integrate them all into a coherent plan.

What is certain is that the building was massive. The whole complex was about 130m (426ft) long from north to south. The hall was over 24m (80ft) long and over 13m (43ft) wide.

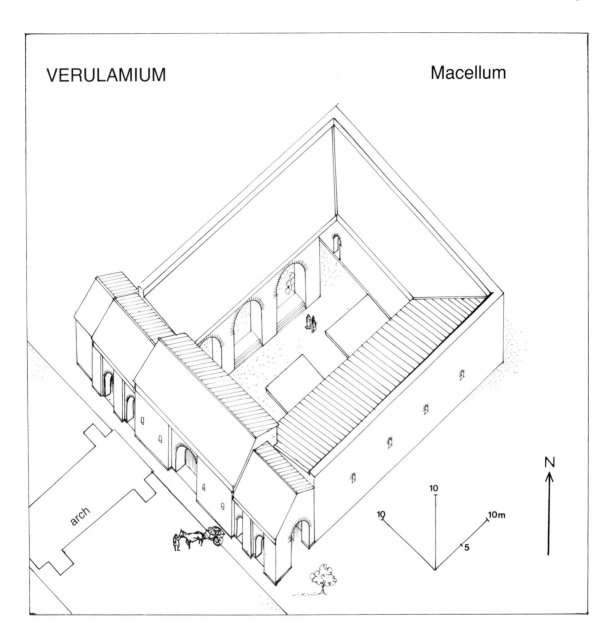

VERULAMIUM

Macellum

arch

N

10
10
10m
5

70 The market building at Verulamium (final phase – fourth century; axonometric reconstruction). The site was a long-lived one and it lay immediately across Watling Street from the theatre. It was built in the first century on a much larger plan with two rows of nine 'shops' facing one another. By the second century it had been reduced in size to two rows of five shops. More reconstruction work followed in succeeding years and by the later fourth century it had been remodelled with a monumental façade. There is no specific evidence for its use at any period but it is similar to more certain examples on the Continent. It may also have served a quasi-religious function, perhaps incorporating a shrine for the *genius* of particular trades.

The excavator believed that the central area may have been covered like the hall of a basilica. This is possible but unlikely. The piers of the aisles would probably have needed strengthening to withstand the lateral forces of a central roof. Such strengthening as did take place would have improved tolerance of forces in the opposite direction, i.e. towards the inside of the building. The drawing shown here reflects this.

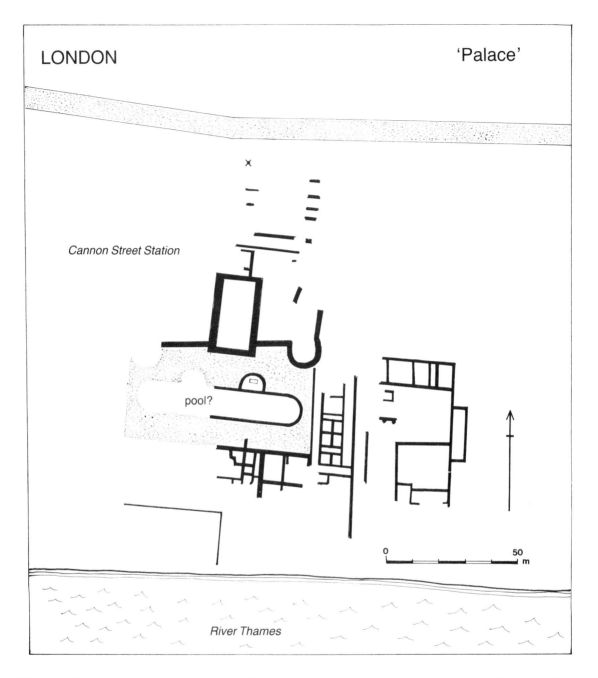

LONDON   'Palace'

Cannon Street Station

pool?

River Thames

0   50
m

71 Plan of the so-called 'governor's palace' at Cannon Street, London (after Marsden). This remarkable building is only known from tantalizing traces and seems to have consisted of a main hall with ornamental garden as well as a series of surrounding ranges of rooms and wings. It was built in the late first or early second century and was terraced on three levels on the slope down to the Thames where there would probably have been a substantial watergate and wharf. More recently it has been suggested that the baths complex at Huggin Hill to the west may actually be the palace of the provincial governor (figs. 4, 84). Both sites are associated with tiles stamped for the provincial government: P P BR LON ('procurator of the province of Britain at London'). By the late fourth century the site was derelict though there may have been casual occupation of the ruins.

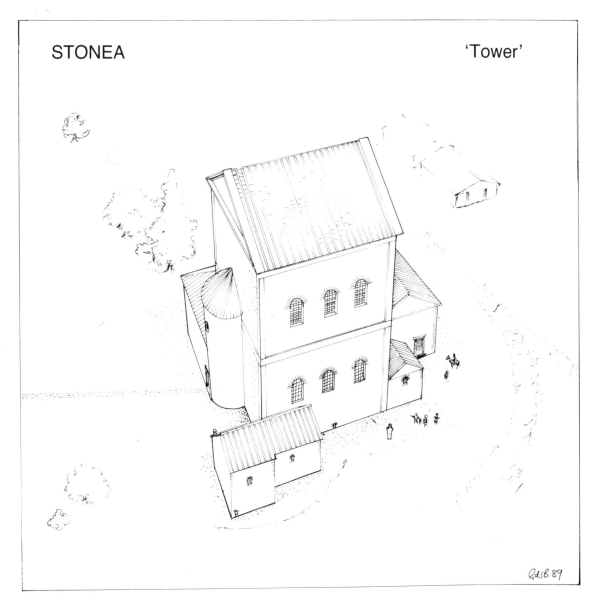

STONEA   'Tower'

QdIB 89

72 Tower(?) at Stonea Grange, Cambridgeshire. This enigmatic site was discovered in 1980 and involves extensive traces of settlement in the Cambridgeshire Fens. The most remarkable building is what appears to have been a monumental tower with colossal foundations. Built in the Hadrianic period it had an apse, a hypocaust, a flanking corridor and attached hall. It may have been a purely commemorative building (following the defeat of Boudica?), a kind of land-locked lighthouse for guidance in a comparatively featureless landscape, or even a central administrative and observation post for what may have been an imperial estate. However, by c. 200 the tower had been demolished though settlement continued.

Other circumstantial evidence suggests that there were colonnades and a bath suite as well as the garden, pool and various rooms. Underlying deposits do not post-date the late first century so it seems reasonable to conclude that this was yet another in the series of monumental buildings erected in Roman Britain during the Flavian period. Of its subsequent history little is known but it was evidently mostly ruinous by the late Roman period because dumps of late-Roman rubbish lay in a number of the rooms. The terracing of the building probably also meant that there was some kind of substantial water gate or wharf on the river bank. The Huggin Hill bath complex is only about 300m (1000ft) to the west,

and it is possible that a number of major public buildings were strung out along the riverbank.

There are a small number of monumental buildings which are very difficult to interpret. The enigmatic complex of structures in the Fens at Stonea in Cambridgeshire includes a building with such massive foundations that it has been assumed that it must have been a tower (fig. 72). It had an apse, was heated and seems to have had a hall and gallery attached to it. It was built in the Hadrianic period but interpretation is extremely difficult because it falls into no familiar category and, apart from the surrounding buildings, stands in virtual isolation. It has been suggested that the building commemorates an early battle against the Iceni, but this is obviously quite uncertain and in any case by *c.* 200 the building had been completely demolished. Another possibility is that it was a facility for over-looking the surrounding area which is of course very low-lying – there are few villas in the region and it has been suggested that, following drainage, the Fens were operated as an imperial estate which would have been managed by a procurator. Alternatively it may have provided a convenient landmark in a comparatively featureless landscape. Indeed it may have served all or none of these functions. Perhaps even more remarkable is the monumental winged building of palatial proportions on the edge of the Fens at Castor, near Peterborough.

---

73 Monumental building at Castor, near Peterborough. Little is known about this building but in terms of scale and appearance it is comparable with the stately homes of eighteenth– and nineteenth-century England. It stood on a hillslope and looked west across the river Nene and east across the Fens. It is quite possible that it functioned as a residential headquarters for an imperial estate but this is pure speculation and it is equally possible that it was a private establishment. Extensive Roman settlement in the Fens which grew up after the area was drained has been noted but is rarely associated with villas, apart from a small concentration near the town at Water Newton.

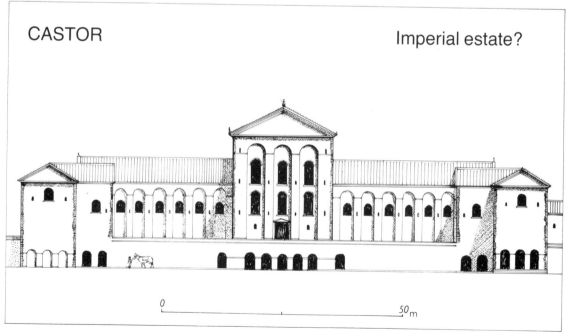

CASTOR

Imperial estate?

0   50m

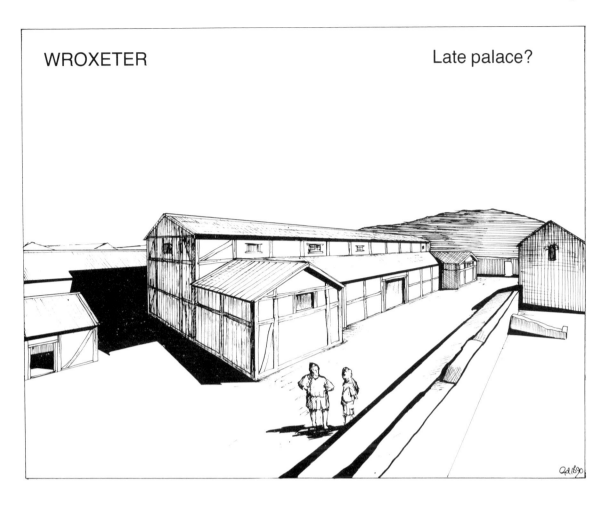

WROXETER   Late palace?

74 Late building at Wroxeter. Careful excavation on the site of the baths (see fig. 83) has revealed the presence of a complex of timber buildings built on the ruined site during the fifth century. In most cases nothing more than the rubble platforms survived but these suggest that the buildings were carefully designed to emulate long-established 'Roman' styles. The centrepiece was a symmetrical winged structure with central entrance. Its identity is completely unknown but its size and central location suggest that it may have served as either an administrative centre for the sub-Roman town or perhaps the stronghold of a civic leader who was effectively functioning as a king. This has been interpreted as evidence for the survival of Roman ways but it is equally significant that the public baths were in ruins.

Like the Stonea tower it seems curiously displaced in such a comparatively remote area of the province and it is tempting to interpret it as the headquarters of an imperial estate (fig. 73).

The history of Roman Britain in the early fifth century and the subsequent decay of a romanized form of life is very obscure. One possibility is that the towns continued to function for several decades with some sort of centralized local authority. At Wroxeter careful excavations have revealed a series of timber buildings erected on the site of the baths' palaestra. One of these is sufficiently large to suggest that it was of some importance (fig. 74). Its purpose is entirely unknown but it may be that it was either an administrative centre or even the headquarters of a man who was a local leader. This is not a purely fanciful idea – such evidence as exists (and this includes the Arthurian legends) suggests the gradual emergence of regional kings or chiefs.

Theatres and amphitheatres

The semi-circular classical Roman theatre (used for plays or religious displays) or elliptical amphitheatre (used for gladiatorial contests or military displays) could be something of a triumph of arcading and vaulting. These weight-relieving techniques made it possible to support the auditorium and provide a series of passage-ways through which crowds could be channelled. If a hillside was available then the theatre could be set into the slope.

Theatres and amphitheatres often survive in a very reasonable state of preservation partly because they have continued to serve as public meeting places and partly because of their very substantial construction. This was not always the case – an amphitheatre collapsed at Fidenae in Italy during the reign of Tiberius, killing 20,000 people (Suetonius – who was probably exaggerating – *Tiberius*, 40). A number of major sites around the Mediterranean can boast magnificent examples, such as the amphitheatres at Pompeii in Italy and El Djem in Tunisia, and the theatres at Ephesus (built into a hill) and Aspendos (free-standing) in Turkey.

Amphitheatres

Amphitheatres are known at a number of Romano-British sites, mostly towns. Commonly associated nowadays with the slaughter of animals and gladiators they were probably just as important as centres of public ritual ceremony where the whole community could witness the display. Romano-British amphitheatres which survive in recognizable form were built on earth embankments with stone revetments and timber seats. They were similar to the military *ludus* (figs. 47-9). At Dorchester in Dorset a neolithic henge monument now known as Maumbury Rings was adapted (fig. 75). Henge monuments were circular or oval mounds with an internal ditch. The Dorchester example was already around 2000 years old when the Romans adapted

75 Maumbury Rings, Dorchester, Dorset, looking north. The site lies outside the Roman town walls and began life as a Neolithic 'henge' monument *c.* 2000 BC. The Romans dug a deeper central area and used the spoil to raise the banks. Timber seating and revetments completed the conversion into an amphitheatre during the late first century. (Photo: author, 1989.)

76 Recess in the arena wall of the amphitheatre at Silchester. There were two such recesses aligned on the short axis of the elliptical arena. They may have served as preparatory chambers for gladiators but it is more likely that they were vaulted and contained altars dedicated to Nemesis (Fate). See fig. 49 for a more elaborate example at Caerleon. (Photo: author, 1989.)

it in the late first century. The central area was lowered and the earth used to raise the banks to around 9m (30ft). Timber was used to reinforce the banks. The site seems to have had a relatively short life and may have been disused by the late second century.

Silchester's amphitheatre also consisted of earth banks and timber revetments but was put up in the third quarter of the first century. Repairs during the second century did not change this basic design, and it was only during the third century that stone revetments for the banks were incorporated when the arena was enlarged. Its design was probably fairly typical and included two entrances opposite one another, and two niches in the arena walls (fig. 76). These were almost certainly religious, perhaps containing altars or statues, perhaps to Nemesis (Fate) who

had an obvious association with winners and losers (see also fig. 49).

The amphitheatre at Cirencester also lies outside the town and was also based on earth banks. It, too, was built in the late first century but was revetted in stone by the beginning of the second century. Unlike the one at Dorchester which was so rapidly disused, this one seems to have remained in use until the fifth century. The recently discovered amphitheatre at London lies within the city walls. This can be explained by its proximity to the south-east corner of the fort in London built in the first half of the second century and incorporated into the early-third-century walls. It therefore probably began life as a military *ludus* but at present very little of the building has been uncovered and very little can be said about its history. Even small settlements could enjoy such facilities. The mining community at Charterhouse in the Mendips had been founded by 49 and at some point a modest amphitheatre (so small it may only have been used for bear-baiting or as a cock-pit) had been added to the associated town. Charterhouse is probably not unusual and many minor settlements may have had amphitheatres, attracting

101

visitors from the surrounding countryside. Elsewhere more economical examples have been found like the simple elliptical enclosure within the walls at Caerwent, though the identification here is uncertain – it is just as likely to have been a corral for a cattle or horse market.

All these examples suggest that the amphitheatre was a relatively early introduction into Roman Britain though subsequent histories could be very different. No doubt this reflected local tastes but unfortunately we have practically no specific evidence for the kind of entertainments which went on. That gladiatorial conquests were known is evident from the appearance of a series of matched pairs of cupids on mid-fourth century mosaics at Bignor villa in West Sussex (plate 1). A much earlier gladiator's helmet has been found, but not even in association with a Roman settlement, let alone an amphitheatre (see *Finds*, fig. 79e). Curiously no evidence of any kind of gladiatorial or other gaming equipment has been found in association with an amphitheatre in Britain, even at Silchester which has been completely cleared only in the last decade. It is worth recalling Vitruvius' comment that in first-century BC Italy it was customary to give gladiatorial shows in the forum (v.1.1) – obviously there is no direct connection with Britain but it does mean that we need not assume that a lack of an amphitheatre meant that local people went without such displays.

Theatres

Even fewer theatres are known than amphitheatres. The best-known examples have been identified at Canterbury, Colchester, Gosbecks (Colchester) and Verulamium. We can be almost certain that they existed at other major towns, particularly London, York, Cirencester and Gloucester, though it is worth bearing in mind that Silchester has yielded no trace of one at all, despite having been almost completely excavated. Recent detective work in London has isolated a probable site in the far south-western corner of the city where the medieval streets of Ludgate Square and St Andrew's Hill curve to the east, perhaps preserving the line of the auditorium; the rear wall of the theatre's stage would have been incorporated into the city wall. Only excavation will confirm the theory. The minor town of Brough-on-Humber had a theatre; we know because a local *aedile* (magistrate)

called Marcus Ulpius Januarius commemorated his donation of a new stage to the theatre in *c.* 140-4 on an inscription (see Appendix 2). However the theatre has not been found and it may very well be that it was built only of timber; this may explain the lack of evidence for theatres in Britain – they may have been largely temporary affairs, built of wood and only erected when they were required. Theatrical masks have been found at a number of sites in Britain which have yielded no other evidence for theatres, such as Catterick and Baldock (*Finds*, fig. 79b).

Theatres were very far from being purely secular buildings. They were inextricably linked with religious activities because they were used for displays during religious festivals. The Verulamium theatre was associated with a Romano-Celtic temple. The Gosbecks theatre formed part of the religious complex outside Colchester. Within the walls of Colchester another theatre lay adjacent to the precinct of the Temple of the Deified Claudius – indeed we know that a theatre (not necessarily the same one, or the same site) existed here by the Boudican Revolt of 60/61 because Tacitus mentions it (*Annales*, xiv.32). The theatre at Canterbury also probably lay next to a temple precinct (figs. 77, 78). It is a virtual certainty that the temple precinct at Bath would have been accompanied by a theatre though we have no specific evidence for it yet. We should not forget that there was also a rich tradition of secular, sometimes very bawdy, Latin plays which may have become popular as Latin became more widely spoken in Roman Britain.

The Roman theatre was almost invariably a semi-circular auditorium facing a stage. A certain amount of activity took place in the *orchestra* (between the auditorium and the stage). In Britain we have only the traces of wall footings, and none of these supplies any particularly useful information about the superstructure as the plans show (fig. 77). The reconstruction of the theatre at Canterbury gives an idea of what the building may have looked like in the third century, but the drawing is completely hypothetical and is based only on the dimensions of the plan. The best-known theatre, at Verulamium, also the only one visible to any useful degree (figs. 79-81), seems to be something of an exception because it lies somewhere between an amphitheatre and a theatre, and apparently employing elements of each.

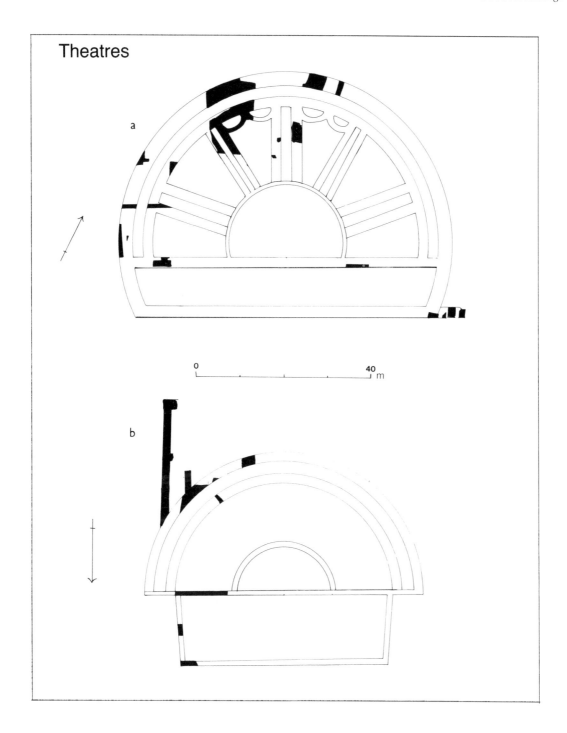

Theatres

a

b

0   40
                   m

77 Plans of the theatres at Canterbury (Period 2, *c.* 210-20, see also fig. 78) and Colchester (second century?; see plate 6). It is apparent that while on one hand very little of the plans of either of these buildings has actually been located, on the other the distinctive form of the theatre makes restoration of the general outline relatively straightforward. The Colchester theatre was built into a north facing slope while the Canterbury theatre was free-standing on a level site.

103

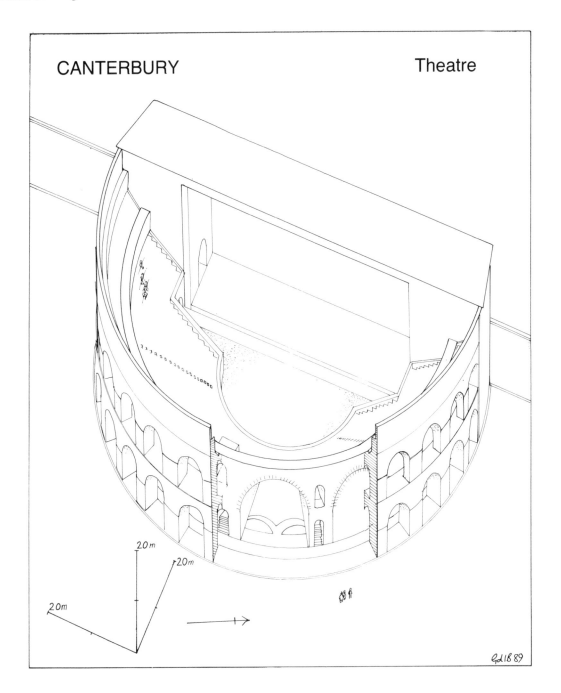

CANTERBURY

Theatre

78 The Period 2 theatre at Canterbury, built *c.* 210-20 (axonometric reconstruction). Rather less well-known than the theatre at Verulamium, Canterbury's developed theatre seems to have been classical in form though apart from its probable dimensions little more has been discovered. The curious curved walls within the auditorium may have acted as buttresses to support the outer walls. The earlier theatre, built in the late first century, is known to lie beneath and resembled that at Verulamium in having an auditorium built of gravel banks held in place with a retaining wall. The stage is hardly known at all but it flanked a road, on the other side of which seems to have been a temple precinct. The two were probably used together for religious rituals and festivals.

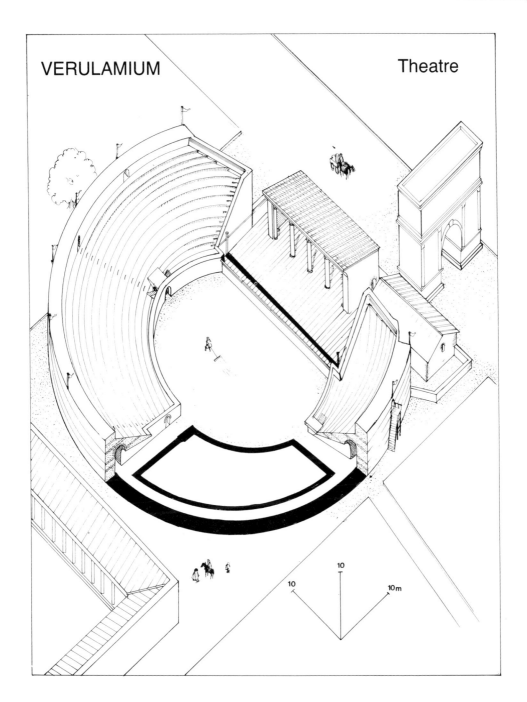

VERULAMIUM Theatre

79 The theatre at Verulamium (axonometric reconstruction) in period 4 (see fig. 80). The best known of all the theatres found in Roman Britain, this site was excavated many years ago. Nevertheless the broad pattern of development seems fairly clear. The site, north of the town's administrative centre, seems to have been reserved from an early date. Although the theatre was not put up until the middle of the second century the space was apparently empty, curious for the centre of a large town, so the theatre's construction must have been anticipated. The area set aside is immediately east of a large temple precinct in Insula xvi, and it can be assumed that the the theatre was designed to play a role in religious ceremonies.

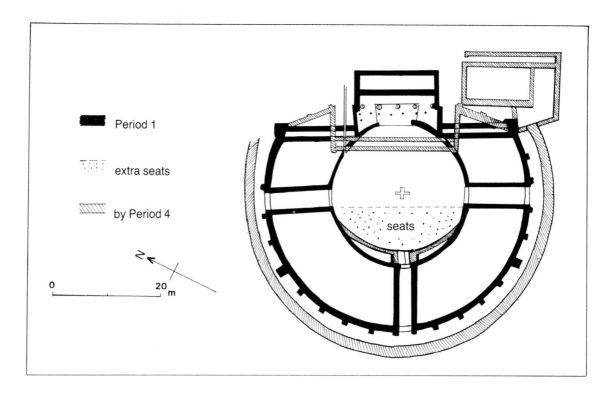

Period 1

extra seats

by Period 4

0   20
                       m

seats

80 Plan of the Verulamium theatre.

In its original form (Period 1) the orchestra was almost circular, and was surrounded by stage buildings, and earthen banks supporting wooden seats. The banks were revetted with stone walls.

By *c*. 160-80 (Period 2) the theatre had been altered to accommodate extra wooden seats within part of the orchestra, and an enlarged stage which further reduced the orchestra area. If the theatre had previously been used in part for activities more appropriate to an amphitheatre (such as bear-baiting) it can be assumed these pastimes had been removed elsewhere. Seat access was improved and the stage itself was now rebuilt in Corinthian style.

During the third century (Period 3) the building was kept maintained and external staircases were added. In the early fourth century (Period 4) the building was altered. The extra seats in the orchestra were removed, though the retaining wall of the auditorium was moved eastwards to provide extra seats on the ramps. A new perimeter wall was put up and connected to the old with a vault. This allowed a new, higher tier of seats to be added to the auditorium. However, before the end of the fourth century the building had become redundant and was used as a public rubbish tip; this may have been because the pagan activities associated with the building had ceased.

Seating capacity is difficult to estimate. In Period 1 the area of the auditorium was about 750 sq. m (8070 sq. ft). Each person needs at least 0.3 sq. m (about 3½ sq. ft) to sit comfortably – this allows seats for about 2500. In Period 4 the available area had been roughly doubled so a capacity of 5000 can be suggested. However, this does not allow for unusable areas such as structural components, stairs and so on.

What little evidence we have suggests that very early theatres in Roman Britain were initially built out of solid banks and timber. This was the case at Canterbury where gravel banks supported wooden seats in the first period building, put about 80-90. Only in a reconstruction during the second decade of third century was the theatre rebuilt in stone (figs. 77, 78). No comparable evidence for Colchester exists but the known stone remains probably belong to the second century, perhaps replacing the one which Tacitus mentions (fig. 77, plate 6). The theatre at Verulamium has been excavated completely and this has revealed an interesting sequence of activity (figs. 79-81). The visible building was put up after *c*. 155 on a site in the town centre which

81 The theatre at Verulamium looking south towards the site of the basilica and forum (beneath the church). The stage buildings lie behind and to the left of the surviving column. The track at the left represents the line of Watling Street, the main route through the town. The market building (fig. 70) lay to the left of the picture across the track. The Insula xiv shops (fig. 111) lay immediately beyond the theatre. (Photo: author, 1989.)

found in the vicinity, possibly a souvenir, suggests that the local impresarios were not entirely concerned with elevated themes (see *Finds*, fig. 60f).

was almost certainly reserved for it because no traces of earlier buildings have been found beneath it; this does not mean that the site was unused, and it may well be that theatrical activities took place using facilities which have left no trace. The new theatre was not semi-circular and resembled an amphitheatre in being based on an ellipse; however the stage was inserted into one of the long sides. Although it was revetted in stone the auditorium was built out of earth banks. At the beginning of the fourth century it was substantially enlarged suggesting that considerable demand for its services still existed. We have no specific evidence for what these may have been apart from its being sited next to a temple. However, an erotic knife handle

Bath buildings

The process of bathing in Roman times is well known and briefly discussed in Chapter 2. Substantial public bath buildings are known to have existed in Roman Britain but none survive to such an extent that we can confidently reconstruct their original appearance, even though the remains at Leicester and Wroxeter (figs. 82, 83, plate 7) include some of the highest standing Roman walls in Britain. Recently more of the huge bath building complex on Huggin Hill in London has been uncovered (fig. 84) and the recovery of tiles stamped P.P.BR.LON (for the procurator of the province of Britain at London) confirm that this establishment was a major public facility.

107

LEICESTER

Baths

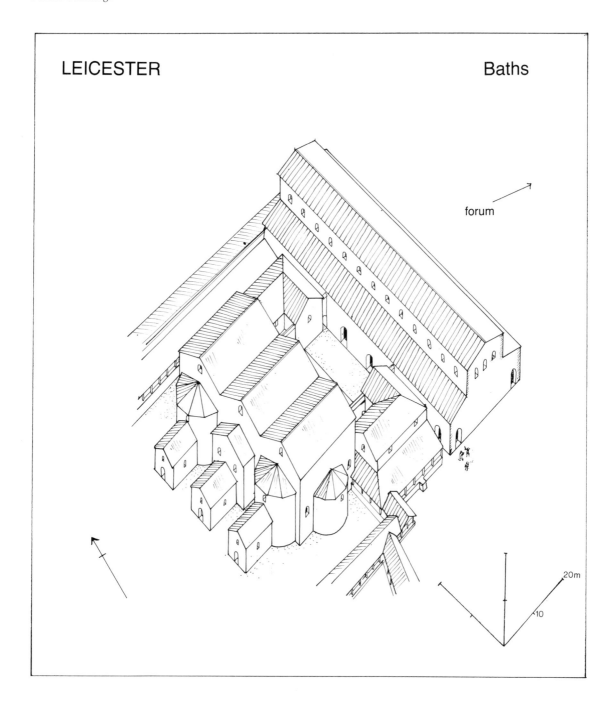

forum

20m

10

82 The baths at Leicester (axonometric reconstruction; after Neal), *c*. 140 and later. The complex was begun in the Hadrianic period *c*. 125 when the exercise hall and adjacent rooms were erected. The three parallel rooms (all hot rooms) extending the range were put up in the next fifteen years or so. Part of the exercise hall's west wall survives to an impressive 9m (30ft) in height and is visible along with part of the baths today, known as the Jewry Wall. The buildings undoubtedly formed the town's main baths, lying adjacent to the forum and basilica.

83 The later baths at Wroxeter (isometric reconstruction). The complex was a large one and has not been built on since Roman times which has allowed extensive long-term excavations to take place. The baths were built in the second half of the second century, replacing an earlier project on an adjacent site which was itself demolished to make way for the civic basilica. The new baths included an exercise hall which so resembles a basilica that it has been suggested that it was originally designed to be just that. The change-over of site function may have been connected with problems over water supply.

The main sequence of baths was entered from the south side of the exercise hall (Pl) through a door. The section of wall with a gap for the door survives *in situ* and is known as the 'Old Work' (plate 7). This led the bather to the cold bath (F) with its plunge baths at either end, and on to the warm and hot baths (T, C). An extension suite of baths ran westwards from the main sequence towards the short-lived outdoor swimming pool (Ps). This was used as a rubbish tip by the beginning of the third century, perhaps because of the weather. Very few have been identified in Britain (for example at Caerleon and Bath – the latter obviously having the advantage of naturally heated water). By the fifth century the site was ruinous and had been built over with an enigmatic complex of timber buildings (see fig. 74).

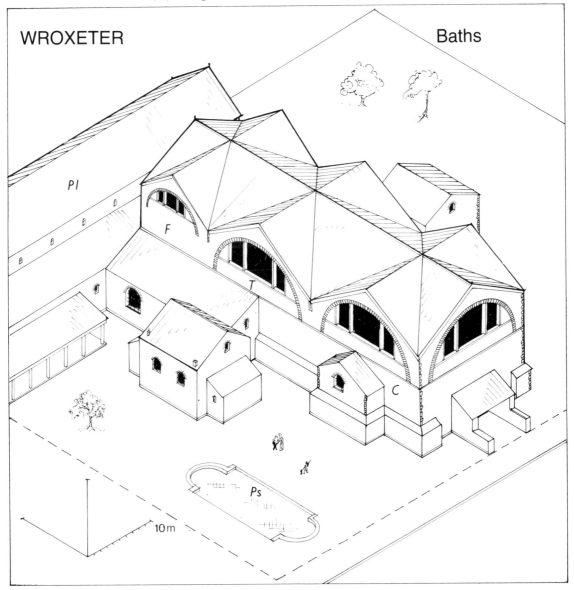

WROXETER

Baths

Pl

F

T

C

Ps

10 m

Roman baths were traditionally associated with large open exercise areas known as the *palaestra*. A particularly good example survives at the Stabian baths in Pompeii where separate bath suites for men and women were ranged around a colonnaded palaestra. This emphasizes the social nature of the bath building, but obviously the design reflected not just a Mediterranean way of life but also a Mediterranean climate. Some of the early public bath-houses in Britain retained the open colonnaded palaestra, for example in the first century versions built at Silchester and Wroxeter (later buried beneath the forum), though in both

these cases the bath-suites and exercise areas were laid out in a linear sequence rather than the former being ranged around the latter. In the second century this idea, common to a number of baths in Gaul, was still in use, but the palaestra was built as a covered hall, resembling a basilica, for example at Leicester (fig. 82), Wroxeter (fig. 84) and Caerwent. It has been suggested that the Wroxeter palaestra is so large that it may have been intended as the town's basilica but that for some reason plans were changed. However, as such similar buildings exist at Leicester and Caerwent this seems unlikely. The Huggin Hill baths in London have not been excavated in their entirety but the remains uncovered so far suggest that the lay-out may have been modelled on the more traditional design, even during substantial reconstruction work in the Hadrianic period. As the building was almost certainly designed as much for members of the provincial government as the public this is hardly surprising.

Bath buildings followed a pattern with various rooms for functions such as changing, and the sequence of warm, hot and cold rooms (see fig. 44). Sense can usually be made of their remains, but no Romano-British example gives any idea of internal decorations. At Pompeii and Herculaneum in Italy the rooms were decorated with stucco, and had statues, wash-basins and benches of carved stone or bronze. We can be sure that this was the case in Roman Britain. The vaults raise an interesting problem: the bath-house at Beauport Park undoubtedly had vaults in two of its rooms because parts of them were found on the floors where they had fallen (fig. 44); the same occurred at the Great Bath at Bath (figs. 10, 11). Vaults were important because the warm damp atmosphere was unsuitable for timber roofs. In small bath-houses and private houses this was not as important because timber was plentiful. However with substantial bath-buildings the problems involved in repairs become rather more complicated. It seems very likely that most of the major baths in Roman Britain would have been vaulted. This creates a further problem because the vault would be exposed to British weather. It is probable that vaults were protected by walls and timber super-structures supporting tiled roofs. This has formed the basis for the reconstruction of the second-century baths at Wroxeter (fig. 83), modelled on reconstructions of baths found in Rome and Asia Minor.

84 The Huggin Hill baths, London, under excavation in 1989. This is only a small part of what appears to have been a huge complex of public baths built close to the river bank during the Flavian reconstruction of the city. A number of tiles stamped P·P·BR·LON have been found as well as painted wall-plaster and evidence of sophisticated drainage. Stacks of tiles for supporting the floor can be seen. The room shown was tri-apsidal in form, and the shape of the robbed curved wall of one of them can be seen in the foreground. The site has been re-buried under rammed sand and polythene. See fig. 4 for a detailed view of the walls. (Photo: author, 1989.)

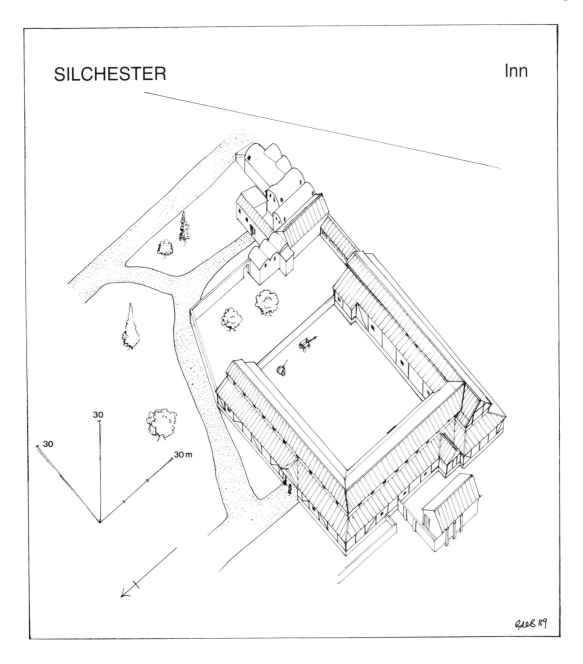

SILCHESTER   Inn

85 The inn at Silchester (axonometric reconstruction). A number of these buildings are known from Roman Britain (for example at Caerwent and Chelmsford). They would have existed in most towns and are best understood as hotels or inns, serving official messengers travelling on the *cursus publicus*, a system which provided facilities like accommodation and horses on major routes throughout the Empire. They were often sited close to the town wall, are similar in plan to courtyard villas and usually have substantial bath-suites. The Silchester example appears to date to the third century and lies close to the south-east gate. Unlike a courtyard villa though there were a large number of small rooms flanked by two corridors around the three wings and these were mostly poorly decorated. The bath building seems to have had twin suites, presumably for the use of both sexes, and a substantial latrine. Note what appears to have been a granary in the foreground.

Inns

Roman administration throughout and between provinces was dependent on the *cursus publicus*, literally 'public passage'. Throughout the Empire inns and staging posts provided accommodation and facilities for people travelling on state business. Apart from the incidental evidence of official lead seals which probably accompanied goods or papers connected with the government we have no specific evidence for the *cursus publicus* in Roman Britain. Nevertheless in a number of towns a large courtyard building has been found and this has usually been interpreted as an inn (*mansio*) connected with the *cursus*.

At Silchester a large courtyard building faces the end of a road which led to the forum (fig. 85). The complex included a substantial bath-house and what appears to be a granary. Within the building rooms were arranged in groups of three and access seems to have been available from corridors on both sides of the north and south wings. It was probably built at a comparatively

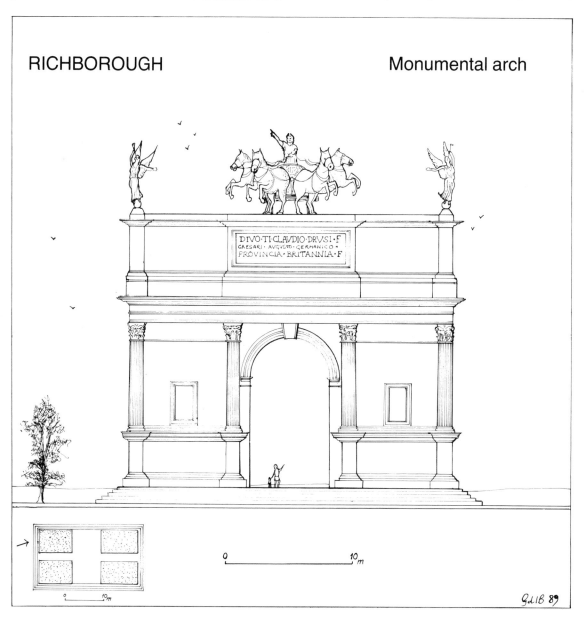

RICHBOROUGH

Monumental arch

DIVO·TI·CLAVDIO·DRVSI·F
CAESARI · AVGVSTO · GERMANICO ·
PROVINCIA· BRITANNIA·F

0   10 m

0   10 m

GdIB 89

early date because it matches the orientation of the street grid which seems to have been established by the early second century. A similar building is known at Chelmsford, though in rather less detail. Here the size of the building is even more obviously disproportionate to the area of the settlement. Two houses at Caerwent might be identified as a mansio. Both are larger than most of the other houses and both lie immediately within the town walls beside a main gate (the west and the south). Obviously, identification of these buildings is very tenuous and it remains quite possible that they are all simply the residences of affluent families. However, as we will see in Chapter 4 they are somewhat atypical of house development within towns.

The small settlement of Wall lies on Watling Street in Staffordshire. It was one of a number of minor towns on the major route from London to north Wales via Verulamium and Wroxeter. Although the site is known to have had a military origin, its principal importance in subsequent years was probably as the location of a mansio with an elaborate bath-house. A bath-suite was erected here before the end of the first century but was demolished before ever being used.

---

86 Monumental arch at Richborough. This building seems to have been one of the few truly impressive classical structures erected in Roman Britain. Sadly only its foundations have survived along with a number of fragments of the arch itself. The reconstruction here is therefore purely hypothetical, but the original would have been of similar scale and appearance.

Assumed to be the site of Aulus Plautius' landing in 43 Richborough would have been of obvious political significance. By *c.* 85 or shortly after, with Agricola's activities in the north at their climax, a decision seems to have been taken to build an arch at the gateway to Britain. From this point Watling Street ran west to London and into the heart of Roman Britain. Arches were frequently used to celebrate military success and to embellish a major route.

This arch was *quadrifons* (a four-way arch). Traces of its superstructure show that it was encased in marble and topped by monumental bronze statuary. It is impossible to recreate accurately its precise appearance because the fragments of columns are too small, and were too dispersed. By the middle of the third century the arch was converted into a signal tower and surrounded by ditches. Within another generation the whole site had been cleared to make way for the Saxon Shore fort (see figs. 50, 51).

Subsequently a much more complicated replacement was erected in the second century which was effectively a small version of major civic public baths. Recent excavations on the site suggest that the baths were connected with an adjacent courtyard building which has been interpreted as the mansio proper. Built in stone *c.* 120 with painted wall-plaster and window glass, it is unlikely to have been a private project and along with its baths is probably the best preserved example of a type of building which would have been commonplace throughout Britain and the Empire.

Monumental arches

The monumental arch is one of the simplest but most expressive architectural statements of Roman civilization. The arch symbolizes the principal element of Roman architecture while its use to commemorate some event, usually a military success, embodies the basis of Roman expansion and power. The arches of Titus, Septimius Severus and Constantine the Great in Rome are amongst the city's finest monuments – as a group they are complemented by a host of equal and lesser examples known elsewhere in Italy and in other provinces.

At least six are known to have existed in Roman Britain but only one is known in architectural detail. Its original site is unknown but was somewhere in London. The sculptures which survive from it suggest that it was actually an entrance into a religious precinct (fig. 163). Of the other five, three stood in Verulamium and a fourth formed the first period of the Balkerne Gate at Colchester (fig. 87). The fifth formed a dramatic gateway to the province of *Britannia* at Richborough. The Richborough arch was probably the most impressive at around 28m (90ft) in height but it was demolished in the late third century to make way for the Saxon Shore fort (fig. 86). It was probably built in the late first century but within two centuries was being used as a signal tower before finally being cleared away. Now only the concrete base for the passageways through the arch survive but a few architectural fragments were found during excavation. Reconstruction is extremely difficult because these fragments are so small that a number of possibilities exist. However, it is certain that it was a four-way arch, had marble veneer and a bronze statue group on top. The

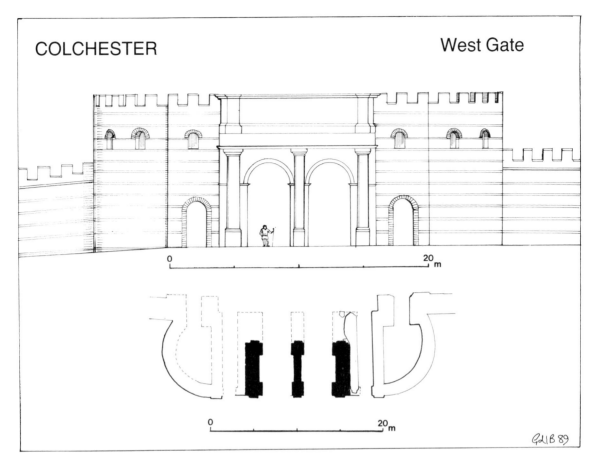

COLCHESTER

West Gate

0   20 m

GdB 89

87 Elevation and plan of the west gate (Balkerne Gate) of Colchester. Originally excavated by Wheeler, his interpretation has now been revised to show that the gateway started life as a monumental free-standing twin portalled arch/gate on the main road to London, built *c*. 75. Two Romano-Celtic temples built on either side of the approach road would have enhanced its appearance to a traveller. When the city walls were built in the early second century (?) the gate was enlarged with pedestrian passages and flanking gatetowers and incorporated into the walls. In the fourth century the gate was made redundant by extending the ditch of the defences across the old London road, cutting off vehicular access. This may have been because the new gatetowers did not project and because the temples had forced the ditch out too far from the walls. Some of the gate has survived and can be seen today though the bulk of the central part lies beneath a public house (plate 8). A modern road cutting mirrors the effect of the extended ditch by excluding access to all but pedestrians.

Verulamium examples were simpler and smaller single-portal arches, perhaps about 12m (40ft) high. Two were built on Watling Street to mark the town's first-century limits around the time that the third-century walls were put up. The other was built in the fourth century, also over Watling Street, between the theatre and macellum (fig. 79).

Defences

Like the forts of the Saxon Shore, the walls of the towns of Roman Britain have survived in part because they continued to serve a purpose long after they were originally built. The walls either formed the defences of medieval successors or proved less easy targets for stone robbers. So at Silchester and Verulamium the city walls are the main visible survivals of the towns though they are for the most part only ragged, fragmentary cores.

114

Town defences consisted of walls, gates, ditches and ramparts. This simple format conceals the fact that Romano-British town defences, remain a very awkward archaeological problem, made worse by a modern tendency to try and interpret them as a unified provincial or civic response to a single problem. It is as well to make it clear that we have no inscriptional or literary evidence for the erection of any town defences, gates or walls at any time. All we have is Tacitus' record of how Colchester fell easily to Boudica in 60 because it had not been provided with fortifications (*Annales*, xiv.31). Archaeology has confirmed that the defences of the former legionary fortress were filled in after the colony was established in *c*.47. When Vitruvius described city walls, he did not perceive them as a response to an immediate threat, rather they are described as a routine part of establishing a town once the site had been chosen and communications established (v.5.1).

Unfortunately, walls are not generally associated with much in the way of archaeological evidence except for material swept up in earth banks behind walls, and, naturally, this includes mixed-up rubbish of almost any earlier date that happened to be lying around. Tolerably reliable evidence can only be found where the walls, or gates, overlie some earlier building or feature, and where a component of the defences such as a gate-tower contains dateable evidence of occupation. The underlying feature will give a 'time after which' (*terminus post quem*) the defences were built complicated by the presence of earlier, residual, pottery; the occupation evidence will give a 'time before which' (*terminus ante quem*) the defences must have been built. Needless to say such evidence is rare, especially as underlying evidence is generally available only by demolishing part of the defences. Worse still is the fact that it is clear that gates and walls were not necessarily contemporary. The 'London' gates at Colchester (the Balkerne Gate, originally a triumphal arch; fig. 87) and at Verulamium were both built before the walls.

Walls and ramparts

It does seem to have been the case that some first-century towns were defended by earth ramparts, for example at Chichester, Silchester, Verulamium and Winchester. Verulamium seems to have been founded by *c*. 49, but its early earth defences were rapidly outgrown. The other towns may have all been settlements within the client kingdom of the Atrebates, led by Cogidubnus, up to the late first century. These early examples, and also towns which grew up in former forts and fortresses, like Lincoln and Gloucester, were the only settlements to have defences. There does not seem to have been any concerted policy to build them; instead Romano-British towns were able to spread naturally along the roads and rivers which gave them life.

Towards the end of the second century many of the major settlements were surrounded by an earth rampart and ditch; there are exceptions, for example Leicester, but here the ramparts may just not have been located yet. Subsequently, and this may have been much later, stone walls were added by cutting back the rampart and installing a stone revetment. This meant that the towns generally retained the size to which they had grown except in a few cases, like Caistor-by-Norwich where the walled area was smaller. It may well be that the Romano-British earthworks reflect a more leisurely precautionary approach to an unsettled northern frontier during the second half of the second century. As official permission was necessary for building town defences this suggests that the decision was a provincial one rather than a series of individual schemes. But the later second century was not notably more unsettled than the early second century, and we should not necessarily feel the need to connect an archaeological fact with what little historical information we have. It is equally conceivable that the building of town 'defences' (after all, we do not know that they were specifically defensive) was connected with civic prestige or even the control of traffic for the purpose of levying local taxes.

Evidence from stone gates does not necessarily date stone defences because stone gates were often erected at around the same time as the earth defences, for example the 'London' and 'Chester' gates at Verulamium. But fortunately Verulamium is one of the very few places which has produced evidence for a 'time before which' the stone walls must have been built. The 'Silchester gate' was built in one with the stone walls, and one of its towers contained a coin hoard ending in 273; clearly the tower was in existence by 273 or within a few years after. A tower on the walls of London contained a coin-forger's equipment which included a mint

88 The north gate of Lincoln. This is the only Roman gate in Britain to retain an arch from one of its main thoroughfares. However, even this was knocked down in recent years by a lorry and has had to be reconstructed. It was built in the third century and rising ground levels have diminished its scale. Note how the pedestrian way drops to allow access through the foot traffic arch. The view is from within the city. The smaller blocks of stone in the higher courses are medieval work. There would probably have been a corresponding pair of arches on the left for wheeled and foot traffic going in the opposite direction. The house on the right probably sits on top of a projecting tower. (Photo: author, 1989.)

condition coin of Caracalla struck *c*.213-17; while hoards are unlikely to be left for very long after the date of the latest coin without being added to, a coin forger may have deliberately used 'older coins' because of their metal content. So it could have been 10, 15 or more years old when lost. At any rate it is unlikely that London's walls were much later than *c*.225-30. Consequently it seems likely that, if there was a general policy of adding

stone walls, it took place during the first half of the third century or later. If we bear in mind Vitruvius' attitude towards city walls, mentioned above, it is equally plausible to interpret them as just the next project on the list once all the public buildings were up. This fits the broad time scale for the erection of the basilicas and forums; in fact if we take Vitruvius at face value Romano-British city walls were put up really rather late, they should have been built when the towns were laid out (v.5.1).

As far as the walls are concerned we have very little evidence for their original appearance, except for the remarkably well-preserved remains at Caerwent (fig. 92). Stone-robbing has left us with rubble cores while medieval repairs have often long concealed Roman work. They may have been brightened up with decorative patterns of brickwork, well known on the Continent, for example at Le Mans in France. The church of St Mary Northgate in Canterbury incorporates part of the Roman city wall into its north wall, including crenellations which may be of Roman date. If correct this suggests that the walls could be patrolled. Excavations on the

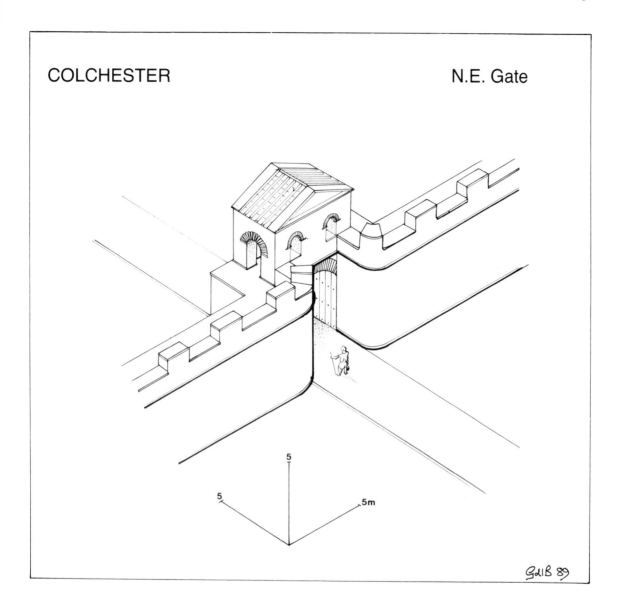

COLCHESTER   N.E. Gate

5

5

5m

G∂lB 89

89 The north-east gate ('Duncan's Gate') at Colchester (isometric reconstruction based on the revised elevation by Hull; see Bibliography). This was a single portal gateway built behind the line of the city wall (built in the early second century) which turns in to meet it. A large portion of the fallen superstructure remained *in situ* and showed that there was a guardroom with at least two windows above. Whether it extended right across, or just above the arch (as shown) is unknown as is the type of roof. Hull restored it with crenellations – this illustration shows an alternative.

Bishop's Palace site in Chichester showed that the stone wall had been built without foundations. Some of the lower sections of the London walls have been well preserved behind later deposits and show, for example at Tower Hill, that the wall, built of squared ragstone facing blocks, a rubble core and double or triple courses of bonding tiles, stood on a chamfered sandstone plinth.

A particularly interesting development of late date is the so-called riverside wall in London. The early-third-century wall enclosed the city on the east, north and west. The River Thames formed

90 Elevation and plan of the south gate at Caerwent from within the town walls (after Ward but reconstructed). This gate has survived in excellent condition largely because it was completely blocked up in antiquity. As a result a number of the arch stones survive *in situ*. The detailed lower part of the drawing shows the section which is still visible today. The rest of the tower is hypothetical. The walls were at least as high as shown because the south wall of Caerwent stands in part to a height of 5.5m (17ft). The stone curtain seems to have been added to a pre-existing earth rampart by the late second century. A drain ran beneath the roadway.

When the gate was blocked up a new drain was built through the blocking, and it seems likely that the external part of the gate was demolished. Much of the blocking and the new drain is still in the gate but has been omitted here to show the gate's original appearance (see fig. 91).

118

the southern defence, but in the fourth century a new wall was added right along the river front. It included a great deal of re-used masonry, preserving a large quantity of sculptured stone from buildings we would otherwise have no knowledge of. It was up to 3m (10ft) high and was built in part on timber piles which have made it possible to use radio-carbon and dendrochronology dating techniques, suggesting that it post-dates 330. It was not necessarily built all at once because some parts were built carefully from new masonry and does not appear to have had a rampart because it collapsed northwards, back onto the slope up from the river. It was probably part of the same phase of defensive work as the bastions (see below) commonly associated with Theodosius in 367.

Gates

Gates are more complicated because it is even more difficult to be certain of their original appearance, and a large number of different types of plan have been recovered. Gates need not always have been defensive – they could form impressive statements of civic pride. The incorporation of masonry gates into earth defences suggests this, for example the 'Balkerne Gate' at Colchester (fig. 87, plate 8) and the 'London' gate at Verulamium. Typically a major town gate had four passages: two large ones for wheeled traffic in the middle, and two smaller on either side for foot traffic. Only the north gate at Lincoln retains an example of each still standing (fig. 88). These were flanked themselves by two 'towers' which could project in front of the passageways, but this was not always the case. There may have been guardrooms above the passageways, but even if so we do not know if these were as high as the towers. The Balkerne Gate at Colchester is particularly interesting because it seems to have begun life as a free-standing monumental gate in the manner of a triumphal arch with two portals, built *c*.75. Only in the second century were the foot passages and towers added when the gate was incorporated into the new city walls.

Towns often had minor gates too and these were usually of 'single portal' design. Sometimes the walls turned in to meet the gate, as for example at Duncan's Gate in Colchester (fig. 89), or they stood more or less flush with the wall, for example at the south gate in Caerwent (figs. 90,

91). Such minor gates could be added at quite late dates. The west gate of the lower town at Lincoln was cut through the city wall in the early fourth century as a straightforward archway; subsequently projecting rectangular towers were added which made use of redundant carved stonework from other buildings.

Bastions

In *c*.367 Count Theodosius began the re-organization of the defences of Roman Britain. This has been thought a likely explanation for the addition of bastions to town walls; the effect would have been to make them resemble the forts of the Saxon Shore (see Chapter 2) and it is reasonable to assume that they too were designed to support defensive artillery. Of course dating is simply not precise enough and there are no relevant inscriptions, which are even rarer from this date than any other time. Bastions could be solid or hollow (fig. 92). They were built out of any available stone and projected from the existing walls in either semi-circular or polygonal form. London's bastion 10 in Camomile Street was found to contain not just building blocks from former buildings but also tombs; bastion 2 in Trinity Place contained the blocks from the tomb of the first-century procurator Classicianus

91 The south gate at Caerwent from within the town walls as it appears today. (Photo: author, 1989.)

92 Caistor-by-Norwich, bastion in the west stretch of town wall now half lost in the wood that clings to the ramparts. The bastion stands to a height of 3m (10ft) and although robbed of all its facing stones shows the method of construction with flint nodules, cement and tile courses. (Photo: author, 1986.)

(see *Finds*, p. 177). This does tend to suggest an element of crisis, and it is perhaps more legitimate to associate the bastions with a specific historical episode than the building of the walls. The bastions on the north and south walls at Caerwent (fig. 93) are particularly interesting because they survive to heights of up to 3m (10ft). They do not bond in with the existing walls, thus demonstrating that they were a later addition, and holes in the stonework show where the scaffolding was inserted during construction.

Other defensive works

The division between military and civil building is very fine when it comes to discussing any other defensive building. Signal towers have been discussed in Chapter 2, but it is worth noting that civil defences may have been augmented by signal towers at some distance from the towns. Any decision to build them probably came at the same time as the decision to build the bastions. Only one is known for certain – at Shadwell, 1.4km (0.9 mile) east of the Roman city wall, where the 8m (26ft) square stone tower, surrounded by a timber palisade, had a view downstream and of the city. It may have been one of a series but no others have yet been located. Dating is very uncertain but the tower may have been built as early as the late third century.

93 The south wall of Caerwent looking east showing one of the six prominent semi-octagonal bastions. The bastions are not bonded to the wall and were therefore built later. There were more bastions on the north wall, but apparently none on the east and west walls. These are the most outstanding remains of Romano-British civic defences, not only because much of the circuit survives but also because so much of the original facing remains. (Photo: author, 1989.)

4

HOUSES

Introduction

The houses of Roman Britain were of many different types. Not only did these dwellings reflect the relative wealth of their owners, but they also reflected the cumulating or declining wealth of individuals and their families. Consequently some houses were both substantial and extravagant while others were extremely modest. In between there is a very large number of houses which represents an almost infinite range of variations on a few basic schemes. While most of the larger houses are of third or fourth century date and had their origins in simple buildings, houses at all levels of sophistication appear throughout the period. From a structural point of view they present a number of problems arising from the lack of any surviving examples and the fact that most excavated plans consist of nothing more sophisticated than variations on rows of square or rectangular rooms.

Problems of interpretation

We do not know for certain the name of a single owner of a specific house in Roman Britain so we cannot know if any house remained in the possession of a single family. Tantalizingly the Antonine Itinerary (an early-third-century route book of the Empire) preserves the name *Villa Faustini*, a place somewhere between Caistor-by-Norwich and Colchester, but we do not know where the actual site lies. Presumably Faustinus was the owner or builder of a large villa estate. A building stone carved with the name *Firmini* from the house at Barnsley Park may conceivably represent the owner's name (i.e. *[Villa] Firmini* = 'the villa of Firminus') but is equally likely to indicate the name of the mason or builder (i.e.

[Officina] Firmini = 'the workshop of Firminus').

We do not even know if any one particular house was owned by someone and let to another. We do not know if country houses were usually owned by town dwellers who employed bailiffs to manage the estate (if one existed). In cases where the houses were particularly big, or where there were at least two distinct residential blocks (for example Sparsholt), we are almost certainly dealing with the homes of two or more families who may have been related, or perhaps one employing the other. Such evidence as exists from other parts of the Empire (mostly graffiti from Pompeii and papyri from Egypt) suggests that letting parts of urban property to various different tenants was quite normal. These might be shops downstairs and accommodation upstairs. An alternative was to purchase a share in a fraction of a property, similar to the way in which several people might club together to buy a flat in a block today. Evidence from rural sites is even rarer. The first-century writer Columella, in describing the operation of country farm property, referred to the use of either tenant farmers or slave overseers to run a farm on behalf of the landowner (*On Agriculture*, 1, 6-9). It is clear from what he says that tenant farmers might actually live in a town and use their own slaves to operate the farm, though this was better avoided. Clearly he is describing a situation in which very wealthy landowners were dealing with several dispersed components of their huge estates. There may well have been some families in this position in Roman Britain but we will never know the extent to which the rural houses were occupied by tenants or landowners.

Only one legible 'monumental' inscription has

been recovered which certainly refers to the actual structure. Found on the site of the Combe Down villa near Bath it records the restoration of a headquarters building (*principia*) by an imperial freedman called Naevius during the reign of Caracalla (212-17; see Appendix 2). It is therefore almost certain that the 'villa' was actually the headquarters of an imperial estate, and a long-established one at that. This means that the land had either been inherited by the imperial family or been confiscated. An incomplete inscription which unfortunately cannot be read has been found in the house at Stanwick in Northamptonshire (Appendix 2). Milestones, re-used as building material, have been found at Rockbourne in Hampshire, and an inscription dedicated to Carinus, as Caesar (heir), in 282-3 at Clanville, also in Hampshire, may either be another re-used milestone or indicate imperial ownership. Apart from this we are left only with slogans or couplets on mosaics (and these are generally religious or literary in content) and occasional graffiti on metal vessels, pottery or building materials. We do not even know 'how much' a house was worth, though a cryptic text preserved on a wooden tablet found in a well at the Chew Park villa seems to record the sale of land (Appendix 2).

So all that we have to work from consists of rarely anything more than the foundations of walls, their footings and the rubbish that was left behind. From this an archaeologist has to establish approximately when the first house was built on the site, what it was used for and, if applicable, how it changed in succeeding years. It may be possible to make estimates of the numbers of people who may have lived there at any one time, and perhaps make an assessment of their relative standard of living. For houses involved in farming it may be possible to estimate the size of the estate, but unless there are obvious natural boundaries or traces of man-made boundaries this is particularly difficult. The numbers of rooms may not always be very clear cut because internal divisions, even in a stone-built house, may have been of lathe and plaster and these leave traces that are difficult to identify. Doorways and entrances are elusive in a house which barely survives above its foundations. Even establishing what individual rooms were used for is more difficult than it might seem because unless artefactual or other evidence of say, cooking, is found it will be quite difficult to

be sure which room was the kitchen. However, in the better-appointed houses it is probably reasonable to assume that larger decorated rooms which may be heated were the principal reception rooms such as the *triclinium* (dining room). It is also worth remembering that a single house building may have been only one component of a residence that actually consisted of several different buildings (such as barns, baths and stables). This was certainly the case with many rural villas, but early archaeologists tended to chase walls, which makes it unlikely that extra buildings would be located. The large 'courtyards' at Stroud and Woodchester for example (figs. 102, 121) may really be very misleading. The plan of the Bancroft site may be much more representative (fig. 109). Even apparently separate establishments may have been connected (see Stanwick below).

Emergence of romanized housing

It was not until the late first century that a number of pre-Roman sites began to show a change in living habits. This is hardly surprising; the invasion took place only in 43, and it took the Boudican Revolt in 60 to shake up the Roman administration into a more positive frame of mind. Tacitus tells us that Agricola exhorted the British to build *domos* (= homes; *Agricola*, 21.70) and this almost certainly represents policy well established by this time (*c.* 78-84). Such an approach was designed to encourage the British to perceive Roman rule as beneficial in an obviously material sense; at the same time the level of manufactured imports leapt, a fact

---

94 Brixworth, Northants (isometric reconstruction). The plan (after Turland) shows the interesting sequence of development from a first-century round-house, through the Roman period and finally to traces of Saxon settlement. The first rectangular house, built *c.* 70-100, had painted walls, an unusual feature for so early a date. Despite the addition of a bath-suite in the fourth century this was apparently never used. The final plan is of a slightly haphazard house, an interesting mixture of pretensions and economy. A nearby outbuilding contained traces of bronze working in the late second century and most of the third but whether this was the principal bread-winning activity, or only a peripheral trade is unknown. The building's modest scale suggests that the 'estate' was never an especially rich one even though it survived the period.

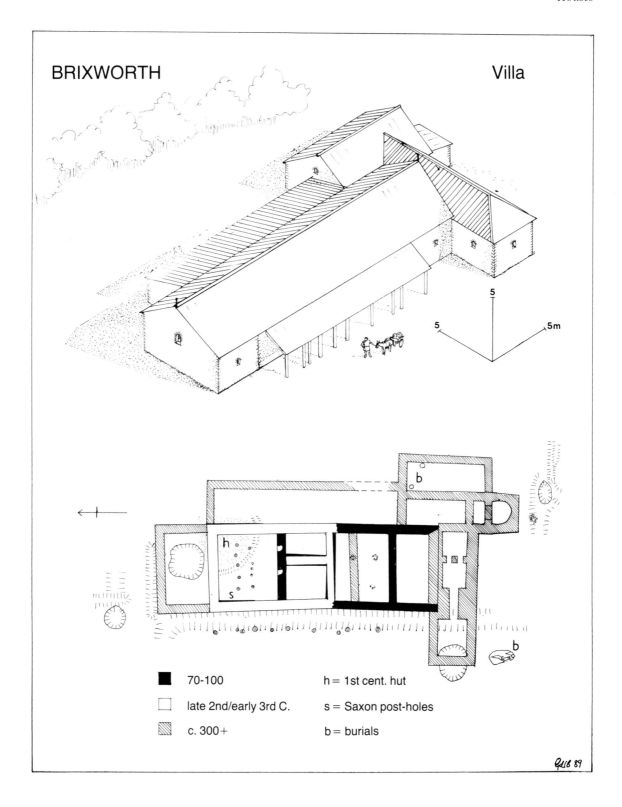

BRIXWORTH   Villa

5m

■ 70–100   h = 1st cent. hut

□ late 2nd/early 3rd C.   s = Saxon post-holes

▨ c. 300+   b = burials

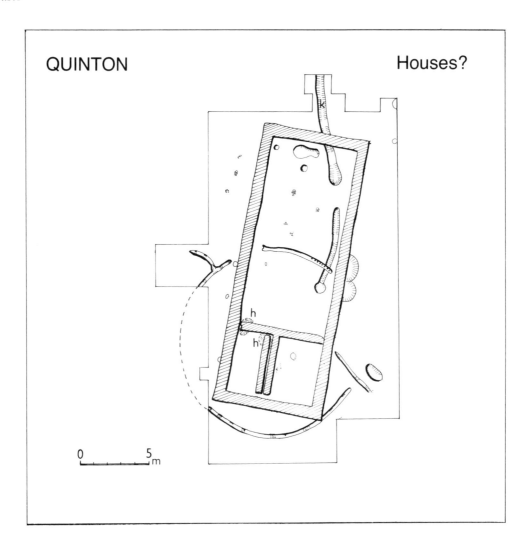

95 Plan of house at Quinton, Northants (after Taylor). A late-first-century rectangular stone building was found to overlie an early-first-century circular timber house. It is clear that the round house would have had to be demolished before the stone house was built. The later house remained in occupation until *c*. 160-70. Such instances probably represent a widespread desire to adopt a new way of building which must have been perceived as superior (but see fig. 110).

testified right across south-eastern Britain but especially in the nascent towns like London and Verulamium. In archaeological terms the change on any particular site from a pre-Roman round house to a rectangular stone structure with room divisions may seem abrupt. The change is often described as an 'early' one if the evidence points to a late-first-century date. On the other hand this also represents the passing of a whole generation. We may know nothing of the ownership of any one house, but a great deal can happen to the fortunes of a farmer in 30 years, and the attitudes of an adult son who had grown up after the year 43 might have been quite radically different in terms of expectations of standard of living.

The majority of known first-century houses are relatively simple and have been identified through analysis of the plan of a later, more elaborate house. There is no convenient way of discerning those belonging to a 'romanized' household but it seems reasonable to begin with those which use approximately straight walls, roughly right-angled corners and also two or more rooms.

This raises the general point of 'influence' and distribution of typologically distinct varieties of houses. When we are dealing with military or public buildings it is easier to perceive the dynamic of influence through official organizations. With private houses this is not so apparent. Certain types of houses like the 'winged corridor' or the 'aisled' appear throughout lowland Britain and in the romanized parts of northern Europe. It is a little too easy to read more into this than can really be justified. As we will see later the plans of most houses in Roman Britain were no more than elaborations on rows of rooms arranged in wings. There is comparatively little one can do with such an arrangement without involving techniques of vaulting or requiring extremely complicated roofing arrangements (see below). And of course we have very little idea of what the houses actually looked like – it is possible that two typologically similar plans were originally two completely different houses. The reconstructions of Stroud (figs. 102, 103) show how different these can be. Even if house types were copied from one area to another we should remember that influence might range from casual observation to professional research and even individual inspiration.

Although they lie outside the brief of this book there are two very important points which must be borne in mind, when considering individual buildings.

The first is that recent archaeological techniques have begun to reveal hitherto unsuspected timber houses in towns. Fourth-century Wroxeter is one of the best examples and it raises the unavoidable conclusion that town plans like that of Silchester are actually very misleading. In other words the density of urban housing, and therefore the population, may have been much higher than we can ever really know. The second is the density of rural settlement. The villa site at Stanwick in Northamptonshire has been the subject of recent close scrutiny. This has revealed a villa with many subsidiary buildings, including a bailiff's headquarters (?), contained within an extensive series of enclosures. This has been described by the excavator as a 'villa and its related "village"'. In other words the population of this one estate may have been much bigger than a simple examination of the villa building and its immediate environs would ever have suggested. This has considerable implications for interpreting the Romano-British countryside as a whole.

The architecture of Romano-British houses

However complicated Romano-British houses became, the large majority of excavated plans are only elaborations of a very simple kind of linear structure: literally a line of rooms. The simple house at Brixworth (fig. 94) and the vastly more sophisticated house at Woodchester (fig. 121) are two versions of the same thing. Most houses began as a handful of rooms laid out in a row in a rectangular plan, for example Quinton (fig. 95). They generally had stone footings, though some early examples of apparently isolated bath-houses with a short period of occupation may have been associated with unlocated timber houses belonging to families who were never able to afford long-term development. Houses in the countryside and of certain first-century date are often found to have succeeded a round-house, possibly of pre-conquest date. Most of these houses underwent some sort of elaboration at some point in their histories. Generally this involved attaching a corridor to one side so that rooms could be accessed individually. The corridor usually had a chamber at either end, creating a symmetrical façade to the house and is now known as the winged-corridor villa (see Plaxtol for example, figs. 96, 97) though what this actually meant in terms of appearance is not quite as clear-cut as orthodox reconstructions imply. Houses that were developed to this extent either stayed as they were or were subsequently enlarged by extending the wings, and eventually a fourth wing might enclose a courtyard. Then the original two wings might be extended further and a second courtyard created.

In architectural terms all that was happening was that the basic format was being extended rather than being radically altered. Instead of rows of rooms being added adjacent to the existing structure, new rows were strung out at right angles. This was probably because of two quite straightforward factors, in addition to some of the points raised in Chapter 1 about Romano-British architects. Firstly there was little pressure on space, or at least this appears to have been the case. We have no evidence for the kind of pressure on space that created the multi-storey

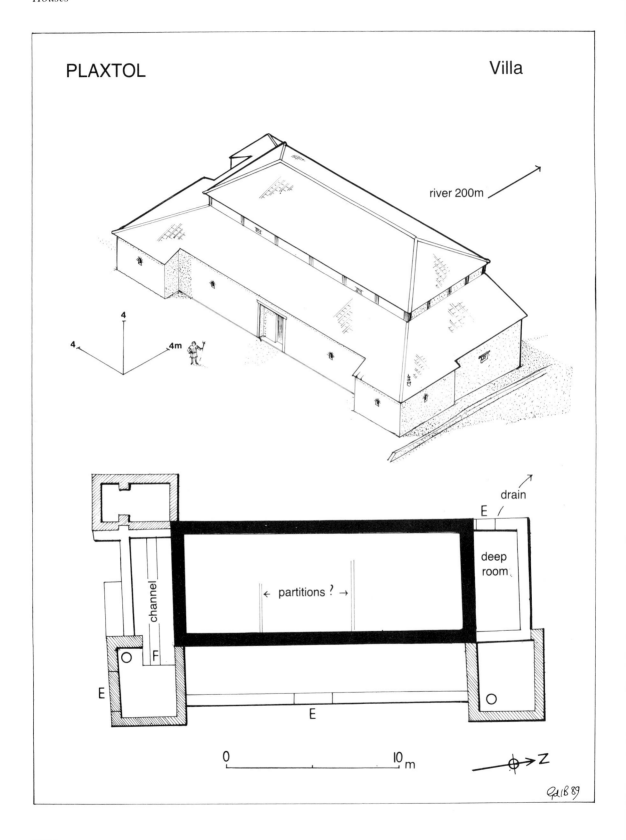

PLAXTOL

Villa

river 200m

4

4

4m

drain

E

deep
room

channel

F

E

← partitions ? →

E

0

10 m

Z

96 The house at Sedgebrook, Plaxtol, Kent (isometric reconstruction) – a typical example of a modest country house, probably associated with farming. The site looks west across the fertile valley of a tributary of the River Medway. Traces of a much more substantial house are known less then a mile to the south, possibly forming the centre of an estate which included this house. In fact a modern road and footpath run between the two sites, perhaps indicating that a connecting route has survived.

The house seems to have been built by the early second century though, as is often the case, traces of earlier occupation were found below the building (but no structural remains). The long central room was built first out of ragstone with a rubble core though upper parts were probably timber. All the other rooms abut this one demonstrating the progress of construction. The next stage was the addition of two rooms, one at either end. The northern room had an excavated cellar, drained by a stone-lined channel, and at some stage this part of the building was gutted by fire. The roof and contents of the northern room collapsed into the cellar where they were left and a new room re-built on top. The wings and corridor were added last and on the southern side formed part of a heated area – a hypocaust channel and iron stumps of a brazier were found here; there was also an entrance here, as well as in the middle of the corridor (E). The northern wing contained remains of a large pottery container which seems to have acted as a hearth (O).

Apart from the cellar which contained several complete (but broken) late-second-century samian vessels the house was disappointingly devoid of datable finds. A handful of barbarous Carausian coins (286-93) found in the roof-fall and a single early-fourth-century coin serve only to indicate that the house may have remained in occupation that long. The house seems to have been carefully cleared before being abandoned. It apparently fell down of its own accord and the entire site was covered with shattered roof tile. The illustration shows the house as it may have appeared in its final stage of development, looking south-west. The precise layout of the rooms makes it exceptionally hard to reconstruct the building in the modern conventional style for winged-corridor villas (see fig. 108 for example) and therefore the opportunity has been taken to show a roof which is actually a great deal simpler.

---

apartment blocks in Ostia (the port of Rome). So a house could spread as space required. This even seems to have happened in a number of Romano-British towns. Secondly there was the question of roofing. The only means of spanning very wide rooms or buildings is to use either exceptionally long timbers or vaults. Vaults required colossal walls to absorb the lateral thrusts, even if the vault was built with hollow tiles (for example at Bath, figs. 10, 11). There is very little evidence for them in Roman Britain apart from bath-houses, both public and private. The only alternative was wood, but until the invention of the hammer-beamed roof at the end of the fourteenth century any roof could be no wider than the length of the longest timbers available. In an island which was probably still undergoing extensive deforestation timber of the right size would have been available. But then there would have been the problems of re-roofing the existing structure to accommodate new rooms and lighting rooms which were now internal. In any case it is quite possible that the additional wings were used to house sons and their families, servants or even tenants, and a degree of separateness would have been desirable.

We have no idea of whether these houses had upper storeys. Sometimes it is claimed that excavated walls in specific cases are too thin to have supported an upper floor. But the walls may have been built with lower courses of stone only, the upper parts being made out of timber frameworks resembling medieval half-timbered houses. And it is quite possible that in any one case there was an upper storey but that the stone supporting walls had not been built strongly enough, creating structural problems for which we would have no evidence. On the other hand the stone walls in another house may have supported only a single storey but had been built more thickly than was strictly necessary (it is of course sensible to make a building capable of absorbing more stress than it is ever likely to have to endure). In other words it is impossible to say that any particular building had an upper storey or not unless there is incontrovertible evidence like the collapsed walls at both Meonstoke and Stanwick. All that can generally be said is that buildings were usually enlarged by adding wings and this implies, but no more, that if space was needed it was gained by growing sideways rather than upwards. A curious building at Chalk, probably an outbuilding of an undiscovered villa, preserved traces of a wooden staircase but this ran down to a cellar. At Littlecote a stretch of wall running from one of the wing towers parallel to the corridor may be the remains of an external staircase (fig. 98). Within a building stair-wells may be represented by narrow rectangular rooms in the plan.

97 The house at Plaxtol under excavation looking south. See fig. 96. (Photo: author, 1987.)

98 Façade of the villa at Littlecote, looking west (c. 360; based on a painting by L. Thompson). The site is famous for the celebrated Orpheus mosaic (fig. 159 and plate 9). By the late second century the house existed in winged-corridor form with a bath-suite. By the late fourth century the baths had been demolished, probably being replaced by the baths associated with the contemporary triconch hall. Remodelling of the wings of the house involved thickening of walls. A wall running north from the south wing may have represented external stair access to the south wing. This and the thickened walls may mean that the wings were in tower form as shown here. The clerestory windows in the main block would have been essential.

The villa was approached through a masonry gatehouse built about 75m (250ft) to the east in c. 300. A barn just south of the midway point between the villa and the gatehouse was built c. 260. It was substantially altered including room divisions and a small bath-suite so it may have been converted into a residence.

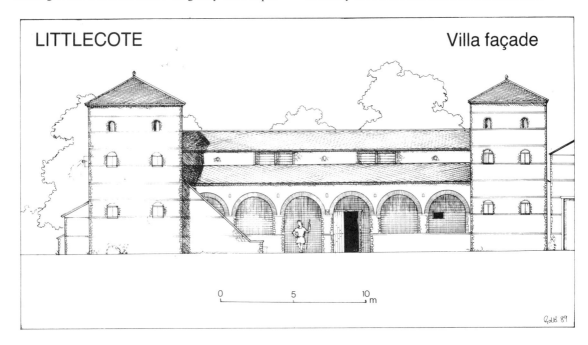

LITTLECOTE   Villa façade

0   5   10
            m

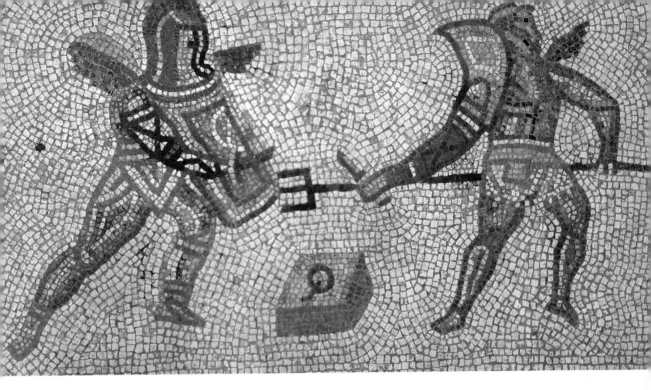

1   Mosaic from Bignor villa, west Sussex, depicting a matched pair of cupid gladiators. A *secutor*, armed with a short sword and shield, fights a *retiarum*, armed with a trident. Between them is a stone with an iron ring where reluctant trainees were tied up. Three other pairs are included in the panel. The composition includes a portrait of Venus in the apse but the central panel has collapsed into the hypocaust beneath. The scene forms part of a floor in the apsidal room at the north-west corner of the villa and was laid during the fourth century. (Author.)

2

Reconstructed wall-painting from a courtyard house at Verulamium built *c.* 180 (Insula xxi, building 2). Forming part of the decoration of the south-west wing this panel covered the south-west wall of room 3 and enough remained of the collapsed plaster to allow a reconstruction by N. Davey. The lower dado consisted of alternate purple and black rectangles. The main panels consist of foliate candelabra framing birds. Although the details are individual the general proportions are probably representative of the kind of material which was becoming increasingly common in Roman Britain at the time. (Courtesy of the Trustees of the British Museum.)

3 The reconstructed Antonine west gate of the fort at South Shields, Tyne and Wear in north-east England. (Author.)

4 Reconstructed view of the interior of milecastle 37 on Hadrian's Wall looking north. The gate survives to its springers but the superstructure shown here is hypothetical. See figs. 56, 57. (Painting: author.)

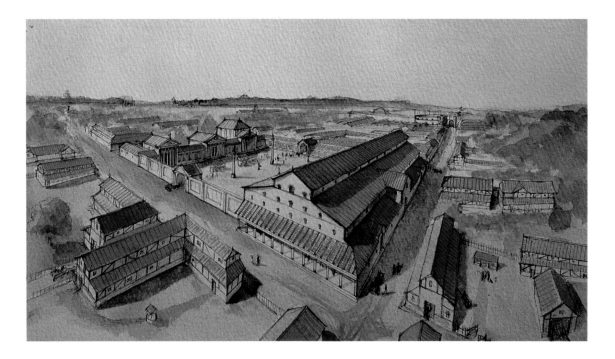

5 Reconstructed view of the basilica and forum at Verulamium looking north-west. In the distance the theatre and its adjacent triumphal arch can be seen. The town's defences run along the ridge to the left and the whole site lies on the east-facing slope of the valley of the River Ver. The basilica has only been examined in very limited detail and its plan presents many problems. Nevertheless it is clear from details of the forum and its temples that Verulamium's civic centre was more continental in plan, and does not resemble the military headquarters building as closely as other Romano-British examples. (Painting: author.)

6

Reconstructed view of Colchester's theatre and temple precinct in the second century, looking southeast. (Peter Froste, reproduced by courtesy of the Colchester Archaeological Trust.)

7 The 'Old Work' at Wroxeter which formed part of the basilican-type exercise hall for the public baths. The gap indicates the former position of the doorway between the hall and the *frigidarium*. The wall is one of the largest surviving fragments of a Romano-British building. (Graham Webster.)

8 The Balkerne Gate at Colchester, view from within the city looking west. On the left is the entrance to the southern tower, to the right is the southern pedestrian thoroughfare. The main body of the gate lay immediately to the right. See fig. 87. (Author.)

9   Reconstructed aerial view of the house and triconch hall at Littlecote from the south in its fourth century heyday. See figs. 98 and 159 for details. (Author.)

10   The surviving remains of the house at Lullingstone, Kent, as consolidated for public viewing beneath a cover building. The view is looking south. In the foreground can be seen a staircase leading down to the 'deep room', centre left, with the later blocking still in place. In the far wall of the 'deep room' is the niche decorated with a painting of nymphs. The Christian house church lay above these rooms. In the upper centre are the mosaic rooms, added after c. 330 and beyond is the bath-suite. See figs. 99, 100 for more details. (Author.)

11 Painting of the temple precinct at Bath in its final form, looking west. Although the temple's appearance is fairly certain the other buildings are no more than wall stumps and fragments of carvings. The precinct would have been dwarfed by the huge north wall of the spring cover building (to left), propped up by buttresses and an arched entrance. See figs. 133-138. (Author.)

12 The Romano-Celtic temple at Lamyatt Beacon, Somerset. The temple was put up in the late third century and was still in use well over a century later. It was comparatively remote and was situated on a ridge about 6km (4m) east of the Fosse Way some 20km (12m) north-east of the town at Ilchester. Few other buildings are known in the surrounding countryside so many of its visitors would probably have been travellers making a detour from their main journey along the Fosse Way. See fig. 151 for a more detailed discussion. (Author.)

13 The central feature of the mid-fourth-century mosaic from Hinton St Mary, Dorset, which appears to show the figure of Christ. If so, this is an exceptional portrayal of Christ on a mosaic in antiquity. Also depicted are four male busts (the Evangelists?) and Bellerophon killing the Chimaera (symbolizing good over evil), a scene also found at Frampton, Dorset, on a floor which includes a Christogram. Even so it is not necessary to insist that the site functioned as a house church – pagan religious figures and motifs were common on domestic mosaics. (Reproduced by courtesy of the Trustees of the British Museum.)

14 Painting of the bridge across the River Irthing at Willowford on Hadrian's Wall, a little to the east of the fort at Birdoswald. The bridge is shown as it may have appeared during the late second and third century with a wooden superstructure which replaced the Hadrianic stone arched version. See figs. 166, 167. (Author.)

15 The drain for the sacred spring at Bath. The arch was a later modification to the drain which actually ran out below the capstone beneath. The arch may have been designed to relieve weight or to allow access to the sluices within. Although the natural hot water passes through the arch now it may not have done so in antiquity. (Author.)

16 The lighthouse at Dover as it survives today in its commanding position overlooking Dover and the English Channel. The uppermost stage is medieval work and much of the Roman ashlar work has been stripped away from the lower courses. The entrance at the bottom is the Roman one. The lighthouse now stands next to the Saxon church of St Mary, which contains much re-used Roman tile, in the grounds of Dover Castle. (Author.)

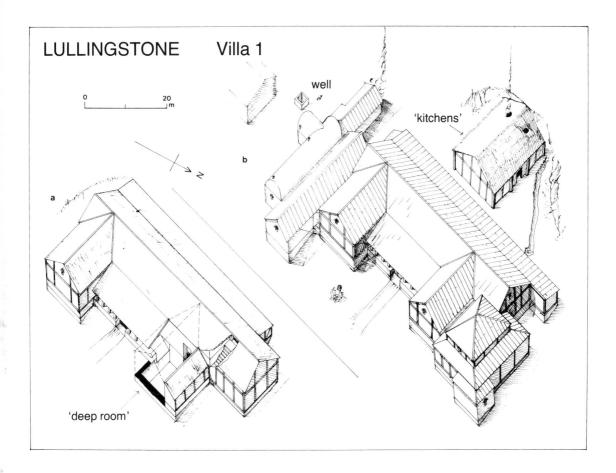

LULLINGSTONE Villa 1

well

'kitchens'

b

a

'deep room'

99 Lullingstone Villa 1. The villa at Lullingstone, Eynsford, Kent, as it may have appeared in the first and second centuries AD. This house is the *only* Roman building in Britain to contain certain evidence for Christian religious activity. However, this belonged to the final phase (see fig. 100).

a the house as built *c.* 80-90. The site lies at the bottom of the western slope to the River Darenth which runs north to the Thames Estuary. The slope was cut back to provide a level terrace for the house above the flood plain. It was almost certainly preceded by more elementary accommodation but no structural evidence was located. The late-first-century house seems to have been a 'winged-corridor' type and included the 'deep room' (here shown cut away) which may have acted as a grain store. Access was on a ramp from the entrance to the house, and a staircase to the west.

b the house in the second century. A number of peripheral features have appeared. A bath-suite has been attached to the south on levelled land gained by cutting further into the hillside – a well further south supplied the necessary water. Beyond that traces of an outbuilding were noted but its length could not be ascertained. Immediately to the west a thatched hut

supported on tree trunks seems to have contained the kitchens – subsequently it became a tannery (during the third century while the rest of the house was apparently unoccupied). The northern side of the house was radically altered to adapt the 'deep room' as a cult chamber. A niche was cut into the wall to contain a painting of nymphs, and a deep pit sunk into the floor. Adjacent to this, but on the higher level, an ambulatory surrounding a rectangular room recalls a Romano-Celtic temple and it has been reconstructed in this form here. To the north-west on a higher terrace a simple circular shrine was built (not shown here, but its site is shown on fig. 100).

Occupation of the house proper is thought to have ceased by the beginning of the third century. However the later owners found possessions of their predecessors left behind. These included two marble portrait busts of second century style and fine workmanship (see *Finds*, plate 22). They portray two aristocratic Roman men, probably relatives, and suggest that the second century occupants were of high status. The combination of a modest house and such remarkable objects implies that it may have been occasional residence of a wealthy person.

129

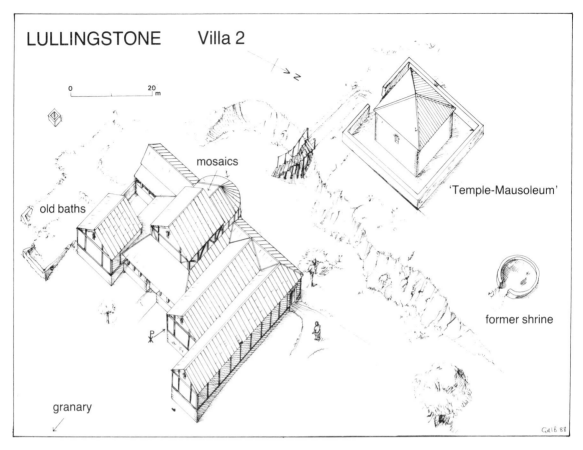

LULLINGSTONE   Villa 2

0 ——— 20 m

mosaics

old baths

'Temple-Mausoleum'

former shrine

granary

100 Lullingstone Villa 2. This illustration shows the site as it may have appeared towards the end of the fourth century, in its final phase (see also plate 10). During the third century only the old kitchens were in use as a tannery, but by its close the house had been reoccupied and altered. Firstly the marble busts were placed in the deep room together with evidence for cult activity (see *Finds*, p. 149). Access from within the house was sealed off (but see below). A granary was built between the house and the river with a long axis at right angles to that of the house. It was about 25m (80ft) long by 10m (32ft) wide with a raised floor to allow the grain to dry.

About the year 300 a man and a woman, in their early twenties, were buried in lead coffins along with grave goods and were placed in a wooden chamber at the bottom of a pit. A mausoleum was constructed, likened by the excavator to a temple though there were no traces of ritual activity (see text). The circular shrine was dismantled.

After *c.*330 the house itself was radically altered though these changes were largely confined within the old structure, reflecting the constrained site. The reconstruction of the central range of rooms included pushing out the west wall in order to build an apse. This

room and the central room were decorated with mosaics, clearly forming the focal part of the house. A room in the northern range was adapted for use as a kitchen (the old kitchen/tannery having long since fallen out of use), and it seems the house was still only an occasional residence.

About 40 years after the mosaics had been laid down the house entered its final phase. Its use as a residence of any sort seems to have ended and its new function makes it a Romano-British building of outstanding importance. The baths were demolished and the mausoleum became derelict. The granary was allowed to decay and was also eventually demolished. The chamber above the deep room seems to have become a Christian house chapel (marked **p x**). Wall-plaster was found depicting people engaged in Christian worship. This impression is strengthened by an access room which contained wall-plaster with the chi-rho symbol. The cult activities associated with the marble busts continued beneath – new pots, open for libations, were placed in a fresh clay floor. By the early fifth century the whole house had been burnt down and it was abandoned. The nature of the place must have remained in local lore because the ruinous mausoleum was eventually built over by a Saxon church.

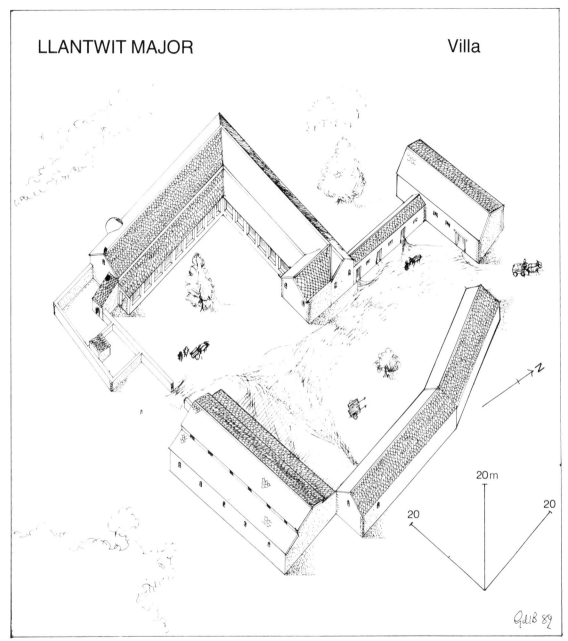

LLANTWIT MAJOR

Villa

20m

20

20

Z

GdB 89

101 Llantwit Major villa (axonometric reconstruction). The site had a long history dating back possibly to the first century though the first stone house was not built until the second century. It is a particularly interesting site because of its remote situation in south Wales, far removed from most Romano-British country houses in a military area. Development was slow and the site may even have been abandoned in the third century. The drawing shows the whole site as it may have appeared in the fourth century when the L-shaped house had been augmented with a number of additional structures creating a semi-enclosed courtyard. The basilican-type building in the foreground may have been a residence for workers on the estate and belongs to the category of aisled buildings sometimes found on their own (see figs. 102-4 for example). The ditch was either a defensive precaution or, more likely, a simple way of controlling livestock. The impression is of an estate large enough to require a number of persons and with accommodation for them, animals and equipment.

131

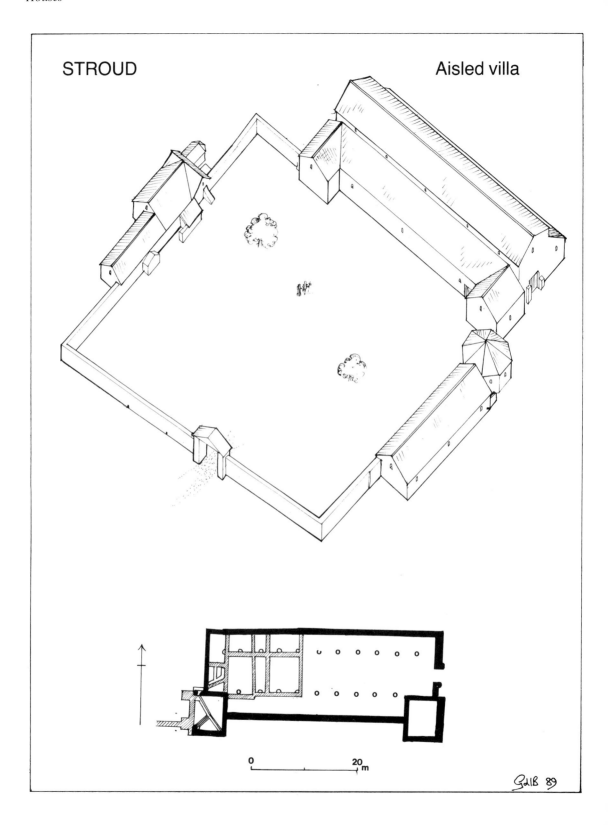

STROUD

Aisled villa

GalB 89

0   20
               m

102 Aisled villa and accompanying buildings at Stroud, near Petersfield, Hampshire. Unfortunately little dating evidence is avaliable for this site because it was excavated around the turn of the century. The main feature was the aisled house with wings which would have given an outward appearance similar to the winged-corridor villas. In its original form the building apparently had no internal rooms apart from the wings, though the excavators may have overlooked timber partitions. At this stage it was accompanied only by the eastern building which may have been a barn or granary. Subsequently a number of internal divisions created separate rooms in the west end of the aisled house, some of which were heated (hatched walls on plan). A separate bath suite was built and faced the barn across a now enclosed courtyard. An octagonal structure of unknown purpose was built by the barn (see Bancroft, fig. 107).

The site is interesting because it seems to show how a structurally unambitious house could be remodelled to create a more sophisticated residence. It also shows an unusual blend of styles which are normally considered distinct. The Bancroft villa by contrast was preceded by an aisled house which was demolished to make way for a more conventional winged-corridor house on a different orientation. It also had an octagonal building of unknown purpose close to the main house. The site was excavated a long time ago and it is quite possible that the empty looking courtyard actually contained a large number of smaller structures which were not identified (compare with the plan of the site at Gorhambury, *Current Archaeology*,

87, 116). See also fig. 103 for a different restoration of the house.

Many houses had at least one 'cellar' like the Chalk example. Here the room had niches for lighting from lamps and a ramp which probably served for rolling barrels down into storage. At Lullingstone the so-called 'Deep Room' began life in the late first century probably as a similar storage area (fig. 99). By the late second century a re-modelling of the house involved converting this chamber into a cult room containing a niche painted with water nymphs (fig. 100, plate 10). Subsequently it became a repository for marble ancestor busts (see *Finds*, p. 149). Such rooms created problems of their own: at Plaxtol the cellar was prone to flooding and had to be equipped with a drain which when cleared helped the excavation of the site (fig. 97).

As ever there are exceptions. The aisled houses, or at least those which appeared to be

103 The house at Stroud, restored isometric view based on a wall-painting at Trier (see fig. 1). The painting shows that 'winged-corridor' villas might have had towers at the wings, as opposed to the conventional reconstructions (see fig. 102).

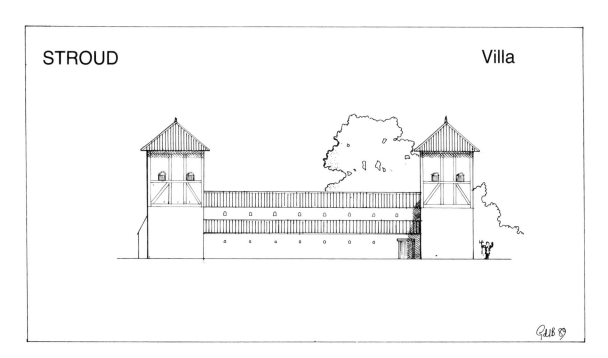

STROUD   Villa

'aisled' or 'basilican' in form, are the most important group. The building type appears elsewhere in Britain as the military principia, the public basilica, and the Mithraic temple and as part of the Fishbourne house, its earliest manifestation in a 'domestic' context. The type is known throughout Britain but curiously it usually appears as an outbuilding to the main house (and as such is assumed to have served a non-domestic purpose) for example at Llantwit Major (fig. 101). There are three areas, however, where examples which seem to have been dwelling houses are grouped: in Hampshire, the Fens, and around the River Humber. In the houses concerned part of

104 The aisled house at Meonstoke, Hampshire. During the early fourth century it was extended with a new east end. Light came in through three round-headed lights, but these were then blocked up. Later the whole new east end collapsed, probably due to inadequate foundations and bonding, but large sections were left where they fell. The remains of the gable seem to have been quite steep, something which is difficult to reconcile with the considerable weight of roof tiles. A house at Stanwick, Northants, has recently been discovered to have suffered a similar collapse; here the gable had a gentler gradient, and it is also clear that there was an upper storey (fig. 8. (After S. Crummy.)

MEONSTOKE   Aisled villa

the aisled 'hall' appears to have been fitted with rooms and in some cases equipped with a bath-suite. In many of these cases it is quite likely that the resident family shared their roof with the farm animals. This is not unusual in other cultures right up to modern times – it is both convenient and secure. The Stroud house is one of the most curious for, despite its aisled interior, it seems to have been built to look like a 'winged-corridor' villa, or one with wing towers (figs. 102, 103). The aisled house at Meonstoke was extended at one end but the new wall collapsed, preserving a façade of decorative brickwork (fig. 104).

The remarkable villa at Lullingstone is also one of the most unusual in structural terms (figs. 99, 100; plate 10) because alterations to the original winged-corridor version were very compressed and the end-product was a far from conventional plan. However, the site is severely restrictive. The first house on the site was at least as early as mid-first century but it occupied a narrow terrace between the River Darenth and a steep hillside. Some later expansion of the Roman house involved cutting back the hillside, but it would have been quite impossible to extend the house in the conventional manner. Radical alterations in the fourth century changed its appearance but it actually grew very little in absolute size. Even the bath-suite fell into disuse long before the rest of the house. In the fourth century it contained a strange combination of pagan mosaic material alongside rooms which seem to have been used as a Christian house church. Lullingstone's site is highly unusual and hence it is a highly unusual house. There may have been far more houses like Lullingstone, but building into a hillside almost inevitably means that the ruins are eventually covered by material running off the hill, making the site almost unidentifiable. Lullingstone was only located by the excavator because he was looking for a building to explain a gap in an otherwise regular series of Roman structures in a single river valley. Houses built on flat open sites are more likely to be found, and those were the ones with room to grow.

Even if most known Romano-British houses were variations on elementary themes their owners sometimes incorporated very extravagant extensions. These were usually the bath-suites and their designs may, in a few cases, have dwarfed the main house. The villas at Lufton and Holcombe (figs. 105, 106) are the best examples, particularly at Lufton where the octagonal plunge bath seems outrageously ostentatious compared to the house. At Ashtead the bath-house formed a separate structure altogether (fig. 107) which reminds us that rural houses in particular were usually only one component, albeit the main one, of a complex of buildings. Of course this would have depended on the kind of estate which was being operated. At Ashtead one of the sources of income seems to have been the manufacture of tiles and a kiln is associated with the house. The house at Gatcombe seems to have been involved in exploiting local iron ores, and at Chew Park lead extraction seems to have taken place. At Bancroft (figs. 108, 109) extensive stripping and excavations have revealed a number of out-buildings which also include a mausoleum (fig. 183). At Llantwit Major the house was one of several buildings which bordered an L-shaped courtyard (fig. 101). We have no knowledge of the size of any estates though it has been suggested that the capacity of granaries or natural boundaries may be helpful. Frere has quoted a possible figure of 400 ha (1000 acres) for Ditchley based on the granary size, and 800 ha (2000 acres) for Bignor. Research conducted around the house at Ditchley has shown that it is surrounded by stretches of dykes of Roman date mostly about 1.6km (1 mile) away. Some of the dykes have terminals and the space in between is still filled with woodland. Together these suggest that the villa estate was defined by dykes, woodland and the main road of Akeman Street which runs from east to west about 2.5km (1.5 miles) to the south. A modern footpath runs from Akeman Street towards the site of the villa and almost certainly represents the survival of the original approach road to and through the Roman estate. The villa at Barnsley Park has been shown to be surrounded by a network of earthworks on a south-facing slope representing small enclosures which were probably fields and stockyards.

The fact that many houses underwent significant alterations and elaborations in their plans does not mean that rudimentary rectangular and round houses did not continue to be built or lived in throughout the period, and it would be quite wrong to imply otherwise. Indeed, it may even be that they constituted the majority of Romano-British homes, shops and farms at any given period. One need only look at the plans of the settlements outside forts, for

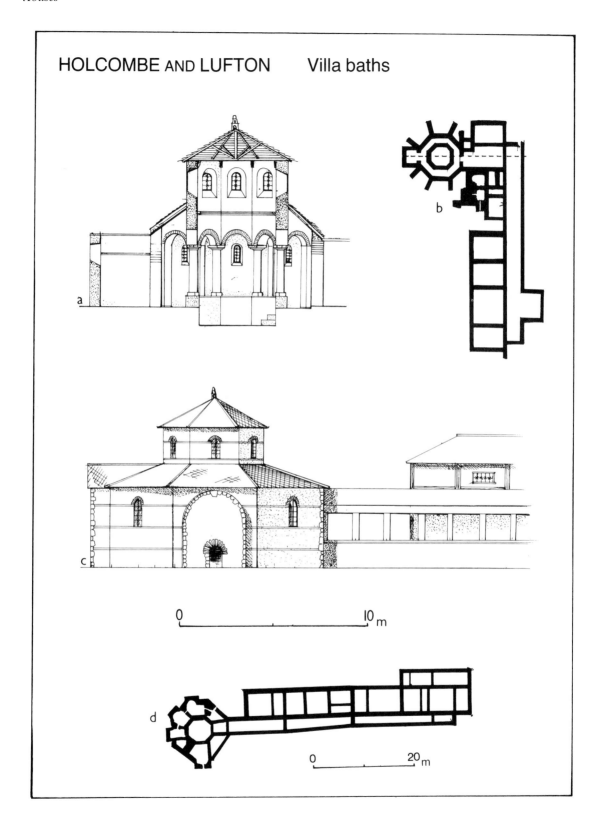

HOLCOMBE AND LUFTON   Villa baths

a

b

c

0 _____ 10 m

d

0 _____ 20 m

105 Holcombe, Devon and Lufton, Somerset villas – the bath-suites.

The house at Lufton was a late foundation – occupation seems only to have commenced in the late third century at the very earliest, and very possibly somewhat later. The house remained a modest establishment consisting of four rooms facing east with a connecting corridor (it may not even have been a house).

This unprepossessing residence was, however, equipped with a large bath-suite to the north. Even this would excite little comment were it not for the astonishing octagonal *frigidarium*. The octagon contained an ambulatory and central plunge bath. The bath walls probably supported a colonnade which may in turn have supported a central lantern. It was undoubtedly of some height because the huge lateral forces generated made it necessary subsequently to strengthen the whole structure with massive buttresses (see fig. 106).

The relative heights of the flanking rooms are less easy to establish but some reconstructions show these as higher than the octagon's ambulatory. This is very unlikely because the effect would have been to diminish the octagon which was obviously the centre-piece of the whole establishment.

The nearby villa at Holcombe (30km/18 miles) has a similarly extravagant fourth-century bath-suite. In this case the various bath rooms are arranged in octagonal form, as opposed to the octagon acting as a single chamber in the sequence.

It is difficult to explain the purpose of such structures unless one sees them as simply the result of grandiose fancies by the owners, either in imitation of one another, or even in competition. There is no reason to deny the Romano-British the trivial pursuits we know so well in our own age. However, there is also the possibility that the buildings actually functioned as commercial rural bathing establishments with cultic/curative reputations.

a the bath-suite at Lufton restored in section

b Lufton villa – plan

c the bath-suite at Holcombe

d Holcombe villa – plan

106 Lufton villa baths (axonometric reconstruction). See fig. 105.

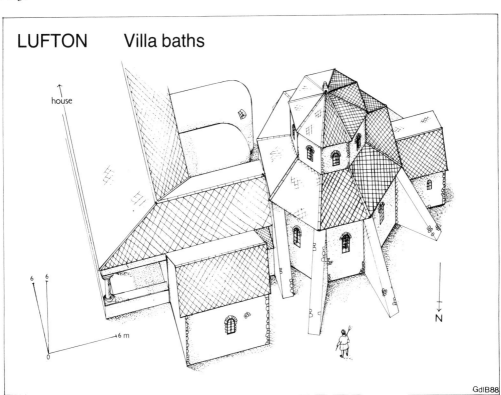

LUFTON   Villa baths

house

N

GdIB88

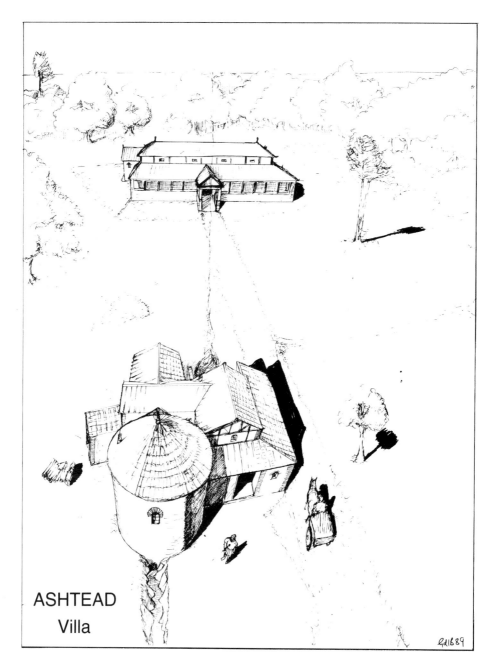

ASHTEAD
Villa

107 The villa and baths at Ashtead, Surrey. One of the very few Roman buildings known to the south-west of London, Ashtead seems to have been a centre of light industry rather than agriculture. Note how the bath-house lies at a substantial distance from the main house. It may therefore have been for the use of workers. There was a kiln for the manufacture of tiles including a distinctive design of box flue-tiles which have been associated with the later part of the second century (see *Finds*, fig. 34d). Tiles made from the same dies have been found at Beddington villa near Croydon. However, the site is comparatively remote and it is difficult to see how finished tiles could have been transported significant distances without an unacceptable level of loss. Despite this, the business was clearly successful enough to be able to support an estate of comparatively early date and of reasonable size.

example Vindolanda, or villages like Catsgore in Somerset to see the kind of far less sophisticated building which continued in use. The Stanwick site in Northamptonshire has already been mentioned – here most of the dwellings are round houses in various enclosures. There may have been far more of the kind of ribbon development settlements like Hibaldstow on Ermine Street in Lincolnshire than we are currently aware of. Here a series of basic rectangular structures fronted the road, presumably offering basic services and accommodation to travellers. There are also a number of 'native settlements' known,

108 Winged corridor villa at Bancroft, Bucks (isometric reconstruction). The drawing shows the house as it appeared after *c.* 340 when the bath-suite was rebuilt and a number of rooms had mosaics laid. In an earlier phase the house was an aisled structure on a different alignment. In the front there was an ornamental garden including an octagonal building of unknown purpose, perhaps a shrine, or simply a garden house. A number of outbuildings have been found (see fig. 109), and these indicate an active and large agricultural estate. Some 300m (1000ft) to the north-west a mausoleum was found, probably built for family members, though it was subsequently robbed out (fig. 183).

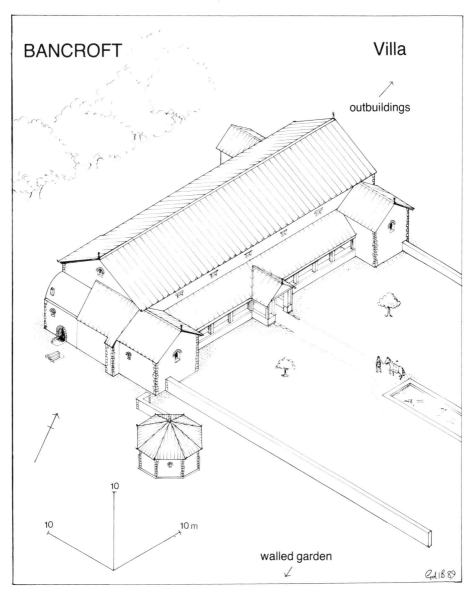

BANCROFT   Villa

outbuildings

walled garden

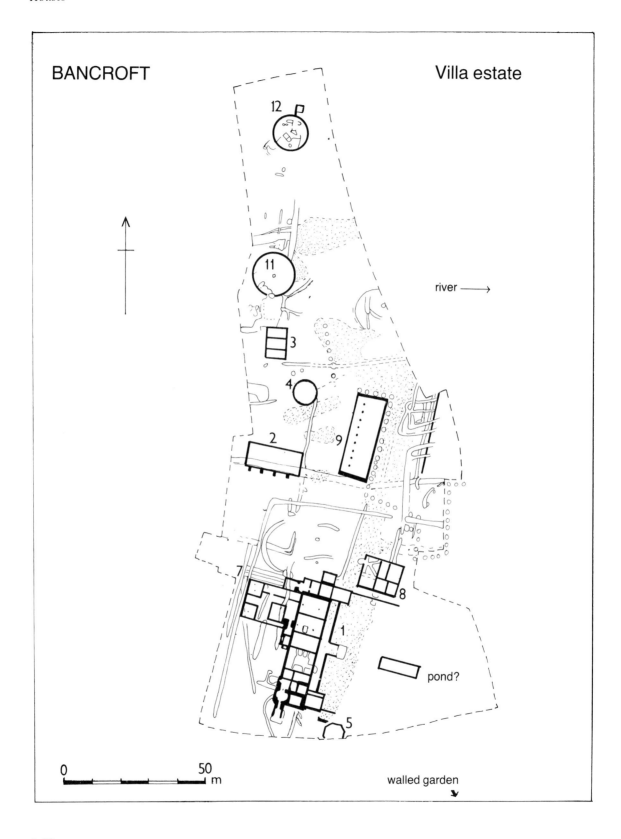

BANCROFT

Villa estate

12

11

river ⟶

3

4

2

9

7

8

1

pond?

5

0   50
     m

walled garden

109 ◄ Bancroft villa estate plan (after Williams), see fig. 108.

110 ▼ Round house at Winterton, Lincolnshire (axonometric reconstruction; 'Building E'). Underlying the substantial villa house this round building appears to date to the second century between about 130 and 180 with two distinct phases. The roof seems to have been supported on four central posts. The house, if this is what it was, is interesting because it shows how even in the later second century, domestic architecture in remote areas of Roman Britain was still quite elementary.

like Chysauster in Cornwall. At Chysauster a pre-Roman settlement of stone-built oval houses remained in use right up to the beginning of the fourth century. Other similar settlements are known in the vicinity of Hadrian's Wall, for example Milking Gap, though these were generally suppressed when the frontier was consolidated. Interesting though these kind of settlements are, their lack of architectural sophistication makes them of little relevance here apart from appreciating that for every Woodchester or even Bancroft there may have been hundreds of simple houses. At Winterton in Lincolnshire round houses were still in use in the second century (fig. 110).

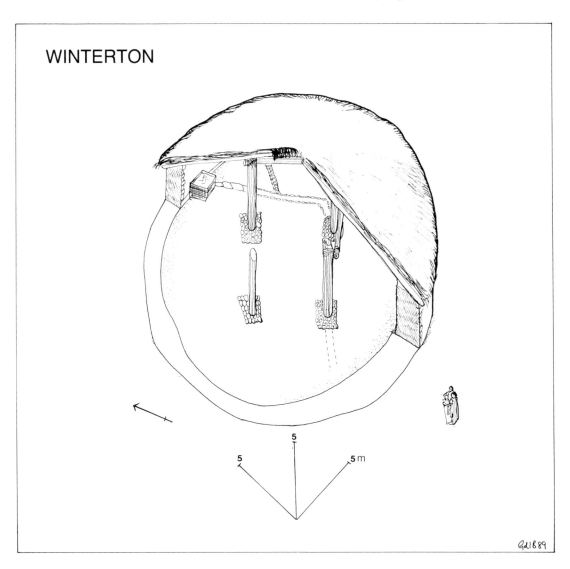

WINTERTON

5

5   5 m

Town houses

In the towns of first-century Roman Britain we have evidence for early living quarters. There are two main types: living quarters adapted from military buildings, and those which were built from new. Roman towns were almost as susceptible to change as their modern counterparts, and it is difficult to distinguish these early dwellings from later structures. However, the three earliest major towns of the province (Colchester, London and Verulamium) experienced considerable destruction during the Boudican Revolt in 60. Subsequent re-building in some cases buried, and protected, the pre-60 structures and supplied a *terminus ante quem*, i.e. the burnt buildings must precede AD 60 (assuming the fire damage has been correctly attributed).

At Colchester the legionary fortress of *legio* XX was given over to the new colony by the late 40s, so its residents were made up of ex-soldiers and their families. On the evidence of excavations at a number of sites within the old fortress, parts of the barrack blocks seem to have been adapted for use as houses, the remainder being demolished and the land being used for farming. The external walls of the barracks were based on mortar and stone plinths which had foundations only of about 4cm (1½ in.). The rest of the wall was made up mainly of sun-dried daub blocks; internal walls were made of timber frames filled with wattle and daub. They were not ideally suited for use as houses because barracks consisted largely of a series of independent rooms for groups of ordinary soldiers; however, each barrack had quarters for the centurion, consisting of a block sub-divided into smaller rooms. In the main these were used, with the independent rooms being demolished. These houses were simple structures with earth, or occasionally timber, floors. The walls were rendered with sandy clay, and in some cases plaster. Roof tiles are easily re-usable and this might explain their absence. However, this would not have occurred during the Boudican sack so it is reasonable to assume that roofing was made out of thatch or shingles (wooden tiles).

Identifying early structures in London is naturally extremely difficult, but a certain amount of basic structural evidence has survived. Three timber buildings were put up *c*. 55 by a probable market place in Gracechurch Street. The best preserved consisted of a rectangular building fronted by a verandah; it seems likely

that it was a series of shops with private quarters behind. It was much more simply built than the ex-barracks at Colchester. The walls were just timber frames filled with mud bricks or wattle and daub and were secured with wooden foundations. The site is similar to the better-known Insula xiv at Verulamium (fig. 111). Here a series of shops housing bronzesmiths seems to have been built as a single timber-framed construction. Again the shops were fronted by a verandah and behind them there seem to have been living quarters. If the interpretation of the structure is correct then we may be dealing with a single entrepreneur landlord putting up a scheme to capitalize on the demand for business premises by craftsmen who themselves wished to supply the demand for their products. The landlord may have been either a private individual, or the government (through the army).

The connecting feature with all these early town buildings is that they were apparently not built or lived in by the indigenous population. They seem to bear more resemblance to the frontier towns of western North America in the nineteenth century. The parallel is not inappropriate – these towns sprang up to service the people who were making it their business to exploit new territory. Britain was probably regarded as a source of easy money, a complacent attitude which proved costly, and there would have seemed little point in making serious investments in buildings. The buildings are not even really houses – on the whole they seem simply to form extensions of shops or craftsmens' workshops, generally belonging to the 'strip'

---

111 Shops at Verulamium, Insula xiv (elevations of Watling Street frontage), selected periods. This remarkable site lies close to the centre of Verulamium, between the theatre and forum and facing north-east. Despite destruction in the Boudican Revolt of 60 and in the Antonine fire of *c*. 155 the site seems to have been used almost continuously as a series of shops and workshops. The fact that periods of rebuilding seem to have involved the whole site suggests that it was in sole ownership throughout. The relative ground levels of **a** and **b** are marked on **c**, showing the build-up of occupation debris.

a the timber shops in Period I, *c*. 49-60
b the timber shops in Period II D, *c*. 150-5
c the masonry shops in Period III, third-fourth centuries

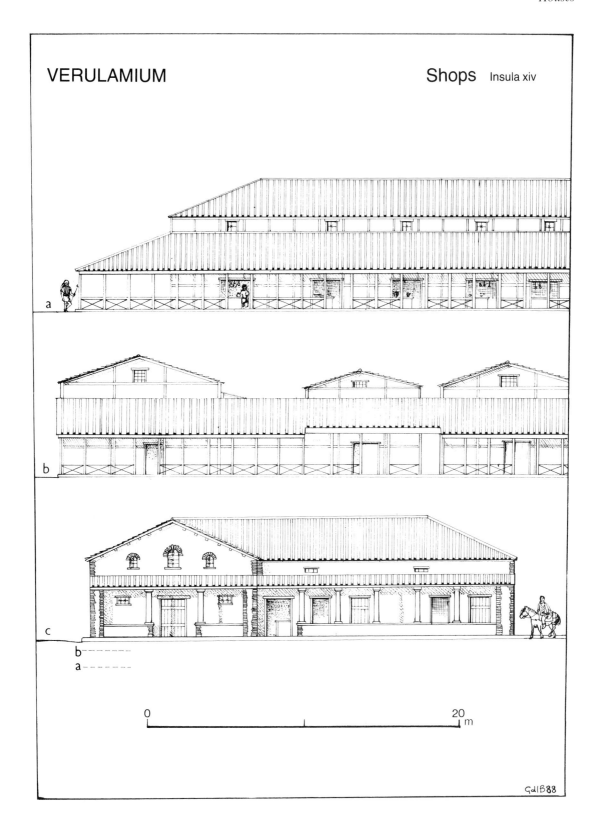

VERULAMIUM

Shops Insula xiv

a

b

c

b ------
a ------

0   20 m

GdlB88

143

form of construction. This contrasts with rural houses where there seems, in relative terms at any rate, to have been more incentive to improve housing.

By the time of the Flavian reconstruction of the province in the 70s the province was already well over a generation old – the sons of soldiers who participated in the invasion and subsequently retired in Britain would have been adults, and the indigenous population in the south-east would have been made up largely of people who had experienced nothing but Roman occupation. Curiously though there seems to have been little incentive to invest time and money in urban living accommodation. At Verulamium the simple timber-framed structures endured, though they were often improved with plastered walls and

opus signinum floors. Here it seems to have taken the Antonine fire of *c.* 155, which destroyed much of the town, to stimulate more robust house building (figs. 112, 113).

---

112 The house at insula iv.10, Verulamium (isometric reconstruction). A fairly typical kind of town-house, this building was one of a number of masonry (or at least with masonry footings) houses put up after the fire of *c.* 155. In the main range a central row of rooms was flanked on either side by a connecting corridor one of which fronted on to the road to the north-west. A single wing projected to the rear with an apsidal termination. By the fourth century the house had been connected by a corridor to another, larger, building which had a street front on the north-east side of the Insula.

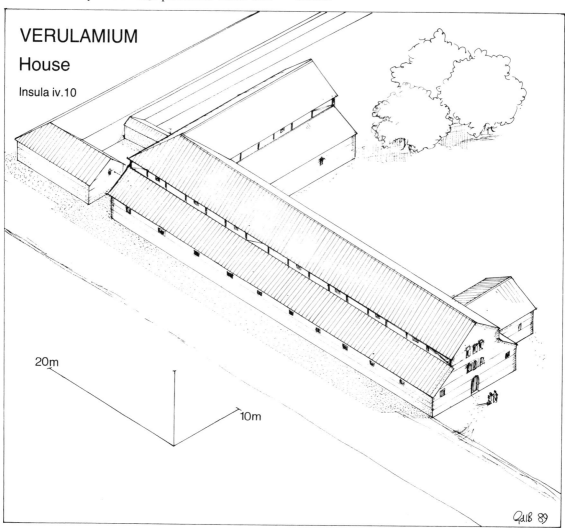

VERULAMIUM
House
Insula iv.10

20m

10m

GdB 89

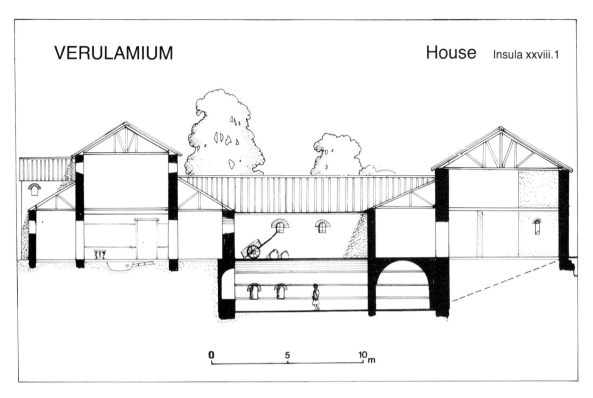

VERULAMIUM House Insula xxviii.1

0 5 10 m

113 Reconstructed section through a town-house at Verulamium, Insula xxviii.1. The drawing should be compared with the published plan (Frere, 1983, fig. 98). The house was built in the third century and included an underground passage with apsidal shrine (?), though this appears to have remained unfinished and instead served as a cellar. The house and apse are visible on site today, near the theatre.

As wealth was accumulated and skills were developed so it became possible for the better-off town dweller to invest in more comfortable accommodation. A similar transition took place in Cirencester. Here too there were simple timber-framed wattle-and-daub shop units, but during the second century more elaborate stone-built houses appeared. A number of basic plans were used which can be identified in most of the towns in which it has been possible to excavate. Not surprisingly the basic strip form remained in use but the corridor type, already well-established in the countryside, became relatively common.

It would be wrong to assume that all these structures *developed* from simple corridor houses. Some may well have been built in this form right from the start. But classical houses were not entirely absent from Britain. The courts built into the various wings of the Flavian Fishbourne house belong to the Mediterranean tradition of internal gardens surrounded by colonnades. By the middle of the second century in Gloucester one such house was put up (fig. 114): it consists of ranges of rooms built around a small central court. Similar houses are known at Caerwent (fig. 115). Both may have had military connections – they certainly resemble houses built for officers in legionary fortresses. Gloucester used to be such a fortress, and Caerwent is close to the fortress at Caerleon. The 'Painted House' at Dover shows the level of sophisticated classical-style decoration which must have been available in Roman Britain but which so rarely survives (fig. 116).

The improvements and sophistication in town house plans went hand in hand with other, perhaps more significant, changes. It became relatively common to equip at least parts of a house with central heating systems, to install timber floors supported on joists and to decorate main living rooms with mosaics. Both Verulamium and Cirencester have produced the most extensive evidence for these expensive

145

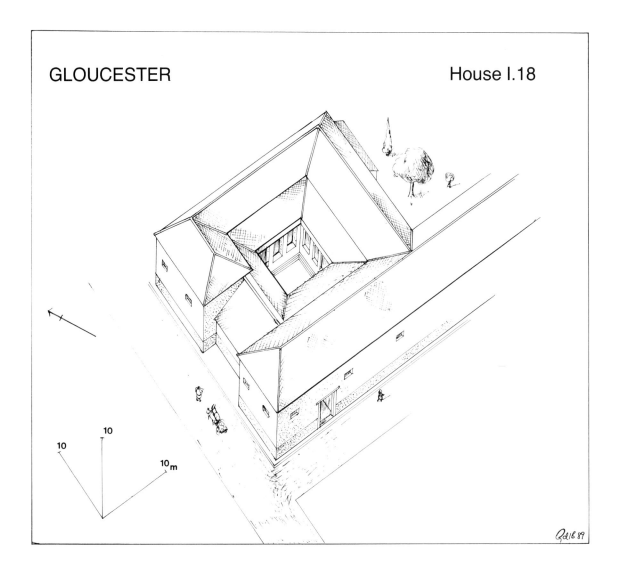

GLOUCESTER

House I.18

10
10
10 m

114 Town-house at Gloucester, Berkeley Street (axonometric reconstruction). This house is particularly interesting because it dates to the mid-second century and resembles military and continental style town-houses with its internal courtyard (see figs. 17, 19). The rooms looked into the court and include a large one in the middle of the east range which may have been a *triclinium* (dining room). It has been suggested that the house was constructed by, or for, someone who had come to Britain from the Continent. However, it was not elaborately decorated and seems only to have had one mosaic. By the third century the house had been dismantled.

investments (plate 2). Not only do these mosaics indicate the growth of a craft industry but also the accumulated wealth which paid for them. However, at Verulamium very few of these new houses had their own bath-suites and none seems to have been connected to water or drainage facilities.

For obvious reasons town houses never expanded to the degree we find in a number of rural cases like Woodchester and Bignor. This was due both to space and to spare money probably being invested in houses outside the towns. Occasionally very large 'houses' are found within town walls and these are normally interpreted as the official inns for users of the

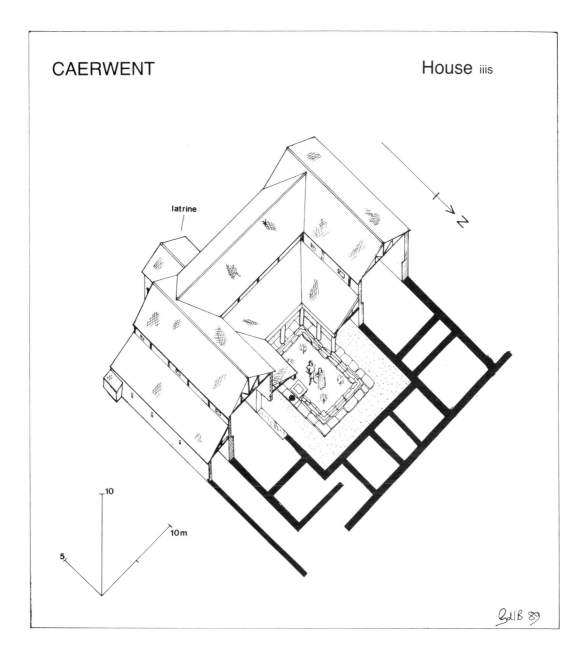

CAERWENT

House iiis

latrine

N

10

10 m

5

GdlB 89

cursus publicus, though it has to be said on very limited evidence (see Chapter 3). Only a single house at Verulamium enclosed a central court-yard with four wings; most of the others barely grew beyond the winged-corridor stage and this was despite the fact that the town exhibits some of the earliest evidence for urban masonry houses. It seems that town houses were slightly more likely to be equipped with underground space for the same reasons. At Verulamium one

115 Town-house at Caerwent, Insula iiiS (cut-away axonometric reconstruction). This house, lying in the south-west area of the town, seems to have been designed on a continental plan as was a house at Gloucester (fig. 114). It may be connected with the nearby legionary fortress at Caerleon, perhaps built by a retiring soldier. Note the central garden surrounded by a colonnaded ambulatory. The gutter around the garden caught rainwater which ran through a drain to the latrine at the rear of the house.

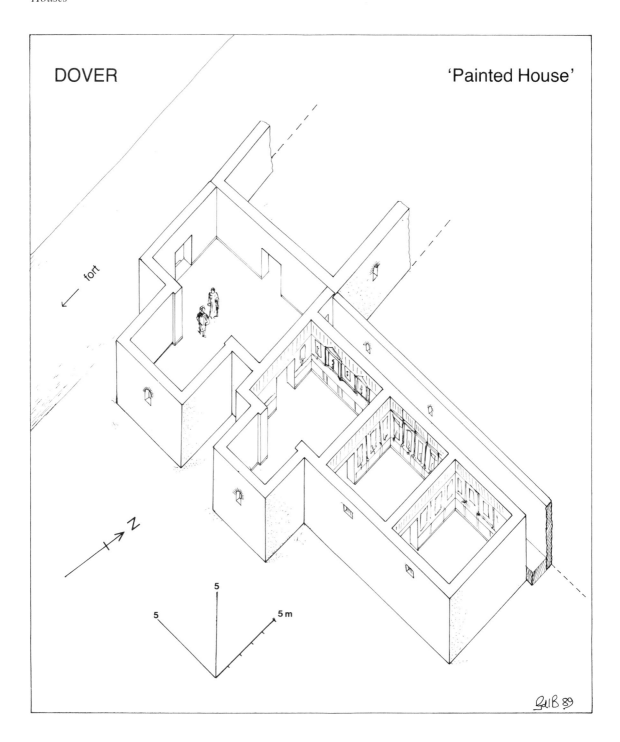

DOVER

'Painted House'

fort

N

5
5   5 m

116 'Painted House' at Dover (axonometric reconstruction). Associated with the fort of the *Classis Britannica* this house appears to have been part of a very substantial complex of buildings beside the road running north from the fort. It owes its preservation not just to the Roman builders of the late-third-century Saxon Shore fort but also to the energetic efforts of the excavators who secured its conservation and display. It is, without doubt, one of the most remarkable buildings of Roman Britain. The reconstruction here shows the building unroofed in order to reveal the rooms within. The 'house' was built *c.* 200, as either a house for a military official or possibly a rest-house for dignitaries on their way to, or from, the Continent. Its walls were decorated with elaborate paintings of the highest quality. Enough of these have survived to make it possible to reconstruct the schemes in some of the rooms. By *c.* 270 the Saxon Shore fort was under construction and, instead of demolishing the part of the house which lay in the path of the fort wall, the builders simply incorporated it into the rampart. However, traces of vegetation on the walls suggest that it had already been ruinous for some time. Neither a town-house nor a villa proper, this building shows the kind of quality work that was available in Britain and it must be certain that many other Romano-British houses were as finely decorated.

The outstanding and well-illustrated excavation report is recommended.

---

house had a subterranean passage and apsidal shrine (fig. 113), and others had cellars. A cellar has also been found in Leicester and, as at Verulamium, there seems to have been provision for lighting these chambers with splayed windows at ground level. Very few town houses had their own bath-suites and it seems likely that their owners must have relied on public facilities. This was the case for most houses at Verulamium, even including the single large courtyard house, in Insula iii.

Whether or not towns became less obviously congested within their walls during the third century and later is not clear. Town plans suggest that houses were fairly widely dispersed, perhaps two to an insula. This would have allowed them to combine reasonable garden space yet still operate shops from their street frontages. Such views are necessarily based on the plans of Verulamium and Silchester, which are the only towns known well enough in detail. It has been suggested that this reflects a social change in favour of the curial class (those eligible in wealth terms to sit on the town's senate, the *curia*) but

equally it may represent the families who were commercially successful in earlier years buying up land and consolidating their wealth in better appointed houses. On the other hand a serious fire in Verulamium in *c.* 155 caused widespread destruction and was possibly responsible not just for the greatly increased use of masonry for construction but also the wider spacing of houses. However, archaeology is beginning to reveal much larger numbers of timber houses in towns, Wroxeter being the prime example, and it may be that in time we will have to re-think entirely ideas about Romano-British towns as fourth-century 'garden cities'.

Even so, there are comparatively few known examples of new houses of significant size in fourth-century Romano-British towns. The curious little house at Dorchester (fig. 117) was built in the early fourth century and had mosaics in almost all its main rooms, glass windows, decorative columns and central heating. In Leicester shops were rebuilt in masonry in the early fourth century and in Insula xiv at Verulamium the long-established row of shops continued to function (fig. 111). In London very few houses of later date are known at all, but there is one particularly interesting site close to the north bank of the Thames in the south-east part of the city (fig. 118). Built in the third century the building had an unusually placed bath-suite, too big for domestic use but neither a grandiose facility (like the example at Lufton) nor big enough for public use. It may have been an inn, perhaps run by a single family, and evidently successful enough to remain in occupation right up to the end of the fourth century at the earliest.

The evidence from some towns suggests that town and country were becoming less sharply defined. In Cirencester a previously unoccupied part of the town (a narrow strip of land between the stream and the city wall, Insula xii) was built over with two houses and several outbuildings. They differ in plan from most other houses appearing as rather compressed groups of rooms, though their outward appearance may have resembled winged-corridor houses. Evidence of agricultural activity was found in one of them, and the complex includes an aisled building in a context similar to those found in country houses. It seems likely that they were at least in part involved in farming though whether this means farming land inside or outside the walls is

117 Fourth-century town-house at Colliton Park, Dorchester, Dorset looking west. There were two ranges of rooms opposite one another and therefore the plan of the building is a little unconventional. The house had a large number of mosaics for its size, every room in the north range having one. The building is almost unique in retaining a window opening though this was reconstructed from collapsed fragments (fig. 12). The south range seems to have been originally separate and may have been either a bath wing or possibly an industrial business, perhaps fulling or dyeing (one of the rooms is adapted to allow surface water to drain off). We might imagine then that the owners of the business had made enough money to allow a fairly luxurious standard of living in the residential part of the complex. (Photo: author, 1989.)

unknown. The Barton Farm house which was found in the early nineteenth century just outside the city walls may be a further indication of a blurring of town and country houses in this period. In fact the town walls may represent a compression of the urban area, and originally the house might have been 'within' the town. Some of the larger houses at Silchester have enclosed yards and outbuildings (for example Insula xix.2) and may have been farms, an idea supported by the lack of villas in the town's vicinity.

Other houses

Romano-British towns were not developed out of any comparable pre-Roman settlement. Settlements there were, but these were not conurbations of permanent structures. In the countryside the situation was different. Farms already existed from sheer necessity and were usually centred on some sort of house, albeit a simple one. As we saw earlier a number of sites have shown a radical transformation in the late first century from Belgic round-houses to rectangular houses consisting of several rooms, sometimes fronted by a verandah which allowed independent access to each room.

How these changes took place is not so clear. It seems strange that a simple lifestyle, unencumbered by the sophistications of provincial classical society, could apparently have become unsatisfactory overnight. The new houses were much larger than the ones they covered and at the same time rubbish begins to include fine pottery wares and other accessories of Roman life. It is difficult to account for this financially because we have no knowledge of how much this sort of activity must have cost. If it cost 'more' to live this way then where did the money come from? It could have come possibly from loans, or possibly because the introduction of a

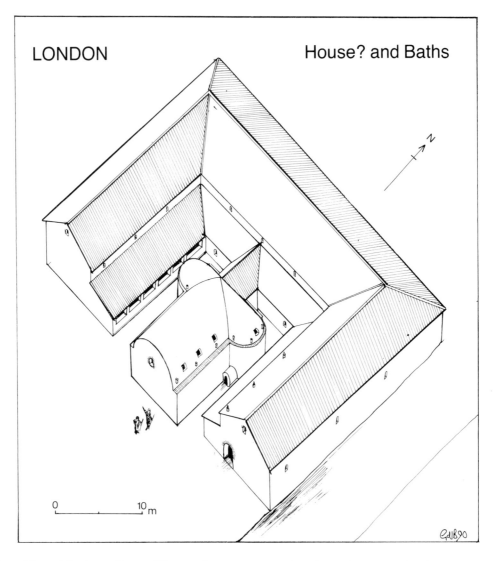

LONDON

House? and Baths

118 House(?) and baths at Lower Thames Street, London. One of the few residential buildings of late date known from London. The central feature is the bath building which seems to have occupied most of what would have otherwise been the courtyard of a winged house. The baths are known in detail but only the eastern half of the house's plan has been recovered – the symmetrical reconstruction shown here is hypothetical. The main room of the baths was the *frigidarium*, with the heated rooms represented by the smaller apsidal chambers and fed by a small furnace. The baths were served by a number of drains and were connected by a short corridor to the house which was built, strengthened by a retaining wall, into the hillside close to the north bank of the Thames during the third century. The house was quite well-equipped, having several heated rooms fed by a furnace in the end of the east wing. It also had painted wall-plaster. Although the baths are small compared to public facilities an alternative possibility is that the buildings served as a small family inn for merchants or sailors, for whom this would have been a convenient resting place, being close to both the river and the commercial and administrative centre of London.

The building survived into the early fifth century on the evidence of a coin hoard with a *terminus post quem* of 395 concealed in the roof. At some point the hoard fell and was scattered but not after the roof collapsed, the remains of which covered the coins. A fifth-century Saxon brooch found amongst debris in the baths indicates that the structure was deteriorating soon after the end of the Roman period. The site has been preserved but is not currently open to visitors on a regular basis.

cash economy was beginning to filter throughout society. As money was received for produce so it could be saved and invested in a new house. But this still fails to explain the motivation: people are notoriously resistant to change. Of course we have no way of knowing if the householders were the same people; it may be that in the cases where we can see a dramatic change in the archaeological record we are actually looking at new money and new people. Yet all but the most conservative types must have seen that multi-roomed houses, sometimes also with *opus signinum* floors, represented an objective improvement in their way of life. In a number of cases, for example at Lockleys, Ditchley and Quinton (fig. 95), the first stone house actually overlies the preceding house. This suggests a break in occupation unless the owners made temporary accommodation arrangements during construction. Perhaps the original site held a certain superstitious significance for the owners who were unwilling to

move away, even a few yards.

But these houses were not the 'villas' which people will now pay to visit. They did not have mosaics or painted walls, and only in a few cases had bath-suites attached. They were really no more than elongated huts. At Gadebridge Park in Hertfordshire the late-first-century buildings consisted of a timber house and an isolated three-roomed bath-suite. Some were slightly more elaborate: at Lullingstone the first stone building, built *c.* 80-90, had a central range of rooms, a rear corridor and a front verandah flanked by two 'wings'. Although built with at least stone footings the lack of associated tiles suggests that it was thatched. Not every late-first-century farm became romanized in this way. At Frocester in Gloucestershire, a long-established Iron Age farm possibly centred on a rectangular house, little seems to have changed. Unlike many contemporary sites the better quality fine wares are conspicuous by their absence, and only in the

---

119 The so-called 'palace' at Fishbourne, near Chichester, West Sussex. The nature of this remarkable building makes it surprising that it remained unknown (at least officially) until 1961. Traces of a Roman building were known but only the extensive excavations of the 1960s revealed that they belonged to a very substantial house of Flavian date with an almost equally impressive predecessor of Neronian date.

Fishbourne was an early military site; lying so close to the sea it would have been ideal as a depot supporting the campaign in the south-west. Traces of military buildings, including a granary, were located. Subsequently it became the site of the Neronian 'proto-palace' which, if it had remained the only house on the site, would still have been of great importance. Built in the 60s it had baths, a colonnaded garden, and rooms decorated with mosaics, marble and stucco – all were remarkable for the date in Britain where such luxuries remained hardly known until the middle of the second century, and even then they were still rare.

However, the proto-palace was short-lived. Within little more than a decade it was demolished to make way for the palace proper which was put up in the years following *c.* 75. Although there are slight eccentricities in the plan, it was oriented around an east-west axis. The main entrance lay in the centre of the east wing and led through a formal garden to the west wing which was built on a higher level. Steps led up into an apsed building. Interpretation of this as an 'audience chamber' and the sheer scale of the whole house led to suggestions that it was built as both a residential and a government centre. The owner is unknown; it may

have belonged to a family of Celtic client kings but it is equally possible that it may have belonged to a Roman administrator of high rank. Like the proto-palace it was lavishly decorated with mosaics in the black-and-white style of the first century, wall-plaster, marble and stucco-work.

The residential quarters were in the north wing, though the main bath-suite was at the south-east corner. It consisted of rooms ranged around enclosed courtyards – these also appear in the east wing. During the second century the north wing was radically altered and new baths were inserted in the west wing (fig. 16). Polychrome mosaics were added, as were hypocausts. The fate of the rest of the building is unknown but shortly after the year 296 the structure had been destroyed by fire. A period of stone-robbing followed and then it was abandoned, ironically just as the first Romano-British villas were beginning to equal its original scale and magnificence. Medieval ploughing took its toll, and little now remains above the floor levels.

As much of the southern part of the structure lies under modern houses and a main road, its form has been largely assumed. Further work has shown that more landscaping took place to the south, probably running down to a jetty. It is also certain that there would have been many 'outbuildings' to service all the various needs of the house.

a the Flavian palace, *c.* 75+
b the north and west wings by the later second century
B baths

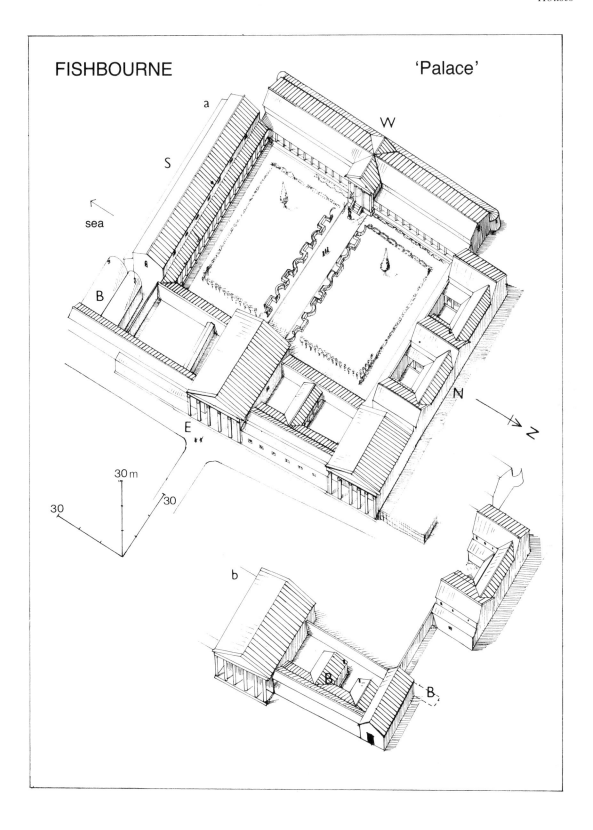

FISHBOURNE

'Palace'

a

S

W

sea

B

E

N

30 m

30

30

b

B

B

late third century were better quality stone buildings put up.

Found (or at least re-discovered) in the early 1960s, the huge house at Fishbourne has earned itself a considerable reputation because of both its size and its supposed association with the tribal king of the Regnenses, Cogidubnus. This it may have been, but the idea is pure supposition and in any case distracts us from the real point, which is that Fishbourne is one of a small number of exceptional and substantial first-century houses known to have existed in Roman Britain. They have nothing to do with the more mundane trends of developments in housing elsewhere because they were built with imported money and craftsmen at colossal expense.

By the late Neronian period a substantial stone house with baths and enclosed garden had been put up on the former military site at Fishbourne. The house was expensively decorated with monochrome mosaics, *opus sectile* floors and a colonnaded verandah. By *c.* 75 the site had been levelled to make way for a much more ambitious project based on four wings built around a garden (fig. 119). Although this bears a superficial resemblance to corridor construction, a closer glance will show how it owes more to the classical tradition of internal courts surrounded by ranges, rather than rows, of rooms. It was built around a formal garden which was itself designed to flank the building's central axis of entrance hall → garden → 'audience chamber' with apse. Like its predecessor the building was fitted with monochrome mosaics, stucco work and architectural embellishments. Below the house towards the sea to the south a further, terraced, garden of more relaxed style led down to a mooring.

Fishbourne is the most remarkable of the large early houses to have been found but it was not the only one, though it may have been the richest. At Eccles in Kent a corridor house with 12 rooms had been put up by *c.* 65; like Fishbourne it was built with mosaics in several rooms and sported an ornamental water basin. Nearby was a detached bath-house which was decorated with painted wall-plaster. Eccles at this period is not remarkable by Fishbourne's standards but it is far closer to Fishbourne than almost all other contemporary houses in Britain. At Rivenhall in Essex rich Belgic occupation is testified by a number of costly items, for example a decorated bronze mirror. During the first century a double courtyard villa seems to have been built on the site (fig. 120). In this case it seems possible that a well-to-do Trinovantian family had found favour with the new Roman administration and had welcomed official encouragement to build a *domus*. On the whole these elaborate houses did not become common elsewhere for over a century. These wealthy first-century houses are found in south-east Britain, and this gives us two possibilities: either they belonged to native aristocratic families who had decided to back the right side (and profited thereby), or they belonged to opportunists or members of the provincial government and army who decided to build themselves houses in the style to which they were accustomed. However, in the absence of specific evidence we can only guess – Rivenhall might equally have been handed over to a wealthy Roman or Gallo-Roman provincial to try to erase the memory of former owners.

During the third and fourth centuries many Romano-British houses enjoyed their greatest periods of expansion. They included a number of the houses which enjoy a reputation in modern times for representing the highest standards of country-house living in Roman Britain, for example Woodchester (fig. 121), North Leigh and Bignor (fig. 127). In general the great houses of the fourth century were elaborations on the corridor house, normally expanded to create four wings around a courtyard though this need be neither symmetrical nor continuous. This may be the result of wealth used to transform a farmyard into a more refined enclosed area. Brading on the Isle of Wight had at least five distinct structures connected by walls. Woodchester seems to have had at least two courtyards, and North Leigh was distinctly trapezoidal in shape. Unlike townhouses, bath-suites were normal, even in the slightly more modest houses like Bancroft (fig. 108) and Brixworth (fig. 94), though the latter was apparently never used. The richer estates would have had large numbers of outbuildings which have not been identified. Aerial photographs of North Leigh show that there were a large number of buildings and compounds very close to the main house. Projecting rooms were added if pretensions and necessity required them, for example the rooms at Keynsham (fig. 122) which is otherwise a simple if sprawling house. The triconch hall at Littlecote, dicussed in more detail in Chapter 5, may be no more than a very extravagant summer dining room just north of the house (fig. 159).

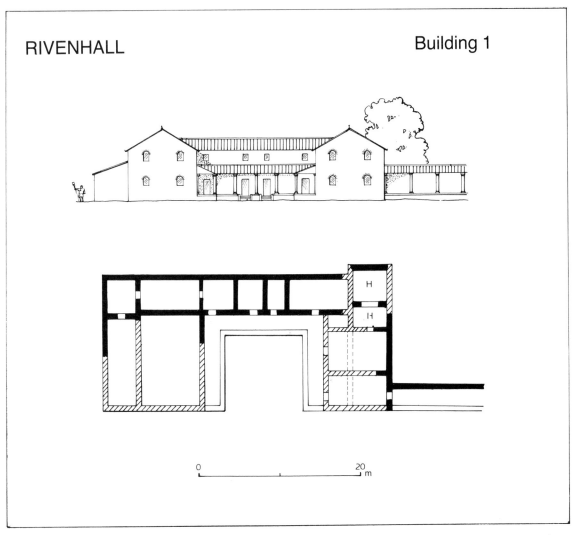

RIVENHALL

Building 1

0   20
                m

120 Rivenhall, Essex, Building I (after Rodwell). Rivenhall, close to the main Roman road running between Chelmsford and Colchester is a particularly interesting site because of the continuity of occupation right through from the prehistoric period to the present day. Late Iron Age residents in the vicinity were wealthy enough to own decorated bronze mirrors which may have been deliberately buried as votive deposits. Stone buildings of Roman type appear around the beginning of the second century apparently forming a large complex arranged around a courtyard. At least two distinct houses, of contemporary date, appear to have been put up one of which (the smaller) is shown restored here. The plan is heavily restored from earlier excavations based on trenches. Speculation on ownership is obviously completely hypothetical, but it has been suggested that the combination of early date and continuity may mean that the house was built by natives. The excavation report is to be recommended as a particularly interesting discourse, not just into the site's history, but also for some of the techniques of design and construction which were involved.

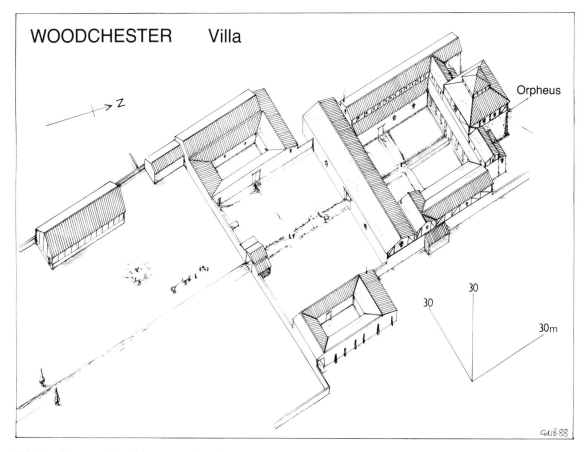

WOODCHESTER Villa

Orpheus

121 Woodchester villa, Gloucestershire (axonometric reconstruction). The plan of most of this villa has been known ever since its excavation by Samuel Lysons in the 1790s, though there are considerable shortcomings in the available evidence.

The villa lies on the western slopes of a valley running north. The vicinity is well known for its numbers of Roman buildings, and the villa is about 16km (10 miles) from Gloucester and Cirencester. The villa complex faced south but it is evident from circumstantial evidence that far more remains to be identified – note for example the walls which continue off the plan. A surviving water conduit fed the building from the west.

The general appearance of the three courtyards and their surrounding buildings is so symmetrical that it might be thought that the villa was built more or less as one unit. But some second-century samian ware, coarse pottery and other material, along with limited excavations in the early 1970s now suggest that the complex represents a longer period. Clarke, the excavator, argues that the site began with the east-west strip of buildings on the north side of the central courtyard in the late first or early second centuries. During the next 150 years the site was extended south-wards around the centre courtyard and beyond to create the outer courtyard.

Throughout these phases the buildings seem to have been lavishly decorated, indicated for example by marble veneers and architectural fragments. Only during the first half of the fourth century, and in common with many other major houses of Roman Britain, did the villa reach its full extent. During this phase the northernmost room, containing the great Orpheus mosaic, was built. Although the villa complex is not the largest in Britain the Orpheus room, at 225 sq. m (2500 sq. ft), is the largest single room known from a villa in the island. Its substantial walls suggest a considerable height and spaces for four columns indicate a possible gallery.

The Orpheus mosaic is one of a series of similar designs known from the Cirencester area. There is a possibility that at least some of the buildings containing these designs were used more as religious centres than domestic premises. However, the rich have never been noted for a lack of ostentation and the size of this house and its facilities may simply indicate a desire to impress, using iconography that was then currently in fashion.

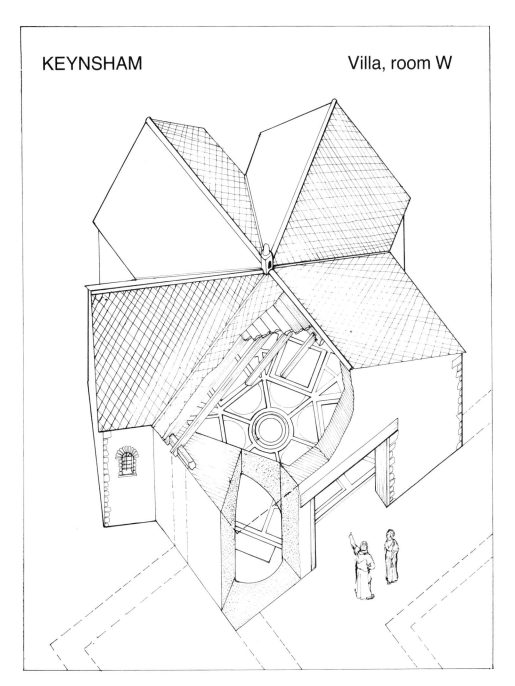

KEYNSHAM   Villa, room W

122 Keynsham villa, room W (cut-away axonometric reconstruction). The villa is essentially a simple, if sprawling, example of a courtyard villa with wings on three sides. However, at the south-west corner a curious hexagonal room with three further chambers protruded from the main block. On the opposite side the entrance to the room was flanked by two niches. The floor was covered with a geometric mosaic. A larger room of similar design was attached to the north-west corner. Their purpose is unknown and they may simply represent an owner's desire to have impressive dining rooms. This room in particular might be compared to the enigmatic triconch hall at Littlecote which may be just an even more extravagant version of the same thing (fig. 159).

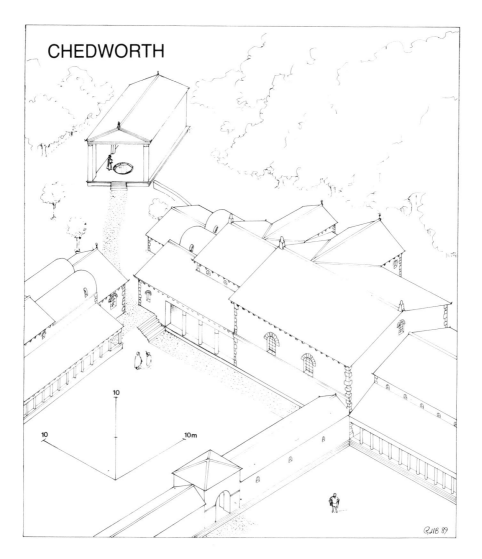

CHEDWORTH

123 Chedworth villa, north-west section (isometric reconstruction, based on a perspective drawing by S. Gibson). Traditionally regarded as one of Roman Britain's finest country houses, Chedworth villa lies in a secluded wooded valley near Cirencester. It was built originally in the late second century and consisted of two houses and a separate bath-suite. Further rebuilding took place in the third century, but only in the fourth century were all the elements combined into a single structure. The result was two parallel east-west ranges connected by a central covered verandah. Another range of rooms, parallel to the verandah, connected with the south range. However, it was not built up to the north range and terminated in a bath-suite. The north range also terminated in an even more elaborate bath-suite, and this is the section shown here. Through the gap led a path and steps up to a small shrine with an octagonal pool.

The presence of the shrine, which marks the source of natural water for the site, and a nearby temple (now destroyed) has led to a suggestion that the villa was actually a guest house and cult centre for the healing god Lenus-Mars. A number of small altars have been found on the site and one of the rooms contained an unusually large number of coins. These could be interpreted as evidence of payments to farm estate staff, fees from pilgrims who wished to use the facilities or even votive gifts. It all depends on how one interprets the site and there is no unequivocal evidence either way. Even if there was a cultic element to the site there is no reason to assume that this precluded normal domestic or agricultural activities. Whatever went on was evidently highly successful as the elaborate bath-suites show – this was a country house of the highest order and represented substantial investment by the owner.

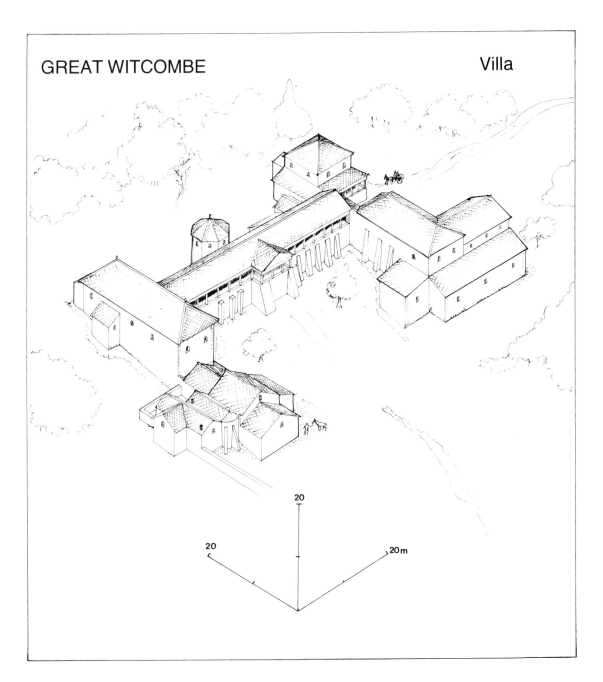

GREAT WITCOMBE   Villa

124 Great Witcombe villa (isometric reconstruction). The house is built of three wings arranged in the form of an 'H'. It was built around the middle of the third century but substantial additions were made within a generation. The site is on a steep hillside riddled with streams. These have made it difficult to imagine why anyone should wish to build a house in a place where the risk of walls being undermined is so great, despite the beauty of the location evident still today.

On the other hand the springs may have formed the attraction – this is another site for which a cult connection has been suggested. However, there is even less evidence here than at Chedworth for such a purpose, and the whim of an eccentric to reside in such a place is no less valid a reason for the house, which had to be propped up with buttresses to resist the effects of the water. The house had a substantial bath-suite, represented by the rooms in the foreground.

125 Room in the middle of the south wing at Great Witcombe. Lying next to the bath-suite this room had a central font and three niches in the wall. It may have functioned as a domestic shrine, perhaps dedicated to water nymphs. The 'deep room' at Lullingstone had a painting of nymphs in a niche – in that case the room undoubtedly served a domestic religious function. (Photo: author, 1989.)

Some of these houses seem so elaborate, particularly in their provision of bath-suites, that it has been suggested that they actually represent hostelries for visitors to a shrine. Chedworth contained a small temple-like structure which stood above and behind one corner of the house. At this point both wings of the house terminate with bath-suites and the gap was filled with steps which led up to the 'temple' (fig. 123). Another temple, now destroyed, lay in the vicinity of the villa. Inscriptions and altars apparently representing Lenus-Mars, a Romano-Celtic version of Mars as a healing god, suggest that, if it was a hostelry for a shrine, then Lenus-Mars was the subject of attention. There is the much more certain hostelry for pilgrims at the shrine to Nodens at Lydney Park in Gloucestershire. More

difficult to understand is the very curious house at Great Witcombe (figs. 124, 125). This house seems to have been built right over a spring. The house, built in the form and 'H' and with various additions, ended up as a very peculiar building which seems to have had bathing facilities quite disproportionate to the available accommodation space.

Gadebridge Park's growth and its associated swimming pool have led to the suggestion that it was operating as a business, perhaps one with a cultic curative significance which funded a substantial house (fig. 126). While this might have applied to Holcombe and Lufton too (figs. 105, 106), such extravagant buildings may have been purely ostentatious displays of wealth and need have no more esoteric reason for their existence; and of course in the ancient world there was far less one could do with spare money than there is now, apart from hoarding it or spending it on property.

These later villas are those popularly associated with mosaics, wall-paintings and a generally luxurious level of facilities. The general subject is covered in Chapter 1 but it is worth noting that even the greatest houses, like Bignor (fig. 127, plate 1) had mosaics in only a small

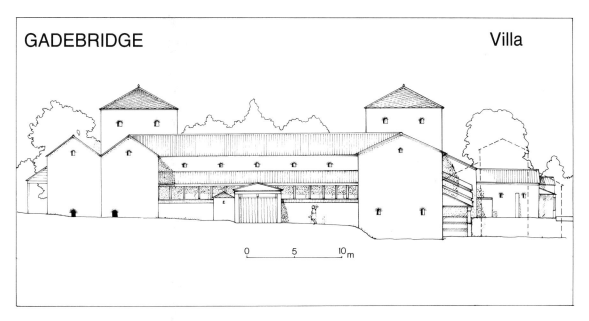

GADEBRIDGE   Villa

0   5   10 m

126 Façade of the villa at Gadebridge Park, Hertfordshire, looking north (periods 5-6, *c.* 300-350; based on drawings by Neal). Another long period site Gadebridge Park seems to have developed from a late-first-century wooden house with detached bath-house into a very substantial variation on the winged-corridor type in the fourth century. The house at this date was set into a slope and may have had towers at either end of the main range. However, the bath-suite had become so elaborate, incorporating a swimming pool (on the very far right), that the excavator has suggested this had become the primary feature of the settlement, which may have operated as a commercial spa. If so it is possible that there was a ritual or cultic element to the site. However, there is no evidence of Roman date for this, and the lack of pre-Roman evidence for the sanctity of the site (as at Bath and Harlow for example) reinforces the possibility that it was more recreational than religious. Interestingly the whole house had been demolished by *c.* 350, but occupation centred on an outbuilding continued into succeeding decades with cattle stockades (?) built over the site of the former main house.

number of rooms. More modest houses might have only a single mosaic, if they had one at all. So the idea that such decorations were commonplace is completely false. The houses which had them tend to be among the more architecturally interesting ones which is why more have been dealt with here.

Not all villas ended up as such extravagant houses. The modest house at Brixworth undoubtedly underwent alterations and extensions but it was little bigger than its original size (fig. 94). The constraints on the site at Lullingstone have already been mentioned. The winged-corridor villa at Frocester was only built in the late third century (and resembles in plan the much earlier house at Plaxtol, fig. 96). By the late fourth century little had altered apart from the addition of a bath-suite. The sprawling house at Rockbourne was never particularly lavish – it had few mosaics and a modest bath-suite (fig. 128) and the impression is more of a working farm than a luxurious country residence.

The distribution of houses

The villas of Roman Britain are found mostly in the lowland zone because, being principally associated with exploiting land, they were bound to reflect the distribution of superior agricultural areas. There were rural settlements in the north of course but presumably the poorer land was less likely to yield the kind of surplus which would fund the building of a better house. Such northern settlements were also less likely to have the advantages of being close to a town, though these are of course as much a consequence of rural settlement as a cause. There are a very few, for example at Maiden Castle outside the modern city of Durham, and the large estate at Llantwit

127 Baths at Bignor, room 55a (cold plunge bath), in the south-east corner of the building. The bath-suite belonged to the fourth-century expansion of the villa which grew from a winged-corridor house into a substantial courtyard house. The baths themselves underwent considerable alterations. The photograph shows the hills of the South Downs to the south which not only provided a natural boundary for the villa estate but were also crossed by Stane Street running from London to Chichester. (Photo: author, 1989.)

Major in south Wales (fig. 101).

Despite this general view villas are distributed unevenly in the south with pockets of concentration and other areas where they are virtually absent. The forests of the Weald of Sussex and Kent are particularly noticeable. The houses at Ashtead and Bignor are amongst comparatively few, which contrasts with the dense concentration of houses in the Darenth and Medway valleys in north Kent. Further north the Fenland had been extensively drained during the Roman period and, although there was a steady growth of village-type settlements from the early second century on, none of the individual farms appear to have developed into substantial houses. This factor, the reclamation works and the remarkable buildings at Stonea (fig. 72) and Castor (fig. 73) all suggest that the whole area was an imperial estate run for the benefit of the state. Under such conditions farmers, who were probably tenants, would have had no opportunity to accumulate wealth in property. A similar situation probably prevailed on Salisbury Plain where small, native-type farmsteads of clustered round-houses exist but no villas.

The largest concentrations of villas were in the Mendips and Cotswolds. Along the River Windrush in Oxfordshire and Gloucestershire for example there are a large number of villas and settlements separated by only 3-5km (2-3miles) at the most, with more to the north clustered around the general path taken by Akeman Street, for example Stonesfield. Other clusters exist around Cirencester, Bath, Water Newton,

Verulamium and Leicester. There are very few examples of villas which are immediately in the vicinity of town walls, though there is usually one, and this suggests that most of the land around towns was owned and farmed by the townspeople. Where such a house does exist, like Gorhambury to the west of Verulamium, it may represent the privileged estate of a particularly important person in the town.

The late fourth and fifth centuries

The period of Roman Britain's decline lasted from the late fourth century until well into the fifth, a period of at least three generations or more. During that time occupation of Roman-type houses seems to have ceased. Settlement of many towns and almost all villas is no longer detectable through conventional artefactual evidence. Traditionally this was associated with the province being overrun periodically by bands of raiders from northern Britain, northern Germany, Denmark and Ireland, particularly during the 'barbarian conspiracy' of 367. The significance of such references was much exaggerated – St Patrick's account of his life

128 The north wing of the villa at Rockbourne showing the octagonal plunge bath attached to the *frigidarium*. This bath-suite was added in *c.* 300 to a house which began life in the second century replacing a first-century predecessor and a late-Iron Age circular house. It was gradually extended to surround a courtyard with three wings, though these were not continuous. Despite its size the building does not seem to have been particularly luxurious and this may reflect its relatively isolated position on the edge of the New Forest, though the setting must have been as enviable as it still is. Nevertheless it had carved stone finials on its roof and amongst the finds was a carved stone table. In its final phase the house seems to have become derelict and eventually it collapsed. (Photo: author, 1989.)

implies that villa owners were continuing to run their estates at least up to *c.* 430, even if they had to suffer the privations caused by intermittent raids. Altogether the evidence was generally interpreted as a violent threat that permanently disrupted the socio-economic structure on which both towns and villas depended as well as eventually resulting in the physical destruction of houses.

There is a certain amount of evidence for the violent destruction of some houses. For example the villa at Brislington in Avon seems to have been destroyed by the late fourth century. Traces of fire are not conclusive on their own, but the fact that the remains of four or five people and a dozen cattle were thrown down the well does suggest that the destruction was caused by a third party. At Keynsham, also in Avon, fire destruction at some time during the fourth century was associated with a wall collapsing and burying an individual whose remains were not recovered. It is extremely difficult to attribute these events, which are only examples amongst many, to specific incidents; they may be just symptomatic of a protracted period of instability. But the period concerned is quite a long one – plenty of time for isolated and unrelated incidents to take place. There are all sorts of possible situations which might result in localized damage: farm-workers responding to years of supervision by a cantankerous foreman, a dropped oil-lamp or even over-heated hay in a tinder-dry wooden barn. Just because we do not have specific evidence of such incidents does not mean that we have an obligation to associate the destruction of a house (or anywhere else for that matter) with the historical references that we do possess. Who, after all, would have guessed that London burned down in 1666 because someone forgot to put a fire out in a bakery if it was not a recorded fact?

But many houses show decline of a more innocuous kind, and it may be more appropriate to look at how the fires or structural decay were *not* followed by repair or reconstruction – this is a much more important perspective. At Keynsham the fire was followed by re-occupation but of a much more low-key nature: a rough hearth platform was laid over the fire debris and a mosaic in a corridor. But this is unusual, more often such damage was simply followed by abandonment. The techniques of construction seem to have been neither available nor desired.

Lullingstone burnt down in the fifth century and was just never rebuilt, despite the presence of a house church which one might have thought would create a kind of vested local community interest in repairing, or at least replacing, the building. Instead the site was abandoned, possibly passing into local lore, and eventually a Saxon church was built over the adjacent 'Temple-Mausoleum'. At Gadebridge Park the substantial fourth-century house was demolished by the mid fourth century, and enclosures marked by post-holes were built across the site. A single small two-roomed outbuilding originally put up around 300 remained in use possibly into the fifth century. This is an interesting case of what seems to be sub-Roman activity during the Roman period, but it may be that the estate had become part of another, unidentified, villa estate. Some villa estates have produced evidence of fifth-century and later occupation in the form of grass-tempered pottery, for example Frocester and Barnsley in Gloucestershire. However, this kind of material is normally associated with fields around the old houses rather than the structures themselves. In any case it is fairly self-evident that the population would have had to feed themselves anyway so it should come as no great surprise that fields were still used in some shape or form, even if the houses were not.

In the towns decay may have been held off longer – some houses in Verulamium were occupied well into the fifth century. One particularly well-known example in Insula xxvii was built in or after 370; subsequent alterations included the laying of mosaics which eventually wore out, one being cut for the installation of a corn-drying oven. Eventually (the time scale is unknown) the house was demolished and built over with a masonry hall which was itself demolished and a water pipe laid across the site. At Cirencester one of the houses in Insula xii mentioned above, built only by the late fourth century, functioned long enough for structural alterations to take place including laying a hypocaust and a new mosaic over another mosaic. This kind of evidence and the presence of a substantial timber public (?) building at Wroxeter (fig. 74) suggests an organized community living, probably in houses, at least into the early fifth century and possibly running on for several decades after the formal end of the province.

Ultimately all these arguments depend on

isolated excavations, many conducted in a period when techniques were not developed enough to identify occupation in periods when artefacts had become rare. The only common thread which ties all the evidence together is that by the late fifth century all traces of occupation of Romano-British type houses had ceased and certainly no new ones were being built. Now, obviously there was a population and it was living somewhere: evidence of this period has been found in early Anglo-Saxon villages like Mucking in Essex or the re-occupation of some hillforts like South Cadbury. Some villa estates, like Orton Hall Farm, near Peterborough, remained in occupation, albeit of a distinctly less romanized nature. But the villas and town houses of Roman Britain belonged to a redundant, if more sophisticated, architectural form: there is practically no evidence of structural continuity into the late fifth century and beyond for domestic buildings of Roman date in Britain.

5

SACRED SITES

Introduction

Religious or ritual activity is a fundamental need of all human societies but it is never quite so clear where religion begins or ends. We live in a more secular age so it can sometimes be difficult to appreciate fully how much cult and culture are the same thing. Conversely it can be easy to use religion as a convenient repository or descriptive term for any artefact or building whose purpose is not otherwise immediately obvious, and archaeologists are often accused of doing this.

But with Roman Britain we are on slightly firmer ground than we are with the anonymity of prehistory or post-Roman times. Inscribed altars and votive gifts make some buildings and associated structures obviously religious in intent. In other cases, especially classical-style temples, the architecture alone makes the intention clear. The range of Romano-British buildings which can be associated with cults is very broad and some are amongst the most interesting of all the structures covered in this book.

Temple types

Most temples were associated with precincts and outbuildings, though excavations, particularly earlier ones, do not always include these. In fact the plan of a temple in isolation is almost certainly misleading – they should normally be seen as components of a religious zone. In towns like Verulamium, or special places like Gosbecks near Colchester, this extended to including theatres which were closely associated with religious rituals. Temples themselves were not generally devised as buildings for the public performance of ritual and so were private and enclosed. Public ritual was generally performed outside around an altar. There are exceptions, and the most obvious of these are temples associated with exclusive eastern mystery cults, especially Mithraism. These are almost invariably isolated structures which were self-contained.

The types of precincts and associated buildings are very varied and reflect the type of cult and its location. Where a temple was located within a town like Verulamium the precinct, or *temenos*, was usually marked out with some sort of wall, perhaps colonnaded. This could be very modest in extent, for example the 'Triangular Temple' (fig. 129), or even be large enough to accommodate more than one temple, as at Springhead (fig. 130). Such precincts focused attention on the main altar. At Colchester's Temple of Claudius, the altar seems to have been a substantial example, in keeping with the outright classicism of the temple itself (figs. 131, 132). In rural areas temples might be associated with a scatter of buildings – the roadside Shrine of Apollo at Nettleton is a particularly good example (fig. 150). In these cases it is not quite so clear where the precinct began and ended, though the neat symmetrical lay-out at Harlow shows that careful planning was possible even where there were no urban buildings to impose a constraint (fig. 139). Some sites may have served for occasional fairs, attracting traders and customers alike from a wide area. At Lamyatt Beacon in Somerset the temple was sited on the narrow crest of a steep hill, and apart from a single outbuilding there seems to have been little more (fig. 151).

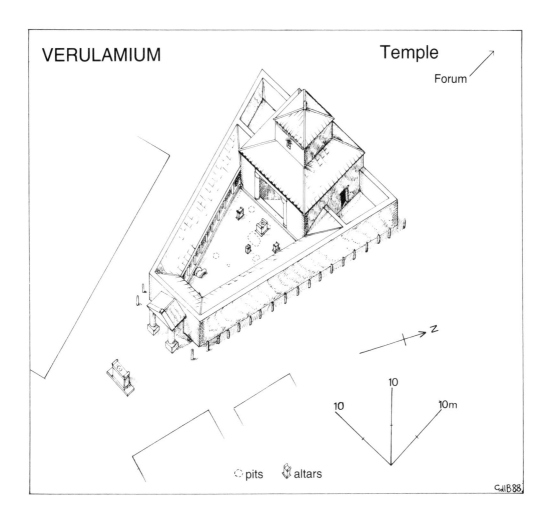

129 Verulamium, the 'Triangular Temple' Insula vii (axonometric reconstruction). Watling Street, running north from London, entered Verulamium at an angle to the established street grid, creating an intersection where the so-called 'Triangular temple' was built.

The building resembles more conventional temples in Britain, for example at Harlow (see fig. 139). The cella was surrounded by an ambulatory extended to flank the colonnaded open court in front of the building where public ritual activities took place. At some point the external wall was painted red. The cella was flanked by two rooms both of which contained water tanks; they may have acted as additional cellas, possibly left open to catch water. In front of the porch entrance to the enclosure was a chalk foundation which may have supported an altar. The only serious anomaly with other temples is the way in which the temple lies so far back in the enclosure; however, bearing in mind the peculiarities of the location, this is almost certainly just a practical solution to a practical problem. It was built around the beginning of the second century.

Excavation revealed a number of pits containing animal bones including an ox skull behind an altar. Many miniature pots were also found and several bases may have supported altars and/or statues of the gods or goddesses. There was no specific evidence for the deity (or deities) worshipped here, but it has been suggested that the water tanks (for ritual purification), and carbonized pine cones, indicate an oriental cult. This may have been the cult of Cybele and Atys, or even Bacchus with whom pine cones were also associated, but this is purely speculative and we should not discount the possibility of local gods being involved as well. Nevertheless there seems to have been a guild of *dendrophori* ('branch-bearers' attached to the Cybele cult) in the vicinity. The temple probably fell out of use in the fourth century.

The peculiar nature of this building makes it difficult to reconstruct and there are a number of different ways of doing this. This version is based on the conventional Romano-Celtic temple, roofed accordingly.

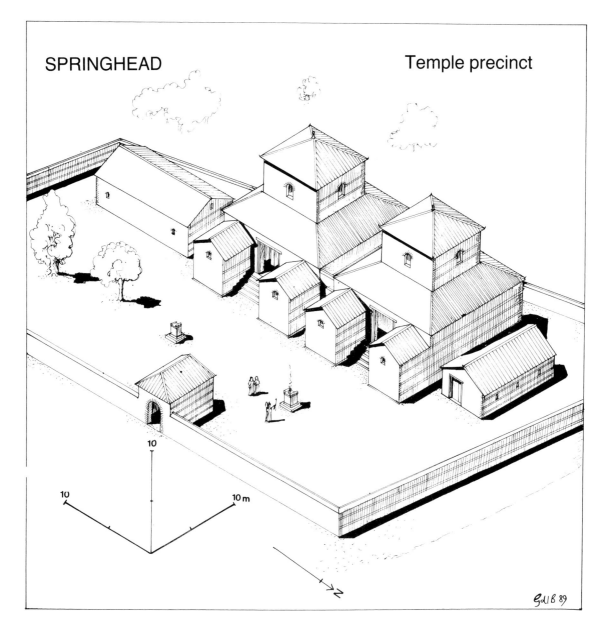

SPRINGHEAD

Temple precinct

130 The temple precinct at Springhead, Kent (isometric reconstruction), an important stopping point on a journey to London. The spring almost certainly had pre-Roman religious significance. Although the site is now crossed by the dual carriageway of the A2 trunk road and a disused railway embankment it is still possible to appreciate that the place must have originally been convivial and intimate. The two Romano-Celtic temples visible here are known as Temples III and II respectively (left to right). They succeeded an earlier temple, Temple I, which lay to the south-west of Temple II. The presence of projecting wings has been taken to indicate that the ambulatory walls were solid. That there were windows in the cellas is suggested by the fact that an iron window grille was recovered from Temple II. The precinct boundary is known but the siting of the altars shown is hypothetical.

131 Façade of the Temple of Claudius at Colchester, Essex, about the mid-first century, looking north. The core of its podium survives beneath the eleventh-century castle keep and was identified by Wheeler and

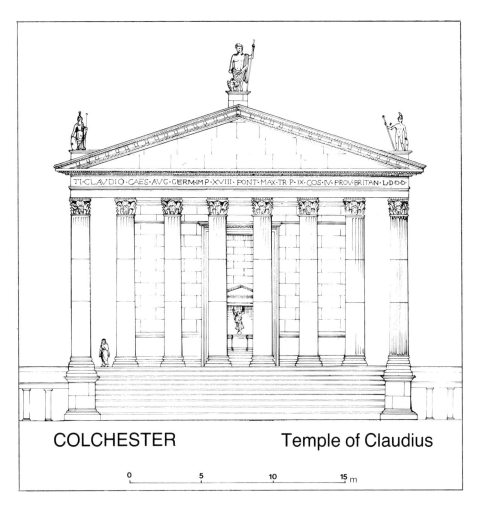

TI·CLAVDIO·CAES·AVG·GERM·IMP·P·XVIII·PONT·MAX·TR·P·IX·COS·IV·PROV·BRITAN·L·D·D·D

COLCHESTER **Temple of Claudius**

0   5   10   15 m

Laver in 1920 who showed that the vaults were structurally separate from the castle walls. There are four rectangular vaults built in pairs whose relative proportions suggest those of a classical temple's *cella* and *pronaos*.

It is clear that we cannot now be certain of the dimensions of the Roman temple. The podium survives to nearly 3.5m (11ft) above the Roman ground level and was probably about 32 x 24m (105 x 79ft). It seems likely that the temple was surrounded by 36 Corinthian columns, eight at each end, though there was a second row at the pronaos.

In front of the temple there was an altar, as was customary. It stood on a podium which was approximately 10m (33ft) wide and was surrounded by the pedestal bases of statues. Traces of the precinct have been identified; combined with the street plan of Roman Colchester they indicate that it was about 150 x 120m (492 x 393ft).

The reconstruction here is imaginative but is based on standard proportions and decorations of classical temples though no exact detail is known. There may

have been a series of sculptures within the pediment, probably illustrating the conquest of Britain. Fragments of marble and limestone veneers found on the site suggest that the building was impressively decorated.

Tacitus says the temple was dedicated to the divine Claudius. Claudius died in 54, just six years before the Boudican Revolt when the temple was destroyed. It seems unlikely that the temple could have been built in six years and so it is more probable that the first temple was begun well before 54 and subsequently re-dedicated. The inscription shown here, again hypothetical, lists Claudius' titles for the year 49-50 and represents the building as it may have appeared some time in the 50s. It would have been re-built after 60. It has been suggested recently that in the late Roman period the temple was demolished. Traces of reconstruction bear comparison with government audience halls known at Trier, and in fact many traces of the more exotic stones on the site seem to belong solely to this phase.

169

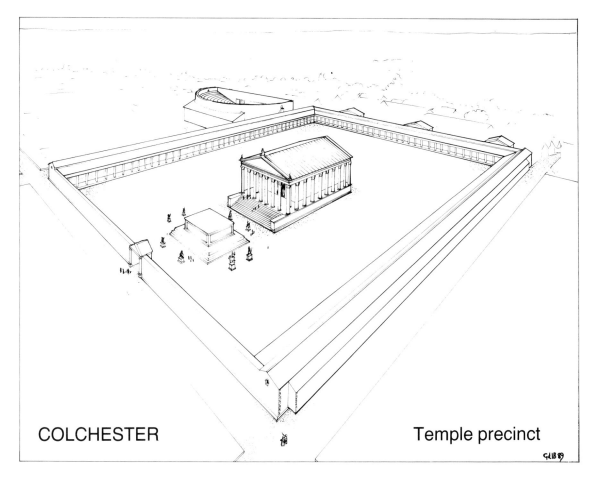

COLCHESTER   Temple precinct

132 The temple precinct at Colchester, Essex. This shows the classical style temple within a colonnaded precinct (see fig. 131 for the temple façade). Note the large scale of the altar which is based on excavated evidence. Much of the rest of this reconstruction is hypothetical but the theatre is shown in its correct position adjacent to the precinct.

Classical temples

There are very few certain examples of classical temples in Roman Britain. In general those which are known seem to have been founded in the first century, apart from the recent discovery at York, but underwent considerable alterations in succeeding periods. Only the celebrated Temple of Sulis-Minerva at Bath is known in any architectural detail even though very little of the actual building has been explored.

Impressive though it must have been, the Bath temple would have seemed tiny compared to the arrogant magnificence of the Temple of Claudius at Colchester. This temple's existence is mentioned by Tacitus in his account of the Revolt of Boudica so we know that it must have been in existence by 60, though it may very well have still been under construction. Had it survived, even in a ruinous state, to early modern times this temple would bear comparison with some of the more famous ruins in France, Italy and North Africa. However, it does not, and we are left with the circumstantial evidence of its vaults which now form the substructure of the eleventh-century Norman castle.

The Temple of Claudius seems to have stood in a monumental precinct which befitted its status as the home of the imperial cult of Claudius, conqueror of Britain (figs. 131, 132, plate 6). It was an outright political statement and there is little likelihood that it was sited on a place of pre-Roman religious importance. The site at Gosbecks to the south of the settlement probably marks this – it grew to have both a Romano-Celtic temple and a theatre. The temple at Bath is of particular interest because of its association with the sacred spring of Sulis and the substantial suite of baths which was developed. This gave the town its name, *Aquae Sulis* – ancient temples were generally sited somewhere for a specific purpose, usually because the site had a traditional status as the home of a god, perhaps a minor local one. It was Roman policy to tolerate, synthesize and absorb local cults. Thus a Celtic sacred grove, tree, pool or spring was often transformed into a place where a god could boast more than just a name. The temple and its altar became the

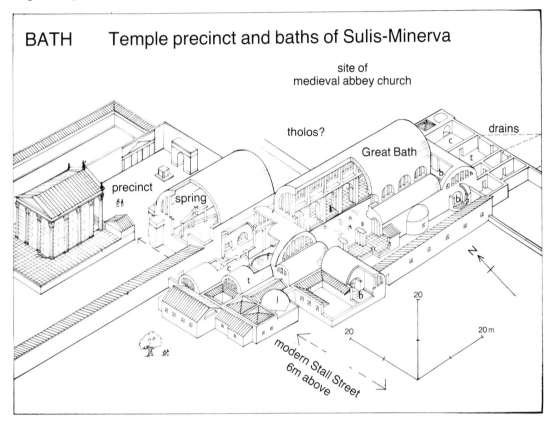

133 The temple and bath complex at Bath looking north-east in its final, fourth-century phase (after Ronayne but adapted and extended). Although much of the temple precinct remains unexplored, as does the area to the north-east of the baths (which lies under the medieval abbey), the bath complex and spring are now well-known.

The focal point was the sacred spring where the hot water emerges at a temperature of 46.5°C (125°F) from underground. It had been a place of great importance for generations. When the site was developed by the Romans the spring had to be harnessed to supply the baths. A reservoir was built of stone walls on timber piles and lined with lead. By the early third century the reservoir had been roofed with a vault (as had the Great Bath – see figs. 10, 11).

The baths form the largest part of the religious complex. They were built around the Great Bath, a lead-lined swimming pool. Water was supplied from the spring except for the western suite (nearest the viewer – these were heated with furnaces). The water passed through a series of pipes and drains supplying the various rooms and pools. On the eastern side they all joined together and the water ran off into the River Avon.

The extent of the site can be appreciated from the drawing, emphasizing the wealth of the site and the numbers of people who must have visited it. Some fragmentary structural evidence suggests that a circular temple, a *tholos*, may have been situated to the east, under the medieval abbey. There was almost certainly a theatre nearby. The known buildings dominate the town centre, so it seems likely that the walls contained little more than the baths, its temples and theatre, accommodation for pilgrims and the homes of those who worked there.

171

BATH   Temple

134 The Temple of Sulis-Minerva at Bath. This perspective view shows the temple as it may have appeared shortly after construction in the late first century. The façade of the temple is known from collapsed fragments (see fig. 135), but apart from its basic dimensions the appearance of the rest of the building is unknown. The statues on top of the pediment are hypothetical, but likely, accessories.

This type with a pediment supported by four columns is known as 'tetrastyle'. As the diameters of the base (about 9m/29ft) and the columns (about 0.8m/2.6ft) are known it can be shown that this example is built in the 'sistyle' version (where the gap between the columns is equal to twice the diameter of a column).

The height of the columns is not so certain, and in fact there is a certain amount of variation in surviving temples. Vitruvius said that the ideal for a tetrastyle temple with sistyle divisions is a height nine and a half times the diameter – the conventional reconstruction (see Cunliffe, 1984, fig. 14) shows this. However, the product is a building which appears a little high for its width so this reconstruction shows columns equal to about eight times the diameter (as with the Temple of Fortuna Virilis in Rome). Either alternative may be correct, or something in between. A single surviving capital from one of the columns shows that they were carved in Composite style (adapting elements from the Corinthian and Ionic orders).

172

focus of ritual, and other buildings may have housed priests or pilgrims. The god then became the subject of carved reliefs and statues.

At Bath this took a particularly dramatic form. The nature of the hot spring and the huge quantities of healing water which were produced meant that engineering works were needed to control and channel the supply. The spring itself was given a stone-built pool which created a head of water to supply the baths. The commercial possibilities were huge, and whatever the religious nature of the site there is absolutely no doubt that those who controlled the spring and

the baths must have stood to make a great deal of money. From an architectural point of view the peculiar nature of the site produced a curiously quaint and cluttered temple precinct. Despite being several metres below modern street level Bath has been the subject of numerous excavations since the nineteenth century, and the site is now known in tantalizing detail. Cunliffe's recent excavations have made sense of the large and complicated site, and it is now possible to appreciate some of the history of the site as well as actually walk through the temple precinct itself (figs. 133-8, plate 11).

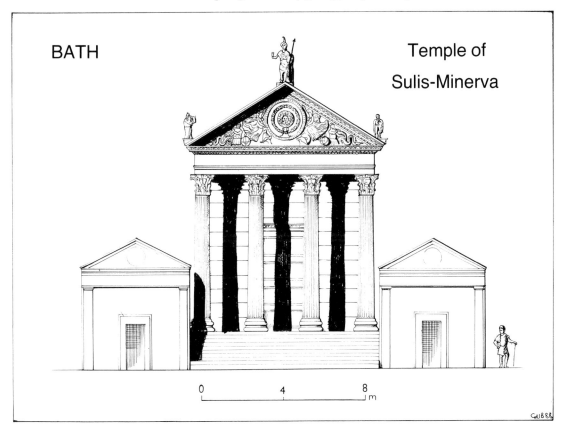

135 Façade of the Temple of Sulis-Minerva at Bath (adapted and extended from Cunliffe) in its final phase during the fourth century looking west.

Much is known about the pediment sculptures and these have been reconstructed from the surviving fragments (see *Finds*, fig. 82). The most important feature is the overtly Celtic nature of the central face juxtaposed with the classical references to Minerva around it. Behind the porch with its columns lay the cella in which the cult statue was probably stored. This was reached through a doorway, reconstructed here,

though as with all ancient sanctuaries public rituals took place on the altar which lay outside.

By *c.* 200 the precinct was substantially altered: a number of sculptured façades and structural additions were made around the precinct. The podium of the temple was enlarged to create a raised area around the building which enclosed a new set of steps. These steps, heavily worn by the steps of pilgrims, are the only part of the temple visible *in situ*. Two small 'chapels' were incorporated into the new podium on either side of the steps. Their form is uncertain.

173

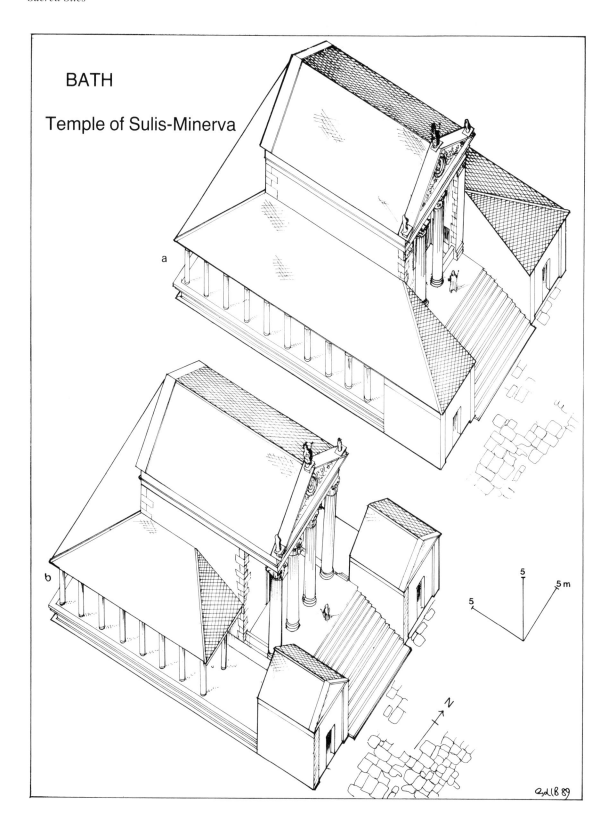

BATH

Temple of Sulis-Minerva

136 ◄ The Temple of Sulis-Minerva at Bath, final phase. Cunliffe has argued that the expansion of the temple podium may have involved surrounding the temple with an ambulatory. This creates certain problems particularly if the flanking chapels are given normal pitched roofs. There are parallels for such ambulatories which convert a classical temple into a Romano-Celtic temple, for example the Temple of Lenus-Mars at Trier (for a reconstruction see Ward-Perkins, 1981, 229, fig. 139b). These two illustrations give two possibilities for Bath though neither are particularly satisfactory either aesthetically or practically.

137 ▼ The Temple precinct at Bath in the fourth century (axonometric reconstruction; based on views by S. Gibson, but adapted). Very little is known of the buildings' superstructure and much shown here is hypothetical (see plate 11).

The precinct is dominated by the covered sacred spring. The roof is shown broken away in order to reveal the spring itself within. In the south wall three windows (two of which have survived complete) allowed pilgrims and dedicants to hurl their offerings to the goddess of the waters. A number of statues may have stood around in the water. The vaulted cover building was put up in the late second century, or early third century (the huge buttresses were put up later – see fig. 138); parts of it were found in the spring where it had collapsed in post-Roman times. Prior to that the spring was probably open to the sky though Roman engineers in the late first century had enclosed it to form a walled pool. This created the necessary head of water to supply the baths.

In the middle of the precinct itself the base of the altar has been found *in situ* (see fig. 138). The modern visitor to the site is currently able to enter the precinct at the west, just between the temple and the western buttress. The steps of the temple are visible in a recess in walls which support modern levels above. The raised walkway then runs along the precinct between the altar and the porch.

The temple itself is shown with pilasters around the cella, an alternative to fig. 134.

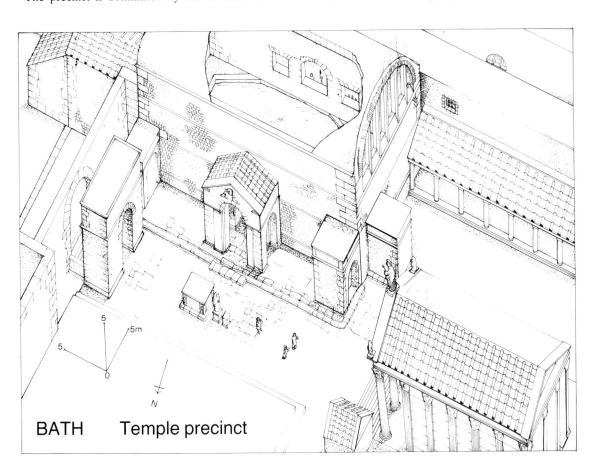

BATH   Temple precinct

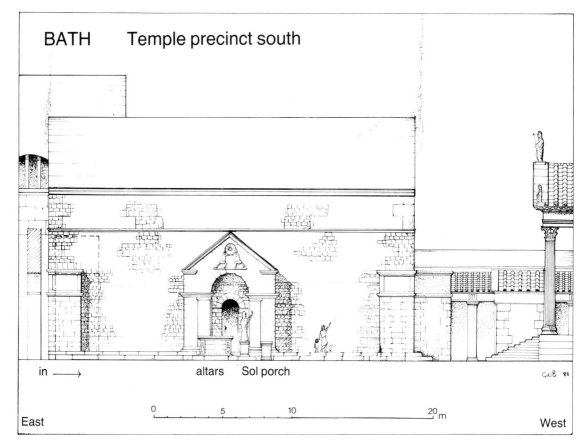

BATH   Temple precinct south

in ⟶   altars   Sol porch

GdlB 88

East

0   5   10   20 m

West

138 The temple precinct at Bath looking south. The view is taken from a line running continuously with the north side of the temple cella. The main feature is the north wall of the building covering the sacred spring. The spring was enclosed and covered somewhere around the late second century. Access to the precinct was through the little door just visible in the centre beneath the Sol porch.

The vault of the spring cover-building created lateral forces too great for the massive walls of the cover-building to bear. By the early fourth century the northeast corner had given way.

Three massive buttresses were added on the north wall, and one on the west. The central northern buttress was constructed as a porch to the spring, with entrances on the west, east and north. It seems to have been decorated with a pair of water nymphs holding up a bust of the sun god, Sol, though the surviving pieces are very fragmentary. The buttresses on either side were probably plain, but the north-west one may have incorporated an arch. However, as so little remained, it is quite possible that the buttresses may have been part of a much more complicated façade, perhaps including a vaulted portico. The reconstruction shows those components which are certain (though not necessarily their exact form). It seems to have been balanced by a façade depicting the moon-goddess, Luna, on the northern side of the precinct (not shown).

Between these façades stood the main altar – the focal point of public ritual. Two of the corner slabs, decorated with Jupiter and Hercules, and Bacchus and an unknown female deity, have been located on the site. A third depicting Apollo and an unknown god was removed in the Middle Ages and built into the church at Compton Dando about 13km (8 miles) away. The plinth of the altar was found *in situ*. Immediately to the west of the altar stood a statue base dedicated to the goddess Sulis ('DEAE SULI') by the augurer ('HARUSP[EX]'), Lucius Marcus Memor.

The precinct was entered by an arch to the east, indicated here by a dotted line. In the background on the left can be seen the vault of the Great Bath, and behind the temple to the south can be seen the portico surrounding the temple.

Other classical temples are known to have existed elsewhere, for example at London adjacent to the Flavian forum and at Wroxeter. Neither is known in any detail and they were obviously modest structures. However, it is virtually certain that more existed epecially at London and in the other major cities such as Cirencester. Hadrian visited Britain early in his reign and may have been involved with the construction of London's second-period basilica and forum. Whether or not he was, it is likely that some sort of temple would have been dedicated as a commemorative gesture. If so it may have been a circular classical temple, known as a *tholos*, which would have suited Hadrian's penchant for Greek styles. Remains of the entablature from such a building have been found at Bath but its site is unknown. A temple to Diana is known to have existed at the legionary fortress of Caerleon because an ansate tablet commemorates its restoration around the middle of the third century. The dedication was by the legion's legate, Postumius Varus, who was eventually promoted to be prefect of Rome (Appendix 2). All this suggests that it was likely to be classical in form but it has not yet been found. The structural remains of several buildings at Corbridge have been interpreted as temples. Some of these were almost certainly classical in form. The exciting remains of a classical style temple were discovered in York in 1989 and were associated with extensive remains of cult activity including votive coins scattered around the base of a statue plinth outside the temple and a number of ritual pits containing animal remains within the temple. The building seems to have been put up by the 180s but was wrecked by fire within a generation. It was subsequently reconstructed and a monumental gateway was added to the precinct.

Romano-Celtic temples

Much more common than classical temples in Roman Britain were the so-called Romano-Celtic temples. These temples are found in Gaul as well and they form a distinctive regional form of religious architecture. None seems to have had political foundations, but many, other than those found within towns, seem attributable to a pre-Roman cult and sacred place.

The excavated plans of these buildings are usually very simple, amounting to no more than two concentric squares. The term 'Romano-Celtic temple' was coined by Mortimer Wheeler in a study of the temple at Harlow (fig. 139). He was interested in a series of temples with square or rectangular plans which contained an inner chamber and a concentric outer one. The inner is normally interpreted as the sanctuary (*cella*) and the outer as an ambulatory or series of rooms. Wheeler noted that there were other temples which followed a similar pattern but which had circular or polygonal plans. It seems quite reasonable to consider them altogether because they probably belong to the same general type of building. Even so buildings with very similar plans are found in different contexts, and the modern enthusiasm for classifying according to the available information has led to the assumption that all such plans must belong to the same kind of building. The so-called 'Temple-Mausoleum' at Lullingstone (fig. 100) is one of better-known examples though it is apparent from the site report that there was no evidence to support the idea either that it was a religious shrine or it looked like what we assume a Romano-Celtic temple to have done (see Chapter 6).

Romano-Celtic temples are mainly distributed in central and northern France and Britain. This suggests in itself that they may belong to an earlier tradition because much of the material of Roman date from these sites has a very distinctive regional flavour. A very important discovery was made at Heathrow (on the site of the airport) of a late Iron Age (or possible early Romano-British) building of similar plan but built in timber. A similar example is also known from South Cadbury in Somerset. A circular Romano-British temple built over an Iron Age penannular ditched structure at Frilford in Berkshire emphasizes the point of continuity though neither the Heathrow nor the South Cadbury examples were built over in this way. At Hayling Island an Iron Age wooden circular temple was succeeded by a very early-Roman stone temple built on the same plan immediately above (fig. 140). It seems likely that the Romano-Celtic temple grew out of local tradition, though being stone they are far better preserved and far more are known. It may well be that closer examination of stone examples of Roman date might reveal pre-Roman buildings beneath, but this would involve some destruction of higher levels.

HARLOW

Temple

139 The temple (of Minerva?) at Harlow, Essex in its final phase. The Harlow site seems to have been sacred in the pre-Roman period as the Bronze Age burials and large numbers of late Iron Age coins found here testify. Recent re-excavation has revealed an Iron Age round-house within the temple precinct. The site itself occupies the brow of a small low hill which rises only about 6m (19ft) above the flood plain of the River Stort – it may have been regarded as a sacred wood, perhaps centred on a particular tree.

In the late first century the cella and ambulatory were put up, surrounded by a cobbled area. Later the rectangular area around the temple was enclosed with a timber palisade, probably with a dividing wall which ran in front of the temple.

By the early third century the complex had been improved. The timber palisades were replaced in stone and rooms were added to the temple building to bring

it up to the dividing wall. The open area seems to have had buildings added to the east and west walls (the division into rooms is hypothetical), and an imposing entrance added to the south wall. An altar base was found just outside the entrance to the temple. By the fourth century the site seems to have fallen into disuse. The building materials were probably used to help build the medieval church at nearby Latton.

The recent re-excavation of the site produced a large limestone head of Minerva which may have been the cult statue and a carving of a warrior god. Earlier excavations produced a fragment of an altar reading INI * A which is interpreted as reading NUM]INI · A[VGVSTORUM, 'the spirits of the emperors', but while this is perfectly normal for the Roman period it can hardly account for the site's original religious importance, which must, therefore, remain a mystery.

The plan of a Romano-Celtic temple is usually very simple, for example at Maiden Castle (figs. 141, 142), though the more ambitious projects like Nettleton had more complicated plans (figs. 147-9). On the whole the Romano-British examples are very poorly preserved, but fortunately evidence from the Continent is available to help reconstruct them. This includes a coin reverse (though this is rather dubious), a carved relief and the remarkably well-preserved remains of the so-called 'Temple of Janus' at Autun, near Dijon in France (fig. 143a-c). The cella at Autun still stands high enough to show that it was at least 13m (43ft) high, had three

---

140 Circular temple and temenos at Hayling Island, near Portsmouth, built *c*. 55-60 over an Iron Age shrine retaining the circular plan. The Iron Age shrine seems to have been built of timber, wattle and daub and was surrounded by a fenced courtyard.

The new temple was probably built of dressed local limestone and rendered internally and externally with painted wall-plaster. It had a porch though the entrance into the courtyard has not been certainly located. The temple entrance may actually have faced a large niche in the courtyard. The early date of the temple and the presence in the vicinity of the remarkable first-century house at Fishbourne suggests that the project was undertaken by either the Roman authorities or local Celtic aristocracy who were already influenced by Gallo-Roman tastes. The temple is certainly unusual for Britain though similar examples are known in Gaul.

The temple's later history is rather obscure though the porch was enlarged. Coin and pottery evidence, combined with traces of burning suggest that the temple was no longer in use by the early third century though sporadic finds of later date indicate that it was still visited. In post-Roman times the site seems to have been re-occupied by Saxon peoples. During this time and later stonework from the temple was almost entirely robbed out.

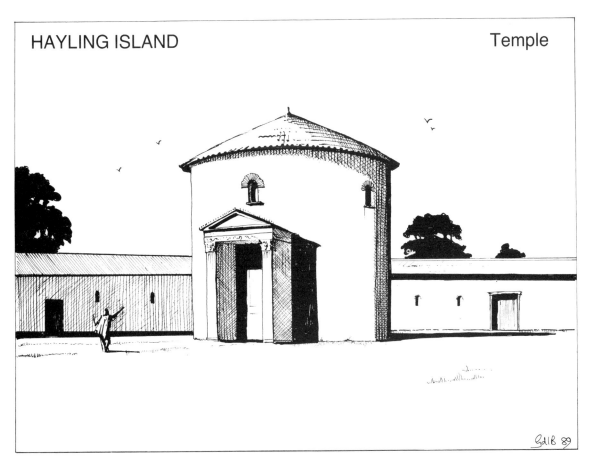

HAYLING ISLAND   Temple

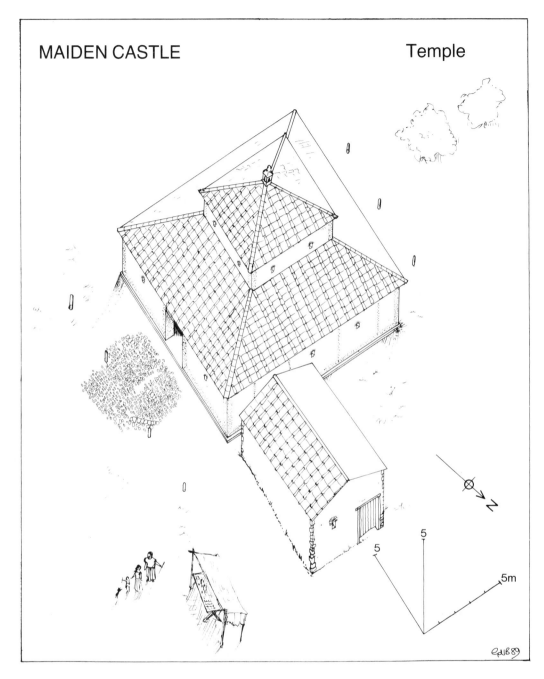

MAIDEN CASTLE   Temple

141 The late Romano-Celtic temple and 'priest's house' at Maiden Castle, Dorset (axonometric reconstruction). Built in the late fourth century on the north side of the Iron Age hill-fort, this temple is one of the best preserved in Britain (fig. 142). There were probably a number of deities worshipped here because the small finds indicate several different gods, for example Taurus Trigaranus (a Celtic bull-god), Minerva and Diana. In addition to the structures shown here an oval hut was identified nearby. Built of dry-stone walling the hut contained a large number of coins, pottery, a steelyard weight, a bronze statue base and a fragment of a marble statue of Diana. It is tempting to interpret this as the place where the enterprising establishment made its sales to pilgrims of various suitable souvenirs and votive gifts.

142 The temple at Maiden Castle today, looking south-east. See fig. 141. (Photo: author, 1989.)

windows in each side above the ambulatory and was built with decorative brickwork, though it was probably plastered over originally. Recesses in the cella wall about half way up show the height of the ambulatory roof and that it was pitched. The circular temple of Vesunna at Périgueux survives in a similar state. A few examples show that this Romano-Celtic external ambulatory with a lean-to roof could even be applied to classical temples, for example at the Temple of Lenus-Mars in the Altbachtal sanctuary of 70 temples at Trier. Together these pieces of evidence help to create an impression of a general type (fig. 144). There were exceptions, as there always are, for example the Hayling Island temple which seems to have lacked an ambulatory (fig. 140) and the temple at Uley where there was an ambulatory around three sides only (fig. 145). The late temple at Lydney Park resembles the Romano-Celtic type in certain respects but also has some similarity to basilican forms as well as a few quite individual features which set it apart from other temples (fig. 146).

While Romano-Celtic temples conformed to a similar pattern they most probably differed in detail. For example the ambulatory may have had a lean-to roof supported by columns sitting on an external dwarf wall, or it may have been solid – the latter would have been more secure. Sometimes the presence of columns or their remains may help, but the absence of columns may not be indicative either way. In fact, Romano-Celtic temple sites have yielded very little in the way of carved stonework. Nettleton is probably the most helpful site in this respect, where a number of dwarf columns and various other fittings were found. At other sites traces, if at all, tend to be fragmentary, for example at Pagans Hill where small pieces of columns were found in a nearby well – obviously one cannot even be certain that these came from the temple. The problem is unfortunately that this kind of material would have been particularly attractive to stone robbers and/or church builders in later periods, so we therefore can have no real idea of the original distribution of such material.

181

144 A typical Romano-Celtic temple showing suggested details of roofing.

143 ◄ Romano-Celtic temples – evidence from other sources (after Lewis):

a reverse of a *denarius* struck by Augustus between *c.* 29 and 27 BC depicting the façade of a building. It may represent a Romano-Celtic temple despite the apparent lack of a roof for the ambulatory. The coin was struck in the east but this would not have precluded showing a building found in the west. However, the coin is identified elsewhere as depicting the Curia Julia (the Senate house) in Rome which is perhaps a little more likely; the building, restored by Diocletian, still stands intact and the resemblance is considerable.

b restored elevation of the Temple of Janus at Autun (about 70km/45m south-west of Dijon in France). Much of the cella survives, and beam-holes exist to show where the ambulatory pentice roof was fitted.

c relief from Titelberg which may also depict a Romano-Celtic temple. Doubt has been expressed over what seems to be a lack of an ambulatory at the front but equally it could represent a temple with entrance-flanking annexes known in plan at a number of Romano-British sites, for example Springhead, fig. 130, and Lamyatt Beacon, fig. 151.

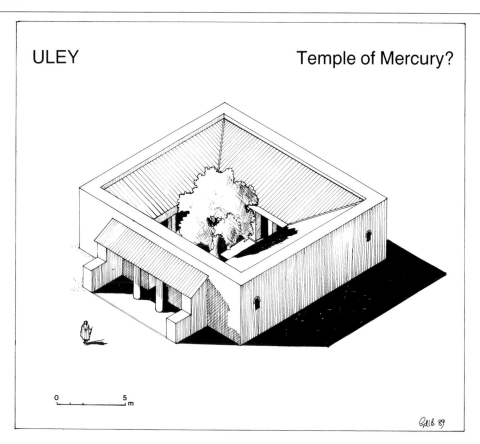

ULEY   Temple of Mercury?

0   5 m

145 ▲ Temple (of Mercury?) at West Hill, Uley, Gloucestershire. As with so many Romano-British temples this site seems to have been used for religious purposes in the late Iron Age. It remained in occupation, but by the fourth century the cult became centred on a new stone-built temple. It was not of conventional plan. The ambulatory surrounds only three sides and a separate porch appears to have formed the entrance. A pit in the cella contained several hundred coins. This may have contained water or even a sacred tree in which case the cella may have

been unroofed. However, with no provision for drainage it is hard to see how this would not have swiftly become a bog as rainwater accumulated. More than 200 curses have been found on the site which, along with a carved head of Mercury and two altars depicting him make it certain that he was the object of devotion here. Interestingly, despite the partial collapse of the temple *c.* 380 it remained in use and one subsequent structure built on the site resembles an early church.

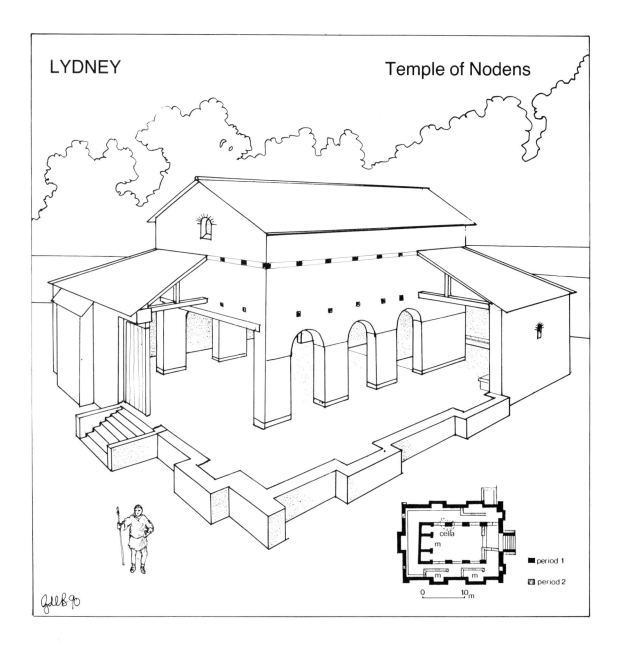

LYDNEY

Temple of Nodens

cella

m

m

m

■ period 1

▨ period 2

0   10m

146 The Temple of Nodens, at Lydney Park in Gloucestershire, period 1 (as built). The site of this shrine and its associated buildings were excavated in the 1920s by Wheeler following earlier efforts by antiquarians. Since then there has been a reassessment of the temple's date, but the site remains one of the best documented religious centres of Roman Britain.

The site of the shrine is an Iron Age promontory hill-fort on the western slopes of the Severn Valley. Until the late third/early fourth centuries the site was used for the extraction of iron ore. Then there was a dramatic change and the site became an important centre of a healing cult (period 1), which is curious because this was a time when pagan cults were generally in decline. Antiquarian records of a mosaic in the temple and a number of inscribed votive goods make it plain that the god concerned was called Nodens, associated with water, hunting and healing. His origins are obscure and it seems odd that, if he had local connections, his cult had been ignored at least since late prehistoric times. He was associated with Mars. It has been suggested that Nodens was 'imported' from Ireland and this would help explain the late date and the location.

Whatever the origins of Nodens, his temple at Lydney is architecturally unique though the plan seems to have been derived from the Romano-Celtic and basilican forms and measures 17m x 10m (56ft x 35ft). At the rear of the cella were three rooms where the cult statues or altars may have stood. In the first period the walls of the cella were supported on piers but unfortunately the builders and architect were unaware of a natural fault in the limestone which chanced to be beneath one of the piers. This 'swallow hole' gave way by the late 360s to early 370s and the pier above collapsed bringing down much of the temple's superstructure. The temple was rebuilt and this time the piers were incorporated into solid walls (period 2).

The cella mosaic no longer exists but an antiquarian drawing exists to show that it consisted of a scene of sea monsters, geometric motifs and a dedicatory inscription (see Appendix 2). The most important feature was an earthenware funnel, forming an integral feature of the design, which contained coins and a bronze dog (see *Finds*, fig. 101f).

Whether the temple had a clerestory or not is uncertain but had it not had one the cella would have had no source of light. It has also been pointed out that if the building had been roofed in a single span then the collapse of the swallow hole would have caused little damage, and merited limited structural alterations.

The most peculiar part of the temple's structure lies in the bays sited around the ambulatory. These project outwards providing recesses within and in the second phase three of these were partially enclosed to provide chambers with mosaic floors. Around part of the ambulatory a stone bench ran against the external wall.

It seems certain that the various buildings in the temple enclosure were intended to house pilgrims to the shrine. The largest is comparable to a courtyard house and lies next to a substantial bath-house. A range of rooms runs by the temple itself, perhaps for the devoted to sleep in whilst awaiting contact with Nodens.

The cella was probably taller than the ambulatory and was usually roofed (on the evidence of collapsed tiles). In Chapter 1 we saw how Romano-British architecture tended to be rather haphazard and how the result was a tendency to over-build in some places and under-build in others. Nettleton is an excellent example: it would be very easy to comment on the lack of external buttressing to support a central octagonal tower and reject this as a possibility (figs. 147-50). However there probably was a tower and precisely because of the lack of provision for the stresses involved it eventually fell down after a history of problems with inadequate internal walls (one only need look at the baths at Lufton villa, fig. 106, to see the kind of provision that might be necessary). In any case, as we have no idea of the timber content of upper parts of walls, we have no idea of the weight involved in any one instance.

The sheer simplicity of Romano-Celtic temples makes it impossible to date them according to their ground plans, and there seems to be no chronological pattern behind the various kinds of modifications which could be built in or added. The basic design seems to have been used almost throughout the period and often it is very difficult even to be certain where the entrance was – there was no specific orientation, though many seem to face east. The walls were almost invariably covered with painted wall-plaster, though none survives over a large enough area to draw up any kind of scheme of decoration. Flooring varied enormously from gravel, old roof-tiles and cement to, very occasionally, mosaics.

A number of 'cosmetic' variations to the plan are known. One of the most frequently encountered is the addition of wing rooms to one side of the temple, usually flanking the temple entrance, for example at Springhead and Lamyatt Beacon (figs. 130, 151, plate 12). In these cases such rooms would seem to preclude the possibility of a colonnaded ambulatory. The temple at Lamyatt Beacon also featured a semi-

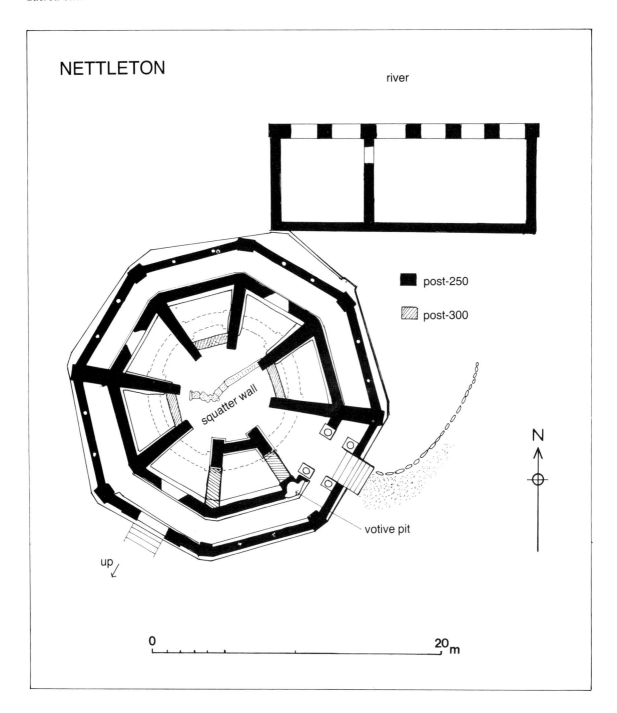

NETTLETON

river

■ post-250

▨ post-300

squatter wall

votive pit

N

up

0   20 m

147 Plan of the octagonal Shrine of Apollo at Nettleton, Wiltshire (after Wedlake). The site lies in a narrow valley which runs west to east crossed by the Fosse Way running north-south which was built *c.* 47. Pre-Roman occupation, probably of a religious nature, seems to have attracted Roman attention and on the higher ground to the south an early Roman ditched military (?) enclosure was built at the same time as the road.

By the Flavian period a small circular shrine had been erected on the slope running to the south bank of the stream about 100m west of the Fosse Way (Period 1). Its plan is indicated here by a dotted line within the later temple. Over the succeeding years the shrine was surrounded by various buildings which were probably designed to house the priests of the cult and serve the various needs of visitors; as the road was a major arterial route, running between Cirencester and Bath, there would probably have been many potential visitors.

By *c.* 230 the shrine was surrounded by an octagonal podium (Period 2) but by *c.* 250 it had been burnt down. It was replaced with a much more ambitious structure. The old octagonal podium was expanded, with a slight eccentricity, to abut a nearby building (Building VII – possibly a *schola* for an inner circle of devotees of the cult). The new temple (Period 3) consisted of a central octagonal cult chamber with a vaulted roof and eight, arched, doorways to eight flared side chambers (walls in black). One of these chambers acted as an entrance passage to the central area; some of the chambers seem to have had windows to the ambulatory. There are problems involved in reconstructing the temple's appearance at this stage (see figs. 148, 149). By *c.* 300+ there seems to have been concern about the building's safety and the two radial piers were replaced with walls. Other alterations involved strengthening walls and closing off four of the side chambers (hatched walls).

Curiously after *c.* 330 the nature of the site, which had become quite a cluster of buildings, seems to have altered from one of great religious veneration to a centre of light industry. Buildings were converted for the use of metal-workers. During this period the temple itself seems to have suffered partial collapse but by *c.* 360 a haphazard arrangement of building debris in the central chamber was used to create a dividing wall (dotted wall on plan). It seems that renewed pagan activity took place here until the remains of the temple's vaults finally came down (Period 5). The upstanding walls on the south side were used to form the basis of a late-fourth-century farmstead. Occupation on the site as a whole seems to have ceased in the early fifth century; a number of skeletons lying where they fell and bearing cut marks suggests violence.

subterranean room attached to the south wall of indeterminate purpose. At Caerwent, Temple I had an apse at the rear of the cella and a portico at its entrance (fig. 152, 153). Temple II at Springhead, instead of having a cella with solid walls, seems to have had one with eight piers. At Wood Lane End in Hertfordshire a particularly enigmatic site has been identified which seems to have involved a number of different types of building centred on a monumental structure which resembles a Romano-Celtic temple (fig. 154).

We even have little evidence of the gods worshipped at any particular site, and where we do have some idea it is clear that almost any god or any number of gods might have been the subject of devotion. Lamyatt Beacon produced a number of statuettes of classical gods, Uley seems to have been dedicated to Mercury, Harlow to Minerva (and possibly the *numen Augusti*), Nettleton to Apollo and Cunomaglos (a Celtic hound prince) – these are all assumptions based upon representations of deities and a few very rare inscriptions. Only one site appears to have been named for its temple – the fort at Bewcastle, north-west of Hadrian's Wall, which was probably called *Fanum Cocidii* according to the Ravenna List. This means 'the Temple of Cocidius' (Cocidius was a Celtic warrior god often associated with Mars). However, the temple building has not been found.

Romano-Celtic temples have been the subject of much debate precisely because it is so difficult to classify them in any kind of really convincing way. Lewis, who wrote the standard work for Romano-British temples of this kind, identified three broad possible variants: the tower cella with ambulatory (the orthodox reconstruction); the continuous roofed-type (a single roof covers cella and ambulatory); and the open cella type. However, we have contemporary evidence for only the first type and virtually none for either of the other two or his various sub-classifications which were divided up according to various combinations of solid and colonnaded walls. This is simply because almost all known examples do not stand above ground height, and no ancient descriptions exist.

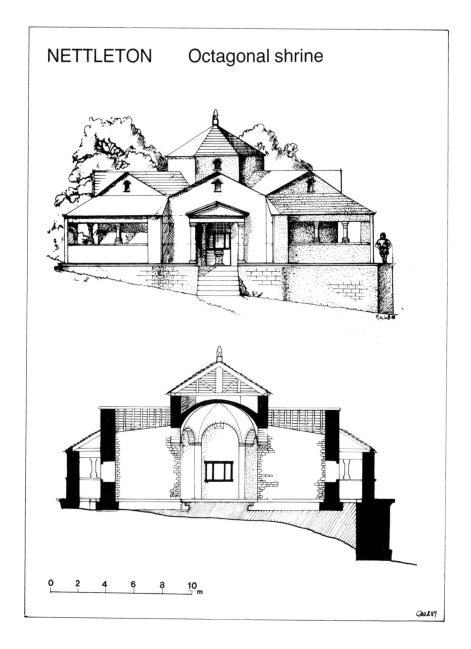

NETTLETON   Octagonal shrine

0 2 4 6 8 10 m

148 The octagonal shrine of Apollo at Nettleton, Wiltshire, as it may have appeared between *c.* 250 and 330, based on the excavator's reconstruction. The excavator believed these radial chambers had vaulted roofs, but during the preparations of these drawings it was found that not only would this be unique but is also extremely difficult to reconcile with the evidence. The radial walls do not increase enough in thickness to support a wider vault. A vault which becomes wider also becomes higher. This would be rather peculiar unless the radial walls became lower to compensate but this does not seem to have been the case. Octagonal buildings from elsewhere in the Empire, for example the Mausoleum of Galerius at Thessalonica, with vaulted radial chambers, have completely different ground plans. Their radial walls expand in order to create chambers with parallel walls thus avoiding expanding vaults for the chambers. This reconstruction therefore omits the radial vaults but retains the gable ends to the chambers. This is attractive but it is without parallel and still involves remarkably complex roofing. There seems to be no doubt that the central chamber

NETTLETON   Octagonal shrine

0   6 m

was vaulted.

At this period there were only six radial walls, the other two being piers (see plan, fig. 147). Around the whole there seems to have been a roofed ambulatory with open walls, the roof being supported on piers at the angle points. Subsequently the two open radial walls were blocked as were four of the concentric chambers.

149 The shrine of Apollo at Nettleton. This alternative reconstruction shows the temple in a form based on San Vitale at Ravenna in Italy which has a similar plan. Like Nettleton, San Vitale is based on concentric octagons but without the external ambulatory. It too has radial walls and these radial chambers have pitched roofs which rest against the walls of the central octagonal tower. San Vitale was finished by the middle of the sixth century and so was not directly contemporary. The only significant difference was the use of weight-relieving arches in the radial walls. On the whole it seems reasonable to argue that Nettleton looked something like this in its heyday.

189

NETTLETON

150 The Shrine of Apollo at Nettleton with its surrounding buildings (isometric reconstruction). See figs. 147-9 for a discussion of the temple's history and details of construction.

So we are left with many excavated examples which on the whole have very similar plans, though differing in detail, and seem to belong to all kinds of different cults at different places and at different times. From a general point of view very little else can be said, and, it only remains to examine sites more closely to trace their individual histories. English medieval parish churches offer a parallel because they all belong to a similar type with similar function yet are all unique in detail and patterns of repair, alterations and rebuilding. The scattered evidence available suggests that Romano-Celtic temples were similar in this respect. Having recognized this as a general probability there is no need to substitute for the lack of exact information a series of classifications which cannot really be supported by surviving structural evidence from a single site and which gives an illusion of knowing more than we really do.

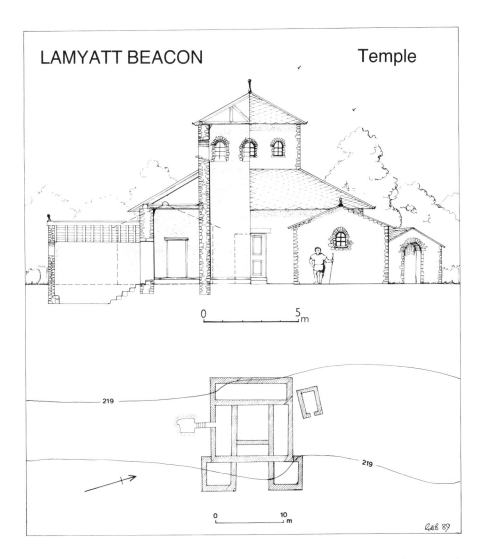

LAMYATT BEACON　　　　　Temple

0 — 5 m

219

219

0 — 10 m

GdB 89

151 The Romano-Celtic Temple at Lamyatt Beacon, Somerset (see also plate 12). The illustration shows a reconstructed elevation with section and plan. The temple was built in the late third century and remained in use up to the early fifth century.

The plan is fairly typical for this type of temple but includes two annexes on the east which probably flanked the entrance. To the south was a sunken room but this had suffered particularly badly, both from robbing and earlier excavations. The temple itself had also been heavily robbed but enough survived to indicate that the cella was buttressed by internal walls in the ambulatory. It therefore seems reasonable to assume that the cella walls stood higher than the ambulatory. The structure had stone walls except for the annexes which were probably timber-framed internally. The roof was covered with hexagonal limestone tiles.

The site has produced a large number of votive objects, mostly buried in pits in and around the temple, including fragments of stone statuary and small bronze figurines of Jupiter, Mars, Mercury, Minerva and a Genius. Mars seems to have been the most important and other circumstantial evidence implies that his worship here may have been conflated with a horned Celtic deity, perhaps Cernunnos.

There was a small building just to the north of the temple proper. It may have been of later date, especially if it was associated with the small cemetery. Radio-carbon dates from some of the human remains indicate a period from the late sixth to eighth centuries. Such an association of 'Dark Age' burials with a Romano-British religious site is not uncommon. There is no specific evidence to indicate a pagan or Christian context, though there are obvious parallels with small 'oratories' in Ireland and south-west Scotland.

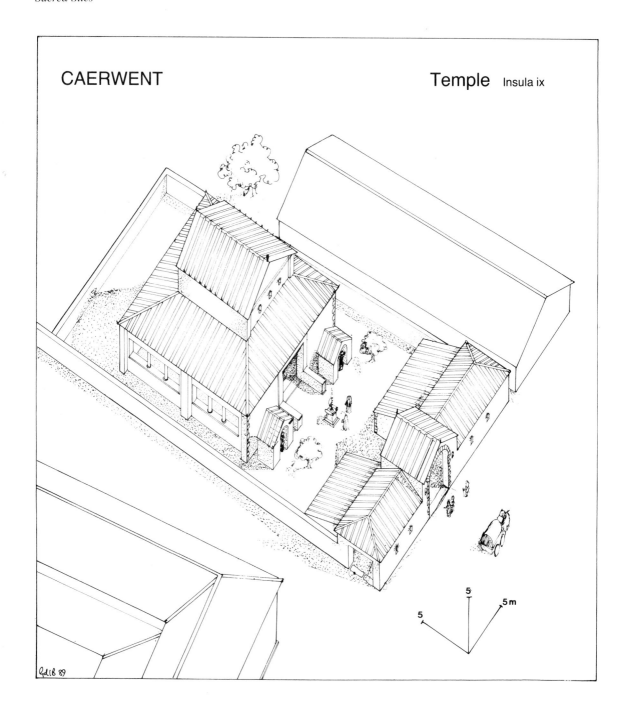

CAERWENT

Temple Insula ix

GdlB 89

152 The temple at Caerwent in Insula ix (axonometric reconstruction). The temple was built in the late third century or later across the street from the forum but on a slightly different alignment. It replaced earlier stone and timber buildings. The precinct was entered through a forehall. During the fourth century rooms were built on to the north side of the forehall which have been interpreted as quarters for the priest(s) and as small shops selling votive gifts and religious souvenirs. Unusually for a Romano-Celtic temple the cella had an apse on the north side. See also fig. 153.

153 View of the surviving remains of the temple at Caerwent looking north. See fig. 152. (Photo: author, 1989.)

Temples associated with eastern religions

Roman civilization and society were very catholic in attitude towards cults of any sort so long as they did not conflict with state cults. This is not always an easy attitude for us to appreciate fully because it is so different from the Christian tradition of intolerance developed during the Middle Ages. Throughout the Roman period there was a penchant amongst certain groups of people for religions which had grown up in the eastern part of the Empire or beyond. These spread across the Empire and included the worship of Cybele and Atys, Mithras, Christ, and Egyptian gods such as Isis and Osiris. We traditionally separate Christianity and explore it as a different phenomenon but it shared with Mithraism a promise of salvation and a life to come. But Christianity was initially just a troublesome cult whose more enthusiastic disciples refused even to pretend to worship official gods and emperors. For many others Christ may have seemed a useful deity, worshipped literally as the mood took them along with any other god who seemed a convenient solution to the problem at hand.

Christianity

There is a reasonable amount of evidence in the form of ritual equipment and inscriptions for the worship of a number of eastern gods in Roman Britain (see *Finds*, Chapters 6 and 8). A scratched reference on a flagon and an inscription make it certain there was a temple to Isis in

193

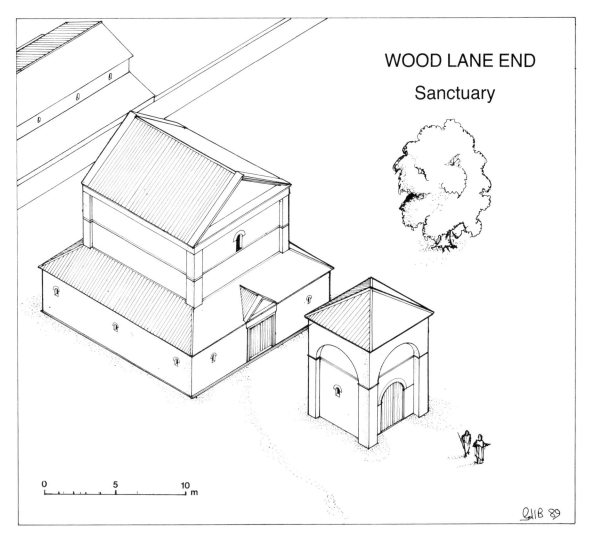

WOOD LANE END

Sanctuary

0   5   10
m

154 'Sanctuary' at Wood Lane End, Hemel Hempstead, Hertfordshire. This structure and a number of associated buildings 5km (3 miles) west of Verulamium have now been identified as a religious sanctuary. The central structure, Building 1, probably resembled a Romano-Celtic temple but with a classical pediment-type façade. The massive walls of the cella with reinforced corners suggest a considerable height. The vault within the cella may have been either a tomb or a repository for valuables – no evidence survived. In front stood Building 6, constructed on the same axis. Behind stood a basilican structure, Building 4, and a number of other structures, including a small bathhouse, formed part of the complex. If this was a cult centre it was rarely visited, as the small number of finds testifies. It may have been the private centre of a guild of worshippers who met in Building 6. Such dating evidence as exists suggests a main period of activity in the second century, but by the third century the whole site had been completely demolished. The excavator has noted the contemporary abandonment of the nearby Gorhambury villa and suggests this may be connected with the re-organization of land ownership around Verulamium.

London, though the building has not yet been located (Appendix 2). There is no certain evidence of a Christian church of Roman date, but structural remains at Icklingham, Lincoln, Richborough, Colchester and Silchester are considered as possible candidates. The most likely places are shrines built around the tombs of martyrs within a cemetery. The abbey of St Albans is almost certainly the final product of a line of untraceable buildings on the site of St Alban's tomb outside the town of Verulamium. A church-like building at Icklingham is surrounded by an inhumation cemetery, and the settlement as a whole has produced some of the most important evidence for Christianity in Roman Britain in the form of lead baptismal (?) tanks (see *Finds*, fig. 118). But the only building which has exhibited what must be incontrovertible evidence for the actual practice of Christianity is the villa at Lullingstone in the late fourth century. This takes the form of wall-paintings in one wing of the villa house and seems to have involved no specific architectural planning or design (fig. 100). The mosaic from Hinton St Mary in Dorset (plate 13) may be evidence of another house church. However, a mosaic from Frampton, also in Dorset and possibly by the same mosaicist (but now lost), combined a number of mythological scenes with a Christogram showing how difficult it is to interpret these floors. In any case interpretation of a building's function from mosaic iconography is a rather dubious and very unsure practice.

Even so we can be fairly sure that churches existed in Roman Britain. By the beginning of the fourth century an episcopal framework existed in the province because three British bishops (from York, London and Lincoln or Colchester), a priest and a deacon attended the Council of Arles in 314. They must have had churches in their respective sees. Gildas, who wrote in the middle of the sixth century, refers to the rebuilding of churches which had been destroyed ('renovant ecclesias', *De Excidio Britonum*, 12 and 24). Bede's eighth-century description of Augustine's mission to Canterbury in 597 includes a number of references to the repair and recommissioning of Roman churches in and around the town (*Historia Ecclesiastica*, i, 26 and 33). Interesting though these examples are, they are very hard to match with evidence on the ground. The extra-mural churches at Canterbury, for example St Martin's, are built partly out of Roman material though cannot be associated with

artefactual evidence of Roman occupation. At Stone-by-Faversham a late-Roman mausoleum seems to have been used later as part of a Saxon church, and it is possible that part of St Martin's is a Roman mausoleum rather than a church. Only St Pancras at Canterbury seems possibly to have had a church-like form during the Roman period, though local tradition held that before 597 it was a pagan building.

The Silchester 'church' has been described as such ever since it was discovered but the truth is that there is no positive evidence for this description apart from its form (fig. 155b). It does indeed resemble a church or a *martyrium* (a chapel commemorating the site where a martyr died) and traces of a small structure outside its entrance have been interpreted as a baptistry. But we have to remember that the church shape belongs to a long-established type of Roman building which includes basilicas and pagan temples (particularly mithraea, see below). Consequently it is rather unwise to extrapolate backwards.

Much the most convincing church site so far discovered lies outside the south-west corner of the town walls of Colchester in Butt Road. Here an extensive cemetery used for most of the Roman period has been known since the nineteenth century. Graves dating to the fourth century are orientated east-west, something normally associated with Christian burials (though the occasional appearance of grave goods and coins suggests that some pagan practices were maintained). Recent excavations have uncovered several hundred graves and a rectangular building 7.4m (24ft) wide by 24.8m (81ft) long with a simple apse at the east end. Post-holes within indicate that the east half of the 'church' had been separated by a screen and contained a nave with two side aisles (fig. 155a). Coinage in and around the building suggested a period of use between *c.* 320 and the early fifth century. There were no finds of wall-plaster or inscribed artefacts which would confirm its identification as a Christian building, but here the combined circumstantial evidence of structural form and the cemetery means that it is reasonable to suggest that this was a cemetery chapel.

Mithraism

The temples of Mithras, or *Mithraea*, are rather better known than Christian churches, though in

Churches?

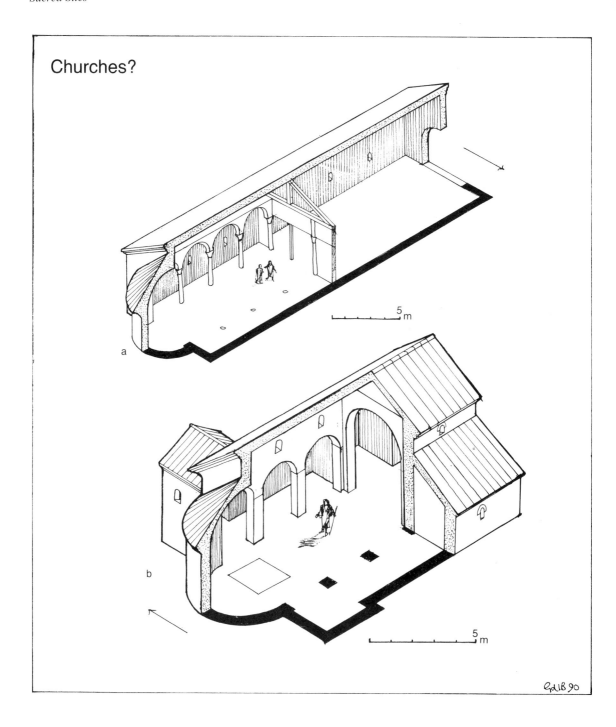

a

5 m

b

5 m

GdlB 90

155 Churches? (isometric reconstructions):
a extra-mural 'church' at Butt Road, Colchester. Built *c.* 320 and remaining in use into the early fifth century. The building was surrounded by several hundred graves oriented east-west in Christian style and itself conforms to church convention with the apse to the east.
b 'church' at Silchester by the forum. Although conventionally described as a church since its discovery in 1892 this curious little structure, while church-like in form, has produced no evidence at all for Christian activity. Although it has an apse, nave, aisles and a narthex, these also make it similar to temples of known pagan dedication in Rome (like mithraea). It also faces west which creates certain problems because churches usually (but not always) face east. A brick base near the entrance of the building has been interpreted as the site of a font, possibly standing within a baptistry of which no certain trace remained. However, even the evidence for a font is much less convincing than that found at Richborough. It lacks the circumstantial evidence of the Colchester site so we cannot attribute the building to any particular cult, even though it was almost certainly religious.

---

actual fact only three have been explored in detail and publication of the most famous, at London, is still awaited (fig. 156). Others are known near the forts at Carrawburgh (figs. 157, 158), Rudchester and Housesteads on Hadrian's Wall, and also at Caernarvon in north Wales. Another one must have existed at Caerleon because an inscribed column found there refers to the god, but no building has yet been located. This reflects the popularity of a cult which was exclusive to men and which was associated with themes of a righteous killing, endurance, virility and salvation of believers. Even the London example seems to have had military associations – one small relief was dedicated by an ex-soldier (see *Finds*, fig. 85a). The temples of Mithras show how mystery cults were completely different from mainstream classical and native religions. In most of the latter cases there was usually an element of 'place' – the site itself was of primary importance and came first, the temple second. For Mithraism, and Christianity, this was not the case. The ritual itself and the temples were the principal factors. They were sacred because that was where the rituals took place. These depended on the active participation of the devotees and required intimate enclosed surroundings. The basilican design with an

apsidal end was ideally suited and therefore they could be built wherever was convenient. For Mithraism running water was needed for purification. So the London mithraeum was beside the Walbrook stream and the Carrawburgh mithraeum was on a slope below the fort by a stream. In both cases the temples were liable to flooding, which caused some structural problems, particularly in London.

The theology of Mithraism is complex. In its simplest form Mithras emerged from the ground and engaged in a conflict which was essentially one of good versus evil presented as a brave and virtuous act of ritual killing. Mithras pursued and killed a bull which had been created at the beginning of time. In doing so he released the creative essence of all life which was contained in the bull's blood. Mithraea were normally built without windows to represent the cave in which Mithras sacrificed the bull. A possible mithraeum was excavated at Burham in Kent in 1894. Unlike the other examples it was built underground in a hillside and was reached through a winding passage, like a real cave. However, no Mithraic cult items were recovered and only its form suggests what it once may have been. The focal point of the mithraeum was the carved depiction of the bull's death. All Romano-British examples were damaged in antiquity, probably deliberately (the creation aspect was regarded with particular distaste by the early Christian church). Occasionally such attacks were foreseen – in London followers of Mithras carefully buried some of the votive statues and gifts which were stored in the temple. During excavation it produced a rich haul of statuary and other items used in the ritual (see *Finds*, p. 140-4).

As a mystery cult, atmosphere was of the highest importance and this was enhanced by lighting effects. At Carrawburgh lamplight shone through holes in an altar, and at London it is clear from scorching on statues that these had had flames held close to them. This was all part of the attraction of a mystery religion which prided itself on exclusivity and endurance. At one point in the history of the Carrawburgh mithraeum an initiation pit was incorporated into the narthex where the would-be faithful could lie, covered with flag-stones, for however long was considered proof of their suitability (fig. 157). No doubt other uncomfortable and bizarre experiences were incorporated into the agenda of the initiation ceremony, but by the final phase the pit

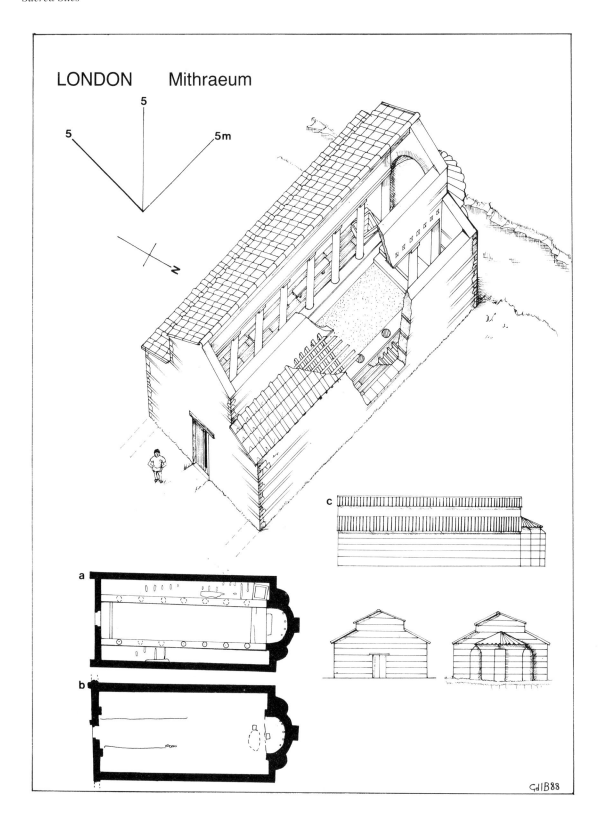

LONDON   Mithraeum

5

5   5m

a

b

c

GdIB88

156 The mithraeum, Walbrook in London. The discovery of this building in 1954, on the site of what is now Bucklersbury House, caused considerable excitement amongst archaeologists and public alike. A number of sculptures were found during the excavation and, together with others found in the vicinity in the nineteenth century, confirmed this as a temple to the eastern god Mithras.

The temple was built in the first half of the third century in basilican form with an apse at one end. In its original form the nave was at a lower level than the aisles and was flanked by two colonnades which can be seen in the cut-away illustration; its length was 17.8m (58ft), width 7.9m (26ft). It was built on top of accumulated rubbish on the east bank of the Walbrook stream, but despite the location the presence of a number of Italian marble and English limestone sculptures must suggest that the people responsible for its construction were wealthy.

By the fourth century the unsuitable location of the temple had led to a decline in its original appearance. The building seems to have been subject to flooding and the floor of the nave was raised, with the columns being removed. During the fourth century the building was ransacked, something anticipated by the faithful who had buried the sculptures and other material used during the rituals.

a mithraeum period I with sunken nave, wooden seats in aisles and well in south-western corner (after Marsden).
b mithraeum period II with columns removed and floor raised (after Marsden).
c side, front and rear elevations of the building in period I.

seems to have fallen out of use. Perhaps lying under the floor had become *passé* and more ingenious variants on self-flagellation had been devised – whatever these were they are not represented in the architecture. Alternatively a cult which excluded women could only grow by attracting followers from outside, so standards may have been lowered to attract newcomers.

Other cults

No other temples have been found which can be positively identified with other eastern cults. That they existed is certain. A well-known flagon from Southwark carries a scratched graffito mentioning a temple of Isis. The flagon is a late-first-century form and interestingly an inscribed altar of mid-third-century date, also from London, records the rebuilding of a temple of Isis

(not necessarily the same one) by the governor Marcus Martiannius Pulcher (see Appendix 2 for both). Of course we have no idea at all what such a temple would have looked like, though its location, and a possible first-century date for its construction, suggest it may have been classical in appearance

Other temples

There are buildings which do not conveniently fit into the categories already discussed. They present particular problems of their own and are not always automatically identifiable as temples. The Littlecote triconch hall is probably the most remarkable (fig. 159a, plate 9). Discovered in the eighteenth century and re-excavated in modern times, the site is known to consist of a dwelling house and a separate barn-like building. The latter was adapted and enlarged over the years, and by the middle of the fourth century a triconch hall bearing a mosaic depicting figures and attributes associated with Apollo and Orpheus had been built into it (fig. 159b).

A triconch hall consists of a conventional rectangular chamber with three apses at one end arranged like the apse and transepts of a church. Much has been made of the building's shape. It has been described as a unique example of a type later represented by some of the churches built in the Eastern Roman Empire during the fifth century and later, for example the cathedral at El Ashmunein (ancient *Hermopolis* in Egypt), built c. 430-40. There is also a certain amount of resemblance to the tomb of Galla Placidia at Ravenna in northern Italy but this building, which stands intact, has square 'apses' instead of polygonal ones; it was built in c. 420. The sheer separation in time and place means that it would be ridiculous to try and link the buildings in terms of architectural tradition though a broad similarity in terms of superstructure is a possibility. However, the plan of the Littlecote building is not quite as unusual as it appears: the earlier *frigidarium* of the Huggin Hill baths is now known to have been similar (fig. 84). Although the apses of the latter are circular and not polygonal, this is really only a cosmetic difference – the structure may have been very similar. Dining rooms of very similar plan are known as integral features of some villas in the Mediterranean area, for example Piazza Armerina in Sicily. So we have to be very careful

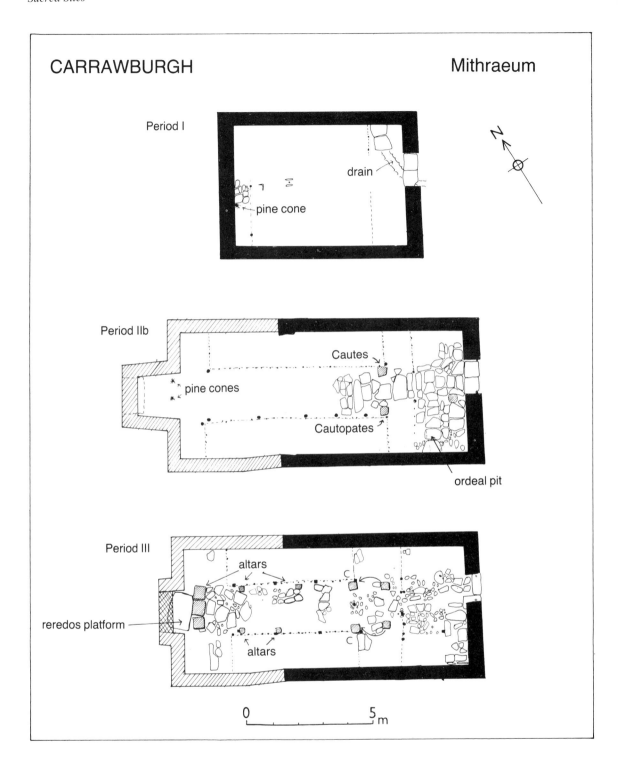

CARRAWBURGH

Mithraeum

Period I

drain

pine cone

Period IIb

Cautes

pine cones

Cautopates

ordeal pit

Period III

altars

C

reredos platform

altars

C

0   5 m

157 Plans of the mithraeum at Carrawburgh on Hadrian's Wall (after Richmond and Gillam). The temple was built on the slope below the south-west corner of the fort near the stream in the second century. At this date it was a simple, modest rectangular structure. Subsequent alterations extended the nave and included a rectangular apse. An ordeal pit was incorporated near the entrance. In its final fourth-century phase the apse was compressed and the statues of Cautes and Cautopates were moved further up the nave. The internal structural components were made of wood and these included the pillars to support the roof; these were well-preserved by the waterlogged conditions on the site. The ordeal pit was no longer in use. Finally it was deliberately destroyed, perhaps by iconoclasts. The site can be visited today and is probably the most instructive religious site in Roman Britain after Bath.

about attaching too much significance to the ground plan.

Part of the problem in understanding the Littlecote building is that its purpose is really quite obscure. It was attached to a bath-suite, but the mosaic has led to the suggestion that the building was a temple used by an Orphic cult. Orpheus was a mortal associate of Apollo who

---

158 The mithraeum and shrine of the Nymphs at Carrawburgh. This drawing shows the temple as it may have appeared in the fourth century. Note the altars within and the reredos sculpture of the sacred act of killing the bull. The Shrine of the Nymphs lay immediately outside the entrance.

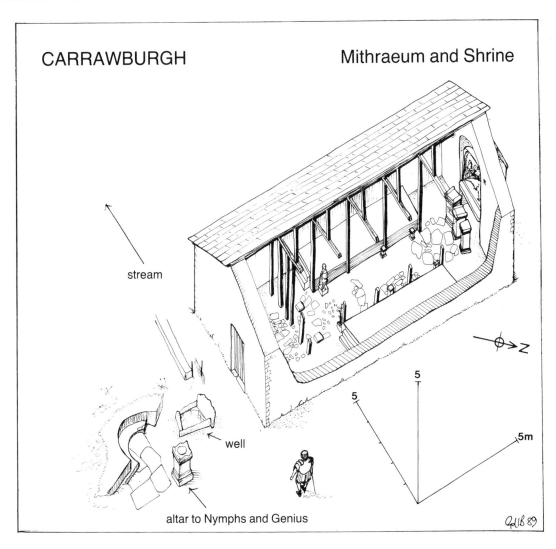

CARRAWBURGH   Mithraeum and Shrine

stream

well

altar to Nymphs and Genius

5m

LITTLECOTE

Triconch hall

0   5 m

159a The triconch hall at Littlecote, Wiltshire, originally discovered in 1727 when the remarkable mosaic was revealed (fig. 159b). Its site was subsequently lost and found again only in 1977. Unfortunately the mosaic had been badly damaged during the winter of 1727-8 but the recent programme of excavations has included the mosaic's restoration.

The site lies astride the main Roman road between Silchester to Mildenhall. Nearby the River Kennet flows east to join the Thames. Roman occupation dates from the late first century in the form of a round house, followed by an open-sided timber barn at the beginning of the second century. Subsequently this was replaced with a flint aisled-barn on an overlapping site a few metres to the east around the year 180. The new barn was associated with a contemporary winged-corridor villa about 30m (100ft) to the south-west (fig. 98 and plate 9). In between the villa and barn was a simpler building, perhaps used to house estate workers. At the beginning of the fourth century a small set of baths was installed at the western end of the barn.

After the year 357 the baths were enlarged and the south-eastern corner was removed to make way for the enigmatic triconch hall. The mosaic that was laid has excited much academic debate (see fig. 159b). The old barn's walls seem to have been reduced to create an open, but enclosed area. The triconch hall probably had a square tower supported by four piers with arches. Three arches led to the apses, the fourth to the nave. Access seems to have been from the baths to the north. Considering the symmetry of the structure it is strange that it was 'tacked on' in such an asymmetrical way; none of the existing walls were exploited and even more curiously it was actually built across the road. Even if the road was disused it is surprising that the architect was prepared to risk subsidence into the old north ditch of the thoroughfare which indeed seems to have affected one of the apses.

had been granted special powers by him over animals and inanimate objects with a magic lyre. He rescued his wife Eurydice from the Underworld, and after he was killed his head and lyre floated out to sea, still playing. The cult was concerned with the concept of punishing the soul before it could be purified. This, combined with the idea that the soul had an independent existence, obviously has similarities to Christianity and it has been suggested that the mosaic and the building's church-like form are discreet references to Christianity. However, it is not certain that the mosaic depicts Orpheus at all, and this speculation may be rather an unjustified elaboration of not very much (see fig. 159b).

159b The Littlecote triconch hall mosaic as recorded in 1730 (omitting a dog or fox accompanying the central figure which has now been restored). Although normally described as an Orpheus mosaic there are problems with this interpretation: a typical Orpheus mosaic depicts Orpheus with his lyre charming animals marching in circles around him (for example Woodchester and Withington). However, the figure's dress is thought by some to be more appropriate to Apollo, perhaps seen here 'entertaining' diners in the apses (which he is facing – rather than a 'congregation' in the nave). Such discussions are very involved and there are arguments either way, none of which is conclusive and none of which helps us decide if the building was secular or religious. The mounted figures are probably the Four Seasons, a common motif, while the sea-dogs and dolphins are not associated with any specific cult or activity. Indeed the innocuous nature of these components does suggest that rather too much significance has been attached to the rest of the floor which may be no more than a decorative feature. (Courtesy of the Trustees of the British Museum.)

The Littlecote building lies very close to a villa (fig. 98) and may be just an elaborate summer dining room, *triclinium*, built by a wealthy man who happened to think the mosaic design was an attractive one and perhaps one which reflected his own interests in iconography, culture and philosophy. The Keynsham, Lufton and Holcombe villas all show the kind of extravagant extensions that some Romano-British were prepared to install. Of course there is the problem that at Littlecote the villa house was quite separate, but all three ideas are quite valid. As ever we do not know for certain, and the subject remains open. It always seems a little unwise to place undue emphasis on a feature of a building which was underfoot and possibly even under furniture – and of course we have no idea what was on the walls either; these may have had paintings portraying something else entirely.

Less sophisticated and unfortunately now entirely destroyed was the beehive temple known as 'Arthur's O'on' just north of the Antonine Wall at Carron (fig. 160). Its identification as a temple is rather more certain even if the evidence is circumstantial. It seems that the building was one of a number in the northern frontier zone dedicated to Victory and presumably built by the army, though whether this was a collective or an individual dedication is quite unknown.

Even simpler is the quaint little temple or shrine dedicated to an obscure god called Antenociticus at Benwell on Hadrian's Wall (fig. 161). Its identity is without doubt because it contained the head from the cult statue and two altars with dedications from the unit. However, it is so small and so irregularly built that it bears all the hallmarks of a kind of home-made temple, and it is difficult to believe that it was even built by a soldier. Nevertheless its structural form and apse at one end are just the kind of clues that might have led to its identification as a church in the absence of other evidence and serves as a salutory warning.

Some prehistoric monuments like Neolithic long barrows and Bronze Age stone circles attracted Romano-British attention, though they would have had little idea of their true age or purpose. They were probably regarded with a mixture of curiosity and awe, and for many communities local lore would have provided an explanation for their importance. Near the villa at Stanwick, Northamptonshire, a Bronze Age round barrow was surrounded by a polygonal

temenos wall during the first century. A modest but decorated entrance led into an enclosure where an ambulatory allowed visitors to walk around the barrow. Several hundred coins were found around the ambulatory, and the vicinity of the barrow was surrounded by deposits of oyster shells. Together these suggest votive gifts and ritual meals. There is no evidence that the cult was connected with a god, but it may be that the community was continuing to venerate the tomb of an ancestor on into the Romano-British period. This is an interesting but tantalizing glimpse of local Celtic myths and legends based on the half-truths of a folk history which is almost completely lost to us.

Rural shrines

Romans were particularly fond of setting up shrines in a rural context where local gods associated with hunting or water might be worshipped in an attractive context. We do not know very much about these shrines because their simplicity means few survive in recognizable form. At Carrawburgh a small shrine to local nymphs and genius was established outside the mithraeum and seems to have consisted of a semi-circular seat and an altar (fig. 158). A pair of shrines, one circular and one rectangular, on Bowes Moor in County Durham were dedicated to a local god associated with hunting called Vinotonus. Like the Carrawburgh shrine they were dedicated by the commander of the local fort, in this case at Bowes. It may well be that these little shrines were dotted all over Britain but only those in remote northern areas have half a chance of surviving in identifiable form.

Civic religious monuments

It was quite normal for the state, the town government or even local people to erect 'religious' monuments within a town. Many are known amongst the remains of the great classical cities around the Mediterranean, but such public monuments to pagan worship were especially prone to re-use in the late Roman period in Britain, or after.

One of the commonest forms was the so-called Jupiter column (fig. 162). Cirencester has produced remains of two, and part of another has been found at Great Chesterford. Their form is

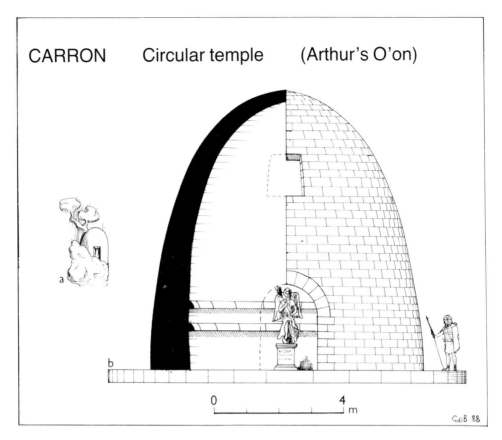

CARRON   Circular temple   (Arthur's O'on)

160 Circular 'beehive' temple at Carron, 3km (2 miles) north of Falkirk, Scotland; also known as Arthur's O'on (Oven). The tragedy of this remarkable building is that it survived until 1743 when it was demolished. Fortunately antiquarian drawings do survive, as does a replica built in 1763.

'Arthur's O'on' was built of dressed stone in beehive form and had an arched entrance and a window above. The diameter was about 9m (30ft) with a similar height. It may have had an *oculus* (an open space) at the top but this is unlikely for a number of reasons. Firstly the *oculus* was designed to let light in: at this latitude (56° north) it would have been unsuitable because at midday on midsummer's day the sun will shine down at an angle of approximately 67°, this is roughly the angle required for the sun to shine through the window known to have existed on to the centre of the floor on midsummer's day. During the rest of the year the sun would shine further and further back on the floor and gradually up the rear wall. This is all based on the assumption that the window was south-facing. Secondly the relatively heavy rain in the area might have made a central *oculus* hopelessly impractical.

It is not certain that the building was a temple but it is difficult to imagine an alternative function and there is the circumstantial evidence of a relief from Rose Hill, Gilsland, Cumbria.

This relief, part of which is shown here (**a**), depicts a similar building on a rocky knoll next to which is a flying Victory. Early reports of Arthur's O'on mention carved Victories and Eagles on the walls within, so it may have been a temple to Victory which would have been appropriate for the location. There was almost certainly a statue within because a pedestal existed and a fragment of bronze statue was also found. It is restored here but the scale of the figure and its posture are purely speculative.

The fact that the temple was so close to the fort at Falkirk on the Antonine Wall, and the quality of its masonry, make it virtually certain that the army was responsible for its construction. The whole of *legio* II *Augusta* is known to have built the wall along with detachments of the VI and XX. Any of these could have been the builders and this does not affect a likely construction date of post *c.* 140. The temple would probably have fallen out of use by the late second century, at the same time as the abandonment of the Wall.

205

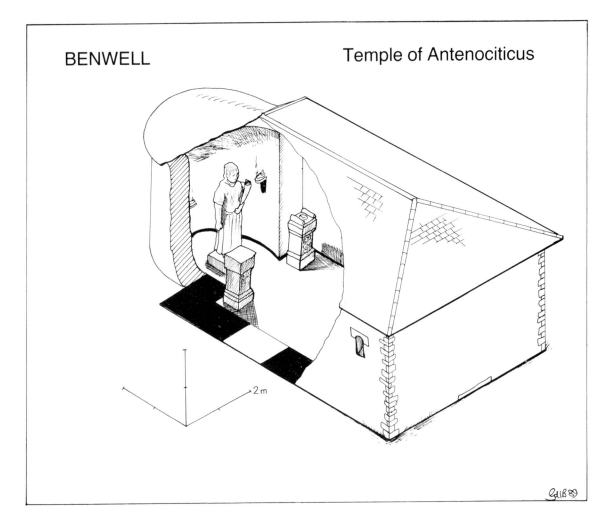

BENWELL   Temple of Antenociticus

161 Temple of Antenociticus at Benwell on Hadrian's Wall. This curious little temple with its apse and irregular walls was identified outside the east wall of the fort at Benwell in 1862. Its dedication to Antenociticus is certain because two altars record the fact. One can be dated to 179 or 180 because it was given by one Tineius Longus who had been designated *quaestor* in that year (such titles can usually be dated from surviving records). The cult statue's head survives (see *Finds*, fig. 81b). Little comment can be made about the structure apart from the fact that its quaint eccentricity suggests a very home-made type of shrine. It is also worth noting that had the altars and statue not been found this is the type of building which might have been described as an 'early church'. As this is palpably not the case here it serves as a warning.

known from more complete examples found elsewhere in the north-west provinces. They consisted of free-standing columns resting on bases which recorded the dedication to *Jupiter Optimus Maximus*. The capital was usually decorated with deities or personifications connected with Jupiter and supported a statue of the god himself (Appendix 2).

Remains of a monumental arch decorated with carvings of various gods has been found in London (fig. 163). It is unlikely to represent a triumphal arch such as that found at Richborough and has been interpreted as a possible entrance to a temple precinct. Unfortunately its original site is quite unknown. It was erected probably in the late second or early third centuries but by the fourth had been demolished to provide stone for the new riverside wall. This fate probably befell

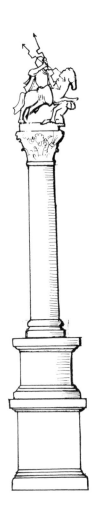

many pagan monuments in the late Roman period elsewhere in Britain (fig. 13). The same riverside wall contained other religious carvings which probably came from temples or shrines nearby in the city, including a screen depicting four mother goddesses and two altars. They may all have formed part of a complex of religious buildings not far west of the so-called governor's palace (fig. 71) and the baths at Huggin Hill (fig. 84).

162 Capital, from Cirencester, probably forming part of a Jupiter column. Such columns were free-standing and would have stood in a prominent public place, perhaps the forum. The surviving capital has four figures associated with Bacchus, who was Jupiter's son: Bacchus himself, Silenus, a female *maenad* or priestess, and Lycurgus, King of Thrace shown here. There would have been a statue of Jupiter on top of the capital while at the base an inscribed block would have recorded the dedication. Such a base has survived from Cirencester but is probably from a different column (see Appendix 2). The restored column shown is based on examples from Germany (see **Schutz, H., 1985,** *The Romans in Central Europe*, figs. 49, 57 and 58).

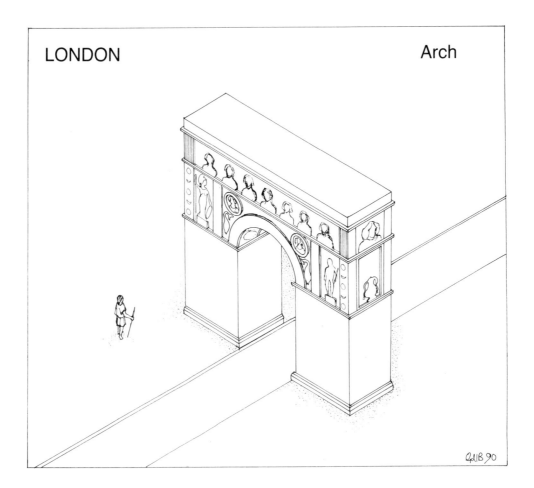

LONDON   Arch

163 Arch from London. The sites of a number of arches are known from Roman Britain – at Verulamium (two) and at Richborough – but practically nothing of their decoration or design is known, though they were almost certainly triumphal arches (see Chapter 3 and fig. 86).

Ironically some of the decoration from the London arch has survived, but its original site is unknown. Sculptured stones were recovered from the late-fourth century defensive wall built along the riverbank. A number of older monuments were re-used in this wall but the arch stones all come from the Blackfriars area in the west of the city.

T. Blagg has restored the arch and the illustration is based on his work. The upper panel seems to have depicted the gods of the week (Saturn, Sol, Luna, Mars, Mercury, Jupiter and Venus – these names survive better in the French than English). The four seasons may have been represented by busts in roundels on either side of the arch (as in many mosaics). On the pillars there seem to have been full length figures, including Minerva and Hercules. At one end a panel showing a wind god appeared above a winding scroll. The whole structure seems to have been about 8m (26ft) high.

If there was an inscription it was on the other side and we have no knowledge of its content. It has been suggested that the arch was actually an entrance way to a temple precinct – evidence of other substantial religious sculpture from the same part of the riverside wall suggests there may have been such an area nearby (these include a stone screen depicting a number of gods). Alternatively the arch may just have been an altruistic gift to the city by some wealthy resident who wished to see his name as a benefactor high above a London road.

The date of the arch can only be estimated on stylistic grounds. These have been used by Blagg to attribute the arch's erection to somewhere between the middle of the second century and the end of the Severan period in the early third century. However, dating is always difficult and it is not unknown for later sculptured material of the third century to emulate earlier work so the possible date range could be much greater.

208

6

OTHER BUILDINGS

Transport

The conquest and exploitation of Britain depended on adequate communications. The Roman army was pre-eminent at organizing this in the ancient world, and by the second century most of the conquered part of Britain seems to have been criss-crossed by a network of roads. Much of the modern road system has its origin in Roman road-building (fig. 164). However, we know far less about the exploitation of waterways even though simple economic considerations mean that transport by water must have been not only cheaper than road transport, but sometimes the only feasible way of moving bulky goods. There must then have been a great deal of building work involving the artificial raising of river levels to make them navigable in their higher reaches, and the drainage of low-lying areas to create canals, though the use of narrow low draught barges would have made even quite small streams usable. Extensive drainage works took place in the Fens and the Somerset Levels, and some ditches of Roman date have been identified such as the Car Dyke in Cambridgeshire and Lincolnshire (though this particular example was not navigable). In general, however, very little tangible evidence for engineering works has been located, though a certain amount of controversy surrounds the so-called bridge at Piercebridge which may in fact be a dam.

Roads

Road-building is the skill which is most popularly associated with Roman civilization. Communication between Roman forts and settlements was essential for the operations of government and trade. Clues lie in not just routes connecting settlements of known Roman date, but also the presence of an *agger* (a raised road surface), wide berms and side ditches (fig. 164). The last items in particular have usually been obscured by the passage of time, and modern wide trunk roads can completely obscure all other traces. However, most major routes between towns have been identified largely because these settlements have endured to the present day and the roads have remained in use ever since the Roman period.

The main roads were almost certainly laid out during the military conquest of Britain in the first century. This even included the principal routes into Scotland, associated with the campaigns of Agricola (78-84). Most of the roads continued in use as the towns and commerce of the civilian province developed. Remains of milestones indicate that repairs of roads continued throughout the period into the fourth century, for example the milestone from Rockbourne villa (re-used as building stone) which mentions the emperor Trajan Decius (249-51) and another from near Carlisle which was erected under Carausius (286-93) but was subsequently inverted and re-carved with the titles of Constantine I, as Caesar, for the year 306-7 (Appendix 2). Another, of the same date and dedication, survives from the other end of the province at St Hilary in Cornwall. A glance at the Ordnance Survey map of Roman Britain shows how little evidence we have for roads and romanized settlements in the far south-west beyond Exeter yet the St Hilary milestone shows that maintained roads did exist in remote areas.

Our knowledge of these minor routes is consequently rather poor, so we really have no

164 Dere Street between Risingham and Hadrian's Wall, looking north. It is a commonplace remark to state that Roman roads are straight; this is only partly true and it is more accurate to say that Roman roads were normally built in a series of straight stretches. Although a modern road now runs along this section of Dere Street two features can be seen which help identify it as a Roman road: the wide berms between the modern road and the field walls, and the height of the curved road surface relative to the adjacent fields. (Photo: author, 1988.)

idea of their extent. A good example is the Darenth Valley in Kent. Here a number of houses of Roman date separated by only a few miles lie close to the river. There would have been some sort of track running north between them to join Watling Street (the main route between Canterbury and London). However, any such track has yet to be found. The majority of all villas lie at some distance from any known road, even though general distribution is biased to the main 'trunk' routes which suggests that access to those roads was of some importance. In a few cases the houses lie very close to the main road – Stonesfield villa in Oxfordshire lies only a few yards north of Akeman Street running between Alchester and Cirencester. The site of the villa is a commanding one looking down

across the road (the agger of which is still visible at this point). At nearby Ditchley a footpath seems to preserve the original track from Akeman Street up to the villa.

Dating roads is particularly difficult because it is unlikely that evidence will be recovered which provides a reliable *terminus post quem*. More useful is the kind of evidence from towns which shows that urban lay-outs took into account a pre-existing road. At Silchester the town baths seem to have been built according to a late-first-century street grid; subsequent reorganization resulted in a re-orientation of the grid, and the bath-house lost its portico which was now covered by a re-directed road. At Verulamium, Watling Street entered from the south making for the early settlement and thereafter was clumsily accommodated into the street grid of the developing town. This created a triangle junction marking the site of the 'Triangular Temple' (see fig. 129). But of course it may be that a Roman road was simply replacing an earlier Celtic track which may have already been in use for generations at the time of the Roman Conquest.

Major Roman roads were designed to cope with the heavy wheeled and hoofed traffic of the day. A sound foundation was essential, and this usually began with large stones embedded in the subsoil. Where the site was poorly drained or low-lying, more support could be gained by

210

ramming in piles. The road network south of the Thames at London was particularly dependent on this because during the period Southwark was made up of a number of low-lying areas separated by marshy areas, quite unlike its modern state. Above the foundations a series of layers of rammed gravel made up the surfacing though this could be augmented with stone if it was available. In Sussex iron slag from local iron works was used because it rusted into a solid surface. Drainage was vital if the road was to be able to cope with the elements and traffic and this was why the raised agger was used with side ditches to carry the water off the berms. The whole effect is rather hard to appreciate in Britain today apart from at a few exceptional sites such as Ackling Dyke in Dorset. Much more impressive are the roads in North Africa, Tunisia in particular, where modern road surfaces form no more than a thin central veneer on an otherwise unaltered Roman road.

The heaviest wear came from wheeled traffic due to the effect of loads transmitted directly to the road surface through the wheels, unrelieved by suspension. Roads which were in long-term use had to be re-surfaced regularly. At the legionary fortress of Inchtuthil waggon ruts were especially concentrated in the vicinity of the

---

165 Bridges:

a reconstruction of the Severan bridge at Chesters on Hadrian's Wall crossing the Tyne. The superstructure was almost certainly made of stone, on the evidence of arch blocks found in the vicinity. The Hadrianic bridge probably had a wooden superstructure supported on more narrowly spaced, smaller piers. Traces of these have been identified within the Severan piers. One is still visible today in the eastern abutment which now lies some metres from the river.

b the bridge at London with wooden piers and superstructure; hypothetical elevation (after Milne) based on finds near Fish Street Hill in 1981. In deeper water the bridge may have been supported on piles.

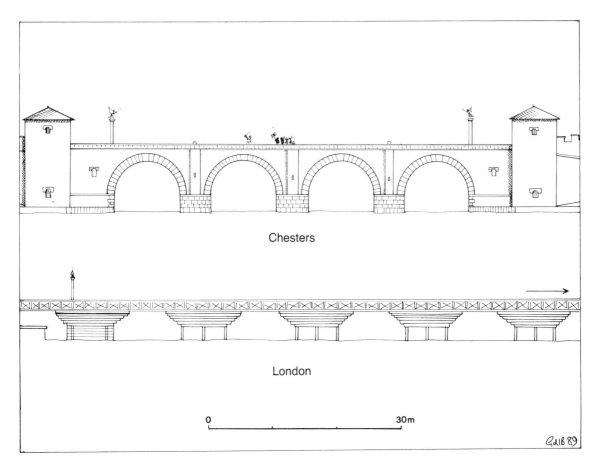

Chesters

London

0   30m

workshop and granaries (see figs. 36, 40) which is not surprising. The streets had never been re-surfaced because the site was abandoned after only about three years of occupation. The road running west from Cirencester by the town amphitheatre towards Bath (the Fosse Way) was found to be heavily rutted.

Roman roads were both recorded and mapped for official use. Some of these records have survived and they supply useful information

about the routes used and the ancient names of the settlements that lay along them. The Antonine Itinerary was drawn up in the early third century, and the Ravenna Cosmography was assembled in the seventh century from earlier records. The Antonine Itinerary is particularly useful because it lists the distances between settlements. While these sources name many of the settlements they do not name the roads – titles such as 'Stane Street' or 'Watling Street' belong to the Saxon period and later. Some of the settlements have yet to be located like *Villa Faustini* which lay between Colchester and Caistor-by-Norwich while others such as Asthall in Oxfordshire are omitted from the list.

The history of roads in Britain after the period of Roman occupation is as hard to trace as the history of almost anything else in the so-called 'Dark Ages'. However, for the most part the major Roman roads of Britain seem to have been

---

166 Plan of the bridge abutment at Willowford on Hadrian's Wall (see also plate 14). The river has moved west since Roman times and the site is now some metres from the present bank. The wall terminated here and it appears that the abutment supported a mill fed by water directed by the pier. A pair of sluices helped control the flow (see fig. 167). As the river gradually moved west so new abutments were constructed.

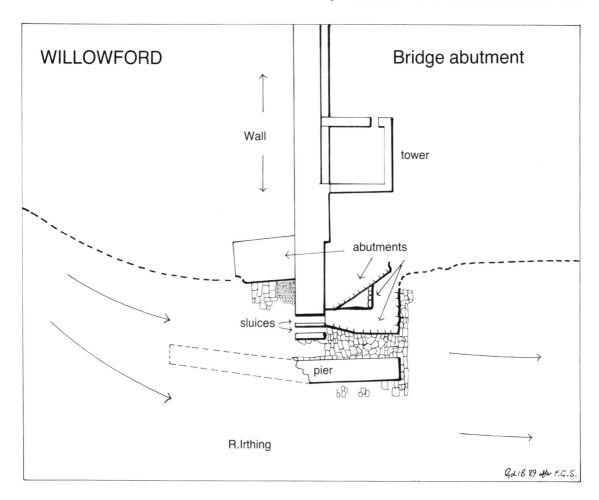

WILLOWFORD

Bridge abutment

Wall

tower

abutments

sluices

pier

R.Irthing

GdlB 89 after F.G.S.

167 The abutment at Willowford looking south showing the north face of Hadrian's Wall with two sluices and a channel for the mill race to right (see fig. 166). (Photo: author, 1988.)

retained as routes and of all the building works of Roman Britain they show the greatest continuity to modern times. Up until the eighteenth century this would have been in the form of ill-kept tracks and lanes. The construction of turnpike roads and subsequently modern metalled roads have preserved the routes, though often with breaks in continuity. The reasons are probably to do partly with simple convenience and partly with land ownership, because throughout the period field boundaries took into account the roads and often the wide berms too – it is quite common to find a modern road running through countryside with what appears to be an unusually wide space between the metalling and the adjacent fields. Although this does not always mean that the road is Roman, or pre-Roman, in origin, it can often be a clue.

Bridges

In a small island criss-crossed by rivers and streams it may well be that most bridges were simple timber affairs which needed regular maintenance and replacement. Many such crossings may have been fords, for example at Iden Green in Kent where flagstones placed across the stream bed provided a firm footing for wheeled and hoofed traffic alike.

At other sites the evidence is hard to interpret. At Asthall in Oxfordshire Akeman Street appears to make a small diversion in order to approach the River Windrush at right angles. The *agger* running from the north is obvious today. It ends abruptly a few yards short of the river, presumably at a point representing the Roman river bank. A few feet further south a number of stones, carefully placed to form a rectangle, may be a small pier for a wooden bridge. A rare case of survival was found at Aldwinkle near Thrapston in Northamptonshire where a gravel quarry revealed the remains of a Roman timber bridge which had once crossed the River Nene. The unusual state of preservation showed that the timber piles were up to 0.5m (1½ft) in

213

168 The River Wear at Binchester. No Roman bridges still stand in Britain and the remains of only a few have actually been identified. These worked stone blocks may represent traces of a Roman bridge below the fort at Binchester at the point where the Roman road from the south crossed the river. The stone in the middle appears to include a groove, perhaps for a sluice gate. The site has not been examined closely but this kind of evidence is of great importance because so often such convenient pieces of stone have been removed. (Photo: author, 1988.)

thickness and had been strengthened with iron sheaths. Even the bridge across the Thames in London seems, on current evidence, to have been built of a timber superstructure supported on timber piers in the shallower water near the banks, and piles across the middle (fig. 165).

The only comprehensive evidence for masonry bridges exists on the northern frontier. The best known is the Chesters bridge, which was built under Hadrian to carry the Wall across the Tyne, apparently just preceding actual construction of the curtain. At this date it was carried on eight piers (possibly with a wooden superstructure) but a later rebuilding remodelled the structure completely so that it was carried on only three larger piers (fig. 165). The remains of stone masonry in the vicinity have been taken as evidence that the bridge was built entirely of stone, rather than having a wooden super-structure supported by stone piers as was the case with the bridge over the Danube depicted on Trajan's Column. Another bridge further west took the frontier across the Irthing at Willowford, just east of the fort at Birdoswald. In its first period the bridge probably resembled the one at Chesters, but here a later rebuilding, complicated by the river's rapid erosion westwards, seems to have involved a timber superstructure (figs. 166, 167, plate 14). Both bridges incorporated mills into their eastern abutments. Other bridges undoubtedly existed in the Wall system. The Roman name for Newcastle upon Tyne, *Pons Aelius*, is proof of one, and altars found in the River Tyne in the general area probably come from it: they were dedicated to Neptune and Oceanus respectively by the VI legion (*RIB* 1319/20). At Binchester colossal pieces of masonry lying in the River Wear below the fort almost certainly come from a completely demolished bridge. Grooves on some blocks may be from sluices (fig. 168).

The most controversial site is at Piercebridge (fig. 169). The site of the Roman bridge across the River Wear has long been known. It lay on the path of the main road (Dere Street) which ran to the east of the fort; and its final traces were swept away only in early modern times. However, a monumental structure has been discovered about one hundred metres to the south-east, and some metres south of the present course of the river. It consists of a rectangular area of flagstones on top of which lie tumbled piles of large blocks. These were identified as the remains of bridge piers, the flagstones acting as a paving to restrict river scouring. There are a number of problems here. Firstly, the second 'bridge' is not on the road alignment; secondly, why should the settlement need two bridges so close to one another?; thirdly, the second 'bridge' is in such a position that one is required to believe that here the river has moved some yards north horizontally and then rather abruptly down-wards, yet has not moved at all on the site of the other bridge. The recovery of rubbish and votive deposits from the whole period on the site of the other bridge makes it unlikely that one bridge

169 Remains at Piercebridge. This controversial site to the south-east of the fort, and across the River Tees, was discovered in 1972. It was identified as the remains of a Roman bridge, constructed as an artificial riverbed with piers. This is, however, hard to reconcile with another Roman bridge a few metres to the west which actually lies on the main Roman road from the south. Moreover this site now lies some metres to the south of the river and it is necessary to account for the fact that the river would have had to move north and then cut a deep channel to find its present course, whereas it has not moved at the point of the other bridge. A much more interesting, if unproven, explanation is given by R. Selkirk who has argued that the stone blocks formed part of a dam, created to raise water levels in the interests of freight transportation. This has the advantage of explaining the other bridge, the road, and avoiding having to explain why at this point the river's rate of erosion should have exceeded that further west. However, no other traces of any possible dam have been located. Unfortunately while Selkirk's case is available in published form the excavators' case is not and it is therefore currently difficult to form a conclusion. (Photo: author, 1989.)

replaced the other. An extremely interesting interpretation of the remains as part of a dam and its associated overspill has been suggested. This would have formed part of a system of dams and locks which would have made higher reaches of rivers navigable. If correct, though there is very little in the way of confirmatory evidence, the implications for interpreting and understanding Roman freight transportation within the province are considerable.

Wharfs and quays

As an island province Roman Britain was particularly dependent on waterborne trade, though in the ancient and medieval world transport by any other means was so inefficient that almost everywhere would have relied on shipping of some sort. The evidence for trade with the rest of the Empire has been known ever since the sources of fine pottery wares in Germany and Gaul were identified along with the sources of amphorae around the Mediterranean. The sources and nature of perishable goods which did not require ceramic containers are unknown.

All these items had to be shipped in, and

215

Britain's products shipped out. The most intensive period of trading was during the late first and early second centuries. By the third and fourth centuries there was much more of a tendency to manufacture goods within the province. Shipping in goods required not just quays on which to unload goods but also warehouses for storage. Not surprisingly most of Roman Britain's major ports have remained as ports, and there has been little opportunity to examine remains of the Roman period except as a result of the colossal redevelopment which has taken place in the City of London in recent years. Archaeological examination of waterlogged sites, especially the St Magnus House (New Fresh Wharf) and the Customs House sites, have revealed the massive timber wharfs and revetments which were built along the north bank of the Thames in association with warehouses

170 Port buildings by the bridge in London, *c.* 100. Recent excavations on a number of sites around the bridgehead in London have revealed traces of a complex and thriving port with many warehouses, containing remains of an extensive series of imported goods. The riverbank was embanked with a series of revetments which created quaysides. Behind the quays rectangular warehouses were built. They contained a number of rooms which may have served as entrances and shops with storerooms on an upper storey. Each building probably had a single owner with a number of merchant tenants. In later years the quays were moved further into the river to create more dockside space. This process continued right on into medieval times, so the Roman riverfront now lies some way inland, though waterlogged conditions have preserved large stretches of the quays. The site must have been the prime commercial location for the province at the time. A well-known reference in Tacitus' Annals suggests that it was an important port by 60 (xiv.33).

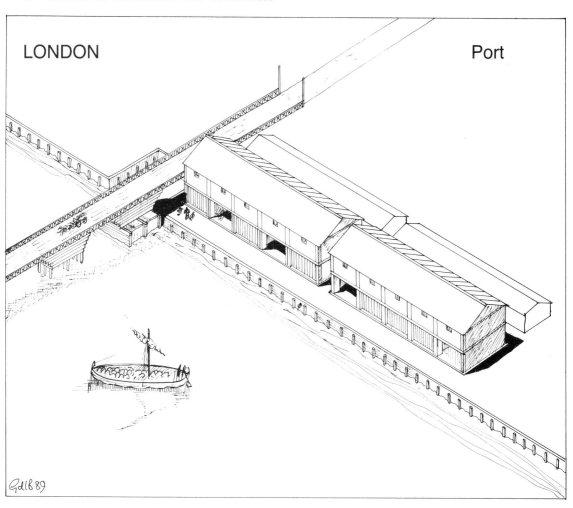

LONDON   Port

Gd1B 89

Wharfs

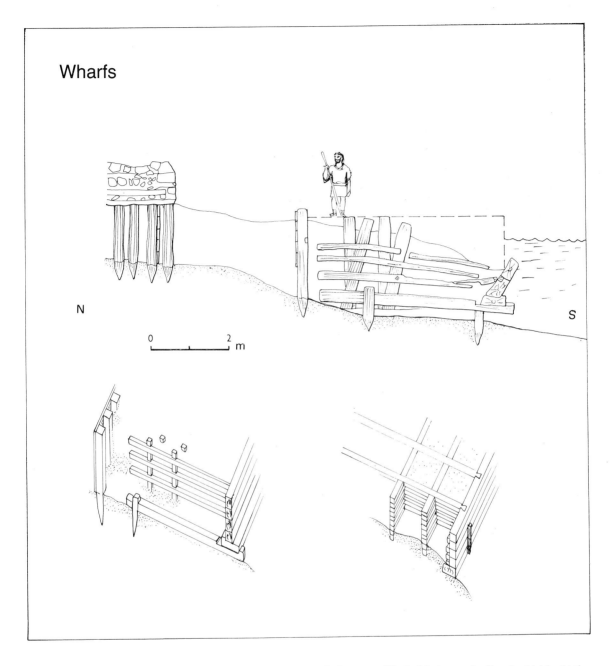

N

0   2

m

S

171 Riverside wharfs in London (after Miller *et al.*). The upper view is a section through part of the third-century wharfs excavated at New Fresh Wharf in London. The foundations and piles at the left represent the footings of the riverside wall, erected in the late Roman period. The quay to right (phase 4) was built with a front wall of oak beams held back by braces strengthened with piles. The space between the timbers was filled with dumped soil and rubbish. At the rear (between the quay and the riverside wall) stood a further revetment, possibly involved with the construction of the phase 4 quay. At lower left is an axonometric view of the same quay. At lower right is an axonometric view of the second-century quay on the Customs House site to the east, built out of a box frame.

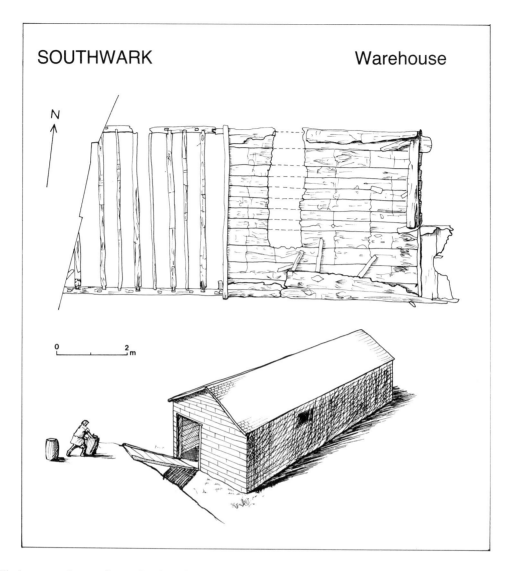

172 Timber warehouse from Southwark, London (after Dillon). Southwark is known to have been the site of an extensive suburb of Roman London, covering at least 12ha (30 acres). It grew up around the southern end of the bridge which crossed the Thames to the provincial capital. In ancient times the area was low-lying marshland with a number of islands separated by streams. Centuries of settlement and embanking of the Thames have completely obscured this. In 1987/8 a remarkable timber building was found sealed in silts on the edge of one of the islands.

The land was originally reclaimed with timber piles in the late first century, and at some point in the early second century a rectangular pit about 80cm (32in.) deep was dug. Into this pit the building was erected directly onto the ground surface. It was based on sill-beams which supported the walls and joists which in turn supported the internal floorboards. It was 4.75m (16ft) wide and at least 11m (36ft) long (the building's full length did not survive). It was probably roofed with timber shingles. Access to the building was down a wooden ramp, part of which survived. The semi-subterranean nature of the building and the ramp suggest that it was a warehouse designed to create a damp cool environment, suitable for storing food and drink. However no evidence of its use survived. It was eventually buried by waterborne silts carrying pottery of the late second and early third centuries so it may be that a flood caused its demise, but also its preservation. The building has been lifted for conservation and permanent display. Such a rare survival is an important reminder that Roman Britain must have contained far more timber buildings than is commonly recognized.

(fig. 170). The technique of dendrochronology (tree-ring) dating has made it possible to associate these wharfs with a long period of building and re-building running from the late first century well into the third. Techniques differ from site to site but broadly speaking the actual quayside consisted of a number of horizontal timbers laced into timbers that ran back into the natural riverbank to the rear, thus bracing the riverfront itself. The spaces between the bracing timbers were filled with rubbish, flint, stone and tile rubble to create a level wharf surface (fig. 171). In time more land was reclaimed by advancing the riverfront forwards by creating a new quayside and filling in the space with rubble again. This does not seem to have taken place after the early third century, though there is evidence for continued use of the wharfs up to the late fourth century.

A number of buildings were associated directly with the wharfs. For the most part they have been identified as warehouses, though their precise function in terms of storage (whether long-term or short-term, pre- or post-voyage) and dispersal is obviously unknown. Fairly typical seem to have been rectangular buildings sub-divided into separate rooms all opening onto the wharf. In this respect they resemble a row of shops like those known at Ostia or Pompeii in Italy, which of course they may actually have been. In later years some of these warehouses seem to have been remodelled with the individual components being redeveloped independently. This may suggest a move from single ownership and renting to merchant tenants, to individual ownership of units. On the south bank of the Thames recent excavations have revealed an exceptionally well-preserved timber building, possibly a warehouse (fig. 172).

More circumstantial evidence exists in the form of a huge dump of burnt samian ware found on the Regis House site. It was associated with burnt building rubble, and it seems likely that the warehouse, which must have been nearby, burnt down and subsequently the debris was swept away and dumped into the quayside. Other material from the general area indicates storage of considerable quantities of pottery goods, for example samian from Billingsgate Lorry Park which was largely unused and may represent warehouse sweepings of damaged goods dumped in the river. Of course we have little idea of perishable goods apart from amphorae: one from the Thames contained olives while others bear inscriptions referring to contents such as wine, oil or brine. All these would have required some sort of storage.

Water

Exploiting water as an energy source and bringing it into settlements by artificial means seem to have been new ideas for Britain. However, the widespread availability of water meant that aqueducts and other examples of hydraulic engineering never had to be quite as elaborate as elsewhere in the Empire, though of course once again we may simply lack the evidence.

Aqueducts, drains and sewers

Aqueducts are popularly believed to consist of a water channel suspended on stone arches carried from a natural source to a settlement. Their remains in Spain, France, Italy and North Africa are amongst the most impressive of all Roman feats of engineering skill. However, they were usually built in this form only to carry water across steep valleys or wide plains. In Britain's undulating terrain it was possible to exploit natural contours to carry the water down through channels cut in the ground. Also, it was rarely necessary to bring water any great distance so aqueducts would never have been as important as they were further south, though the demands of major military and public baths may have made them essential for the fortresses and larger towns.

Several towns were supplied at least in part by aqueducts. At Dorchester (Dorset) contours in surrounding hills were used to carry water in a leet around 1m (3ft) deep over a distance of about 19km (12 miles) into the town. A similar arrangement at the fort of Greatchesters on Hadrian's Wall carried water for 10km (6 miles) into the fort. The circuitous route was made necessary by the lie of the land, and the source of water is actually only about 3.5km (2 miles) away. At Lincoln a rare case of water piped under pressure brought water uphill into the town. At Pompeii a special building at one of the highest points in the town contained tanks to provide a head of water – a large platform in the northern part of Lincoln may have provided the foundation for a similar structure. At street corners in

Pompeii the water seems to have been stored within suspended tanks on brick towers in order to create a head of water. Within settlements water was channelled through pipes (see *Finds*, fig. 68) which made it possible to supply individual houses and water fountains. Lincoln had an ornamental octagonal tank. The inn's courtyard at Catterick contained an ornamental water fountain with a run-off conduit and another can still be seen in Corbridge adjacent to the east granary (see fig. 38). It was embellished with a carved pediment and statues, though in later years the stone walls of the trough seem to have become excessively worn down by knife sharpening.

---

173 Sewer in Church Street, York, in the south-east section of the legionary fortress (after Whitwell).
a section through side passage 4 showing how water enters from above and runs out into the main channel (length of section, about 3m/10ft)
b side passage 4 from above
c elevation of the main channel; in the middle vaulting gives way to a flat roof; height about 1.5m (5ft), or just enough for a small man to walk through with some discomfort
d cross-section of the main channel showing the end of the vault as it meets a flat-roofed section

These isolated examples may well be representative of the province as a whole though we cannot be certain. There is even less evidence for rural house and minor settlements being supplied in this way – they probably used wells (lined with timber if necessary), for example at Lullingstone. However, the house at Woodchester does seem to have been supplied with water by an underground stone conduit. The conduit survives and apparently still carries water, recently actually supplying modern houses. It runs towards the Roman house from a stream some 550m (about 1800ft) away and while its exact date is uncertain the circumstantial evidence points to it being ancient.

Getting rid of water was almost as much of a problem as obtaining it, though it all formed part of a single system. At Housesteads the latrine was flushed by water which simply ran off out through a hole in the fort walls (see figs. 41, 42) into a septic tank or soakaway requiring no specific building works. However, within towns there was more of a problem because obviously each house would have had its own waste whereas a fort's occupants could all use a single central facility. York has yielded the best evidence for sewers. The main sewer, an elaborately built tunnel with a vaulted roof, was fed by side tunnels which carried waste from buildings on either side

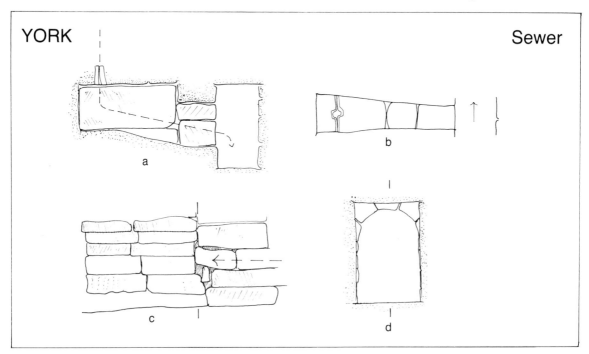

YORK   Sewer

a

b

c

d

HALTWHISTLE BURN   Watermill

174 Haltwhistle Burn watermill. The site is close to milecastle 42 and Greatchesters fort on Hadrian's Wall and was identified as a watermill by F. Gerald Simpson who discovered the site in 1907-8. The stream takes an extreme bend here, and a channel was cut across it with a weir to concentrate the flow of water into the mill. Remains of millstones and use of the north-west wall of the building to form part of the channel suggest that the mill was of the under-shot wheel type, i.e. the water pushes the wheel from underneath, driving a mechanism within.

a reconstructed view based on a photograph by the excavator
b reconstruction of the internal mechanism (after Spain)
c plan of the site (after Simpson)

(fig. 173). Lincoln and Verulamium were similarly equipped, at least in part, but there is very little evidence for comparable facilities elsewhere. A number have been identified at Verulamium, built of either masonry or timber and usually in association with streets. The settlement lies on an east-facing slope, and this may have assisted the civic authorities in arranging such a system. At Silchester the baths had their own drains, and there does not seem to have been any form of sewer network, perhaps because the site's general flatness would have made creating a gradient complicated. At Bath a huge drain helped clear out the reservoir of the sacred spring; when the spring was covered over an arch was built over the drain capstone (plate 15).

Mills

In a world which lacked any form of mechanization the force created by moving water could be of great importance because apart from using animals it was the only means of supplying sustained power. The only certain evidence we have of its exploitation is the existence of watermills. These are known from a number of sites, both military and civil. For example, they are associated with Hadrian's Wall at Willowford, Haltwhistle Burn and Chesters, Ickham in Kent (two), Nettleton in Wiltshire and Great Chesterford in Essex.

The presence of a mill is suggested by a channel and fragments of millstones. The mill race (or head race) was usually an artificial channel which diverted part of a flowing river alongside the mill building so that it could turn the waterwheel, though one Roman writer (Palladius) suggested that the outflow from public baths could be used (*Opus agriculturae*, i, 41). Sometimes the head race was splayed so that the flow was concentrated as much as possible at the point where the waterwheel was sited. It then flowed out on the other side through the tail race to rejoin the main flow. The easiest way of arranging all this was to make a cutting across a bend in a river, for example at Haltwhistle Burn (fig. 174). Alternatively the same effect could be created by building a channel into a bridge abutment, for example at Chesters or Willowford (figs. 166, 167).

The waterwheel would have been made of wood because this was the only feasible way of manufacturing a wheel with paddles. The paddles were pushed by the water which made the wheel turn. The rotating horizontal axis was connected to the vertical axis of the upper and lower millstones through a differential or lantern gear. The millstones or their iron spindles (see *Finds*, fig. 29b) and the bearing stones which housed the shafts are the most likely sort of artefactual evidence for identifying a building as a mill, though of course a building may have housed a waterwheel in order to perform a completely different task such as moving cutting tools for wood or stone, or even hammers for metal-working (see below).

The Hadrian's Wall mills probably helped supply the garrison with food. All three are near forts: Chesters, Greatchesters (Haltwhistle Burn) and Birdoswald (Willowford). Evidence of metal-working at Ickham, remains of what may have been a water-powered hammer and military equipment have been interpreted as possible evidence of a late-Roman military establishment engaged in manufacturing armaments with the help of a watermill. The site was close to several Saxon Shore forts (Reculver, Richborough, Dover and Lympne). However, sites like Great Chesterford or Nettleton may be purely private establishments serving a local community simply as part of the local infrastructure of food supply. Such sites may have remained in use for long after the Roman period and some may have remained in use right through the medieval period though it would be very hard to establish a Roman origin for them.

Kilns and ovens

Although not strictly buildings, kilns and ovens could be quite elaborate structures which required considerable skill to make them serve their desired purpose. They would normally have been associated with some sort of settlement, though it is very rare in Britain for the actual workshops to be located. An interesting example is known from Stibbington, near Peterborough, where a number of kilns are associated with a workshop containing a potter's flywheel (fig. 175).

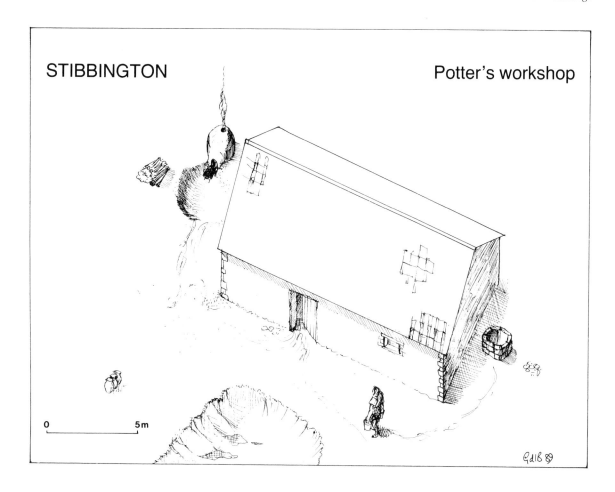

STIBBINGTON   Potter's workshop

0   5m

175 Potter's workshop at Stibbington, Peterborough, restored axonometric view. The structure is simple enough and contained chests for clay. The building yielded remains of a stone flywheel which the potter would have turned with his feet in order to rotate the throwing wheel. Outside in the foreground is a clay pit and to the right a well, supplying two of the three basic requirements for pottery making. The third – fuel for the kiln, sited at upper left – would have come from nearby woodland.

Kilns

The purpose of a kiln is to contain heat in order to fire pottery. This required an effective structure which both retained the heat and kept the direct heat away from the pottery. There are a large number of different types, and for detailed information the reader should consult Vivien Swan's excellent synthesis of the subject (see Bibliography). However, most kilns, apart from surface clamps which were really just bonfires, had three parts: the stokehole, the furnace chamber and the oven (fig. 176). The furnace chamber was usually made by simply digging a suitably sized and shaped pit in the ground. An adjacent pit allowed access to the chamber through the stokehole and flue. The roof of the furnace chamber had to support the load of pottery and also allow the heat through. This was done either with a permanent clay floor pierced with vent holes or by making up the floor each time with fired clay rods which radiated from a central pillar to the walls. The load of pottery was installed and only then was the oven actually roofed over, usually with clay or turves in dome form. If the load was to be 'oxidized' a vent hole was left at the top. If it was to be 'reduced' the dome was completely sealed. Such kilns could be used over and over again but were generally abandoned when a firing went drastically wrong. The samian kiln at Colchester was much more

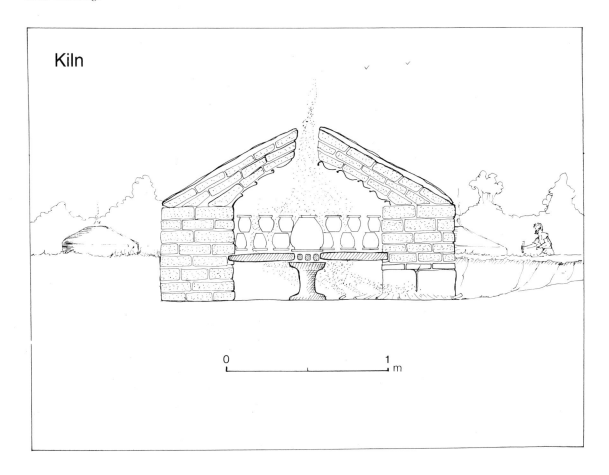

Kiln

0   1
L_____J m

176 Cross-section of a coarse-ware kiln (after Woods). There are many types of these kilns known but their simple structures all reflect an essentially similar technique. The kiln, usually circular, was made by digging a depression in the ground with an extension for the fire. The chamber itself was generally built out of dried bricks. The load was supported on a higher level, in this case by a clay pedestal and radial spars. In this way heat could circulate evenly from below. The kiln was filled and then capped with a 'vault' of turves or bricks. If the pots were to be 'reduced' (starved of air during firing to achieve a black or grey ware) then the cover would be made airtight. If the pots were to be 'oxidized', the opposite to reduction, then a vent was left. The type is broadly typical of the first century and was already in use in Britain in Belgic areas before the Roman occupation.

elaborate because of the technology required to produce high quality fine wares (fig. 177). Large kilns in the Nene Valley were constructed out of specially pre-heated blocks. Tile kilns belong to a special type of kiln and were probably built near the site where a building was being erected or re-roofed so long as suitable clay and water were available (fig. 178).

Ovens

These are best known from military sites where they are usually found close to the ramparts. Each century would have had its own oven. These resembled kilns, but instead of a supply of direct heat being maintained an oven was raised to the temperature required by placing fuel within, this was then raked out, the food loaded and the oven shut fast for the desired time. Consequently they are even simpler and are usually free-standing rather than partially buried (fig. 179).

177 Cross-section of the samian ware kiln at Colchester (after Hull). As a fine ware with a high quality red slip, samian ware required specially elaborate firing equipment to control the distribution of temperature. The ware is 'oxidized', i.e. a supply of air was available in the kiln. The Colchester samian potters seem to have been unsuccessful in their attempts to establish a manufacturing base in Britain (almost all samian came from Gaul; see *Finds*, p. 83). However name-stamp evidence from the site makes it virtually certain that some of the potters were experienced men who had previously worked in East Gaul; the kiln itself resembles types known in that area.

The kiln (number 21) was circular in plan. Hot air entered through a flue beneath the main chamber. It then passed up through tubes around the perimeter of the kiln and nine tubes laid out in a square in the main chamber. The fumes then exited through chimneys at the top. In this way the pots being fired were exposed to the heat but not the dirt of the fire.

Lighthouses

Like a modern lighthouse, the ancient *pharos* served the straightforward purposes of informing and warning mariners. Only two are known for certain in Roman Britain and both overlooked the harbour at Dover, obviously being designed to guide shipping between them, though whether they were built at the same time is unknown. They may have been associated with the Dover forts belonging to the *Classis Britannica* in the second century, or possibly the later Saxon Shore fort built towards the end of the third century. Either way it seems they were military buildings. The western lighthouse is known only from its foundations whereas the eastern one still stands to an impressive height though this is in part due to medieval additions (fig. 180, plate 16). The eastern lighthouse is a simple octagonal tower which rose in a number of stages. Interestingly a

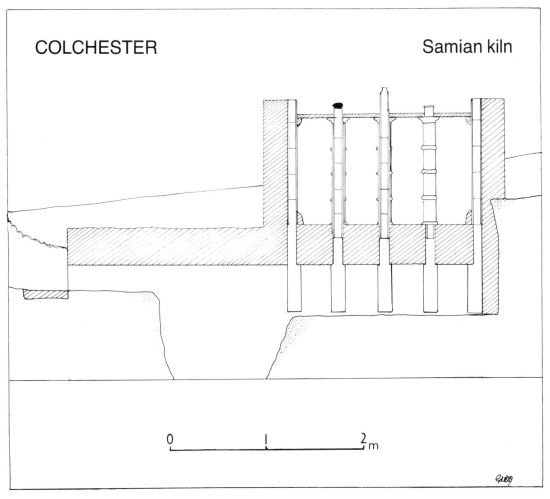

COLCHESTER   Samian kiln

0   1   2 m

tile from London is thought to bear a diagram of a *pharos* though this cannot be certain (fig. 1).

178 Plan of the tile kiln at Great Cansiron Farm, Hartfield, Sussex (after Rudling). The site was probably connected with nearby Roman iron-working and seems to have been established *c.* 100. The thousands of tile fragments found in the vicinity make the kiln's purpose certain. The kiln seems to have had only brief use before being dismantled and back-filled. It may be that it was used for an undiscovered building nearby. Bearing in mind the great weight of tiles it is very likely that most rural buildings or settlements

would have had their tiles manufactured as close as was practicable (availability of clay, water and fuel being determining factors), and the facilities would have been required only for as long as it took to finish the building. Towns would probably have had more centralized establishments, possibly under civic or government control; the army seems to have been largely responsible for its own tile-making.

a plan of the kiln showing the stokehole to left, the main flue and the combustion chamber
b cross-section. The cross-walls were carried over the central main flue by arches
c elevation of the entrance to the flue

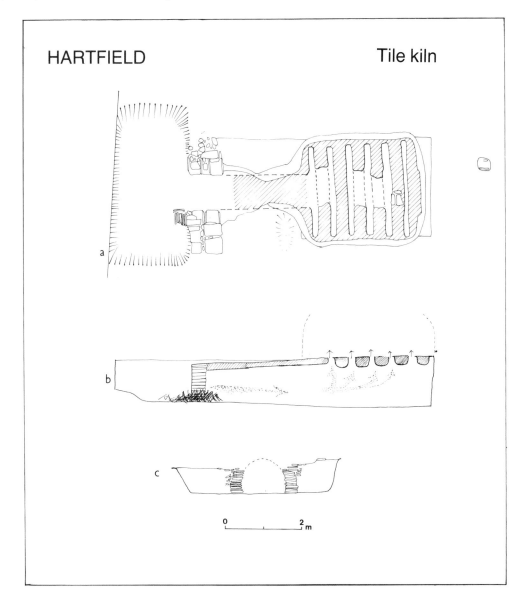

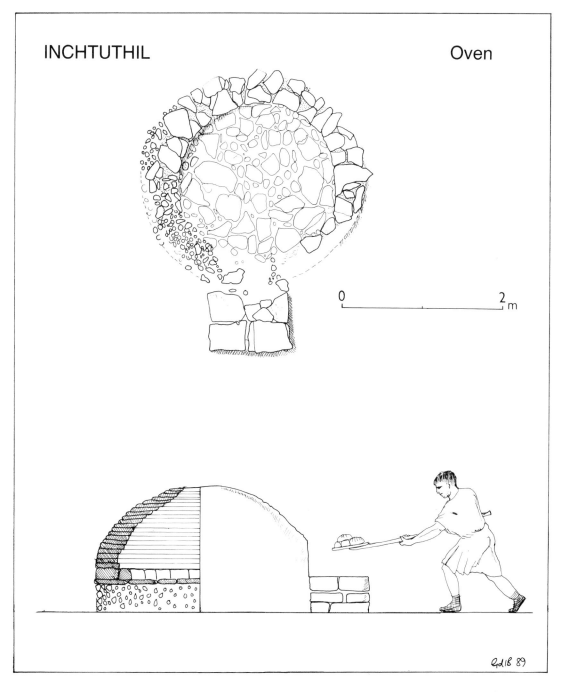

INCHTUTHIL

Oven

0   2 m

179 Oven at the legionary fortress of Inchtuthil for barrack 53, *c.* 84-7. The oven lay in the *intervallum*, the zone between the buildings of the fortress and its ramparts. There it was both sheltered and isolated. Unlike a kiln an oven contained a solid floor and its contents were directly exposed to the heat. The superstructure of a military oven was usually clay but few traces of clay were identified; the oven may therefore have had a stone dome. It was probably used for baking bread and is broadly similar to better-known urban bread ovens found at Pompeii in Italy. Above: plan of the oven (after Richmond); below: reconstruction of the oven.

227

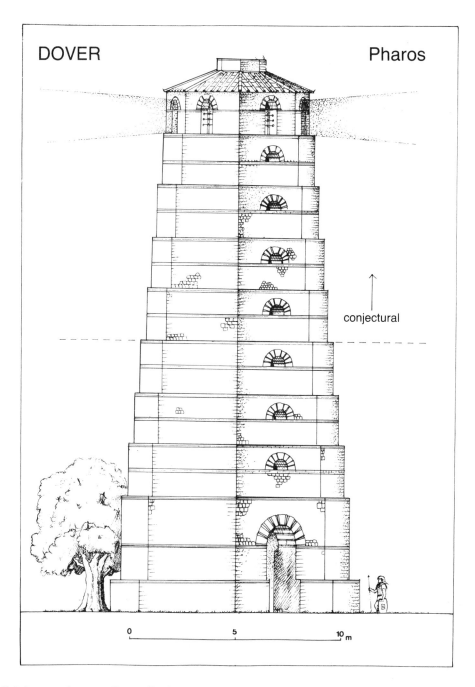

180 The lighthouse, *pharos*, at Dover Castle, restored elevation. One of a pair which overlooked the harbour this building at 13m (43ft) is the tallest surviving Romano-British building (plate 16). It is octagonal externally though the internal chambers are square. It was built in a number of stepped stages and its original height is obviously unknown, though 25m (80ft) is probably a reasonable guess. The tower was built of ashlar-faced rubble with the usual tile courses. At the top a fire beacon would have shone at night. Here the beacon chamber is shown roofed but equally it may have been open. The other lighthouse has not survived beyond traces of foundations. The date of the buildings is not certain but it is likely that they can be associated with the second-century forts of the *Classis Britannica* nearby.

Tombs

During the first and second centuries most of the Romano-British were cremated and their remains buried in simple containers such as earthenware pots or glass jars. The graves were marked with headstones or wooden markers and sometimes were equipped with libation pipes. In the third century and afterwards inhumation became more the norm, but apart from using coffins burial practice seems to have remained unaltered. However, as Christianity spread so

the habit of burying the dead with grave-goods seems to have diminished. Burials were isolated, in groups or in cemeteries depending on the nature of the settlement. A number of burials of these types were discussed in *Finds* (Chapter 7).

However, for the well-to-do, or those who aspired to posthumous prominence, such modest graves were considered insufficient. Their cremated or inhumed remains were interred in tombs, a number of which have been identified in Britain, or beneath earthen barrows. The latter are not really buildings in the sense which would interest us here, but tombs were sometimes quite elaborate structures. They took two forms: a stone revetted tumulus or barrow, or a free-standing walk-in chamber generally with a sub-terranean burial immediately below. Tombs usually lay outside the area of settlement, for example those which stood beside Dere Street as it ran south from the fort of High Rochester (fig. 181), but tombs associated with villas sometimes lay quite close to the house itself, for example at Lullingstone (fig. 100) and Keston (fig. 182). Such buildings were built in a number of different forms, none particularly complex. However, most seem to have fallen into decay during the Roman period and in a few cases were clearly deliberately demolished or their contents robbed

181 Tomb beside Dere Street at High Rochester, Northumberland. To the south of the fort are substantial traces of the cemetery associated with the fort. Most are small mounds covering cremations but a number of more elaborate stone-built tombs seem to have lined the main road, one of which is still visible. Only two lower courses of stone survive, but the tomb may have been as much as 4-5m (13-16ft) in height. One of the surviving stones is carved with the head of an animal. The two figures on the right are standing on Dere Street which runs north from the right past and behind the tomb. The clump of trees in the left centre marks the site of the fort platform a little under 1km (½ mile) away. (Photo: author, 1989.)

out. Evidence from the Continent, for example at Pompeii, shows that tombs were important meeting places for a family where the members would gather to commemorate their dead ancestors, sometimes within the chamber itself if it was designed for access.

The limited evidence that we have certainly suggests that tombs were built for people of wealth and status, for example soldiers of high rank. The High Rochester tombs would fall into this category but were modest structures compared to the substantial tomb known to have existed west of Corbridge. The Corbridge tomb was about 10m square (32 by 34ft) and was surrounded by a substantial precinct wall which was embellished with at least two carved figures

of lions eating prey to symbolize death. It lay in a cemetery beside the Stanegate road.

Other tombs are largely associated with villas, and this implies a certain amount of disposable wealth which could cover the additional cost of what would have been as much of a luxury then as it is now. It has been suggested that rural tombs may have acted as cult centres. The 'Temple-Mausoleum' at Lullingstone was called thus by the excavator because of its presumed resemblance to a Romano-Celtic temple in plan. The principal difference was the sealed chamber which lay beneath the central room containing the inhumed burials of a young man and woman with their grave goods. It seems to have been built around the end of the third century. Nothing whatever is known of the identity of these individuals but it is notable that they are the only burials associated with the house (apart from infant burials) despite its very long period of use (see figs. 99, 100). Others of course may lay further away, but this particular structure was clearly designed to overlook the house which lay only a few metres away down the hillside.

The Lullingstone building has been restored in Romano-Celtic temple form, but it is clear from the excavator's account that no trace of roofing in the ambulatory was found. This is a very important point because it shows how easy it is to assume that a very simple plan represents the same type of building. Consequently the site is

182 Tombs associated with the villa at Keston, near Bromley, Kent. Discovered early in the nineteenth century, the cemetery centres on the buttressed circular tomb which was originally plastered and painted red. Next to this is a simpler rectangular tomb which contained an inhumation in a stone coffin. A third burial was discovered comparatively recently between two of the main tomb's buttresses. This one consisted of a lead casket containing a cremation, sealed in a tile chamber. Other graves were found in the vicinity and it is probably safe to assume that most villas had such cemeteries, though they are not very often located because they can lie several hundred metres away. (Photo: author, 1989.)

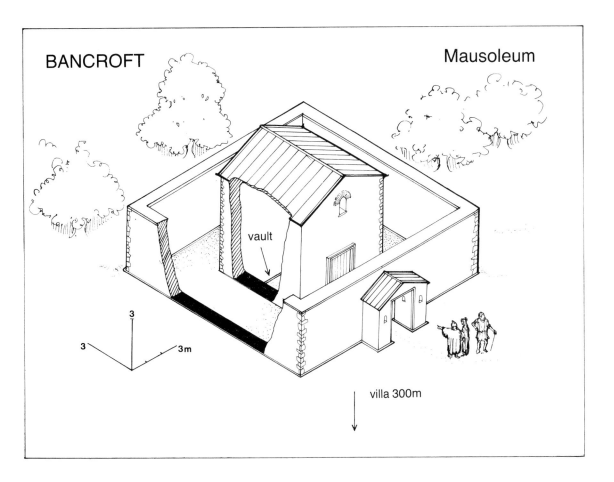

183 Mausoleum at Bancroft, Buckinghamshire (isometric reconstruction). The plan consisting of two concentric squares resembles that of a typical Romano-Celtic temple, but it need not be restored as a similar building. Here the vaulted central chamber has been restored as a separate structure in the manner of surviving tombs at Pompeii, Ostia and Rome with a surrounding wall. Unfortunately the building, put up in the fourth century, had been thoroughly robbed out by the early fifth. However, evidence survived to suggest that the mausoleum had contained painted wall-plaster (also known from other mausolea in Britain, for example at Poundbury cemetery near Dorchester, Dorset), a tessellated floor and a staircase for access to the coffins in the vault.

now quoted as a parallel for others, with a circular argument arising when it is suggested that an assumed religious site like Wood Lane End was centred on a temple-mausoleum (fig. 154) because of its 'resemblance' to Lullingstone in having a vault, even though no evidence of burials was found at the former. The plans may be similar but there is no reason to assume that therefore the superstructures, and by extension the functions, of the two buildings were the same. The central room at Lullingstone was vaulted with tufa blocks and decorated with painted plaster. It may be more accurate to restore the building as a single-chambered tomb within a walled area, and not as a 'temple' at all. Interestingly, it was apparent from the sequence of construction that the burial chamber had been built and sealed prior to the erection of the tomb. By the end of the fourth century the building had fallen into decay and the burials were partially robbed. However, a Saxon church was built directly over the building at an unknown date and it is tempting to suggest that local lore identified the place as one worthy of veneration. But this may actually have been a confusion with the

231

house-church which existed within the main house during the late fourth century. Certainly no votive goods survived to suggest that the 'Temple-Mausoleum' had been anything other than a grave (fig. 100).

A very similar building has been identified more recently at Bancroft though it lies much further away from the main house (fig. 183). Like the Lullingstone example its plan consists of two concentric squares with the central square containing a subterranean chamber. In this case the building had been completely robbed out at a late date, to the extent that a ramp had been constructed to make removal of the spoil easier. A tomb found at Welwyn supports the idea that such buildings need not have resembled Romano-Celtic temples. Here the square tomb was surrounded by a concentric ditch rather than a concentric wall; the ditch itself contained three burials. Concentric walls for tombs may therefore have been boundary walls rather than ambulatories.

The tombs at Keston in Kent were of the simpler stone-revetted tumulus kind but these had their own structural problems. The larger of the pair is circular and around 10m (30ft) in diameter. The earth core created lateral stresses as it settled, and to combat this a number of buttresses supported the outside wall. It was probably capped with an earth cone. A similar, but much larger, example is known at West Mersea in Essex. Here the 20m (65ft) wide rotunda was retained with a masonry wall strengthened by 12 buttresses. The tumulus was further strengthened with six walls radiating from a central hexagonal chamber. But smaller tombs could be very much simpler – the circular tomb at High Rochester and another from Pulborough in Sussex were not big enough to require buttresses, and the smaller tomb at Keston is a simple rectangular chamber (fig. 182).

7

THE RUIN OF ROMAN BRITAIN

If we have little detailed history of the buildings in Britain during the Roman period we know even less about what happened to them afterwards. But, apart from the observations of antiquarians in the sixteenth century and later, there are a few references to the buildings of Roman Britain dating from the fifth century onwards. The sixth century chronicler Gildas referred to the practice of pagan rites amongst 'deserted city walls'. In the early eighth century the monk Bede commented that cities, forts, bridges and metalled roads remained as testimony of the Roman occupation. Later he even observed that Hadrian's Wall (which he thought was built in the fourth century) remained clearly visible in his day and was up to 12ft high (3.6m), and 8ft thick (2.4m). Bede also records that in 685 St Cuthbert visited Carlisle where he was taken on a tour of the Roman city walls and a working aqueduct and fountain. Much further south an anonymous eighth century poet seems to have wandered amongst the ruins of the bath complex at Bath. He was fascinated by the monumental scale of the collapsed vaults and attributed them to giants. Rather later, William of Malmesbury, writing in the twelfth century, referred to an arched building which was still standing in Carlisle and bore an inscription to Mars and Victory.

Probably the most vivid account of Roman remains, however, is that of Gerald of Wales. He wrote towards the end of the twelfth century and recorded his 'Journey through Wales', including a description of remains at Caerleon. The passage is worth quoting in full:

Many traces of its former splendour can still be seen; immense palaces, originally ornamented with gilded roofs, in imitation of Roman magnificence. . . and embellished with splendid buildings; a tower of prodigious size, remarkable hot baths, remains of temples and theatres, all enclosed within fine walls, parts of which remain standing. You will find on all sides, both inside and outside the circuit of the walls, underground buildings and passages, aqueducts; and what I think worthy of note, stoves contrived with wonderful art to transmit the heat insensibly through narrow tubes passing up the side walls.

Gerald's words form the most tantalizing glimpse of the ruins of Roman Britain to survive. Many other Romano-British buildings must have survived in a recognizable state into the Middle Ages. The first serious antiquarians were John Leland (1506-53) and William Camden (1551-1623). Camden published various editions of his *Britannia* in the sixteenth and early seventeenth centuries. He noted that the site of Verulamium had 'ruins of walls, chequered pavements and Roman coins now and then digg'd up there'. In the early eighteenth century William Stukeley visited the settlement at Wall and described walls 3ft (1m) thick and 12ft (3.5m) high running parallel with one another and forming square rooms. The ruins must have resembled those which still stand at Ostia in Italy. Even at Verulamium he was still able to prepare a map showing *Umbra Strati* ('shadow of a street') and *Vestigia cavitas* ('traces of hollows'), the latter probably being the sites of cellars of ruined houses. None are visible now except those which have been excavated in modern times.

Stukeley also visited Hadrian's Wall and graphically described the desecration of the

184 A fanciful view of the temple precinct at Bath in the fifth century and later. In fact the nature of the decay here is documented in Anglo-Saxon poetry and supported by archaeological excavation.

remains during the construction of the Military Road, 'The overseers and workmen. . . demolish the Wall, and beat the stones in pieces, to make the road withal. Every carving, inscription, altar, milestone, pillar etc., undergoes the same vile havoc, from the hands of these wretches'. But the stone was also used by local people. In 1801 William Hutton travelled the Wall: 'Had I been some months sooner I should have been favoured with a noble treat; but now that treat was miserably soured. At the twentieth milestone I should have seen a piece of Severus's Wall [the real date of the Wall was still unknown] 7½ feet high and 224 yards long, a sight not to be found in the whole line: but the proprietor, Henry Tulip, esq., is now taking it down to erect a farmhouse with the materials . . .'. However, further up the Wall at Brunton he was successful in pleading for the curtain's preservation.

But it seems that long before antiquarians began to take an interest in Britain's past, centuries of stone-robbing and the depradations of weather and farming had already exacted a huge toll. There is practically no evidence for any houses remaining in a maintained state after the early fifth century. An arch in the crypt of All Hallows-by-the-Tower, built by the early eighth century, is made entirely of re-used Roman brick and tile. In fact many early churches (being amongst the few Saxon structures built of stone) seem to have been made out of material taken from Roman buildings. Much further north the builders of the eighth-century church at Escomb, County Durham, made use of the remains of the fort at nearby Binchester. The town of Verulamium was gradually abandoned as the settlement moved south-east to cluster round the *martyrium* of St Alban. Subsequently the abbey church was built largely from stone and brick taken from the Roman town. This is even recorded as being due to the abbots Ealdred and Eadmar, who lived around the middle of the tenth century and ransacked the ruins for building materials. Silchester was almost completely abandoned after the Roman period, and the site remains open fields today. But, despite this and its comparative remoteness, the site was almost completely robbed out by the time any serious archaeological attention was paid to it in the nineteenth century.

Many other Romano-British towns like London, Lincoln and York had never really been abandoned and there was very little chance of Roman structures enduring indefinitely, apart from the city walls and gates. The earliest map of London dates from about 1559 and shows nothing that can be related to the Roman city save the Guildhall Yard which is now known to have originally formed the arena of the amphitheatre. Even the site of the huge basilica and forum was split in half by Gracechurch Street running south from Bishopsgate towards London Bridge. At York the great Minster was built over the remains of the headquarters of the legionary fortress.

The consequence of this kind of activity, quite apart from the depradations of nature, sets Britain apart from, say, the west coast of Turkey where the retreat of the sea due to silted rivers has left many of the greatest and richest cities of Asia Minor, like Ephesus, Miletus and Priene, high and dry. Their sites serve no useful purpose any more and their remoteness has ensured that they have largely suffered only from earthquakes and undergrowth. For Romano-British archaeology the challenge has been a huge one – to make sense of the rather undistinguished remains of buildings revealed in modern construction works, by the plough or from rabbits scattering fragments of mosaic from their burrows. Apart from city walls, forts and a few rare instances like the 'Mint Wall' in Lincoln or the bath-house at Ravenglass almost nothing of Roman Britain has been found without having to be dug up.

The result has been that a very wide range of buildings has been excavated over the years, and throughout this book as many different types of building have been looked at as possible with a view to re-creating some of the sense of form. Most of the drawings are fairly rigorous orthographic projections which retain relative dimensions. This has the advantage of retaining much of the original plan yet dispensing with the lifelessness of solid black lines. They are highly subjective and can never be definitive but equally it would be futile to claim that 'more work needs to be done' in order to produce more reliable reconstructions. No amount of work will ever undo the work of generations of rabbits and stone-robbers and no amount of discussion about wall strengths (or lack of) will ever supply certain evidence for an alternative reconstruction, especially as not a single one stands to prove its viability. There are countless ancient buildings scattered around the Mediterranean which defy gravity and make such arguments beyond fairly general observations quite pointless. A centuries-old bath-house in the outskirts of the old Ottoman capital of Bursa in north-west Turkey must surely be one of the most rickety-looking constructions ever erected. Its teetering roofs lean on each other, covered with ancient tiles, some broken, held together with liberal daubs of cement and judiciously placed struts of wood. Yet it has served as a bath-house for longer than most Romano-British buildings would have ever had to serve, and despite its crumbling plaster it serves still.

So these neat geometric drawings are unrealistic in the sense that they can never record the myriad of unrecorded instances and imperfections caused by rotting wood, cracked tiles, stones flung by drunken youths and errors of an architect who had no idea that the ditches of an early fort would cause his basilica's wall to subside. From a structural sense they may be wrong or they may be right – we can never know, and the question is effectively unanswerable.

There are very few cases amongst the buildings discussed in this book where we can associate the structures with testified events. This is a shame but it remains an unavoidable fact. In most respects archaeological and historical evidence are incompatible because archaeology merely dates periods of occupation. Without inscriptions or other written evidence to associate a site with historically testified events or people, such associations are pure supposition. The 'palace of Cogidubnus' at Fishbourne is probably the best-known example where a supposition has become something of a fact with the passage of time.

Nevertheless there is no harm in occasional flights of fancy – throughout the preparation of this book it was very hard to avoid the feeling that some places in Roman Britain must have been amongst the most beautiful, or at least striking, ever created in this island. The temple precinct at Bath was, in its final form, a triumph of cluttered intimacy combining the symmetry of classicism with the irregularity of the site and the Celtic presence of the god of the spring. The valley of Nettleton Shrub is a quiet, isolated place today; the octagonal shrine and its attendant buildings must have seemed almost grotto-like to the visitors approaching from the slopes on either side. Even Hadrian's Wall was built into the landscape rather than over it. All this seems particularly poignant when one considers the controversy which surrounds architecture in Britain today. So this book is an attempt to recreate a little of the lost spirit of the buildings and their nameless builders in and amongst which the Romano-British passed their lives.

APPENDICES

Many of the numerous drawings that form the basis of this book depend on the various techniques of perspective and orthographic projection. Orthographic projection is the presentation of a three dimensional, i.e. solid, object in two dimensions. There are a number of different ways of doing this and they all depend on an accurate ground plan. Representing an upstanding building, of whatever age, is made much easier simply because all the other dimensions and details of the structure are there to be seen and measured. The only consistent feature of Romano-British buildings is, unfortunately, that none of them are upstanding and very few survive above their foundations.

Despite this it is still possible to use the ground plan, together with the better-preserved parallels from elsewhere and common sense, to create a reconstruction which is at least founded on known details. Sometimes the simplicity of a plan makes a reconstruction almost certain. In other cases, like the temple at Nettleton, the remains are so complex that a reconstruction can be no more than an educated guess.

Perspective projection

Perspective drawing creates an illusion of natural depth and realism. The technique is a complex one and the result is not always entirely satisfactory for a variety of reasons. Firstly, a good drawing depends on selecting a suitable viewpoint. Secondly, the distortions involved in using straight lines to represent the effect of what in reality are curves may produce a drawing which is 'accurate' but simply 'does not look quite right'. The reasons for this are very complicated but in short it can often be more effective to exaggerate, or subdue, the effects of perspective in order to produce the desired visual effect.

For the purposes of this book perspective is not always suitable simply because the relative dimensions of the structure are not evident. They are necessary to produce the drawing but do not appear in it. Although perspective sketches and paintings can create a considerable sense of mood and time it can be very easy to fudge details. The end result can be very hard to reconcile exactly with the known plan, if at all. In addition it is not usually simple to find a way of showing a building in such a way that all its various features can be seen. For this reason orthographic projections and elevations have been preferred. They can provide the raw material for perspective reconstructions, as well as supplying exact detail.

Orthographic projection

The most important techniques used in this book are axonometric and isometric projection. The terms are occasionally transposed in error so it is worth discussing them in detail, particularly as they are used so frequently in archaeological books.

Axonometric projection

This technique retains the true plan of the building and is actually drawn straight from it. The precise orientation of the plan is only important insofar as

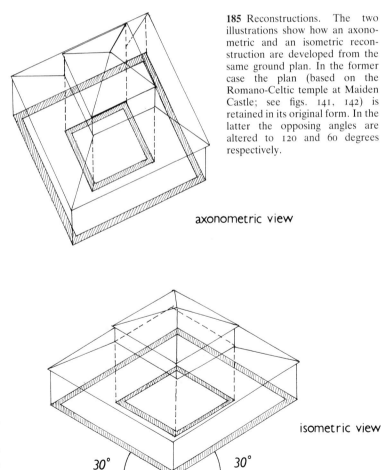

185 Reconstructions. The two illustrations show how an axonometric and an isometric reconstruction are developed from the same ground plan. In the former case the plan (based on the Romano-Celtic temple at Maiden Castle; see figs. 141, 142) is retained in its original form. In the latter the opposing angles are altered to 120 and 60 degrees respectively.

axonometric view

isometric view

30°   30°

the building is presented in such a way that all its features can be appreciated. Once the relative heights of the walls have been decided on (if they are unknown) vertical lines are drawn from all the angle changes in the plan to the chosen heights. The angles of corners remain as they appear in the plan. The roof can then be added, but the technique is especially suitable for illustrating interiors. A single scale then suffices for the whole drawing because the proportions reflect those of the real structure.

Isometric projection

Isometric projection is similar but distorts the plan in order to create an effect which is more realistic for some shapes. Generally these are rectangles and squares. Either shape contains four right-angles at 90 degrees, 360 degrees in total.

In isometric projection the plan is tilted 30 degrees to the horizontal. Within the plan the two pairs of opposite right angles are converted so that one pair becomes two angles at 60 degrees, and the other pair becomes two angles at 120 degrees. The total is obviously still 360 degrees, but what started out as a rectangle has now become a parallelogram, and a square a rhombus. The villa at Great Witcombe (fig. 124) is a particularly suitable subject for this technique but even the octagonal temple at Nettleton can be shown effectively (fig. 150). As with axonometric projection, all the dimensions are in correct proportion, the only difference being the alteration of the angles to emulate some of the effect of perspective.

Elevation

The plan of a building can also be described as a 'vertical view'. An elevation is a horizontal view and is a very good way of depicting monumental buildings which were designed to impress. The technique allows a single façade to be shown in accurate proportion. There were very few such buildings in Roman Britain and hardly any are known in detail. However, so many monumental buildings have survived in other parts of the Roman world that even the barest outline of a plan can provide enough information to create a reconstruction which will be true to the spirit of the original. Adding detail is not always advisable unless there are enough traces to make an accurate restoration. The Temple of Sulis-Minerva is a case in point (fig. 135). On the other hand, a non-committal outline sketch is unlikely to be stimulating, so where the building type is well known it seems quite reasonable to embellish the elevation with likely accessories. This was done with the elevations of the Temple of Claudius at Colchester and the *quadrifons* monument at Richborough. The effect is quite satisfying but it should not be forgotten that both structures survive only in the form of their foundations (figs. 86, 131).

Appendix 2 – Inscriptions

Below are some of the most important inscriptions from Roman Britain which refer to specific buildings. Most are monumental carved inscriptions on stone. A surprising number refer to the repair of existing buildings. A few others have been found scratched on pottery or laid into mosaics. Letters contained within square brackets [ ] are assumed to have been there but are now illegible or destroyed. Letters contained within round brackets ( ) complete words which appear as abbreviations in the original. Due to space some lines have had to be taken over, these are marked with a dash – at the place the break occurs.

Stock imperial titles are abbreviated in Roman inscriptions. See *Finds*, Table VIII, for an expansion of the most important and a list of imperial dates in Table VII. There are also a number or formulaic phrases which are similarly abbreviated. The inscriptions are not literally translated here, but a brief commentary on each points out the significant features.

Architects and masons

1 BATH (spa), Avon (undated)

PRISCUS
TONTI F(ILIUS)
LAPIDARIU[S]
CIVES CAR[NU]TENUS SU[LI]
DEAE V(OTUM) [S(OLVIT) L(IBENS) M(ERITO)]

Dedication to Sulis-Minerva at Bath by Priscus the stonemason, *lapidarius*, son of Tontius, and who came from Carnutenus (Chartres) in Gaul. (*RIB* 149; see *Finds*, fig. 36b.)

2 BEAUPORT PARK (bath-house), East Sussex (third century)

... AU]G ·
... E NOVO...
I]USSIT·VIL[ICUS..
C(URAM)·A(GENTE)·BASSI...
TI[...

Found outside the entrance to the second-century bath-house the inscription seems to refer to the extension built in the third century. The foreman of the ironworks (*vilicus*) seems to have ordered someone called Bassus or Bassianus, the *curam agens* (his agent), to carry out the new work (*novo*). The inscription is so incomplete that it is barely comprehensible but is unique in identifying the name of a man in charge of a specific building project. See Figure 44.

3 BIRRENS (fort), Dumfriesshire (early third century)

BRIGANTIAE S(ACRUM)· AMANDUS ARCITECTUS EX IMPERIO IMP– [ERATUM FECIT]

Statue of Brigantia as Minerva Victrix carved in a niche. Amandus the architect has dedicated the carving to Brigantia in accordance with the command (*imperio*). (*RIB* 2091; see *Finds*, fig. 87a.)

4 PIERCEBRIDGE, county Durham (now lost, date unknown but probably late)

CONDATI
ATTONIUS
QUINTIANUS
MEN EX CC IMP
EX IUS SOL LA

Dedication to Mars Condatus by Attonius Quintianus, surveyor of ducenarian rank, *mensor ex ducenario* (CC = *ducenario*). This means that Quintianus had achieved the rank of *ducenarius* in the army. This was a term used in the late empire for what had formerly been known as *primus hastatus* (the second most senior centurion in the first cohort of a legion which in this case was probably *legio* VI *Victrix* based at York). (*RIB* 1024.)

Military

By far the greatest number of inscriptions come from military sites. Only a small selection of the most important and relevant is given here out of the hundreds known.

1 BIRDOSWALD, Hadrian's Wall (c. 296-300)

[DD]NN·DIOC[LETIANO] ET
M[AXIM]IANO INVICTIS AUGG ET
CONSTANTIO ET MAXIMIANIO
N·N·C·C·SUB V P·AUR·ARPAGIO·PR
PRAETOR·QUOD· ERAT HUMO COPERT
ET IN LABE CONL·ET·PRINC·ET·BAL·REST
CURANT·FL·MARTINO·CENT·P·P·C

A particularly poetic record of the rebuilding of the commandant's house, *praetor(ium)*, the heaquarters building, *princ(ipia)*, and the bath-house, *bal(ineum)* which had been covered with earth (*quod erat humo copert*) and collapsed (*et in labe(m) conl(apsum)*). It also records that the unit (its name is abbreviated beyond recognition) under the centurion Flavius Martinus performed the work during the governorship of Aurelius Arpagius during the rule of the First Tetrarchy, led by Diocletian. (*RIB* 1912; see *Finds*, fig. 22c.)

2 BOWES, County Durham (*c.* 197-8)

D(E)AE FORTUNAE
VIRIUS LUPUS
LEG AVG PR PR
BALINEUM UI
GNIS EXUST
UM COH Ī THR
ACUM RESTI
TUIT CURAN
TE VAL FRON
TONE PRAEF
EQ ALAE VETTONUM

Records the restoration of a bath-house (*balineum...restituit*), dedicated to Fortuna, under the orders of the governor Virius Lupus, after it had been destroyed by fire (*uignis exustem*). The work was carried out by the *alae Vettonum* (a cavalry unit) under the command of their prefect Valerius Fronto, on behalf of the first cohort of Thracians (an infantry unit). (*RIB* 730.)

3 HADRIAN'S WALL (*c.* 122-5)

IMP CAES TRAIAN
HADRIANI AVG
LEG II AVG
A PLATORIO NEPOTE LEG PR PR

Inscription from milecastle 38 (Hotbank) recording the construction of the milecastle during the reign of Hadrian and the governorship of Aulus Platorius Nepos (*c.* 122-5). A similar inscription would have been erected at every milecastle (see fig. 57), carved in wood if the milecastle stood in the Turf Wall section west of the River Irthing. (*RIB* 1638.)

> SILVANI
VALLAVIT
P(EDES) CXII SUB
FLA SECUNDO
[PR]AEF[ECTO]

Building stone from or near the fort at Carvoran indicating that 112ft of rampart had been built by the century (>) of Silvanus, under command of the camp prefect Flavius Secundus (*c.* 136-8). (*RIB* 1820). Similar inscriptions appear throughout the frontier zone and are known at almost all major military sites.

4 HIGH ROCHESTER, Northumberland (218-22)

IMP CAES M AUR[ELIO]
ANTONINO (erased) **PIO FEL [AUG]**
TRIB POT III COS [III PROCOS]
PP BALLIST A SO[LO COH I F]
VARDUL[LORUM ANT SUB CURA]
TIB CL PAUL[INI LEG AUG]
PR PR FEC[IT INSTANTE]
P AEL[IO ERASINO TRIB]

The erased name Antoninus and other titles associates this inscription with the emperor Elagabalus (218-22). The tribune Publius Aelius Erasinus supervised the construction of a new artillery platform, *ballist(arium) a solo*, by the *cohors* I *Vardullorum* during the governorship of Tiberius Claudius Paulinus. (*RIB* 1280; see *Finds*, fig. 22b.)

5 RAVENSCAR, Yorks. (late fourth century)

IUSTINIANUS PP
VINDICIANUS
MABTER TURRE
M CASTRUM FEC[IT]
A SO[LO]

Found on the site of a late signal station the wording records that Justinianus the commander (pp = *praepositus*) and Vindicianus the *magister* (*mabter* = *magister*) built the tower (*turrem*) and fort (*castrum*) from the ground up (*a solo*). (*RIB* 721; see *Finds*, fig. 22d.)

6 RECULVER, Kent (third century)

AEDEM P[RINCI]PIORUM
CU[M B]ASILICA
SU[B A(ULO) T]R[IAR]IO RUFINO
C[O(N)]S(ULARI) [... FOR]TUNATUS
[....DEDICAVI]T

This is the only inscription surviving from any of the Saxon Shore forts. It commemorates the dedication by Fortunatus of the construction of a headquarters building (*principia*) with a shrine (*aedes*) and a hall (*basilica*) under the governor Aulus Triarius(?) Rufinus. The governor's name is not certain but can probably be linked with either Triarius Rufinus or Quintus Aradius Rufinus. Known from elsewhere these two were both active in the early to mid third century. The inscription is the first recorded epigraphic use of the terms *aedes* and *basilica* in this context. (See *Antiq.Journ.*, 61, 1961, 224.)

7 RISINGHAM, Northumberland (*c.* 205-7)

IMP·CAES·L·
SEPT·SEVERO·PIO·PERTIN
ACI·ARAB·ADIAB·PARTHICO·MAXI
COS III ET·M·AVREL·ANTONINO·PIO
COS·II·AVGG·ET·P·SEPT·GETAE·NOB·CAES·
PORTAM · MVRIS · VETVSTATE · DI
LAPSIS·IVSSV·ALFENI·SENECIONIS·V·C
COS·CVRANTE·OCLATINIO·ADVENTO·PROC
AVGG·NN COH·I·VANGION·M·EQ
CVM AEMIL SALVIANO·TRIB
SVO·A SOLO·REST

The inscription describes how the *cohors* I *Vangionum* (9th line) restored this gate and its walls (*portam muris vetustate*, 6th line) under the command of the tribune Aemilius Salvianus, during the governorship of Alfenus Senecio and the procuratorship of Oclatinius Adventus, during the rule of the Emperor Septimius Severus between the years 205-7. The inscription is carved within a circular wreath and held by two soldiers. (*RIB* 1234.)

PUBLIC BUILDINGS

1 BROUGH-ON-HUMBER, Yorks. (140-4)

OB·HONOR[EM]
DOMVS·DIVINAE·IMP·CAES·T·AEL·H[ADRI]
ANI·ANTONINI·A[VG·PII]
PP·COS·I[II]
ET·NVMINIB·A[VG]
M·VLP·IANVARIV
AEDILIS·VICI·PETV[AR]
PROSCAEN·**·DE·SVO·[DEDIT]**

Records the dedication of a new stage (*proscaenium* by the aedile (magistrate) of the town of Petuaria, Marcus Ulpius Januarius, about 140-144 during the reign of Antoninus Pius. (*RIB* 707.)

2 VERULAMIUM, Herts. (79)

[IMP·TITO·CAESARI·DIVI·]VESPA[SIANI·–
]F·VES]PASIANO·AVG]
[PM·TR·P·VIIII·IMP·XV·COS·VII·]DESI–
[G·VIII·CENSORI·PATER·PATRIAE]
[ET·CAESARI·DIVI·VESP]ASIAN[I·F·DO]MI–
[TIANO·COS·VI·DESIG·VII·PRINCIPI]
[IVENTVTIS·ET·]OMN[IVM·COLLEGIORVM–
SACERDOTI]
[CN·IVLIO·A]GRI[COLA·LEGATO·AVG·PRO]–
PR]
[MVNICIPIVM·]VE[RVLAMIVM·BASILICA·OR]–
NATA]

Unfortunately the fragments also allow for two alternatives for the last line. These are:
[CIVITAS·CATV]VE[LLAVNORVM·FORO·EX–
OR]NATA]
or
[RESPVBLICA·]VE[RVLAMIVM·LATIO·–
DO]NATA]

Records the dedication of the forum at Verulamium in 79 during reign of Titus and the governorship of Gnaeus Julius Agricola. Its restoration is an interesting exercise in the standardised formulae of imperial Roman inscriptions. (Frere, 1983, *Verulamium II.*)

3 WROXETER, Shropshire (129-30)

IMP CA[ES]·DIVI·TRAIANI·PARTHI
CI·FIL·DI[VI]·NERVAE·NEPOTI·TRA
IANO·H[A]DRIANO·AVG·PONTI[FI]
CI·MAXIMO·TRIB·POT·XIII[I]·COS·III·PP
CIVITAS·CORNOV[IORVM]

This inscription records the dedication of the forum of the town in 129-30 to Hadrian by the community of the *Cornovii*. The building is not specified but the inscription was found near the main entrance to the forum. (*RIB* 288.)

HOUSES

1 CAMERTON, Avon (third century)

...] ANUS
C]ONDEDIT
..ET·QUINTIANO·COS

Inscription on a statue base found in a room of the villa indicating that ... anus (Name) built (the villa?/part of the villa?) in the year of the consuls ... and Quintianus. This is either 235 or 289, depending on who the other consul was. (*RIB* 180.)

2 CHEW PARK, Avon (undated)

ita uti optimo maximumque iure esse[t n h(abere)–
r(ecte) l(ileat)
quod signis e...res...quae s(upra) s(cripto) est [...]–
partemque quam
quis ex ea euicerit q(uo) m(inus)...[NAME]
...habere possidere ut[i frui recte liceat
id erit quod ita ex ea evic[tum quantum
a ea eta

Included here for completeness this handwritten passage was found on a wooden tablet recovered from a well on the site. It is mostly incoherent and its meaning (which has not been established) need not concern us but the first line is a legal formula known from other sites to refer to the sale of property (real estate or houses) and to guarantee that ownership is free from any kind of bondage or obligation to someone else. As such it may well represent the standard form of contract for house ownership, which would have formed a normal part of the householder's archives. It does not necessarily refer to the site in question, and may even refer to somewhere outside Britain. The restored transcript is that of E.G. Fletcher (see bibliography for Chapter 4).

3 CLANVILLE, Hants. (282-3)

M·AUR
KARINO
N·CAES

Found near the site of the villa this inscription is a dedication to Carinus, as Caesar (282-3). It is not thought to be a milestone and may indicate a building in imperial ownership. (*RIB* 98.)

4 COMBE DOWN, Somerset (now Avon) (c. 212-17)

PRO SALUTE IMP C(A)ES M AUR
ANTONINI PII FELICIS INVIC
TI AUG(USTI) NAEVIUS AUG
LIB ADIUT PROCC PRINCI
PIA RUINA OPRESS A SOLO RES
TITUIT

Found near the villa at Combe Down this inscription records that Naevius, an imperial freedman (*lib(erti) aug(usti)*), and assistant to the procurators (*adiut(or) proc(uratorum)*) – the double 'CC' in PROCC indicates a plural – restored from the ground up (*restituit a solo*), the ruined headquarters building (*ruina principia*). The inscription is not very specific about the nature of the site but it is evident that it was in imperial ownership and therefore

the 'villa' site is more likely to have been the headquarters of an imperial estate though it had clearly been neglected. The imperial titles are those of the emperor Caracalla. (*RIB* 179.)

5 STANWICK, Northants. (undated)

QU]OD
HO]NORAT[US...
...ISCHO...
... NUS...

Found in 1984 in a post-hole packing which had cut into a mid-fourth century mosaic this fragment of mosaic cannot be deciphered but is so rare a find from a Romano-British villa that it seems worthy of inclusion. It seems to be honorific (HONORATUS?) but the main problem is the third line which either represents part of a Greek name, or possibly the word SCHOLA (= a school/fellowship). If the latter, though this seems unlikely at present because of the letter I, this could suggest one of the activities at the site. (*Britannia*, 16, 1985, 324, and 20, 1989, 166, pl. VIb.)

TEMPLES

1 CAERLEON (mid third century)

T·FL·POSTUMIUS
VARUS·V·C·LEG
TEMPL·DIANAE·
RESTITUIT

Inscription on an ansate tablet commemorating the restoration of a temple to Diana by the legionary legate, Titus Flavius Postumius Varus. Postumius Varus is known to have been elevated to the post of Prefect of Rome in 271 which helps date the tablet. The temple is unlocated but the tablet was found in the suburban area to the south-west of the legionary fortress. (*RIB* 316.)

2 CHICHESTER (mid first century)

[N]EPTUNO·ET·MINERVAE
TEMPLUM
[PR]O·SALUTE·DO[MUS]·DIVINA[E]
[EX]·AUCTORITAT[E·TI·]CLAUD·
[CO]GIDUBNI·RE[G·MA]GN·BRIT·
[COLE]GIUM·FABROR·ET·QUI·IN·EQ
[SUNT]·D·S·D·DONANTE·AREAM
[...]ENTE PUDENTINI·FIL

This inscription has provoked much debate over the precise status of the client king Cogidubnus, who ruled over the Regnenses in southern Britain following the Roman invasion. The restoration shown here is that of J.E.Bogaers. However in this context the most interesting point is that a local guild of smiths (*collegium fabrorum*) had donated funds for the building of a temple to Neptune and Minerva with Cogidubnus' permission. It was built on a site dedicated by someone whose name is missing, but was a son of one Pudentinus. (*RIB* 91; see *Britannia*, 10, 1979, 243-54.)

3 CIRENCESTER (mid fourth century)

I O [M]	SI]GNUM ET	SEPTIMIUS
L·SEPT[IMIUS]	[E]RECTAM	RENOVAT
V P PR B [PR]	P]RISCA RE	PRIMAE
REST[ITUIT]	LI]GIONE CO	PROVINCIAE
CIVIS RE[MUS]	L]UMNAM	RECTOR

The three surviving sides of the Jupiter column base from Cirencester record that L. Septimius, governor of B(ritannia) Pr(ima) and a citizen of Rheims, restored the column dedicated to J(upiter) O(ptimus) M(aximus). It had originally been dedicated under the old religion (*prisca religione*) which suggests that the work was done during a period of revived paganism, perhaps during the reign of Julian the Apostate (360-3). (*RIB* 103.)

4 LONDON (late first century)

Londini
ad fanum Isidis

Scratched on a late-first-century flagon this *graffito* is the earliest evidence we have for a temple, *fanum*, dedicated to Isis in London. A recently discovered altar may refer to the repair of this temple or another to Isis (see 5). The flagon was found in Southwark but this does not necessarily indicate that this was where the temple was sited. The lines are evidently meant as an address: 'in London, at (or by) the Temple of Isis'.

5 LONDON (mid third century)

I N H D D
M * MARTIAN
NIUS ▶ PULCH
ER ▶ V ▶ C ▶ LEG
AUGG ▼ PRO *
PRAET ▲ TEMPLUM
ISIDIS ▼ C.....
TIS VETUSTATE
COLLABSUM
RESTITUI PRAE
CEPIT

Altar from Upper Thames Street, London found used as filling in the late riverside wall. It records that Marcus Martiannius Pulcher, possibly governor (or deputy governor) of Upper Britain in the middle of the third century rebuilt a temple which had collapsed. The name of the deity is severely damaged but is probably Isis. It is possible that the temple referred to is the same one mentioned in 4 above. (See *Britannia* 7, 1976, 378.)

6 LYDNEY PARK, Glos. (late fourth century)

D(EO) M N T FLAVIUS SENILIS PR REL EX–
STIPIBUS POSSUIT
O[PITU]LANTE VICTORINO. INTERP(R)[E]
–TIANTE

This cryptic inscription formed part of the mosaic floor in the Temple of Nodens at Lydney Park. It is now lost. An early interpretation of the wording is an excellent example of how educated guesswork became a 'fact'. Collingwood assumed that PR REL stood for *pr(aepositus) rel(iquationis)*, an officer in charge of a military fleet supply base. This was subsequently occasionally used as a basis for arguing that a fleet base must have existed in the area, possibly to act against pirates from Ireland. A new interpretation made by R. P. Wright supplies *pr(aepositus) rel(igionum)*, 'superintendent of religious rites' which has the advantage of fitting the context. It therefore may represent a dedication of the mosaic to Mars Nodens (M N) by Titus Flavius Senilis, in charge of the cult, paid for out of offerings (*ex stipibus*) and assisted by Victorinus, an interpreter (of dreams?). The latter post is testified elsewhere and fits the context of a healing cult where dedicants would sleep in the presence of the god. (See *Britannia*, 16, 1985, 248-9.)

7 YORK (c. 170-95)

DEO·SANCTO
SERAPI
TEMPLUM·A SO
LO FECIT
CL·HIERONY
MIANUS·LEG
LEG·VI·VIC

Inscription recording the building of a temple to the Egyptian god Serapis (a Graeco-Roman Osiris, husband of Isis) by Claudius Hieronymianus, legate of the VI legion. By the reign of Septimius Severus (193-211) he had been promoted to control of the province of Cappadocia which gives us an idea of dates. The temple is unlocated. (*RIB* 658.)

OTHERS

1 LEICESTER (milestone; 119-20)

IMP CAES
DIV TRAIAN PARTH F.DIV NEP
TRAIAN HADRIAN AVG PP TRB
POT IV COS III A RATIS
M II

Milestones do not usually record the building of a road. They marked distances along existing routes and were very possibly renewed when a new emperor took power. This one gives the titles for Hadrian for the year 119-20 and indicates that it is two miles (*m(ilia passuum) II*) to Leicester (*a Ratis*). (*RIB* 2244.)

2 CARLISLE (milestone; 286-93)

IMP C M
AUR MAUS
CARAUSIO PF
INVICTO AUG

and on the other end

FL VA
CONS
TANT[I]
NO NOB
CAES

Found in the River Petteril, 1.6km (1 mile) east of Carlisle, the milestone was evidently erected during the reign of the rebel emperor

Carausius who established independent rule in Britain from 286-93. The milestone was later inverted and recarved with the titles of Constantine I, as Caesar (a junior member of the Tetrarchy) in 306-7. The same stone bears a third, but illegible, inscription. (*RIB* 2291.)

2 SOUTH SHIELDS (c. 222-3)

IMP CAES DIVI SEVERI
NEPOS DIVI MAGNI ANTONINII FIL
M AUREL SEVERUS ALEXANDER
PIUS FELIX AUG PONTIF MAX
TRIB POT PP COS AQUAM
USIBUS MIL COH V GALL IN
DUXIT CURANTE MARIO VALERIANO
LEG EIUS PR PR

Here the emperor Severus Alexander is credited for supplying, via the legate Marius Valerianus, the *cohors* V *Gallorum* with a supply of water (*aquam*). Presumably it refers to the construction of an aqueduct. (*RIB* 1060.)

APPENDIX 3 – Recommended sites

There are numerous Romano-British sites where remains can still be seen today. However, most of these are of military origin and consist of little more than denuded fortifications. This gazetteer lists the best of Roman Britain's sites by type where the remains are reasonably informative and well worth a visit. Outstanding examples are indicated with an asterisk (*). Anyone using the list, which has four-figure National Grid figures, will benefit from using Ordnance Survey maps in the 1:50 000 Series. Basic information about opening times is included but these are subject to change. Ancient monuments (AM) have standard (S) opening hours (Mon-Sat 9.30-6.00, 15 March – 15 Oct, Sundays 2-6.30; Mon-Sat 9.30-4.00 16 Oct-14 March, Sundays 2-4). Some are open on Sunday mornings as well (+ SM) but, unless the information specifically says so, assume they are closed.

People keen to explore more widely are advised to consult books under the heading of Guides to Roman Britain in the bibliography where far more information than can be given here is available. However sites mentioned in the text with visible remains of any sort are indicated in the bibliography.

The reader is reminded that there are many outstanding sites on the Continent with either exceptionally well-preserved remains, or reconstructed buildings. Amongst the former are Rome, Ostia, Pompeii and Herculaneum in Italy; Sbeitla and Dougga in Tunisia; and Aphrodisias, Aspendus, Ephesus, Pergamum and Sardis in Turkey. Amongst the latter are the military buildings at the Saalburg and Xanten in Germany, and the bath-gymnasium at Sardis in Turkey.

Military buildings

1 Fort defences	Grid ref. (OS map)		2 Internal buildings		
* Birdoswald	NY 6166 (86)	AM; any time	Caernarvon	SH 4862 (115)	AM; daily
Brecon y Gaer	SO 0029 (160)	AM; any time (ask at farm)	* Chesters	NY 9170 (87)	AM; S + SM
			* Corbridge	NY 9864 (87)	AM; S
Burgh Castle	TG 4704 (134)	AM; any time	* Housesteads	NY 7968 (86/7)	see above
Caerleon	ST 3490 (171)	any time	Lunt (Baginton)	SP 3475 (140)	see above
Hardknott	NY 2101 (89)	AM; any time	South Shields	NZ 3667 (86)	see above
High Rochester	NY8398 (80)	local permission	Vindolanda	NY 7766 (86)	daily
Housesteads	NY 7968 (86/7)	AM; S + SM	York	SE 6052 (105)	daily, principia beneath Minster
* Lunt (Baginton)	SP 3475 (140)	May-Sept pm (not Mon + Thurs)			
Pevensey	TQ 6404 (199)	AM; any time			
* Portchester	SU 6204 (196)	AM; any time			
Richborough	TR 3260 (179)	AM; S + SM			
* South Shields	NZ 3667 (88)	Easter – Sept daily with restricted times in Oct			

3   Military baths

* Binchester	NZ 2031 (93)	April-Sept, daily except Tues & Wed
* Caerleon	ST 3490 (171)	AM; S + SM
* Chesters	NY 9170 (87)	see above
Ravenglass 'Walls Castle'	SD 0895 (96)	any time

4   Amphitheatres

* Caerleon	ST 3490 (171)	AM; S + SM
Chester	SJ 4066 (117)	AM; any time

5   Frontiers

Hadrian's Wall curtain:

Benwell (vallum)	NZ 2164 (88)	AM; local key (Denhill Park)
Brunton (turret 26b)	NY 9269 (87)	AM; any time
Black Carts (turret 29a)	NY 8871 (87)	AM; any time
Limestone Corner (ditch/vallum)	NY 8771 (87)	any time
* Housesteads west (milecastle 37)	NY 7968 (86/7)	AM; S + SM
* Poltross Burn (milecastle 48)	NY 6366 (86)	AM; any time

Antonine Wall:

Watling Lodge	NS 8679 (65)	AM; any time

Towns

1   Basilica

* Lincoln 'Mint Wall'	SK 9771 (121)	any time (behind hotel in Westgate)

2   Amphitheatres/theatre

Cirencester	SP 0201 (163)	AM; any time
Silchester	SU 6462 (175)	AM; any time
* Verulamium	TL 1307 (166)	daily + SM

3   Public baths

* Bath	ST 7564 (172)	daily + SM
Leicester 'Jewry Wall'	SK 5804 (140)	daily except Fri
Wall	SK 1006 (139)	AM; S (except Mon and Tues)
Wroxeter 'Old Work'	SJ 5608 (126)	AM; S + SM

4   Gates and defences

* Caerwent	ST 4690 (171)	AM; any time
* Colchester	TL 9925 (168)	any time (Balkerne Lane)
* Lincoln	SK 9771 (121)	any time (Bailgate)
Silchester	SU 6462 (175)	AM; any time

Houses

1   Town houses

Caerwent	ST 4690 (171)	AM; any time
Dorchester	SY 6990 (194)	any time (behind County Hall)
* Dover 'Painted House'	TR 3141 (179)	daily Apr-Oct except Mon

2   Villas

* Bignor	SU 9814 (197)	March-Oct except Mon
* Brading (I of Wight)	SZ 6086 (196)	April-Sept daily + SM
* Chedworth	SP 0513 (163)	March-Oct except Mon, Nov-9th Dec except Mon + Tues
* Fishbourne	SU 8404 (197)	March-Nov daily; Dec-Feb Sundays only
* Littlecote	SU 2970 (174)	Apr-Oct daily
* Lullingstone	TQ 5365 (188)	AM; S + SM

Sacred sites

* Bath	ST 7564 (172)	daily + SM
Benwell	NZ 2164 (88)	AM; any time (Broomridge Ave)
* Carrawburgh	NY 8571 (87)	AM; any time
Colchester	TL 9925 (168)	temple vaults summer season only (Castle Museum). Church; by new police station on ring road, any time
Lydney Park	SO 6102 (162)	occasional and by appointment with Lydney Estate Office (Tel: 0594-42844)

Others

Ackling Dyke (road)	SU 0116 (195)	any time
* Chesters (bridge)	NY 9169 (87)	AM; any time
* Dover (lighthouse)	TR 3141 (179)	AM; S + SM
High Rochester (tombs)	NY 8398 (80)	local permission (ask for directions at fort farm)
Keston (tombs)	TQ 4163 (177)	any time but access private
Mersea (barrow)	TM 0214 (168)	local key
Piercebridge (bridge?)	NZ 2115 (93)	AM; any time
* Willowford (bridge)	NY 6266 (86)	AM; any time (foot from Gilsland)

BIBLIOGRAPHY
AND REFERENCES

This is a select bibliography. The first section lists works under a number of general headings; the second follows the chapter headings with a general section for each followed by sites referred to in alphabetical order. The reader is advised also to examine the pages of *Current Archaeology* which is often the only illustrated source of detailed information and illustrations for sites excavated in recent years prior to their formal publication (publishing address: 9 Nassington Road, London NW3 2TX). Useful information will also be found in the pages of *Britannia*, a journal published by the Society for the Promotion of Roman Studies (31-4 Gordon Square, London WC1H 0PP) under the section headed '*Roman Britain in* 19—'.

All sites with visible remains listed in the bibliography are indicated * along with a four figure National Grid reference. Many are in private ownership (though most of the outstanding sites are in the guardianship of official bodies or the National Trust) and the reader should not assume that access is freely available. Ancient monuments in the care of English Heritage, Cadw or the Scottish Development Department are indicated AM (ancient monument). Appendix 3 lists a number of recommended sites which can be visited today with brief details of access.

Abbreviations

AA[2, 4] *Archaeologia Aeliana* (second, fourth series etc.), Society of Antiquaries, Newcastle upon Tyne.
Antiq. J. Antiquaries Journal, Society of Antiquaries, London.
Arch. Journ. Archaeological Journal, Royal Archaeological Institute.
Arch. Camb. Archaeologia Cambrensis, Cambrian Archaeological Association.
Arch. Cant. Archaeologia Cantiana, Kent Archaeological Society.
B.A.R. *British Archaeological Reports*.
BBCS Bulletin of the Board of Celtic Studies, University of Wales, Cardiff.
CAM Pottery forms published by C.F.C. Hawkes and M.R. Hull, *Camulodunum*, 1947 and M.R. Hull, *Roman Colchester*, 1958.
C.B.A. Council for British Archaeology, London
J. Brit. Arch. Assoc. Journal of the British Archaeological Association, London.
JRS Journal of Roman Studies.
LACTOR *London Association of Classical Teachers Original Records*.
LAMAS London and Middlesex Archaeological Society.

PSAS Proceedings of the Society of Antiquaries of Scotland, Edinburgh.
RRCSAL Report of the Research Committee of the Society of Antiquaries, London.
RIB Collingwood, R.G., and Wright, R.P., 1965.
RIC Mattingly H. and Sydenham E.A., *Roman Imperial Coinage*, London, 1923, etc.
TBGAS Transactions of the Bristol and Gloucestershire Archaeological Society.
TCWAAS Transactions of the Cumberland and Westmorland Antiquarian and Archaeological Society.

Note on Classical sources

As a general note on sources a number of the historical texts including those by Suetonius and Tacitus are available in translation in the Penguin Classics series. Almost all can be found in the Loeb Classical Library but these are expensive and usually confined to specialist libraries. Extracts from many authors can be found in Lewis and Reinhold, 1955, (see below) which is easily available.

General background works
Romano-British history and background
Clayton, P., 1980, *A Companion to Roman Britain*, Oxford.
Esmonde Cleary, A.S., 1989, *The Ending of Roman Britain*, London.
Frere, S.S., 1987, *Britannia*, London, third edition.
Johnson, S., 1980, *Later Roman Britain*, London
Jones, B., and Mattingly, D., 1990, *An Atlas of Roman Britain*, Oxford.
Millet, M., 1990, *The Romanisation of Britain*, Cambridge.
Salway, P., 1981, *Roman Britain*, Oxford.
Todd, M., 1981, *Roman Britain* (55BC-AD400), London.
Wacher, J.S., 1979, The Coming of Rome, London.

Guides to Roman Britain
Clayton, P., 1980, *A Companion to Roman Britain*, Oxford.
Clayton, P., 1985, *A Guide to Archaeological Sites*, London.
Ottaway, P., and Cyprien, M., 1987, *A Traveller's Guide to Roman Britain*, London (excellent photographs but lacking in precise detail).

Wilson, R.J.A., 1988 (3rd edition), *A Guide to the Roman Remains in Britain*, London (this book is outstanding and indispensable for anyone seriously pursuing sites as it supplies exact descriptions of locations down to the last field gate, as well as serving as a universal site guide book).
H.M. Ordnance Survey, 1978 (4th edition), *Map of Roman Britain*, Southampton.

Architecture and reconstruction (including a number of well-illustrated books about Pompeii, Herculaneum and Ostia in Italy)
Drury, P.J., 1982, *Structural Reconstruction*, B.A.R. 110 (British Series), Oxford
Calza, G., and Becatti, G., 1977, *Ostia*, Nr.1 in the series of Itineraries of the Museums, Galleries and Monuments of Italy, Rome
Carpiceci, A.C., 1977, *Pompeii 2000 Years Ago*, Florence.
Connolly, P., 1979, *Pompeii*, London.
Fletcher, B., 1896 (and numerous subsequent editions), *A History of Architecture on the Comparative Method*, London.
Grant, M., 1971, *Cities of Vesuvius; Pompeii and Herculaneum*, London.
Ling, R., 1983, 'The Insula of the Menander at Pompeii', *Antiq. J.*, 63, 34-57.
MacDonald, W.L., 1986, *The Architecture of the Roman Empire. Volume II: an Urban Appraisal*, Yale.
Maiuri, A., 1977, *Herculaneum*, Nr.53 in the series of Itineraries of the Museums, Galleries and Monuments of Italy, Rome.
Maiuri, A., 1977, *Pompeii*, Nr. 3 in the series of Itineraries of the Museums, Galleries and Monuments of Italy, Rome.
Meiggs, R., 1960 and 73, *Roman Ostia*, Oxford.
Sorrell, A., 1969, *Roman London*, London.
Sorrell, A., 1976, *Roman Towns in Britain*, London.
Sorrell, A., 1981, *Reconstructing the Past*, London.
Ward-Perkins, J.B., 1981, *Roman Imperial Architecture*, Pelican History of Art series, Harmondsworth.
Ward-Perkins, J.B., 1988, *Roman Architecture*, History of World Architecture series, London.
Wheeler, R.E.M., 1964, *Roman Art and Architecture*, London.

243

Archaeology

Collingwood, R.G, and Richmond, I.A., 1969, *The Archaeology of Roman Britain*, London.

de la Bédoyère, G., 1989, *The Finds of Roman Britain*, London.

Frere, S.S., and St Joseph, J.K.S., 1983, *Roman Britain from the air*, Cambridge.

Greene, K., 1986, *The Archaeology of the Roman Economy*, London.

Rivet, A.L.F., 1964, *Town and Country in Roman Britain*, London.

Rivet, A.L.F., 1969 (Ed), *The Roman Villa in Britain*, London.

Wacher, J.S., 1966, *The Civitas Capitals of Roman Britain*, Leicester.

Wacher, J.S., 1974, *The Towns of Roman Britain*, London.

Ward, J., 1911, *Romano-British Buildings and Earthworks*, London.

Sources

Collingwood, R.G., and Wright, R.P., 1965, *The Roman Inscriptions of Britain*, Oxford.

Goodburn, R., and Waugh, H., 1983, *The Roman Inscriptions of Britain I: Epigraphic Indexes*, Gloucester.

Greenstock, M.C., 1971, *Some Inscriptions from Roman Britain*, LACTOR 4, London.

Ireland, S., 1986, *Roman Britain – a Sourcebook*, London.

Lewis, N., and Reinhold, M., 1955, *Roman Civilisation. Sourcebook II: the Empire*, New York.

Mann, J.C., and Penman, R.G., 1978, *Literary Sources for Roman Britain*, LACTOR 11, London.

Moore, R.W., 1954, *The Romans in Britain – a Selection of Latin Texts with a Commentary*, London.

Rivet, A.L.F., and Smith, C., 1979, *The Place-Names of Roman Britain*, London.

Vitruvius, *The Ten Books on Architecture*, New York, 1960 (Dover Press, translation by **M.H. Morgan**).

1   Construction techniques

References to sites mentioned in this chapter will be found under the relevant chapter headings below; for example Caerleon will be found under Chapter 2 for Military buildings, Bignor villa will be found under Chapter 4 for Houses and so on.

General

Adam, J.-P., 1984, *La construction romaine*, Paris.

Barry, R., 1980, *The construction of buildings. Volume 1: Foundations, Walls, Floors, Roofs*, Oxford.

Chapman, H., 1979, 'A Roman mitre and try square from Canterbury', *Antiq. J.*, 59, 403-7.

Ling, R., 1985, 'The mechanics of the building trade' in **Grew, F., and**

Hobley, B., (Eds) 1985, *Roman Urban Topography in Britain and the Western Empire*, CBA Res. Rep. 59, London.

Strong, D., and Brown, D., 1976, *Roman Crafts*, London.

Vitruvius, *The Ten Books on Architecture*, New York, 1960 (Dover Press, translation by **M.H. Morgan**).

Wacher, J.S., 1971, 'Roman Iron Beams', *Britannia*, 2, 200-2.

Surveying

Dilke, O.A., 1971, *The Roman Land Surveyors*, Newton Abbot.

Walthew, C.V., 1978, 'Property Boundaries and the Sizes of Building Plots', *Britannia*, 335-50.

Walthew, C.V., 1987, 'Length-Units in House-Planning at Silchester and Caerwent', *Britannia*, 18, 201 ff.

Timber

McCarthy, M.R., 1986, 'Woodland and Roman Forts' in *Britannia*, 17, 339-43.

Richmond, I.A., 1961, 'Roman Timber Building' in **E.M. Jope (ed.)**, *Studies in Building History*.

Stone, brick and tile

Blagg, T.F.C., 1976, 'Tools and Techniques of the Roman Stonemason in Britain' in *Britannia*, 152-72.

Brodribb, G., 1987, *Roman Brick and Tile*, Gloucester.

Darvill, T., and McWhirr, A., 1984, 'Brick and tile production in Roman Britain', *World Archaeology*, 15, 239-61.

Dunning, G.C., 1949, 'The Purbeck Marble Industry in Roman Britain' in *Archaeological News Letter*, 1, 11, 15 ff.

Greene, K., 1986, *The Archaeology of the Roman Economy*, London, 149-56.

McWhirr, A., and Viner, D., 1978, 'The production and distribution of tiles in Roman Britain with particular reference to the Cirencester region', *Britannia*, 9, 357-77.

McWhirr, A., 1979 (ed.), *Roman Brick and Tile. Studies in Marketing, Distribution and Volume in the Western Empire*, B.A.R. (International Series) No.68, Oxford.

Peacock, D.P.S., 1977, 'Brick and tiles: petrology and origin', *Britannia*, 8, 235-47.

Pritchard, F.A., 1986, 'Ornamental Stonework from Roman London' in *Britannia*, 17, 169-89.

Williams, J.H., 1971, 'Roman building-materials in South-East England', *Britannia*, 2, 166-95.

Williams, J.H., 1971, 'Roman Building-Materials in the South-West', *TBGAS*, 90, 95-119.

Woodfield, P., 1978, 'Roman Architectural Masonry from Northamptonshire', *Northamptonshire Archaeology*, 13, 67-87.

Mosaics

Johnson, P., 1982, *Romano-British Mosaics*, Shire Archaeology No. 25, Aylesbury.

Neal, D.S., 1981, *Roman Mosaics in Britain*, Soc. Prom. Roman Studies, London.

Rainey, A., 1973, *Mosaics in Roman Britain*, Newton Abbot.

Wall-painting

Davey, N., and Ling, R., 1982, *Wall-Painting in Roman Britain*, Soc. Prom. Roman Studies, London.

Ling, R., 1985, *Romano-British Wall-Painting*, Shire Archaeology No. 42, Aylesbury.

2   Military building

General works

Breeze, D.J., 1983, *Roman Forts in Britain*, Shire Archaeology No. 37, Aylesbury.

Campbell, D.B., 1984, '*Ballisteria* in first to mid-third century Britain: a reappraisal', *Britannia*, 15, 75-84.

Frere, S.S., and St Joseph, J.K.S., 1983, *Roman Britain from the Air*, Cambridge.

Gentry, A.P., 1976, *Roman Military Stone-Built Granaries in Britain*, B.A.R. (British Series) No. 32, Oxford.

Holder, P.A., 1982, *The Roman Army in Britain*, London.

Jarrett, M.G., 1969 (ed.), *The Roman Frontier in Wales*, Cardiff.

Johnson, A., 1983, *Roman Forts*, London.

Lepper, F., and Frere, S.S., 1988, *Trajan's Column*, Gloucester.

Manning, W.H., and Scott, I.R., 1979, 'Roman Timber Military Gateways in Britain and on the German Frontier', *Britannia*, 10, 19-61.

Webster, G., 1985 (3rd edn), *The Roman Imperial Army*, London.

Webster, G., 1988 (ed.), *Fortress into City. The Consolidation of Roman Britain*, London.

Welsby, D.A., 1982, *The Roman Military Defence of the British Province in its Later Phases*, B.A.R. (British Series) 101, Oxford.

Wilson, D.R., 1984, 'Defensive Outworks of Roman Forts in Britain', *Britannia*, 15, 63-74.

Wilson, R., 1980, *Roman Forts*, London.

Sites

ANTONINE WALL *

Breeze, D.J., and Dobson, B., 1987 (3rd, revised, edition), *Hadrian's Wall*,

London, 86-111.

Hanson, W.S., and Maxwell, G.S., 1986, *Rome's North-West Frontier, the Antonine Wall*, Edinburgh.

Keppie, L.J.F., 1982, 'The Antonine Wall 1960-1980', *Britannia*, 13, 91-111.

Robertson, A.S., 1979, *The Antonine Wall*, Glasgow.

BAGINTON (The Lunt)   SP 3475 *

Hobley, B., 1971, 'An experimental reconstruction of a Roman military turf rampart', *Roman Frontier Studies 1967*, Tel Aviv, 21 ff.

Hobley, B., 1971-3, 'Excavations at the Lunt Roman military site, Baginton, 1968-71, *Trans. Birm. and Warwicks. Arch. Soc.*, 85, 30 ff.

Hobley, B., 1974, 'The Lunt fort, 1966 experimental rampart and ditch: years 1-3' (Appendix 1), *Roman Frontier Studies 1969*, (eds. E. Birley, B. Dobson, and M.G. Jarrett), Cardiff, 79 ff.

BEATTOCK   NS 9915

Maxwell, G.S., 1976, 'A Roman Timber Tower at Beattock Summit, Lanarkshire', *Britannia*, 7, 33 ff.

BEAUPORT PARK   TQ 7814 *

Brodribb, G., 1979, 'Tile from the bathhouse at Beauport Park', *Britannia*, 10, 139 ff.

Brodribb, G., and Cleere, H., 1988, 'The Classis Britannica Bath-house at Beauport Park, East Sussex', in *Britannia*, 19, 217 ff.

BRECON Y GAER *Cicutio*   SO 0029 *

Wheeler, R.E.M., 1926, *The Roman Fort near Brecon*, London.

BIRRENS *Blatobulgium*   NY 2175 *

Robertson, A.S., 1975, *Birrens. Blatobulgium*, Edinburgh.

CAERLEON *Isca*   ST 3390 * (AM)

Boon, G.C., 1972, *Isca, the Roman Legionary Fortress at Caerleon, Monmouthshire*, Cardiff.

Boon, G.C., 1987, *The Legionary Fortress of Caerleon-Isca*, Caerleon.

Nash-Williams, V.E., 1957, 'Prysg Field II' in *BBCS*, 15.

Zienkiewicz, J. David, 1986, *The Legionary Fortress Baths at Caerleon, I. The Buildings*, Cardiff.

Wheeler, R.E.M., 1928, 'The Roman Amphitheatre at Caerleon, Monmouthshire', *Archaeologia*, 78, 111 ff.

CHESTER *Deva*   SJ 4066 *

Thompson F.H., 1975, 'The Excavation of the Roman Amphitheatre at Chester', *Archaeologia*, 105, 127-240.

See also *Britannia*, 9, 1978, pl.xxiiiB latrine.
Current Archaeology, no. 84, 1982, 6-12.
Britannia, 20, 1989, 283, pl.xxB cornice stone.

CHESTERHOLM see VINDOLANDA

CHESTERS *Cilurnum*   NY 9170 * (AM)

MacDonald, G., 1931, 'The Bath-house at the Fort of Chesters (Cilurnum)', *AA⁴*, 8, 219-304.

CIRENCESTER *Corinium Dobunnorum*
                            SP 0201 *

Wacher, J., and McWhirr, A., 1982, *Early Roman Occupation at Cirencester*, Cirencester Excavations I, Cirencester.

CORBRIDGE *Corstopitum/Coriosopitum*
                    NY 9864 * (AM)

Bishop, M.C., and Dore, J.N., 1988, *Roman Corbridge: the Fort and Town*, London.

DOVER *Dubris*   TR 3141 *

Philp, B.J., 1981, *The Excavation of the Roman Forts of the Classis Britannica at Dover, 1970-1977*, Kent Monograph Series No. 3, Dover.

EASTER HAPPREW   NT 1940

Steer, K.A., 1956-7, 'The Roman Fort at Easter Happrew, Peeblesshire, *PSAS*, 90, 93-101.

ELGINHAUGH   NT 3267

Hanson, W.S., 1987, 'Elginhaugh', *Current Archaeology*, 104, 268-72.
see also *Britannia*, 19, 1988, 428-9 [annexe].

EXETER *Isca Dumniorum*   SX 9192

Bidwell, P.T., 1979, *The Legionary Bath-House and Basilica and Forum at Exeter*, Exeter Archaeological Report No. 1, Exeter.

Bidwell, P.T., 1980, *Roman Exeter: Fortress and Town*, Exeter.

GELLYGAER   ST 1397

Ward, J., 1903, *The Roman Fort of Gellygaer*, London and Derby.

GOLDSBOROUGH   NZ 8315

Hornsby, K., and Laverick, W.D., 1933, 'Roman Signal Station at Goldsborough, near Whitby', *Arch. J.*, 89, 206 ff.

GLOUCESTER *Glevum*   SO 8318 *

Hurst, H.R., 1985, *Kingsholm*, Gloucester Archaeological Report No. 2, Gloucester.

Hurst, H.R., 1986, Gloucester, *Roman and Later Defences*, Gloucester Archaeological Report No. 2, Gloucester.

GREAT CASTERTON   TF 0009

Manning, W.H., and Scott, I.R., 1979, op. cit. (under general references above), 31.

Todd, M., 1968, *The Roman Fort at Great Casterton, Rutland*, Nottingham.

HADRIAN'S WALL * (AM;NT)

Breeze, D.J., and Dobson, B., 1987 (3rd, revised, edition), *Hadrian's Wall*, London.

Collingwood-Bruce J., 1853, *The Roman Wall*, London.

Collingwood-Bruce J., 1885, *The Hand-Book to the Roman Wall*, London.

Daniels, C., (ed.) 1978, *Handbook to the Roman Wall*, 13th edition, Newcastle.

Graham, F., 1984, *Hadrian's Wall in the Days of the Romans*, Newcastle upon Tyne.

Jones, G.D.R., 1976, 'The western extremity of Hadrian's Wall: Bowness to Cardurnock', *Britannia*, 7, 236-43

Johnson, S., 1989, *Hadrian's Wall*, London.

Simpson, F. Gerald, 1976, *Watermills and Military Works on Hadrian's Wall. Excavations in Northumberland 1907-1913*, (edited by Grace Simpson), Kendal.

See also:
Current Archaeology, 96, 1985, 16-19 (foundations and whitewashing).
Current Archaeology, 116, 1989 (special edition concerned entirely with recent work on the wall at Carlisle, Birdoswald, Vindolanda, Wallsend and South Shields).

HIGH ROCHESTER *Bremenium*
                            NY 8398 *

see **Daniels, C., 1978**, *op. cit.* under Hadrian's Wall above, 295-301.

HOD HILL *Dunium?*   ST 8510 *

Brailsford, J.W., 1962, *Hod Hill, I: Antiquities from Hod Hill in the Durden Collection*, London.

Richmond, I.A., 1968, *Hod Hill II*, London.

HOLT *Bovium?*   SJ 4054

Grimes, W.F., 1930, *Holt, Denbighshire: The Works Dept of the XXth Legion at Castle Lyons*, Y Cymmrodor 41, London.

HOUSESTEADS *Vercovicium*
                    NY 7868 * (AM)

see works listed under Hadrian's Wall above.

INCHTUTHIL   NO 1239

Pitts, L., and St Joseph, J.K., 1985, *Inchtuthil, the Roman Legionary Fortress*, Britannia Monograph Series No. 6, London.

LINCOLN *Lindum*   SK 9771 *

Webster, G., 1949, 'The Legionary Fortress at Lincoln' in *JRS*, 39, 57-78.

LONGTHORPE   TL 1597

Dannell, G.B., and Wild, J.P., 1987, *Longthorpe II: the military works depot: and episode in landscape history*, Britannia Monograph Series No. 8, London.

Frere, S.S., and St Joseph, J.K., 1974, 'The Roman Fort at Longthorpe' in *Britannia*, 5, 1-129.

LUNT, THE (see BAGINTON)

LYMPNE *Portus Lemanis*   TR 1134 *

Cunliffe, B., 1980, 'Excavations at the Roman fort of Lympne' in *Britannia*, 11, 227-88.

MARYPORT *Alauna*   NY 0337

Jarrett, M.G., 1976, *Maryport, Cumbria: a*

Roman Fort and its Garrison, Kendal.

NEWSTEAD *Trimontium* NT 5734
Curle, J., 1911, *A Roman Frontier Post and its People: The Fort of Newstead in the Parish of Melrose*, Glasgow.

PORTCHESTER *Portus Adurni?*
SU 6204 * (AM)
Cunliffe, B.W., 1975, *Excavations at Portchester Castle, I: Roman*, RRCSAL No. 32, London.

RAVENGLASS *Glannoventa* ST 0895 *
see Daniels, C., 1978, op. cit. under Hadrian's Wall above, 284-6.

RICHBOROUGH *Portus Rutupiae*
TR 3260 * (AM)
Bushe-Fox J.P, 1949, *Fourth Report on the Excavation of the Roman Fort at Richborough, Kent*, RRCSAL No. 16, London.
Cunliffe B.W, 1968, *Fifth Report on the Excavations of the Roman Fort at Richborough, Kent*, RRCSAL No. 23, London.

SAXON SHORE (Bradwell, Brancaster, Burgh Castle, Dover, Reculver, Richborough, Lympne, Pevensey, Portchester)
Johnson, S., 1979, *The Roman Forts of the Saxon Shore*, London.
White, D.A., 1961, *Litus Saxonicum*, Madison, Wisconsin.

SCARBOROUGH (see also GOLDSBOROUGH) TA 0589 * (AM)
Rowntree, A., 1931, *History of Scarborough*, Scarborough, 40-50.

VINDOLANDA (Chesterholm)
NY 7766 *
Bidwell, P.T., 1985, *The Roman Fort of Vindolanda at Chesterholm, Northumberland*, London.
Birley, R., 1977, *Vindolanda: A Roman frontier post on Hadrian's Wall*, London.

YORK *Eburacum* SE 6052 *
Addeyman, P.V. and Black, V.E., 1984, *Archaeological Papers from York presented to M.W. Barley*, York. Arch. Trust.
Hope-Taylor, B., 1971, *Under York Minster*, York Minster.
RCHM, 1962, *Eburacum – Roman York*, Volume I, London, 15 fig. 8 (Multangular Tower).

3 Public buildings

General Works

Duncan-Jones, R.P., 1985, 'Who paid for public buildings in Roman cities?', *in* **Grew, F., and Hobley, B., (eds.) 1985**, op. cit.
Esmonde Cleary, S., 1987, *Extra-Mural Areas of Romano-British Towns*, B.A.R. (British Series) 169, Oxford.
Frere, S.S., 1987, *Britannia*, London, 229-256.
Grew, F., and Hobley, B., (eds.) 1985,

Roman Urban Topography in Britain and the Western Empire, CBA Res. Rep. 59, London.
Johnson, S., 1973, 'A Group of Late Roman City Walls', *Britannia*, 4, 210-23
Mackreth, D.M., 1987, 'Roman public buildings' in **Schofield, J., and Leech, R., 1987**, *Urban Archaeology in Britain*, CBA Res.Rep. No.61, London.
Maloney, J., and Hobley, B., (eds.) 1983, *Roman Urban Defences in the West*, London.
Sorrell, A., 1976, *Roman Towns in Britain*, London.
Wacher, J.S., 1966, *The Civitas Capitals of Roman Britain*, Leicester.
Wacher, J.S., 1974, *The Towns of Roman Britain*, London.
Wacher, J.S., 1985, 'The functions of urban buildings: some problems' in **Grew, F., and Hobley, B., (eds.) 1985**, op. cit.
Yegül, F. K., 1986, *The Bath-Gymnasium at Sardis*, Archaeological Exploration of Sardis Report 3, Harvard University Press (a fascinating account of the excavation and partial reconstruction of a monumental public building in Turkey).

Sites

CAERLEON *Isca* ST 3390 *
for *ludus*/amphitheatre see reference under Chapter 2

CAERWENT *Venta Silurum*
ST 4690 * (AM)
Ashby, T., 1906, 'Excavations at Caerwent, Monmouthshire, on the site of the Romano-British City of Venta Silurum, in the year 1905', *Archaeologia (second series)*, 10, 112-117 (South Gate).
Frere, S.S., 1989, 'Roman Britain in 1988', *Britannia*, 20, 264.
Nash-Williams, V.E., 1953, 'The Forum and Basilica and Public Baths of the Roman Town of *Venta Silurum* at Caerwent in Monmouthshire', *BBCS*, 15, 159, ff.

CAISTOR-BY-NORWICH (also Caistor St Edmunds) *Venta Icenorum*
TG 2303 *
Atkinson, J., 1931, *Caister Excavations*, London.
Frere, S.S., 1970, 'Caistor-by-Norwich forum and basilica' in *Britannia*, 1, 1 ff.

CANTERBURY *Durovernum Cantiacorum*
TR 1457 *
Bennett, P., 1984, 'The Topography of Roman Canterbury: a brief re-assessment', *Arch.Cant.*, 100, 47-56.
Frere, S.S., Stow, S., and Bennett, P., 1982, *Excavations on the Roman and Medieval Defences of Canterbury*, Maidstone, Canterbury Arch. Trust (Arch. of Canterbury vol. II).

CASTOR TL 1296
Mackreth, D., 1984, *Durobrivae: A Review of Nene Valley Archaeology*, ix, Peterborough.

CHARTERHOUSE ST 5056 *
Campbell, Elkington, D., Fowler, P., and Grinsell, L., 1970, *The Mendip Hills in Prehistoric and Roman times*, Bristol Arch. Research Group.

CIRENCESTER *Corinium Dobunnorum*
SP 0201 *
McWhirr, A., 1981, *Roman Gloucestershire*, Gloucester, 28-36.
McWhirr, A., 1988, 'Cirencester' in Webster, G., op. cit. above (general), 81-3.

COLCHESTER *Camulodunum*
TL 9925 *
Crummy, P., 1977, 'Colchester: the Roman Fortress and the Development of the Colonia', *Britannia*, 8, 65-105 [Balkerne Gate revision].
Crummy, P., 1982, 'The Roman theatre at Colchester' in *Britannia*, 13, 299-302.
Hawkes, C., and Hull, M.R., 1947, *Camulodunum*, RRCSAL No. 14, London.
Hull, M.R, 1958, *Roman Colchester*, RRCSAL No. 20, Oxford (Balkerne Gate, Duncan's Gate, defences general).

DORCHESTER (Dorset)
Durnovaria SY 6990 *
Bradley, R., 1975, 'Maumbury Rings, Dorchester: The Excavations of 1908-13', *Archaeologia*, 105, 1-97.

GOSBECKS (near Colchester) TL 9622
Dunnett, R., 1971, 'The Excavation of the Roman Theatre at Gosbecks', *Britannia*, 2, 27-47.

LEICESTER *Ratae Coritanorum/*
Corieltauvorum SK 5804 *
Hebditch, M., and Mellor, J., 1973, 'The Forum and Basilica of Roman Leicester', *Britannia*, 4, 1 ff.
Kenyon, K.M., 1948, *Excavations at the Jewry Wall site, Leicester*, London.
Wacher, J.S., 1974, *The Towns of Roman Britain*, London.

LINCOLN *Lindum* SK 9771 *
Jones, M., Gilmour, B., and Camidge, K., 1982, 'Lincoln', *Current Archaeology*, 83, 366-369.
Jones, M., 1988, 'Lincoln', in Webster, G., (Ed), *Fortress into City*, London, 145-65.
Thompson, F.H., and Whitwell, J.B., 1973, 'The Gates of Roman Lincoln' in *Archaeologia*, 104, 129-207.

LONDON *Londinium* TQ 3881 *
Brigham, T., 1990, 'A Reassessment of the Second Basilica in London, AD 100-400', *Britannia*, 21, 53-98.
Hill, C., Millett, M., and Blagg, T., 1980, *The Roman Riverside Wall and Monumental Arch in London, Excavations at Baynard's Castle, Upper Thames Street, London, 1974-76*,

LAMAS Special Paper No. 3, London.

Johnson, T., 1975, 'A Roman Signal Tower at Shadwell, E1', Interim Note, *LAMAS*, 26, 278-80 (see also Merrifield, 1983, below, 192-4).

Marsden, P., 1975, 'Excavation of a Roman Palace Site in London, 1961-72' in *LAMAS*, 26, 1-102.

Marsden, P., 1976, 'Two Roman public baths in London', *LAMAS*, 26, 1-102 [Huggin Hill and Cheapside].

Marsden, P., 1978, 'The discovery of the civic centre of Roman London' in *Collectanea Londiniensia*, LAMAS Special Paper No. 2, 89 ff.

Marsden, P., 1980, *Roman London*, London.

Marsden, P., 1987, *The Roman Forum Site in London – Discoveries before 1985*, London.

Merrifield, R., 1983, *London, City of the Romans*, London.

Perring, D., 1985, 'London in the 1st and early 2nd centuries' in **Grew, F., and Hobley, B., (eds.) 1985**, *Roman Urban Topography in Britain and the Western Empire*, CBA Res. Rep. 59, London.

Philp, B., 1977, 'The forum of Roman London' *Britannia*, 8, 1 ff.

Royal Commission on Historical Monuments (England) 1928, *An Inventory of the Historical Monuments in London, Volume III, Roman London*, London.
See also:
Current Archaeology, 109, 1988, 49-50 [amphitheatre].
Current Archaeology, 115, 1989, 244-45 [Huggin Hill baths].

RICHBOROUGH *Rutupiae*
                         TR 3260 * (AM)
Cunliffe B.W, 1968, *Fifth Report on the Excavations of the Roman Fort at Richborough, Kent*, RRCSAL No. 23, London.

ST ALBANS see VERULAMIUM

SILCHESTER *Calleva Atrebatum*
                         SU 6462 * (AM)
Boon, G.C., 1957, *Roman Silchester*, London.

Boon, G.C., 1974, *Silchester: The Roman Town of Calleva*, Newton Abbot.

Fulford, M., 1985, 'Excavations on the sites of the Amphitheatre and Forum-Basilica at Silchester, Hampshire. An Interim Report.' *Antiq.J.*, 65, 39-81.

Fulford, M., 1989, *The Silchester Amphitheatre excavations of 1979-85*, Britannia Monograph 10.

STONEA GRANGE   TL 4493

see *Current Archaeology*, 81, 1981, 298-301.

VERULAMIUM (St Albans) TL 1307 *
Kenyon, K.M., 1934, 'The Roman Theatre at Verulamium' in *Transactions of the St Albans and Hertfordshire Architectural and Archaeological Society*.
Frere, S.S., 1983, *Verulamium*

Excavations II, RRCSAL No. 41, London.

Richardson, K.M., 1944, 'Report on Excavations at Verulamium, Insula XVII, 1938' [Macellum], *Archaeologia*, 90, 81.

Wheeler, R.E.M., and Wheeler, T.V., 1936, *Verulamium, a Belgic and two Roman Cities*, RRCSAL No. 11, Oxford.

WALL *Letocetum*   SK 1006 * (AM)
Webster, G., 1958, *The Roman Site at Wall, Staffordshire*, London (site booklet) see also various references in the 'Roman Britain in . . . ' section of *Britannia*, vols. 3 (1972), 6 (1975), 7 (1976), 8 (1977), 9 (1978).

WROXETER *Viroconium Cornoviorum*
                         SJ 5608 * (AM)
Atkinson, J., 1942, *Excavations at Wroxeter 1923-27*, Oxford.

Barker, P., 1975, 'Excavations on the Site of the Baths Basilica at Wroxeter 1966-74: an Interim Report', *Britannia*, 6, 106-117.

Barker, P., 1985, 'Aspects of the topography of Wroxeter (Viroconium Cornoviorum)' in **Grew, F., and Hobley, B., (Eds) 1985**, *Roman Urban Topography in Britain and the Western Empire*, CBA Res. Rep. 59, London.

Bushe-Fox, J.P., 1913, *First Report on the Excavations on the Site of the Roman Town at Wroxeter, Shropshire, 1913*, RRCSAL No. 1, Oxford.

Bushe-Fox, J.P., 1914, *Second Report on the Excavations on the Site of the Roman Town at Wroxeter, Shropshire, 1914*, RRCSAL No. 2, Oxford.

Webster, G., 1987, 'Wroxeter', *Current Archaeology*, 107, 364-68.

YORK *Eburacum*   SE 6051 *
Royal Commission on Historical Monuments (England) 1962, *An Inventory of the Historical Monuments in the City of York, Volume I, Eburacum, Roman York*, London.

4 Houses

General Works

Black, E.W., 1987, *The Roman Villas of South-East England*, B.A.R. (British Series) 171, Oxford.

Branigan, K., 1976, *The Roman Villa in South-West England*, Bradford-on-Avon.

Branigan, K., and Fowler, P.J., 1976, *The Roman West Country. Classical culture and Celtic society*, Newton Abbot.

Casey, J., 1985, 'The Roman housing market' in **Grew, F., and Hobley, B., (eds.) 1985**, *Roman Urban Topography in Britain and the Western Empire*, CBA Res. Rep. 59, London.

Johnston, D.E., 1988 (3rd edition), *Roman Villas*, Shire Archaeology No. 11, Aylesbury.

Neal, D.S., 1981, *Roman Mosaics in Britain*, London.

Percival, J., 1976, *The Roman Villa. An Historical Introduction*, London.

Rainey, A., 1973, *Roman Mosaics*, Newton Abbot.

Rivet, A.L.F., 1964, *Town and Country in Roman Britain*, London.

Rivet, A.L.F., 1969 (ed.), *The Roman Villa in Britain*, London.

Smith, J.T., 1963, 'Romano-British Aisled Houses' in *Arch. J.*, 120, 1 ff.

Smith, R.F., 1987, *Roadside Settlements in Lowland Roman Britain*, B.A.R. (British Series) 157, Oxford.

Todd, M., 1978 (Ed), *Studies in the Romano-British Villa*, Leicester.

Walthew, C.V., 1975, 'The Town House and the Villa House in Roman Britain', *Britannia*, 6, 189-205.

Walthew, C.V., 1978, 'Property Boundaries and the Sizes of Building Plots in Roman Towns', *Britannia*, 9, 335-50

Walthew, C.V., 1987, 'Length-Units in House-Planning at Silchester and Caerwent', *Britannia*, 18, 201 ff.

Webster, G.W., 1983, 'The Fall of Magnentius' in **Hartley, B., and Wacher, J., 1983**, *Rome and Her Northern Provinces. Papers presented to Sheppard Frere in honour of his retirement from the Chair of Archaeology of the Roman Empire*, Oxford.

Wilson, D.R., 1974, 'Romano-British villas from the air', *Britannia*, 4, 251-62.

For references to house ownership elsewhere in the Empire and the Columella passage the simplest source of information is **Lewis, N., and Reinhold, M., 1966**, *Roman Civilisation, Sourcebook II: The Empire*, New York City, 167-75, 213-14.

Sites

ASHTEAD (Surrey)   TQ 1760
Lowther, A.W.G., 1928, 'Excavations at Ashtead, Surrey' in *Surrey Arch. Coll.* 37, 144-63.

Lowther, A.W.G., 1929, 'Excavations at Ashtead, Surrey. Second Report' in *Surrey Arch. Coll.*, 38, Part 1, 1-17.

BANCROFT (Bucks)   SP 8240 *
Mynard, D.C., 1987 (Ed.), *Roman Milton Keynes: excavations and fieldwork 1971-82*, Buckinghamshire Archaeological Society Monograph Series No. 1, Aylesbury, 60 ff.
See *Britannia*, 15, 1984, 306 for a detailed plan.

BARNSLEY PARK (Glos.)   SP 0806
Webster, G., 1967, 'Excavations at the Romano-British Villa in Barnsley Park, Gloucestershire', *TBGAS*, 86, 74-87.

Webster, G., and Smith, L., 1981, 'The excavation of a Romano-British rural settlement at Barnsley Park: Part I', *TBGAS*, 99.

Webster, G., and Smith, L., 1982, 'The excavation of a Romano-British rural settlement at Barnsley Park: Part II',

TBGAS, 100, 65-190.

Webster, G., and Smith, L., 1985, 'The excavation of a Romano-British rural settlement at Barnsley Park: Part III', *TBGAS*, 103, 73-100.

BASTON MANOR, HAYES (Kent)   TQ 4064
Philp, B., 1973, *Excavations in West Kent 1960-1970*, Dover, 80-93.

BIGNOR (West Sussex)   SU 9814 *
Applebaum, S., 1975, 'Some Observations on the Economy of the Roman Villa at Bignor, Sussex', *Britannia*, 6, 118-132.
Frere, S.S., 1982, 'The Bignor Villa', *Britannia*, 13, 135-196.

BRISLINGTON (Avon)   ST 6170
Branigan, J., 1972, 'The Romano-British Villa at Brislington', *Som. Arch. Nat. Hist.*, 116, 78-85.

BRIXWORTH (Northants)   SP 7471
see *Britannia*, 3, 1972, 322 and fig. 7.

CAERWENT (*Venta Silurnum*)
          ST 4690 * (Cadw)
Martin, A., and Ashby, T., 1901, 'Excavations at Caerwent', *Archaeologia*, 57(II), 301-310.

CHALK (Kent)   TQ 6773
Johnston, D.E., 1972, 'A Roman building at Chalk, near Gravesend', *Britannia*, 3, 112-48.

CHEDWORTH (Glos.)   SP 0513 * (NT)
Goodburn, R., 1986, *The Roman Villa: Chedworth*, National Trust.
Webster, G., 1983, 'The Function of the Chedworth Roman Villa' in *TBGAS*, 101, 5-20.

CHEW PARK (Avon)   ST 5751
Turner, E.G., 1956, 'A Roman Writing Tablet from Somerset', *JRS*, 46, 115-18.
Rahtz, P., and Greenfield, E., 1976, *Excavations at Chew Valley Lake*, London, 63 and pl.xxviii.

CIRENCESTER (*Corinium Dobunnorum*)
          SP 0201
McWhirr, A., 1986, *Houses in Roman Cirencester*, Cirencester Excavations III, Cirencester Excavation Committee, Cirencester.
McWhirr, A., 1988, 'Cirencester', in Webster, G., op. cit. (see general bib. for Chapter 3), 85-7.

CLANVILLE (Hants.)   SU 3148
Victoria County History Hants, (i), 1900, 296.

COLCHESTER (*Camulodunum* TL 9925
Crummy, P., 1977, 'Colchester: the Roman Fortress and the Development of the Colonia', *Britannia*, 8, 65-105.
Crummy, P., 1988, 'Colchester', in Webster, G., (ed.) 1988, *Fortress into City*, London, 42-43.

COMBE DOWN (Avon)   ST 7662
Branigan, K., 1976, op. cit. above

(general), 45.

DITCHLEY (Oxon)   SP 3290
Ralegh Radford, C.A., 1936, 'The Roman Villa at Ditchley, Oxon', *Oxoniensia*, 1, 24-69.

DORCHESTER (*Durnovaria*) SY 6990 *
Drew, Lt. Col. C.D., and Collingwood Selby, K.C., 1938, 'Colliton Park Excavations: First Interim Report', *Proc.Dorset Nat. Hist. Arch. Soc.*, 59, 1-14.
Drew, Lt. Col. C.D., and Collingwood Selby, K.C., 1939, 'Colliton Park Excavations: Second Interim Report', *Proc.Dorset Nat. Hist. Arch. Soc.*, 60, 51-65.

DOVER (*Dubris*)   TR 3141 *
Philp, B., 1989, *The Roman House with Bacchic Murals at Dover*, Kent Monograph Series, Volume V, Dover.

ECCLES (Kent)   TQ 7260
Detsicas, A., 1983, *The Cantiaci*, Gloucester, 120-126.

FISHBOURNE (West Sussex) SU 8304 *
Cunliffe, B.W., 1971, *Excavations at Fishbourne, Vols. I & II*, RRCSAL No. 26, London, 1971.
Cunliffe, B.W., 1971A, *Fishbourne, a Roman Palace and its Garden*, London.

FROCESTER (Glos.)   SO 7703
Gracie, H.S., 1970, 'Frocester Court Roman Villa; First Report', *TBGAS*, 88, 15-86.
Gracie, H.S., and Price, E.G., 1979, 'Frocester Court Roman Villa; Second Report', *TBGAS*, 97.
See also *Current Archaeology*, 88, 139-145.

GADEBRIDGE PARK (Herts.) TL 0508
Neal, D.S., 1974, *The Excavation of the Roman Villa in Gadebridge Park, Hemel Hempstead, 1963-8*, RRCSAL No. 31, London.

GLOUCESTER *Glevum*   SO 8318
Hurst, H.R., 1988, 'Gloucester' in Webster, G., (ed.) 1988, *Fortress into City*, Gloucester, 56-60.

GREAT WITCOMBE (Gloucestershire)
          SO 8914 * (AM)
Clifford, E.M., 1954, 'The Roman Villa, Witcombe, Gloucestershire', *TBGAS*, 73, 5-69.

HOLCOMBE (Devon)   SY 3193
Pollard, S., 1974, 'A Late Iron Age and a Romano-British Villa at Holcombe, near Uplyme, Devon', *Proc. Devon Archaeol. Soc.*, 32, 59-161.

HUCCLECOTE (Gloucestershire)
          SO 8617
Clifford, E.M., 1933, 'The Roman Villa, Hucclecote', *TBGAS*, 55, 323-76.

Clifford, E.M., 1961, 'The Hucclecote Roman Villa', *TBGAS*, 80, 42-9.

KEYNSHAM (Avon)   ST 6469 *
Bulleid, A., and Horne, E., 1926, 'The Roman House at Keynsham, Somerset', *Archaeologia*, 75, 109-138.

LEICESTER   SK 5804
Wacher, J.S., 1974, *Towns of Roman Britain*, London, 352, pl. 70.

LITTLECOTE (Wiltshire) SU 2970 *
Toynbee, J.M.C., 1981, 'Apollo, Beasts and Seasons: Some Thoughts on the Littlecote Mosaic', *Britannia*, 12, 1-5.
Walters, B., 1981, 'Littlecote', *Current Archaeology*, 80, 264-268.
See also *Britannia*, 15, 1984, 322-3 and fig. 26, and 20, 1989, 315-6 and figs. 26, 27 for plans of the whole complex.

LLANTWIT   MAJOR   (South Glamorgan)   SS 9569
Hogg, A.H.A., 1974, 'The Llantwit Major Roman Villa: a reconsideration of the evidence' in *Britannia*, 5, 225-250.
Nash-Williams, V.E., 1945, 'The Roman Villa at Llantwit Major' in *Arch. Camb.*, 102, 21 ff.
Webster, G., 1969, in Rivet, A.L.F., 1969 op. cit. (general section), 238-243.

LOCKLEYS (Herts)   TL 2316
Ward-Perkins, J.B., 1938, 'The Roman Villa at Lockleys, Welwyn', *Antiq. J.*, 18, 339-76.

LONDON *Londinium*   TQ 3281 *
Marsden P., 1980, *Roman London*, London, 151-155.
Merrifield, R., 1983, *London, City of the Romans*, London, 47, fig. 5.
Perring, D., 1985, 'London in the 1st and early 2nd centuries' in Grew, F., and Hobley, B., (eds.) 1985, *Roman Urban Topography in Britain and the Western Empire*, CBA Res. Rep. 59, London.
See also *Britannia* 15, 1984, 309 & pl.xixB for Lime Street damp course (Chapter 1).

LUFTON (Somerset)   ST 5118
Hayward, L.C., 1952, 'The Roman Villa at Lufton, near Yeovil, Somerset' (baths), *P. Som. Arch. Soc*, 97, 91-112.
Hayward, L.C., 1972, 'The Roman Villa at Lufton, near Yeovil, Somerset' (house), *P. Som. Arch. Soc*, 116, 59-77.

LULLINGSTONE (Kent)
TQ 5365 *(AM)
Meates Lt.-Col. G.W, 1979, *The Lullingstone Roman Villa, Kent, Volume I – the Site*, Maidstone.
Meates Lt.-Col. G.W., 1987, *The Lullingstone Roman Villa, Kent, Volume II – The Wall Paintings and Finds*, Maidstone.

NORTH LEIGH (Oxon.) SP 3915 *(AM)
Wilson, D.R., and Sherlock, D., 1980, *The Roman Villa at North Leigh*, HMSO, London.

PARK STREET (Herts) TL 1403
O'Neil, H.E., 1945, 'The Roman Villa at Park Street, Near St Albans, Hertfordshire', *Arch.J.*, 102, 21-110.

PIDDINGTON (Northants) SP 7954
see *Current Archaeology*, 117, 1989, 316-321; and *Britannia*, 20, 1989, 290 for summaries

ROCKBOURNE (Hants) SU 1217 *
RCHM, 1983, 'West Park Roman Villa, Rockbourne, Hampshire', *Arch.J.*, 140, 129-50.

QUINTON (Northants) SP 7753
Taylor, R.M., 1973, 'Quinton' in *Bulletin of the Northamptonshire Federation of Archaeological Societies*, 8, 15-17. See also *Britannia*, 3, 1972, 322.

RIVENHALL (Essex) TL 8217
Rodwell, W.J., and Rodwell, K.A., 1986, *Rivenhall: investigations of a villa, church, and village, 1950-77*, Chelmsford Archaeology Trust Report No. 4; CBA Research Report No. 55.

ST ALBANS see VERULAMIUM

SILCHESTER *Calleva Atrebatum*
SU 6462
Boon, G.C., 1957, *Roman Silchester*, London.
Boon, G.C., 1974, *Silchester: The Roman Town of Calleva*, Newton Abbot.

SPARSHOLT (Hants) SU 4130
See **Johnston, D.E., 1988**, op. cit. (general section), fig.23 and plate 5.

STANWICK (Northants.) SP 9771
Neal, D.S., 1989, 'The Stanwick Villa, Northants.: An Interim Report on the Excavations of 1984-88', *Britannia*, 20, 149-168.

STROUD (Hants.) SU 7223
Morley Watson, A., 1909, 'The Romano-British Settlement at Stroud, near Petersfield, Hants', *Arch. J.* 66, 33 ff.

VERULAMIUM (St Albans) TL 1307 *
Frere, S.S, 1972, *Verulamium Excavations I*, RRCSAL No. 28, London.
Frere, S.S, 1983, *Verulamium Excavations II*, RRCSAL No. 41, London.
Wheeler, R.E.M., and Wheeler, T.V., 1936, *Verulamium, a Belgic and two*

Roman Cities, RRCSAL No. 11, Oxford.

WINTERTON (Lincs.) SE 1118
Stead, I.M., 1977, *Excavations at Winterton Roman Villa and other Roman sites in North Lincolnshire*, 1958-67, Department of the Environment Archaeological Reports no. 9.

WOODCHESTER (Glos.)
SO 8303 * (very occasionally)
Clarke, G., 1982, 'The Roman Villa at Woodchester' in *Britannia*, 13, 197 ff.
Lysons, S., 1797, *An Account of the Roman Antiquities discovered at Woodchester*, London.

5 Sacred Sites

General works

Barley, M.W., and Hanson, R.P.C., (eds.) 1968, *Christianity in Roman Britain 300-700*, Leicester.
Green, M.J., 1986, *The Gods of the Celts*, Gloucester.
Henig, M., 1984, *Religion in Roman Britain*, London.
Henig, M., and King, A., (eds.) 1986, *Pagan Gods and Shrines of the Roman Empire*, Oxford University Committee for Archaeology Monograph No. 8, Oxford.
Horne, P.D., 1981, 'Romano-Celtic Temples in the Third Century' in **Henig, M., and King, A., 1981**, *The Roman West in the Third Century*, B.A.R. (International Series) 109, Oxford, 21-26.
Horne, P.D., 1986, 'Roman or Celtic Temples?' in **Henig and King, 1986**, op. cit.
Lewis, M.J.T., 1965, *Temples in Roman Britain*, Cambridge.
Milburn, R., 1988, *Early Christian Art and Architecture*, Aldershot.
Morris, R., 1983, *Churches in British Archaeology*, CBA Res. Rep. 47, London.
Muckelroy, K.W., 1976, 'Enclosed Ambulatories in Romano-Celtic Temples in Britain' in *Britannia*, 7, 173-191.
Rodwell, W. (ed.), 1980, *Temples, Churches and Religion in Roman Britain*, B.A.R. (British Series) 77, Oxford [contains a number of useful papers discussing various related topics].
Thomas, C., 1981, *Christianity in Roman Britain to AD500*, London.
Webster, G., 1986, *The British Celts and their Gods under Rome*, London.
Wheeler, R.E.M., 1928, – see reference under Harlow below for a survey of Romano-Celtic temples.
Wilson, D.R., 1975, 'Romano-Celtic Temple Architecture', *J. Brit. Arch. Assoc.* 38, 2-27.

Sites

BATH *Aquae Sulis* ST 7564 *
Blagg, T.F.C., 1979, 'The Date of the Temple at Bath' *Britannia*, 10, 101 ff.
Cunliffe, B., 1986, 'The Sanctuary of Sulis-Minerva at Bath: a brief review' in **Henig and King 1986**, op. cit.
Cunliffe, B.W., 1984, *Roman Bath Discovered*, London, 1971, revised edition, London.
Richmond, I.A., and Toynbee, J.M.C., 1955, 'The Temple of Sulis-Minerva at Bath' *JRS*, 45, 97 ff.
Cunliffe, B., and Davenport, P., 1985, *The Temple of Sulis Minerva at Bath, Volume 1*: The Site, Oxford University Committee for Archaeology Monograph No. 7, Oxford.

BENWELL *Condercum* NZ 2164 * (AM)
Simpson, F.G., and Richmond, I.A., 1941, 'The Roman Fort on Hadrian's Wall at Benwell', *AA^4*, 19, 37 ff.

BOWES MOOR (Scargill Moor; Durham)
NY 9910 *
Hanson, W.S., and Keppie, L.J.F., 1980, *Roman Frontier Studies*, 1979, B.A.R., Oxford, 233-54.

BURHAM (Kent) TQ 7262
Ward, J., 1911, *Romano-British Buildings and Earthworks*, London, 245-6, fig. 70.

CAERNARFON *Segontium* SH 4862
Boon, G.C., 1960, 'A Temple of Mithras at Caernarvon-Segontium', *Arch. Camb.*, 109, 136-72.

CAERWENT *Venta Silurum*
ST 4690 *(AM)
Ashby, T., Hudd, A.E., and King, F., 1910-11, 'Excavations at Caerwent, Monmouthshire, on the Site of the Romano-British City of Venta Silurum in the year 1908', *Archaeologia*, 62, 4.

CARRAWBURGH *Brocolitia*
NY 8571 *(AM)
Allason-Jones, L., and McKay, B., 1985, *Coventina's Well*, Chesters.
Richmond, I.A., and Gillam, J.P., 1951, 'The Temple of Mithras at Carrawburgh', *AA^4*, 29, 1-92.
Smith, D.J., 1962, 'The Shrine of the Nymphs and the Genius Loci at Carrawburgh', *AA^4*, 40, 59-81.

CARRON (Arthur's O'on; Central)
NS 8782
Henig, M., 1984, op. cit. above (general section) 208-9, 227.
Steer, K.A., 1958, 'Arthur's O'on: A lost shrine of Roman Britain', *Arch. J.* 115, 99-110.
Steer, K.A., 1976, 'More light on Arthur's O'on', *Glasgow Arch. J.* 4, 90-2.

COLCHESTER *Camulodunum*
TL 9925 *
Crossan, C., and Crummy, N., forthcoming, *Butt Road cemetery and church*, Colchester Archaeological Reports, Colchester.

249

Crummy, P., 1988, *Secrets from the Grave*, Colchester [Butt Road 'church' and cemetery booklet].

Drury, P.J., 1984, 'The Temple of Claudius at Colchester Reconsidered', *Britannia*, 15, 7-50.

Fishwick, D., 1972, 'Templum Divo Claudio Constitutum', *Britannia*, 3, 164-181.

Hull, M.R., 1958, *Roman Colchester*, London, 160 ff (Temple of Claudius).

FARLEY HEATH (Surrey)   TQ 0544 *
Goodchild, R.G., 1947, 'Farley Heath' *Antiq. J.*, 27, 83.

FRILFORD (Oxon)   SU 4396
Bradford, J.S.P., and Goodchild, R.G., 1939, 'Excavations at Frilford, Berks', *Oxoniensia*, 4, 1-70.

Hingley, R., 1982, 'Recent Discoveries of the Roman Period at the Noah's Ark Inn, Frilford, South Oxfordshire', *Britannia*, 13, 305-9.

GODMANCHESTER *Durovigutum*
          TL 2470
Green, H.J.M., 1986, 'Religious Cults at Roman Godmanchester' in **Henig and King**, op. cit., 1986, 29 ff.

HARLOW (Essex)   TL 4612 *
France, N.E., and Gobel, B.M., *The Romano-British Temple at Harlow, Essex*, Gloucester, 1985.

Wheeler, R.E.M., 1928, 'A "Romano-Celtic" temple near Harlow, Essex', and a note on the type', *Antiq. J.*, 8, 300-326.
See also *Current Archaeology 112* for a summary of recent work.

HAYLING ISLAND (Hants.)   SU 7202
Downey, R., King, A., and Soffe, G., 1980, 'The Hayling Island Temple and Religious Connections across the Channel' in **Rodwell, W., (Ed.) 1980**, *Temples, Churches and Religion in Roman Britain*, B.A.R. (British Series) 77 (vol.I), Oxford.

HEATHROW (Middlesex)   TQ 0574
Grimes, W.F., 1961, 'Draughton, Heathrow and Colsterworth', in **Frere, S.S. (ed.)**, *Problems of the Iron Age in Southern Britain*, 21-3.

HINTON St MARY (Dorset)
          ST 7816 * (British Museum)
Painter, K.S., 1966, 'The Design of the Roman Mosaic at Hinton St Mary', *Antiq. J.*, 56, 49-54.

HOUSESTEADS *Vercovicium*   NY 7868
Bosanquet, R.C., 1904, 'The Roman Camp at Housesteads', *AA²*, 25, 255-263 [mithraeum] ff.

ICKLINGHAM (Suffolk)   TL 7872
West, S., 1976, 'The Roman Site at Icklingham', *East Anglian Arch.* 3, 63-126.

JORDON HILL (Dorset)   SY 7982 *
Drew, C.D., 1931, 'Jordon Hill', *Proc. Dorset Nat. Hist. Arch. Soc.*, 53, 265 ff.

LAMYATT BEACON (Somerset)
          ST 6636
Leech, R., 1986, 'The excavation of a Romano-Celtic Temple and a Later Cemetery on Lamyatt Beacon, Somerset' in *Britannia*, 17, 259-328.

LITTLECOTE (Wilts.)   SU 2970 *
Toynbee, J.M.C., 1981, 'Apollo, Beasts and Seasons: Some Thoughts on the Littlecote Mosaic', *Britannia*, 12, 1-5.
See also bibliography for Chapter 4.

LONDON *Londinium*
Grimes, W.F., 1968, *The Excavation of Roman and Mediaeval London*, London [Mithraeum]

Hill, C., Millett, M., and Blagg, T., 1980 *The Roman Riverside Wall and Monumental Arch in London, Excavations at Baynard's Castle, Upper Thames Street, London, 1974-76*, LAMAS Special Paper No. 3, London.

Marsden, P., 1980, *Roman London*, London, 49 [Isis flagon], 50-52 [classical temple], 133 [Isis altar], 134-136 (arch), 137-147 [Mithraeum].

Merrifield, R., 1983, *London: City of the Romans*, London, 179-180 [Isis altar], 183-187 [Mithraeum].

LULLINGSTONE (Kent)   TQ 5365
Meates Lt.-Col. G.W., 1987, *The Lullingstone Roman Villa, Kent, Volume II – The Wall Paintings and Finds*, Maidstone.

LYDNEY PARK (Glos.)   SO 6102 *
Wheeler, R.E.M., and Wheeler, T.V., 1932, *Report on the Excavation of the Prehistoric, Roman and Post-Roman site in Lydney Park, Gloucestershire*, RRCSAL No. 9, London.
See also **Henig, M., 1984**, op. cit. (general section), 253, note 16.

MAIDEN CASTLE (Dorset)
          SY 6688 *(AM)
Wheeler, R.E.M., 1943, *Maiden Castle, Dorset*, RRCSAL No. 12 Oxford.

NETTLETON (Wilts)   ST 8276
Wedlake W.J, 1982, *The Excavation of the Shrine of Apollo at Nettleton, Wiltshire, 1956-1971*, RRCSAL No. 40, London.

PAGANS HILL (Avon)   ST 5562
Rahtz, P., 1951, 'The Roman Temple at Pagans Hill, Chew Stoke, North Somerset', *P. Som. Arch. Soc.*, 96, 112 ff.

RICHBOROUGH *Rutupiae*
          TR 3260 * (AM)
Brown, P.D.C., 1971, 'The Church at Richborough', *Britannia*, 2, 225-31.

RUDCHESTER *Vindobala*   NZ 1167
Gillam, J.P., 1954, 'The Temple of Mithras at Rudchester', *AA⁴*, 32, 176-219.

SILCHESTER *Calleva Atrebatum*
          SU 6462
Fox, G.E., and Hope, W.H. St John, 1892-3, 'Excavations on the site of the Roman city at Silchester, Hants, in 1892' [church], *Archaeologia*, 53, 563.

Frere, S.S., 1975, 'The Silchester Church: the Excavation by Sir I. Richmond in 1961', *Archaeologia*, 105, 277-302.

King, A., 1983, 'The Roman Church at Silchester Reconsidered', *Oxford J. Archaeol*, 2, 225-37.

ST ALBANS – *see* VERULAMIUM

SOUTH CADBURY (Somerset) ST 6325
Alcock, L., 1970, 'Excavations at South Cadbury Castle, 1969', *Ant. J.*, 50, 14-25.

SPRINGHEAD *Vagniacae*   TQ 6172
Detsicas, A.P., 1983, *The Cantiaci*, Gloucester, 60 ff.

Penn, W.S., 1959, 'The Romano-British settlement at Springhead', *Arch. Cant.*, 73, 24 ff.

Penn, W.S., 1964, 'Springhead: the temple ditch site', *Arch. Cant.*, 79, 170 ff.

STANWICK (Northants)   SP 9771
Neal, D.S., 1989, 'The Stanwick Villa, Northants.: An Interim Report on the Excavations of 1984-88', *Britannia*, 20, 156-7.

ULEY (Glos.)   ST 7899
McWhirr, A., 1981, *Roman Gloucestershire*, Gloucester, 156-8.

Woodward, A. and Leach, P., 1990, *The Uley shrines; excavation of a ritual complex on West Hill, Uley, Gloucestershire, 1977-9*, London.

VERULAMIUM (St Albans)   TL 1307
Lowther, A.W.G., 1935, 'Verulamium: Insula XVI', *Trans. St Albans and Herts. Arch. and Arch. Soc.*, 166-72.

Wheeler, R.E.M., and Wheeler, T.V., 1936, *Verulamium, a Belgic and Two Roman Cities*, RRCSAL No. 11, Oxford.

WOODEATON (Oxon)   SP 5312
Goodchild, R., and Kirk, J.R., 1954, 'The Romano-Celtic Temple at Woodeaton', *Oxoniensia*, 19, 15 ff.

WOOD LANE END (Herts.)   TL 0807
Neal, D.S., 1983, 'Unusual buildings at Wood Lane End, Hemel Hempstead', *Britannia*, 14, 73-86.

Neal, D.S., 198, 'A Sanctuary at Wood Lane End, Hemel Hempstead', *Britannia*, 15, 193-216.

WROXETER *Viroconium*   SJ 5608
Bushe-Fox, J.P., 1913, *First Report on the Excavation on the Site of the Roman Town at Wroxeter, Shropshire, 1913*, RRCSAL No. 1, Oxford.

6 Other Buildings

Roads

Bagshawe, R.W., 1979, *Roman Roads*, Shire Archaeology No. 10, Aylesbury.

Margary, I.D., 1973 (revised edition), *Roman Roads in Britain*, London.

See also the *Ordnance Survey Map of Roman Britain*, 4th edition, 1978

Bridges

Bidwell, P., and Holbrook, N., 1989, *Hadrian's Wall bridges*, London (Chesters NY 9170 *(AM); Willowford NY 6266 *(AM)).

Kackson, D.A., and Ambrose, T.M., 1976, 'A Roman Timber Bridge at Aldwincle, Northants' in *Britannia*, 7, 39-72.

Milne, G., 1982, 'Further Evidence for Roman London Bridge?', *Britannia*, 13, 271-6 (see also **Milne G.**, under Quays and wharfs below, p. 44-54).

Selkirk, R., 1983, *The Piercebridge Formula*, Cambridge (NZ 2115 *).

Quays and wharfs

Boon, G., 1978, 'Excavations on the site of a Roman quay at Caerleon', in **Boon, G. (ed.)**, 1978, *Monographs and Collections, I, Roman Sites*, Cambrian Arch.Assoc., 1-24.

Dillon, J., 1989, 'A Roman Timber Building from Southwark', *Britannia*, 20, 229-231.

Dyson, T., (ed.) 1986, *The Roman Quay at St Magnus House, London: Excavations at New Fresh Wharf, London 1974-78*, LAMAS Special Paper No. 8, London.

Milne, G., 1985, *The Port of Roman London*, London.

Aqueducts and water supply

Clarke, G., 1982, 'The Roman Villa at Woodchester' in *Britannia*, 13, 217.

Forster, R.H., (Ed) 1908, 'Corstopitum: Report of Excavations in 1907', *AA³*, 4, 272.

Richardson, K.M., 1940, 'Excavations at Poundbury, Dorset', *Ant. J.*, 20, 435.

Stephens, G.R., 1985, 'Civic Aqueducts in Britain', *Britannia*, 16, 197 ff.

Thompson, F.H., 1954, 'The Roman Aqueduct at Lincoln', *Arch. J.* 111, 106.

Wacher, J.S., 1978, *Roman Britain*, London, pl. 27 [Catterick].

Whitwell, J.B., 1976, 'The Church Street Sewer and an Adjacent Building' in *The Archaeology of York. Volume 3: The Legionary Fortress*, York.

Mills

Simpson, F. Gerald, 1976, *Watermills and Military Works on Hadrian's Wall*.

Excavations in Northumberland 1907-1913, (edited by Grace Simpson), Kendal.

Spain, R.J., 1985, 'Romano-British Watermills', *Arch. Cant.*, 100, (for 1984), 101-28.

Kilns and ovens

Hull, M.R., 1963, *The Roman Potters' Kilns of Colchester*, RRCSAL No. 21, London.

Pitts, L.F., and St Joseph, J.K., 1985, *Inchtuthil*, Gloucester, 195-200.

Rudling, D.R., 1986, 'The Excavation of a Roman Tilery on Great Cansiron Farm, Hartfield, Sussex' in *Britannia*, 17, 191-230.

Swan, V.G., 1984, *The Pottery Kilns of Roman Britain*, RCHM Supplementary Series No. 5, London.

Wild, J.P., 1973, 'A fourth century Potter's Workshop and Kilns at Stibbington, Peterborough' in **Detsicas, A.P., (ed.), 1973**, *Current Research in Romano-British Coarse Pottery*, CBA Research Report No. 10, London.

Woods, P.S., 1974, 'Types of Late Belgic and Early Romano-British Pottery Kilns in the Nene Valley', *Britannia*, 5, 262-289.

Lighthouses

Brodribb, G., 1982, 'Graffito drawing of a Pharos', *Britannia*, 13, 299.

Wheeler, R.E.M., 1930, 'The Roman Light-houses at Dover' in *Arch.J.*, 86, 22ff TR 3141 *.

Tombs

Bancroft (Bucks.): 'Roman Britain in 1983', *Britannia*, 14, 302.

Harpenden (Herts.): *JRS*, 28, 1938, 186

High Rochester (Northumberland): *A History of Northumberland*, 15, 1940, 105 NY 8398 *.

Keston (Kent): *Archaeologia*, 22, 1829, 336 TQ 4163*.

Lullingstone (Kent): **Meates, Lt. Col. G.W., 1979**, *The Roman Villa at Lullingstone, Kent, Volume I – The Site*, Maidstone, 122-132.

Pulborough (West Sussex): **Martin, P.J., 1859**, 'Some Recollections of a part of the "Stane Street Causeway" in its passage through West Sussex', *Sussex, Arch. Coll.*, 11, 141.

Welwyn (Herts.): **Rook, T., Walker, S., and Denston, C.B., 1984**, 'A Roman

Mausoleum and Associated Marble Sarcophagus and Burials from Welwyn, Hertfordshire', *Britannia*, 15, 143 ff.

West Mersea (Essex): **Clapham, A.W., 1922**, 'Roman Mausolea of the Cart-Wheel Type', *Arch. J.*, 79, 93 TM 0214 *

7 The Ruin of Roman Britain

Conclusion

Some of the sources referred to in this short chapter are difficult to find though a small number are available in the Penguin Classics series. Modern general works which include them are also mentioned here.

Anonymous Anglo-Saxon poet in **Kershaw, N., 1922**, *Anglo-Saxon and Norse Poems*, Cambridge [also quoted in **Cunliffe, B., 1984**, *Roman Bath Discovered*, London, 213-4].

Bede, *A History of the English Church and People*, trans. Leo Sherley-Price, 1968, London (Penguin Classics series).

Bede *The Life of St Cuthbert*, trans. By L. Sherley-Price, 1983, London (Penguin Classics Series).

Camden, W., 1586, *Britannia*.

Davies, D.G., and Saunders, C., 1986, *Verulamium*, St Albans (the museum guide which supplies a useful synopsis of references to Verulamium).

Embleton, R., and Graham, F., 1984, *Hadrian's Wall*, Newcastle upon Tyne.

Gerald of Wales [Giraldus Cambrensis], *The Itinerary through Wales and the Description of Wales*, edited by W. Llewellyn Williams, Everyman Library, London, 1908 [or trans. by L. Thorpe in the Penguin Classics Series].

Gildas *The Ruin of Britain and Other Works*, edited and translated by M. Winterbottom, London, 1978 [also quoted in **Henig, M., 1984**, *Religion in Roman Britain*, London, 17).

Hutton, W., 1801, *The History of the Roman Wall*.

Stukeley, W., 1723, *Itinerarium Curiosum*, **1759**, *Carausius*, and **1776**, *Iter Boreale*.

William of Malmesbury *Gesta Regum Anglorum*, ed. W. Stubbs, 1887-9, Rolls Series.

INDEX

Note: italics indicate the page number of an illustration

Places

General